D1095428

WARSHIPS AFTER WASHINGTON

The last of the French 'treaty cruisers', *Algérie*, in heavy weather during the late 1930s. (Courtesy of Robert Dumas)

Warships
After
Washington

The Development of the Five Major Fleets 1922–1930

John Jordan

Seaforth
PUBLISHING

Copyright © John Jordan 2011

First published in Great Britain in 2011 by
Seaforth Publishing,
Pen & Sword Books Ltd,
47 Church Street,
Barnsley S70 2AS

www.seaforthpublishing.com

British Library Cataloguing in Publication Data
A catalogue record for this book is available from the British Library

ISBN 978 1 84832 117 5

Typeset by Mac Style, Beverley, East Yorkshire
Printed and bound in Great Britain by the MPG Books Group

Contents

Preface

The original manuscript for this book was completed some five years ago. It then lay abandoned until the autumn of 2010, when yet another query about the provisions of the Washington Treaty on the web discussion forum to which I belong prompted me to revisit the manuscript and to offer it for publication.

My aim in writing the book was to attempt to bridge the gap between the political and the technical. Much has been written about the political aspects of the interwar naval arms limitation treaties by 'professional' historians. Likewise, much has been written about the technical side of warship development during the same period by reputable naval specialist authors. However, the latter have often been dismissive of the constraints of the treaty, and have generally had a narrow focus on a particular navy. The same authors have often shown a lack of sympathy for (or empathy with) the political aspirations of the period, which, for the decade after Washington, transcended national boundaries, and have also failed either to grasp or to explain the essentially interactive nature of many of the technical developments of the period and the extent to which these were both moulded and guided by the treaty provisions.

In some ways this dichotomy is a reflection of the period in question. Admirals are military professionals whose job is to prepare for (and hopefully win) the next war. This involves the development and the acquisition of weaponry which is qualitatively and – ideally – quantitatively superior to that of their likely next opponent. Any constraint, whether in the form of international arms limitation treaties or domestic financial restraint, is bound to be regarded as an obstruction to that goal and as a threat to national security. This is why, following the failure of the Geneva Conference in 1927, the politicians decided that the admirals should be barred from future direct negotiation, and should again be relegated to their Washington role of 'expert' advisers, free to express their views on the various proposals but powerless to obstruct the process.

Looking back from this point in time, separated from the Washington Conference by a second 'world war' and numerous other lesser conflicts, it takes a leap of imagination to grasp the impact of the speech of US Secretary of State Charles Evan Hughes at the opening session, with its bold proposals for an end to competitive naval building backed by an offer to scrap an entire generation of US battleships and battlecruisers currently on the building ways – a speech received initially in stunned silence and followed by rapturous applause. The admirals present, even if they had strong personal and professional reservations about the likely impact of these proposals, found it impossible to swim against the tide. They would recover their equilibrium only after the conference had created a new international environment governed by codes of behaviour and constraints on naval building. This book sets out to examine in detail how the navies of the five 'Contracting Powers' responded, and the degree to which they were successful in working within (and on occasions subverting) the agreed qualitative and quantitative limits placed on future naval construction and on the modification of existing ships, during the period 1922 to 1930. It begins with the Washington Conference of 1921–22 and ends with the London Conference of 1930, the main purpose of which was to review the original treaty and to plug the holes in it that had become increasingly apparent, and which were viewed by the major powers as opening up new paths of competition in naval armaments.

Drawings and Data

The sixty or so drawings have been specially prepared for this book. Given the nature of the manuscript, the author opted for schematics drawn and labelled in a uniform style to enable the reader to make an informed comparison between the different designs developed by the five navies within the broad parameters laid down by the treaty, often – though not always – to fulfil similar military requirements. This has not been an easy task given the disparity in the quality of published material; where possible I have used either official plans, or redrawings of official plans published in reliable secondary sources. Where sufficiently detailed drawings were not available, any assumptions or 'guesstimates' on the part of the author are recorded in the associated caption.

The tabulated data which accompanies the drawings and the text has been simplified for the purpose of making meaningful comparisons, with figures for dimensions rounded up or down to the nearest foot or metre and displacement figures – which are notoriously variable even between ships of the same class – to the nearest five tons/tonnes. The issue of which units of measurement to adopt was a difficult one to resolve. The British and American navies of the period used imperial units, the other three navies the metric system – although Japan only formally adopted the latter during the early 1920s, from which time previously imperial measurements were converted to metric. Even within the metric system there were anomalies: the Italians and the French – at least in the post-Washington period – expressed gun calibre and torpedo diameter in millimetres, whereas the Japanese (like the Germans) used centimetres, and often rounded the figures up or down. Despite the author's wish to facilitate comparisons there was an issue here of 'authenticity' and respect for the non-Anglo-Saxon navies. The solution adopted was inevitably a compromise: displacements, which are generally 'Washington standard' for all ships and all navies, are given in long tons; dimensions are in imperial units for Britain and the USA (with metric equivalents in parentheses), and in metric for Japan, France and Italy; for guns, torpedoes, armour thickness, boiler pressure, etc., the appropriate units for the navy concerned are used and conversion tables provided at the front of the book. Readers looking for more accurate and comprehensive data about a particular class of ship are referred to the specialist works cited in the bibliography.

There was a similar issue to resolve with regard to the different practices in programming and authorising construction. In all the countries concerned naval construction, together with the necessary funding, had to be authorised before ships could be ordered; in most cases there then followed a short interval before the ship was laid down. Naval 'estimates' were generally voted by the respective parliaments annually. However, in Japan construction programmes generally ran over several years. During the period covered by this book there were only two 'naval replenishment' programmes, dated 1923 and 1927. Ships approved in each of these programmes would be laid down to a schedule determined by the navy, taking into account capacity in the naval dockyards, and some of the units within a single programme would be of improved design (see in particular the submarine authorisation table at the end of Chapter 9).[1] The author has endeavoured to respect these cultural differences in drawing up the authorisation tables in Chapters 6–10. Because estimates were generally voted in advance of the year in question, and because most of the ships laid down during the early 1930s were designed prior to the London Conference, the years run from 1922 to 1930.[2]

Acknowledgements

The author wishes to thank Rob Gardiner of Seaforth Publishing for his support in bringing this project to fruition. Richard Worth and Stephen McLaughlin provided a wealth of research material relating to the treaty period and much encouragement. Many of the photographs reproduced here are from the Leo van Ginderen collection. Other friends and colleagues who kindly provided photographs include: Stephen Dent, David Hobbs, Ian Johnston, Maurizio Brescia, Robert Dumas, Philippe Caresse and Jean Moulin. John Roberts provided substantial support and advice for my drawings of the G3 and F2/F3 battlecruisers, and Ian Johnston kindly gave permission for the use of his pencil drawing of the M2 battleship design. Without the help of these friends and colleagues this book would not have been possible.

Finally, I would like to thank those authors who blazed a trail for the technical analysis I have attempted to apply to the five major navies of the period. Their influence is acknowledged in the selected bibliography published at the end of the book. One name stands out among the rest: Norman Friedman, who, besides his detailed studies on the major categories of warship built for the British Royal Navy and the US Navy, has published a number of more general 'comparative' works illustrating the often very different choices navies make when designing ships for similar missions. Whilst acknowledging these influences the author naturally accepts full responsibility for any errors of fact or judgement contained in this book.

John Jordan
Gosport, UK
8 May 2011

Conversion Tables

Length: feet to metres

ft	m	ft	m	ft	m	ft	m	ft	m	ft	m	ft	m
200	61	300	91	400	122	500	152	600	183	700	213	800	244
210	64	310	94	410	125	510	155	610	186	710	216	810	247
220	67	320	98	420	128	520	158	620	189	720	219	820	250
230	70	330	101	430	131	530	162	630	192	730	222	830	253
240	73	340	104	440	134	540	165	640	195	740	226	840	256
250	76	350	107	450	137	550	168	650	198	750	229	850	259
260	79	360	110	460	140	560	171	660	201	760	232	860	262
270	82	370	113	470	143	570	174	670	204	770	235	870	265
280	85	380	116	480	146	580	177	680	207	780	238	880	268
290	88	390	119	490	149	590	180	690	210	790	241	890	271

Note: conversion to the nearest whole metre

Beam and draught: feet to metres

ft	m	ft	m	ft	m
1	0.30	15	4.57	65	19.81
2	0.61	20	6.10	70	21.34
3	0.91	25	7.62	75	22.86
4	1.22	30	9.14	80	24.38
5	1.52	35	10.67	85	25.91
6	1.83	40	12.19	90	27.43
7	2.13	45	13.72	95	28.96
8	2.44	50	15.24	100	30.48
9	2.74	55	16.76	105	32.00
10	3.05	60	18.29	110	33.53

Note: conversion to two decimal places

Guns

in	mm	in	mm	in	mm
18in	457mm	(9.4in)	240mm	(5.1in)	130mm
16in	406mm	8in	203mm	5in	127mm
15in	381mm	(7.9in)	200mm	4.7in	120mm
14in	356mm	7.5in	190mm	4.5in	(114mm)
13.5in	(343mm)	(6.1in)	155mm	4in	102mm
(13.4in)	340mm	6in	152mm	(3.9in)	100mm
(13in)	330mm	5.5in	140mm	(3.5in)	90mm
(12.6in)	320mm	(5.4in)	138.6mm	3in	75/76mm
12in	305mm	(5.3in)	135mm	2pdr	40mm

Note 1: brackets indicate that this is simply an equivalent measurement; it does not represent an actual gun.

Note 2: the French and Italian navies used millimetres, whereas the Japanese (like the Germans) expressed gun calibres as centimetres (457mm = 45.7cm); some calibres employed by the Imperial Japanese Navy (IJN) were approximations (e.g. the 8cm HA gun – in fact a 76.2mm gun)

Armour

in	mm	in	mm	in	mm
1in	25mm	3in	75mm	11in	280mm
1¼in	30mm	4in	100mm	12in	305mm
1½in	38mm	5in	125mm	13in	330mm
1¾in	45mm	6in	150mm	14in	355mm
2in	50mm	7in	175mm	15in	380mm
2¼in	55mm	8in	200mm	16in	405mm
2½in	65mm	9in	230mm	17in	430mm
2¾in	70mm	10in	255mm	18in	455mm

Note: conversion above 38mm to the nearest 5mm

Torpedoes

in	mm
(17.7in)	450mm
18in	(457mm)
21in	533mm
(21.7in)	550mm
(24in)	610mm
24.5in	(622mm)

Boiler working pressure

in	mm	in	mm
18kg/cm²	255lb/in²	26kg/cm²	370lb/in²
19kg/cm²	270lb/in²	27kg/cm²	385lb/in²
20kg/cm²	285lb/in²	28kg/cm²	400lb/in²
21kg/cm²	300lb/in²	29kg/cm²	415lb/in²
22kg/cm²	315lb/in²	30kg/cm²	425lb/in²
23kg/cm²	330lb/in²	35kg/cm²	500lb/in²
24kg/cm²	340lb/in²	40kg/cm²	570lb/in²
25kg/cm²	355lb/in²	45kg/cm²	640lb/in²

Note: conversion to nearest 5lb/in²

Battle ranges: metres to yards

m	yds
1,000m	1,100yds
5,000m	5,500yds
10,000m	11,000yds
15,000m	16,500yds
20,000m	22,000yds
25,000m	27,500yds
30,000m	33,000yds
35,000m	38,500yds
40,000m	44,000yds

Note: conversion to nearest 500yds

Distances: nautical miles to kilometres

nm	km
1nm	1.85km
50nm	92.5km
100nm	185km
200nm	370km

Introduction

... I believe that America, free from international complications and entanglements, free from the centuries-old prejudices which have kept Europe in a state of turmoil for a thousand years, free from thoughts of aggrandizement or of territorial aggression, occupies the position in the world today which entitles her to the leadership, yea, which compels her to assume the responsibility of bringing about such an international conference. It must not be overlooked that we are in a position also of being able to establish and maintain the largest navy in the world if we so desire it. We have the wealth, the material and the man power to outstrip in a naval program any and all nations. We make no threat; we desire to enter into no ruinous competition. We seek an amicable adjustment of the problem, and will reduce if the nations will join us in an international compact.

Frederick C Hicks (Congressman for New York, member of Naval Affairs Committee, American Academy of Political and Social Science, July 1921)

The Washington Conference on the limitation of naval armaments, convened at the invitation of the US government on 12 November 1921, was to result in a treaty which would become the key reference point for all naval construction over the next fifteen years. The declared purpose of the conference was 'to contribute to the maintenance of the general peace, and to reduce the burdens of competition in armament', and the five key participants – designated the 'Contracting Powers' – were the United States of America, the British Empire, France, Italy and Japan. Each of these countries was represented by high-ranking ministers and officials from their respective administrations, with technical advice being provided by teams of naval officers briefed by their respective admiralties as to desired outcomes, and what could (and could not) be accepted.

The Washington Treaty which emerged three months later, after some hard and at times difficult negotiations, prescribed the total tonnage available to each of the five contracting powers in the 'capital ship' and 'aircraft carrier' categories based on a fixed ratio which placed the USA and Britain at the top of the tree, France and Italy at the bottom, and Japan somewhere in the middle. It also closely defined both of these categories in terms of maximum unit displacement and gun calibre, and at the same time established a new definition of a ship's displacement – termed 'standard' or 'Washington standard' – to ensure that total tonnage allocation was a meaningful concept and not subject to individual interpretation by the respective navies. These agreed limitations were then applied to the existing fleets and construction programmes of the contracting powers. Following further negotiations, annexes were produced detailing those capital ships which could be retained, the ships already under construction which could be completed, and the replacement programmes permitted during the fifteen-year span of the treaty.

The ten-year 'battleship holiday' decreed by the treaty was to be matched by strict controls on the development of new military bases in the Western Pacific with a view to defusing growing political tensions in that region. Under a parallel Four-Power Treaty, the USA, the British Empire, Japan and France agreed to maintain the status quo: the United States agreed not to build new bases or to fortify existing bases west of the Hawaiian Islands, and the British agreed not to develop naval facilities beyond Singapore.

Background to the Conference

The Washington Conference took place in a new era of international relations ushered in by the Treaty of Versailles and the setting up of the League of Nations. Before the First World War the balance of power had been maintained in Europe by a network of bilateral and trilateral alliances which in theory served to deter military aggression by any one power. This system had patently failed to preserve the peace, and the scale of the Great War, which was waged not by standing armies and navies alone but by the mobilisation of entire nations, led to a general desire for a more effective means of securing international stability and prosperity.

It was recognised that if international relations were left to individual nations each would pursue its own narrow national interests, and that sooner or later this would bring them into conflict with other nations pursuing their own equally legitimate political and economic interests. What was clearly required was a set of rules of behaviour to which all the leading nations could subscribe, and which would set clear limits on the future actions and on the political and military ambitions of individual nations. This principle of 'collective security', closely associated with the US Democrat President Woodrow Wilson, was welcomed by the peoples of Europe, who were drained physically, emotionally and financially by the war.

Ironically, considering his postwar 'peace' credentials, it was during Wilson's first term as president that the Naval Expansion Act of 1916 had been passed, with provision for the construction of no fewer than ten new battleships, six large 'battle scouts' – comparable in size and hitting power to the latest British battlecruisers – and ten scout cruisers. Influenced by the belief current in some US foreign affairs circles that the winners of the First World War would automatically become potential rivals of the United States, the programme had the avowed aim of creating naval parity with the greatest foreign power (i.e. Great Britain). The programme elicited an immediate response from Japan, which in 1920–21 laid down two 40,000-ton battleships and four battlecruisers of similar size armed with 16in guns, with plans for eight even more powerful ships armed with 16in and 18in guns to be laid down over the following two years. These developments could not be ignored by Britain, which saw its traditional supremacy threatened by these two new rivals, and in 1920–21 the Royal Navy was preparing to lay down four battlecruisers of 48,400 tons armed with nine 16in guns (the G3s), to be followed by four battleships of similar size armed with nine 18in guns.

The capital ship programmes of Britain, the USA and Japan would have effectively begun a new naval arms race. This was neither affordable nor desirable. The four British G3 battlecruisers ordered in the run-up to the conference were effectively a bargaining chip; the British government of the day fervently hoped it would not need to fund their completion. The US Navy was experiencing similar difficulties securing the necessary funding allocations for its own ambitious programme. A much-changed political climate in the United States witnessed the defeat of Woodrow Wilson and his Democratic Party in 1921. The new Republican administration led by President Warren G Harding responded to an increasingly isolationist public rejection of foreign entanglements and obligations in the United States, and there would be little support in Congress for ever-greater expenditures on military hardware, to the extent that throughout the period covered by the Washington Treaty the US Navy consistently failed to build up to its permitted limits, and therefore never achieved the material superiority over the Imperial Japanese Navy on which it had insisted during the treaty negotiations. A naval arms limitation treaty was seen as necessary not only to protect US security interests but also to reduce expenditure on the navy.

Avoiding Conflict

The Americans were particularly anxious to see an end to the Anglo-Japanese Alliance, which, although not specifically directed against the United States, was felt to give Japan a free hand to pursue its own expansionist agenda on the Asian mainland. The alliance was due to expire in July 1921, but both Japan and Britain initially favoured renewal: the British because they needed Japan as a counterweight to US power in the Pacific and also because they saw the treaty as a means of restraining Japanese imperial ambitions in Asia; the Japanese because of the status an alliance with the world's premier naval power accorded to Japan, and because the British Empire in the Far East was seen as posing no threat to Japanese interests. The United States leaned heavily on the British not to renew the alliance, with strong support from the British Dominion of Canada, proposing in its place the Four-Power Treaty (the 'Big Three' plus France), negotiations for which were conducted simultaneously with the Washington Conference. Under the Four-Power Treaty each of the contracting powers agreed to respect the others' existing possessions in the Far East, and to consult in the event of a crisis. Under a complementary Nine-Power Treaty, which also embraced China, Belgium, Italy, the Netherlands and Portugal, it was agreed that all parties would respect Chinese integrity and sovereignty, and maintain the existing 'Open Door' policy.

When the Washington Treaty was signed on 6 February 1922 there was therefore a general sense of relief that potential sources of conflict in the Far East had been nipped in the bud, and that the concept of collective security had replaced the old system of ad hoc opportunistic alliances which had conspicuously failed to preserve peace in the past. There was also relief that a new naval arms race had been averted, and that the construction of a ruinous new generation of battleships had been halted, thereby releasing funds for the regeneration and reconstruction of Europe and for the further economic development of the United States and Japan. There were many who believed that the naval arms race had been a major factor in the deterioration of relations between Britain and Germany pre-1914, and by the early 1920s 'navalism' was being used as a pejorative term in the United States. The Washington Treaty was thought by many to herald an end to 'competitive building', at least in capital ships – the major naval currency of the day – and therefore made war less likely.

CHAPTER 1

The Navies of the Victorious Powers 1918–1921

Great Britain

In 1918 Britain's Royal Navy remained in size, power and reputation the world's premier fleet. It was a navy befitting a power with a vast empire 'on which the sun never set'. However, during the early part of the twentieth century it had faced increasing challenges from new contenders: first from the Kaiser's Germany, an industrial powerhouse with ambitions to threaten British naval supremacy and build an empire of its own; and subsequently from the United States and Japan – one a potential economic superpower, the other a rapidly developing country whose precocious naval prowess had already shocked and alarmed the powers of 'Old Europe' by defeating a large Russian expeditionary fleet at Tsushima in 1905.

Britain's response to Germany's ambitious naval construction programme had been to concentrate the fleet in home waters, leaving its distant possessions and the sea lanes which tied them to the mother country to be patrolled by a handful of elderly armoured and protected cruisers. This concentration was made possible by two alliances which became the twin cornerstones of British maritime strategy during the early part of the century. The Entente Cordiale with the French in 1904 permitted the Royal Navy to withdraw its most modern capital ships from the Mediterranean, which would henceforth be the operational responsibility of the Marine Nationale. And the Anglo-Japanese Alliance, first signed in 1902 and renewed in 1907, ensured that British possessions in the Far East would be secure against the depredations of the German East Asiatic Squadron, a powerful force of modern armoured and light cruisers, while the largely British-built Imperial Japanese Navy would provide a useful political counterweight to growing American influence in the region.

The Grand Fleet established the pattern of organisation for all the major navies of the dreadnought era. At Jutland in May 1916, at the peak of its power, it was divided into two major components: the 'battle fleet', based at Scapa Flow and comprising three squadrons of 21-knot battleships, each with two four-ship divisions; and the 'battle cruiser fleet', a strategic scouting force based at Rosyth, comprising two three- or four-ship squadrons of 27-knot battle cruisers with four fast battleships of the 5th Battle Squadron in support.

The battle fleet cruised in divisional columns, escorted by destroyers and preceded by a scouting line of pre-dreadnought armoured cruisers, with a three-ship squadron of older battlecruisers and a squadron of fast light cruisers twenty miles ahead of the battle squadrons to provide an eventual link with the battle cruiser fleet. At the approach of the enemy fleet the three squadrons of the battle fleet would deploy into a single continuous battle line, the cruisers and destroyers being positioned ahead and astern to protect it against enemy torpedo attacks. The van squadron was a powerful homogeneous force of super-dreadnought battleships armed with 13.5in guns, while the centre squadron (which included the fleet flagship, *Iron Duke*) was a mix of modern and older ships, and the squadron bringing up the rear was made up of older dreadnoughts armed with 12in guns.

The most impressive battleships of the Grand Fleet were the five ships of the *Queen Elizabeth* class completed in 1915–16. Armed with eight 15in guns in twin turrets superimposed fore and aft, the *Queen Elizabeth*s had side belts and turret armour 13in thick and displaced 27,500 tons.[1] More significantly still, they were the first British battleships to be oil-fired, and the greater thermal efficiency of this fuel was largely responsible for a designed speed of 25 knots, which, although not attained in service due to being overweight, enabled them to be employed in conjunction with the battlecruisers as a 'fast wing' of the battle fleet. These ships caused a considerable stir abroad when first completed. The Japanese, who perceived high tactical speed as a major asset in combat, modelled the postwar *Nagato* class on them.[2]

In May 1916, the month of Jutland, the British also laid down the battlecruiser *Hood*, essentially an enlargement of the *Queen Elizabeth* design with a similar armament and a comparable level of protection but with almost three times the horsepower for a top speed of 31 knots. Three other ships of the same class were laid down in 1916–17, but with an end to the war in

The battleship *Malaya*, one of the five influential fast battleships of the *Queen Elizabeth* class. Their handsome lines would be spoiled by the modifications they underwent post-Washington to improve their underwater protection and anti-aircraft capabilities (see Chapter 5).

The 'Mighty *Hood*' on her completion at John Brown's Clydebank Yard in 1920. At 41,200 tons she would remain the largest capital ship in the world throughout the interwar period due to the 35,000-ton limit imposed on new construction by the Washington Treaty. (National Archives of Scotland, courtesy of Ian Johnston)

sight construction was abandoned, and as it was subsequently acknowledged that the ships reflected pre-Jutland ideas on the disposition of armour they were cancelled in 1918. The director of naval construction (DNC) argued strongly in favour of concentrating resources on new designs which benefited from wartime experience. This assessment was certainly at odds with public perceptions of this impressive 41,200-ton ship, easily the largest in the world at the time of her completion in 1920 and christened the 'Mighty *Hood*' by the British press. *Hood* was also widely admired by Britain's foreign competitors, and influenced the redesign of the US battlecruisers of the *Lexington* class laid down in 1920–21.

Apart from the elderly armoured cruisers, whose protection was to prove totally inadequate in the face of the uniform big-gun batteries of the German dreadnoughts and which were subsequently relegated to less demanding duties, the British cruisers were fast, lightly-armoured ships armed with quick-firing 6in and 4in guns in single, open-backed mountings. The 'fleet' cruisers built prior to the First World War were of two distinct types: a 27-knot fighting cruiser of 5,500 tons with a uniform armament of eight single 6in guns (the 'Towns'), and a smaller, faster type of 3,750–4,200 tons intended to operate with the destroyer flotillas and armed initially with up to ten single 4in guns, but subsequently with two 6in guns and six or eight 4in guns. The later ships had their magazines and machinery spaces protected by 2–3in armoured belts, together with 1in armoured decks. During the war these two types effectively merged, and the 'C'-type fleet cruisers laid down from 1915 had a uniform armament of five 6in guns. A steady increase in beam, together with the lessons of wartime, meant that later 'C'-type ships had four twin 21in trainable torpedo tubes in place of the two fixed (submerged) tubes of the earlier ships, which enhanced their performance when operating with the flotillas, and in the larger 'D' class of 1916 there was an additional 6in gun and the torpedo mountings were triples, for a total of twelve tubes.

In 1915 a new type of larger cruiser was designed to counter the threat of armed raiders in distant oceans. With a displacement of 9,750 tons and a main armament of seven single 7.5in guns, the 'Elizabethans' were expensive ships; only five were built. However, they made a considerable impact abroad, particularly in the United States and Japan, and were to have a major influence on the framing of the Washington Treaty itself and on subsequent cruiser construction.

British development of the torpedo-boat destroyer – subsequently 'destroyer' – was unmatched by any other country. The late-war ships of the 'V' and 'W' classes, which displaced 1,300 tons, had a designed speed of 34 knots, and were armed with four 4in guns and two twin or triple banks of 21in torpedo tubes. Their successors of the 'Modified W' class, which were on the stocks at the end of the war, featured single 4.7in guns in place of the original 4in. Not only were they the best of their type in the world when completed, but they were to become the template for destroyer construction both in Britain and abroad once the renewal of the flotillas began during the mid-1920s.

The Royal Navy had been a reluctant builder of submarines, surmising (correctly) that the proliferation of increasingly capable submersibles armed with torpedoes could ultimately threaten Britain's traditional maritime supremacy. However, developments abroad compelled the British to follow suit, and the Royal Navy produced some of the best submarine designs of the First World War, and some of the most innovative. The standard submarine for overseas deployment was the 670-ton 'E' type, which was succeeded in the latter part of the war by the 890-ton 'L'. These were complemented by a series of 'coastal' boats of 350–430-ton displacement for deployment in the North Sea. Rumours of fast German U-boats, which ultimately proved

HMS *Curacoa*, one of the 4,000-ton 'fleet' cruisers designed to scout for the Grand Fleet and to lead the destroyer flotillas. Armed with five 6in guns and eight 21in torpedo tubes, these ships formed the bulk of the British cruiser force throughout the interwar period, but had insufficient range for trade protection or for service in the Far East. (Leo van Ginderen collection)

The destroyers of the 'V' and 'W' classes were the world's most advanced destroyers of the late war period. Fast, robust and seaworthy they were armed with four single 4in guns and four 21in torpedo tubes in twin trainable mountings. This is *Vanessa*, completed in 1918. (Leo van Ginderen collection)

false, were the driving force behind successive (and abortive) attempts to build a 'fleet' submarine fast enough to keep station with the battle fleet and to operate in the van. The diesel-driven 'J' class approved in January 1915 was followed by the steam-turbine-driven 'K' class, which was designed for a speed of 24 knots on the surface, and featured retractable funnels sealed by watertight hatches and trainable torpedo tubes. The 'monitor' submarines of the 'M' class, of which four were ordered in 1916, were armed with a single 12in gun for shore bombardment – the gun was provided with fifty shells and could open fire within twenty seconds of surfacing. They influenced the design of the French *Surcouf*, the largest 'cruiser' submarine of the interwar period.

All the major navies had shown an interest in the future possibilities of aircraft at sea from about 1910 onwards, but only the Royal Navy had been prepared to make the necessary investment of resources to secure real advances. Seaplane carrier conversions of cross-channel steamers and former liners were followed in 1917 by the fitting of flying-off and flying-on decks for wheeled landplanes aboard the light battlecruiser *Furious*. By the time of the Armistice *Argus*, a 20-knot former liner with a full flush flight deck and a hangar beneath, was nearly complete, the conversion of the incomplete hull of the Chilean battleship *Almirante Cochrane* (subsequently HMS *Eagle*) was underway, and the world's first purpose-built aircraft carrier *Hermes*, based on a cruiser hull, was on the stocks. The primary purpose of these ships was to provide long-range reconnaissance, gunnery spotting, and fighter protection for the battle fleet; they would also carry large torpedo bombers capable of making attacks on the enemy battle line. *Hermes* and *Furious* (which would later undergo a full conversion on the lines of the other ships) had sufficient speed to operate with the strategic scouting forces, in advance of the battle fleet, to give advance warning of the approach of an enemy fleet.

It should be clear from the above that although Britain was herself exhausted and arguably past the apogee of her power and influence in 1918, the Royal Navy was still by some way the most powerful and well balanced in the world, and was in the van of technological developments for all types of ship. At Jutland previously unsuspected flaws had shown up in the ammunition-handling arrangements of the lightly armoured battlecruisers and in the heavy armour-piercing shell, which had a tendency to break up on impact, but these were corrected in the postwar capital ship designs. In cruiser and destroyer construction the Royal Navy had battle-tested designs as good as, and generally superior to, any in the world. Naval aviation developments were well in advance of the competition and influenced the United States, Japan and France in the immediate postwar period. The Admiral Fisher-driven Royal Navy of the pre-war period had been an innovatory force responsible for a plethora of conceptual, tactical and technological developments which had revolutionised naval warfare, and some of these developments had been accorded a further stimulus by the advent of war.

This is not to say that there were not important developments outside Britain. The French and the Americans were influential in the early development of submarines, and the Italians in other aspects of underwater technology such as torpedoes and mines. German optical instruments, naval artillery and submarine diesels were widely admired when their ships were distributed as prizes to the victorious powers postwar, and the larger German U-boats, particularly the long-range 'cruisers', would have a major influence on postwar developments. The 'all-or-nothing' protection system of the most

The 'L' class was the standard British patrol submarine. Laid down towards the end of the Great War, these 900-ton boats proved particularly successful and served throughout the interwar period. (Leo van Ginderen collection)

recent US Navy battleships would be adopted by virtually all the major navies for their interwar designs. However, in general, where the Royal Navy led other navies followed. This would change in the post-treaty era.

US Navy

The US Navy was a 'young' navy, with neither the weight of tradition nor the operational experience of the Royal Navy. It was also in a unique geostrategic position in that there was no local threat to its supremacy; nor did it have a worldwide empire to police. Its composition was therefore very different from the navies of its European counterparts, being notably 'battleship heavy', without the plethora of vessels of intermediate size (in particular, cruisers) which characterised other fleets.

US naval strategy was traditionally predicated on the ability to defeat an expeditionary fleet from one of the major European powers. However, with the acquisition of the Philippines following the Spanish–American War of 1898, the US Navy might also be required to despatch an expeditionary fleet of its own to the Western Pacific. Long range and staying power were therefore essential characteristics for US fleet units. However, these qualities had to be matched by fighting capabilities, for there was little point in despatching an expeditionary fleet if, like the Russian Baltic Squadron of 1905 at Tsushima, it were to be defeated on arrival. US battleship designs therefore emphasised firepower and protection, at the expense of tactical qualities such as high speed and manoeuvrability.

On 16 December 1907 President Theodore Roosevelt (favourite proverb: 'Speak softly and carry a big stick') despatched sixteen of the latest US battleships of the Atlantic Fleet on a fifteen-month world cruise embracing six continents. The 'Great White Fleet', which covered 43,000 miles without a serious breakdown, put down a marker to the other major powers that the United States had arrived on the international scene, and was not to be 'messed with'. It also captured the imagination of an American public traditionally opposed to foreign military adventures, and thereby prepared the ground for later naval expansion programmes.

From 1906 the US Navy would lay down two modern dreadnought battleships per year – a conservative figure compared to Britain and Germany, who at the height of the naval arms race which preceded the outbreak of the First World War were building four or five a year, but an impressive one nevertheless. Moreover, once war began and both European powers reviewed their extensive building programmes with a view to restricting construction to ships already on the stocks that could be completed during the course of the conflict, the United States ploughed ahead with its own programme of two ships per year, each class an incremental improvement on the last. By 1916, even discounting the 18-knot *South Carolinas*, there were twelve modern dreadnought battleships, of which the last six were armed with 14in guns and the last four armoured on the revolutionary 'all-or-nothing' principle.

The US battleship *Nevada* introduced the revolutionary 'all-or-nothing' protection system, whereby armour was limited to the vital areas of the ship, thereby increasing the thickness of both vertical and horizontal protection. A thickly armoured box enclosed the machinery and magazines, and the only areas outside this to receive protection were the turrets, barbettes and conning tower. (USNHC NH45796)

The year 1916 was to mark a turning point for the US Navy. Having struggled to get funding from Congress even for the scouts – which had been shown in war games at the Naval Staff College to be essential for effective deployment of its powerful battle fleet – the US Navy suddenly found itself the focus of the Naval Expansion Act, sponsored by the Democrat administration of President Woodrow Wilson, which promised to place it on a par with the largest and most powerful European navies. Ten new battleships and six large 'battle scouts', all armed with 16in guns, were to be built, together with ten long-range scout cruisers. The latter were the first cruisers to be authorised since 1904, and were to have a full-load displacement of 9,000 tons, a speed of 35 knots and an armament of ten 6in guns and ten 21in torpedoes. There were delays in finalising some of these designs, and that of the 'battle scouts' was substantially recast following the close contact between the US Navy and the Royal Navy in 1917–18. However, in 1920 alone, when the Royal Navy was in the process of consigning large numbers of its pre-war ships to the breakers' yards, the US Navy laid down six 16in gun battleships – five of which displaced 43,000 tons – four 16in gun battlecruisers (ex-battle scouts) with a similar displacement and a designed speed of 33.5 knots, and eight scout cruisers. The 1916 programme, once completed, would put the US Navy on an equal footing with the Royal Navy and thereby ensure the freedom of the seas for its own and 'neutral' merchant shipping carrying American goods, which during the Great War had been subjected to British controls as part of the blockade of Germany and Austria–Hungary. A consequence unforeseen at the time was that it would provide a powerful incentive to bring Britain and Japan to the conference table in late 1921.

US battleship design prior to Washington was solid rather than spectacular. Curtis steam turbines of local manufacture were introduced in the early 12in-gun dreadnought *North Dakota* (completed 1910), but the General Board had strong reservations about their performance, and the *New York* class of 1911–14 reverted to traditional triple-expansion reciprocating turbines. Although the latter were subject to vibration and breakdown at high speed, which meant that exercises and operations were often followed by a lengthy stay in the dockyard, the early, direct-drive steam turbines proved to be uneconomic at cruise speed, and US battleships had to be able to reach the Philippines from the West Coast without replenishment. The US Navy also experienced problems with its astern turbines. The solution to both problems was the adoption of turbo-electric propulsion, first trialled in the battleship *New Mexico* of 1915–18, which was also seen as a means of improving underwater subdivision. Although employed in all subsequent US capital ship construction up to the Washington Conference, turbo-electric propulsion was not adopted by any other navy, and was subsequently abandoned by the US Navy because of its excessive demands in terms of weight and volume.

The US Navy adopted oil-firing technology at about the same time as the Royal Navy, the two *Nevada*s being laid down within a month of their British counterparts of the *Queen Elizabeth* class. The United States, unlike Britain, had no concerns regarding the availability of oil supplies, and was quick to recognise the benefits of oil over coal: greater thermal efficiency, flexibility in the positioning of bunkers, a reduction in complement, easier – and cleaner, less labour-intensive – replenishment. The US Navy was also well to the fore in the development of an effective system of underwater protection; the battleships laid down from 1916 had a combination of liquid-filled and void compartments designed to disperse the force of an exploding torpedo warhead outboard of the machinery spaces; the broad beam of American battleships enabled these systems to be incorporated into the hull rather than being built on as a 'bulge'.

In terms of fighting capabilities the US Navy was an early proponent of long-range gunnery, leading to the development of the distinctive cage mast, a fire control support designed to survive multiple hits by small- and medium-calibre guns. Director firing for primary and secondary batteries was adopted following close contact with the Royal Navy in 1917–18. Other legacies of this period include 'concentration dials' and turret bearing markings for data transmission to other ships in the formation, and the enclosed bridge, which was found to be a necessity in North Sea operations.

The major innovation for which the US Navy was responsible was the 'all-or-nothing' protection system adopted from the *Nevada* class onwards. Other navies had persisted with graduated armour; heavy waterline belts were complemented by upper belts of moderate thickness, and the 'ends' of the ship received similar protection; the multiple decks received only thin plating. This system was a relic of the pre-dreadnought era, when the threat from a plethora of medium-calibre and quick-firing guns at the relatively

By the end of the Great War, the US
Navy had built a formidable fleet
of heavily armed, well-protected
dreadnought and super-dreadnought
battleships capable of power projection
in distant waters. This is the recently
completed *New Mexico* leading other
ships of the US battle fleet in April
1919. (US Navy, Leo van Ginderen
collection)

short engagement ranges of the period was arguably greater than from the
relatively small battery of slow-firing main guns. When 'all-big-gun' batteries
were introduced, it could still be argued that the light upper belt armour
would serve to detonate the heavier shell, and that the light protective decks
would be sufficient to keep out the resulting splinters. However, as gunnery
ranges increased it became more likely that steeply descending shells would
miss out the upper belt altogether and plunge through the thin horizontal
armour, disabling the propulsion machinery or detonating the magazines.
The solution adopted for the *Nevada* was to eliminate all intermediate and
light armour, and to concentrate the weight of protection on an armoured
'box' comprising a relatively high waterline belt of a thickness equivalent to
that of the calibre of the main guns, topped by a 3in armoured deck. A thin
'splinter' deck beneath the latter covered the ship's vitals. All subsequent US
Navy battleships had this protection system, and it was universally adopted
by the other major navies for their postwar designs.

   Apart from the battleship, the only ship type in which the US Navy
invested heavily before 1918 was the destroyer. Early US destroyers were
relatively fragile craft with a small silhouette which favoured torpedo attacks.
However, the destroyers authorised from 1911, at the behest of the General
Board, were larger 1,000-ton ships intended, like their British counterparts,

From 1916 onwards the US Navy ordered some three hundred 1,000-ton destroyers which were promptly christened 'flush-deckers'. Built in private shipyards using mass production techniques these ships would continue, in the absence of new construction, to form the backbone of the US destroyer flotillas until the late 1930s. They carried an impressive complement of torpedoes but were too small and too fragile for ocean operations. This is *Goff* (247) at Boston in July 1922. (Leo van Ginderen collection)

to protect the battle line against enemy torpedo boats. In the absence of the scout cruisers for which the General Board pleaded annually, they would also have been employed in the scouting role in advance of the battle line. Armament was generally four 4in guns and eight or twelve 21in torpedo tubes in trainable twin or triple mountings, and the designed speed was 30 knots. From 1911 to 1915 a class of six new boats, each an incremental improvement on the last, was authorised every year, but as part of the 1916 naval expansion programme no fewer than fifty of a new, mass-produced 'flush-decker' type with a speed of 35 knots[3] were authorised.

Although it was recognised that large numbers of destroyers were needed for anti-submarine (A/S) work, the new design was fundamentally unsuited to slow-speed, long-endurance convoy and A/S patrol work. Moreover, the US Navy had no depth charge and no submarine detection gear prior to its contact with the Royal Navy in 1917; the only measure undertaken to improve anti-submarine performance was a strengthening of the bows to permit ramming. In that same year a special ASW committee proposed the construction of a dedicated anti-submarine destroyer with a speed of 26 knots which prefigured the destroyer escorts (DEs) of the Second World War. However, it was feared that any design change would cause serious delays in the destroyer building programme, and it was decided to proceed with an expanded programme of 'flush-deckers'.

The flush-deckers, which would prove to be wet in service with upperworks liable to sustain damage in heavy seas, were not the world's best destroyers, but the construction of almost three hundred of them over about four years, mostly in private shipyards and using mass-production techniques, was a further indication of the potential of the US military-industrial base.

The Imperial Japanese Navy

The Imperial Japanese Navy (IJN), like that of the United States, was also a comparatively young navy. Closely modelled on the British Royal Navy, which the Japanese greatly admired, the IJN was open to any other outside influence which it deemed of possible benefit to its development, and from its earliest days proved capable of technical and tactical innovation. Most of its early battleships were built in British shipyards, and subsequently in Japanese yards with British expertise and equipment, but the IJN of the early 1900s also operated armoured cruisers built in Germany and Italy, and after 1905 large numbers of ex-Russian vessels were incorporated into the fleet.

Japanese maritime strategy was based on aggressive ocean-oriented defence of the home islands. The only nation which posed a strategic threat to Japan following the annihilation of the Imperial Russian fleet at Tsushima in 1905 – an event which propelled Japan into the front rank of naval powers – was the United States, and from 1908 the IJN adopted a hypothetical naval standard of 70 per cent of US Navy strength. This standard took into account the US Navy's considerable strategic disadvantages: the need to divide its naval forces between the Atlantic and the Pacific, the vulnerability of the Philippines, and the major logistical difficulties inherent in despatching an expeditionary fleet across the Pacific from the West Coast of America (Pearl Harbor had yet to be developed as a fleet base). The IJN would cling to this dogma of a 70 per cent ratio for thirty years, and it would be Japan's failure to achieve it first at the Washington Conference and subsequently at the London Conference of 1930 which would mobilise hard-line nationalist elements of the navy against the resulting treaties.

In tactical terms the Imperial Japanese Navy after Tsushima was to be a scaled-down version of the British Royal Navy, with a battle fleet comprising battleships and battlecruisers backed up by squadrons of small, fast fleet cruisers and destroyer flotillas. The base unit of the fleet was a *sentai* (squadron) of eight capital ships on the British model, which could be subdivided into two or four divisions for maximum flexibility. Experience at Tsushima had shown that two such squadrons could be placed under a single commander, so the optimum battle fleet organisation became sixteen capital ships in two squadrons. Each of the battle squadrons would be supported by two divisions of cruisers, together with flotillas of torpedo boats.

This 'eight–eight' fleet, comprising eight battleships and eight battlecruisers (initially armoured cruisers) was an article of faith in the IJN up to the Washington Conference. The equal weighting given to battleships and battlecruisers was in marked contrast to US naval thinking of the period, and gave even more prominence to the battlecruiser type than Britain and Germany (each of which built battleships and battlecruisers in a ratio of approximately 4:1). It was a reflection of the emphasis on high tactical speed in the IJN, for which the ability to outmanoeuvre the enemy immediately prior to and during combat was perceived as crucial to victory (as at Tsushima). A 'fast' squadron of armoured cruisers or battlecruisers could choose its station relative to the enemy battle line and to its own battle squadron, making possible key manoeuvres such as 'crossing the T'.

The first eight–eight construction programme was proposed by the General Staff in 1910, but was subsequently cut by the Navy Ministry to seven battleships plus three armoured cruisers, and then further amended by the cabinet to only a single battleship plus four armoured cruisers. However, the IJN was able to obtain approval by 1913 for four new battlecruisers and four new battleships, all armed with 14in guns. The first of the battlecruisers, *Kongo*, was built in Britain to ensure that Japanese constructors had access to the latest British technology, and the second ship, *Hiei*, was built at Yokosuka using largely imported materials; however, the remaining six ships were built in Japan using almost exclusively Japanese components.

In 1915, with the economy in recovery, the IJN submitted plans for an eight–four fleet, to include four new battleships. This was rejected by the Diet, but the US Naval Expansion Act of 1916 persuaded it to agree authorisations in 1916–17 which would permit the IJN to attain an interim goal of an eight–six fleet comprising new-build ships armed with 16in guns, and in 1918 two more battlecruisers were added to the programme for a full eight–eight fleet. Of these only the two battleships of the *Nagato* class would be completed.

Like the Royal Navy, the IJN initially favoured a division in the function of light cruisers into a small, fast 'fleet' type capable of leading the destroyer flotillas and a larger, more heavily armed type for scouting. The three-ship *Chikuma* class of the 1907 programme were similar to the British 'Towns',

When first completed, the four battlecruisers of the *Kongo* class were arguably the most powerful and advanced ships of their type in the world. *Kongo*, seen here on sea trials, was built in Britain; the other three units were built in Japan.

and a close study of the *Arethusa* and 'C'-type destroyer leaders led to the two *Tenryus* laid down in 1917. The IJN subsequently opted for an intermediate type to perform both roles, resulting in the eleven ships of the *Kuma* and *Nagara* classes, which displaced 5,500 tons, were armed with seven 5.5in (14cm) guns in single mountings and eight 21in (53cm) torpedoes in twin trainable tubes, and had the exceptionally high designed speed of 36 knots. However, the IJN was concerned that these ships would be outclassed by their foreign contemporaries – the British 'Elizabethans' made a particularly strong impression – and in the immediate postwar period had its constructors draw up plans for new scout cruisers of 7,500–8,000 tons, armed with 19cm or 20cm guns, which became the *Furutaka* and *Aoba* classes (see Chapters 2 and 6).

Where the IJN departed from the Royal Navy was in its more aggressive use of the torpedo boat. Whereas the Royal Navy's own battle line was materially superior to that of any navy it was likely to have to fight, Japan would almost certainly be faced by a more numerous enemy battle fleet (as indeed it had been at Tsushima). Even before the Russo-Japanese war, IJN tactical thinking stressed the importance of using its flotillas of torpedo boats to whittle away at the enemy fleet once night fell after the main surface action, mopping up any ships which had sustained damage in combat and become separated from the main body.[4] This was to evolve during the interwar period into a strategy which involved the use of cruisers and larger, more powerful destroyers for a campaign of attrition against the enemy battle fleet as it made its way through the Western Pacific en route to the Philippines, using night-time torpedo attacks to disable enemy battleships and thereby secure a

Prior to the Washington Conference the IJN laid down a series of small 'fleet' cruisers similar in conception to the British 'C' and 'D' classes. Armed with seven 14cm (5.5in) guns and with a designed speed of 36 knots, these ships would serve as command ships for the destroyer flotillas. This is *Kinu* in 1927. (Leo van Ginderen collection)

Destroyers were a key part of the IJN's strategy when faced by a more powerful battle fleet despatched from Europe or from the west coast of America. It was envisaged that aggressive torpedo attacks on the enemy battle line would even out the disparity in battleship numbers, while under the cover of night the IJN destroyer flotillas would hope to finish off any damaged 'strays' which had become isolated from the main body of the enemy. Armed with six 53cm torpedoes and four 12.7cm guns, the twenty-four destroyers of the F-41 type laid down postwar were among the most powerful ships of their type in the world. This is *Yunagi* of the *Kamikaze* class.

local superiority for the IJN battle line when the major surface battle – which would, theoretically, decide the outcome of the war – took place somewhere to the south of Japan.

The first ocean-going destroyers of the *Umikaze* class were ordered in 1907, but until the ten smaller second-class destroyers of the *Kaba* class were authorised under the war budget of 1914[5] it was the thirty-two 400-ton destroyers of the *Asakaze* class, built under the 1904 war programme, which constituted the backbone of the destroyer flotillas. Spurred on by the US Navy's Naval Expansion Act of 1916 the IJN proceeded to design the F-41 type, arguably the most powerful destroyer of its time. With a normal displacement of 1,350 tons, these ships were armed with four 12cm (4.7in) guns in single mountings and six 53cm (21in) torpedoes in three twin trainable mountings; their geared steam turbines gave them a designed speed of 39 knots, 4 knots faster even than the US Navy's flush-deckers. Laid down from 1918 onwards, twenty-four ships were built (they were subsequently known as the *Minekaze* and *Kamikaze* classes). A second-class type, the F-37, with only three guns, four torpedo tubes, and with slightly reduced speed, was designed and built in parallel with the F-41, and became the twenty-one-ship *Momi* and the eight-ship *Wakatabe* classes. These destroyers were authorised under the 1918–21 programmes, and many had been completed by the time of the Washington Conference.

Japanese naval technology was essentially derivative, based on what was perceived to be the best foreign practice. Although by the early 1900s Japan was capable of building its own ships in its own shipyards, fitted out with guns and torpedoes and other equipment of local manufacture, it still liked to 'touch base' at regular intervals, as with the construction of the first of the *Kongo*s in Britain. The Anglo-Japanese Alliance, with its regular exchange of naval delegations, ensured that the IJN was abreast of the latest British technical and tactical developments.

Early turbine machinery was imported, then built under licence: Mitsubishi installed British Parsons turbines, Kawasaki the American Curtis types. During the First World War the Navy Technical Department began the development and design of its own turbine machinery. The resulting Gihon (subsequently Kampon) turbine made its debut in the *Nagato* class. One consequence of Japan's increasing estrangement from Britain and the United States post-Washington was, however, that the IJN failed to keep pace with developments once superheated steam was introduced.

Oil-firing was adopted relatively late because of concerns about expense and availability. Japan had virtually no natural reserves of oil, and during the 1920s was compelled to import seven thousand oil tanks from the United States in order to build up a reserve sufficient for future military operations. It also initiated an agreement with the USSR for the purchase of oil from northern Sakhalin. However, Japan's dependence on foreign oil for its own industrial growth would be increasingly problematic; it would play a major part both in the decision to go to war in 1941, and in her eventual defeat in 1945.

The Marine Nationale of France

The French Marine Nationale was traditionally the British Royal Navy's principal rival in Europe. However, the absence of any coherent or agreed policy had effectively stymied the development of the Marine Nationale during the latter part of the nineteenth century, and political wrangling continued into the early years of the twentieth.

An unstable political situation – where the primary aim of each incoming navy minister seemed to be to undo the work of the last – was reflected in a navy which itself was unsure how to respond to the unquestioned supremacy of its greatest rival, the British Royal Navy. Whereas the Germans single-mindedly set out to build a fleet which was a mirror image of the British fleet, there was an influential school of thought within the Marine Nationale, the 'Jeune Ecole', which favoured what we would nowadays term 'asymmetric warfare'. Instead of investing huge sums in battleships, the adherents of the Jeune Ecole wanted to use large numbers of cheap submarines and torpedo boats to protect French ports from a potential British blockade, and to build large, fast cruisers to harry the sea lines of communication of the British Empire. Once Britain became a potential ally with the signing of the Entente Cordiale in 1904, France could again contemplate the creation of a balanced fleet centred around squadrons of battleships, which would at least dominate the Mediterranean. However, one of the more interesting side-effects of the

Washington Treaty, which effectively prohibited the construction of a new French battle fleet, would be to breathe new life into the ideas of the Jeune Ecole with a renewed emphasis on the construction of a powerful force of submarines and flotilla craft.

French naval construction during the period which preceded the Great War was dominated by two major long-term programmes, each of which was intended to arrest decline and to give direction and structure to the Marine Nationale: that of 1900 and that of 1912. The 1900 naval programme was largely responsible for the French Fleet which took part in the First World War. Because of its timing and also because of the protracted building times that were endemic in French shipyards, that fleet was essentially a pre-dreadnought fleet. The first of the class of six 'semi-dreadnought' battleships of the *Danton* class which formed the elite 1st Battle Squadron of the Armée Navale in 1914 was laid down seven months after the completion of HMS *Dreadnought*, and took four years to build.[6] By the outbreak of war on 3 August 1914 only two French dreadnoughts were in commission, and these were already outclassed by contemporary foreign construction. The other major component of the 1900 naval programme was the armoured cruiser, of which no fewer than twenty-four were to be built. These were powerful (and expensive) ships, but the seven armoured cruisers completed between 1904 and 1910 were totally outclassed by the British and German dreadnought battlecruisers, and were obsolescent by 1914.

The destroyers built during this period were too small and too fragile to be much use in combat, even in the relatively benign waters of the Mediterranean. Their direct-drive turbines were prone to frequent breakdown, and fuel consumption at cruising speed was too high to enable them to keep company with the battle fleet for long periods. A shortage of modern destroyers for fleet work in 1913 was 'resolved' by the Cartesian subterfuge of reclassifying the old, small 330-tonne and 450-tonne types as *torpilleurs d'escadre* ('fleet' torpedo boats) and padding out the first-line destroyer flotillas with them.

France had been prominent in the development of the submarine, but, as in other areas of naval activity, extensive investment in experimental models failed to deliver viable and effective production types. Most French submarines of pre-war design were small coastal boats, with diving times which were found postwar to be well in excess of contemporary German U-boats; they had unreliable propulsion machinery and fragile electrical switchboards and mechanical linkages. They obtained few successes during the First World War, and there were numerous accidents, many of which resulted in the loss of the submarine.

The *Statut Naval* of 1912 marked France's first attempt to build a modern navy which could compete in quantitative and qualitative terms with Britain and Germany. By this time the big-ship proponents of the Marine Nationale were firmly in the driving seat, and France's first dreadnoughts were well on the way to completion. Under the 1912 programme no fewer than twenty-

The three super-dreadnoughts of the *Bretagne* class, armed with ten 340mm (13.4in) guns in twin turrets and comparable to the British *Iron Duke*s, were the most modern French battleships at the time of the Washington Conference. This is *Provence* shortly after completion in 1915. (Courtesy of Robert Dumas)

eight super-dreadnought battleships were to be in service by 1920, together with ten scout cruisers, fifty-two torpedo boats (of which thirty-two were to be large fleet units of 1,500 tonnes), ninety-four submarines and ten vessels for distant stations. Three battleships of the *Bretagne* class armed with ten 340mm (13.4in) guns were duly laid down in 1912, as well as five even larger ships of the *Normandie* class, armed with twelve 340mm guns in quadruple turrets, in 1913–14. These were to have been followed by four 29,000-tonne ships of the *Lyon* class armed with sixteen 340mm guns, to be laid down in early 1915. Competitive sketch designs for battlecruisers, with two or three quadruple 340mm mountings and a speed of 27–28 knots, were followed by a 1914 proposal from the Naval Staff to build eight *grands éclaireurs d'escadre* (literally 'large fleet scouts') for strategic scouting (cf. the US Navy's proposed 'battle scouts' of 1916). The French Naval Estimates accordingly increased from 415m francs in 1911 to more than 600m francs in 1914.

However, when war was declared on 3 August 1914 not a single ship of this programme had been completed. The early successes of the German Army meant that large tracts of northern France, where much of the country's heavy industry was located, were occupied. The dockyards lost their younger men to conscription, and the efforts of the remaining workforce were increasingly directed to the production of field guns and munitions. The naval infrastructure that remained was sufficient only to maintain the existing fleet, most of which was based in the Mediterranean. The three *Bretagne*s were duly completed in 1915–16, but work was largely abandoned on the following *Normandie* class after October 1914, by which time three had been launched. The battleships of the *Lyon* class were never laid down, nor

Ernest Renan, one of a series of powerful but dated armoured cruisers completed prewar.
During the ten years which preceded the Washington Conference, the Marine Nationale failed to
complete a single modern cruiser of the scout or fleet type. (Leo van Ginderen collection)

were the projected scout cruisers of the *Lamotte-Piquet* class. Only three fleet
torpedo boats were completed during the entire war, and when the navy was
desperate for new destroyers for anti-submarine duties in the Mediterranean
in 1917 they had to be ordered from Japan.

France therefore entered the Washington Conference with the worst possible
negotiating hand.[7] Although Great Britain was drained financially by the war,
she at least had her military-industrial infrastructure intact, and the Royal
Navy was still the most powerful and technologically advanced in the world.
France, by contrast, was left with a rapidly ageing fleet of ships of outmoded
design and with her infrastructure either seriously disrupted or in ruins. The
ambitious 1912 naval programme had been stillborn, and in the immediate
aftermath of the war the twin pressures of demobilisation and obsolescence
compelled the French to dispose of large numbers of existing ships, and to
focus on rebuilding infrastructure while the preliminary planning took place
for a completely new generation of warships. The order of priority established
by the General Staff in 1919 was firstly for 'destroyers' (English terminology
was used to embrace the new flotilla craft under consideration), secondly for
light cruisers, and thirdly for battleships. When the Washington Conference
took place there was no new generation of capital ships on the drawing board,
and the Marine Nationale was a pale, exhausted shadow of its former self.

In terms of technology, too, France had slipped well behind the other
major naval powers by the time of the Washington Conference. The Marine
Nationale was slow to adopt the 'all-big-gun' battleship, and when it did
so failed to appreciate the radical changes in protection and fire control
systems which would inevitably follow. Thus the dreadnought and

super-dreadnought battleships laid down prior to the Great War had the same graduated all-over armour plating as the pre-dreadnoughts, with a substantial upper belt and heavy plating which extended to the bow and almost to the stern.[8] This distribution of armour was the antithesis of the US Navy's 'all-or-nothing' system; it was effective against the medium-calibre guns of pre-dreadnought battleships and armoured cruisers, but could be easily penetrated by large-calibre shells. Moreover, the French persisted in the belief that gunnery actions between the main battle lines would be conducted at relatively short ranges, generally 8,000–12,000m. This belief not only underpinned French persistence with upper armour belts,[9] but obviated the need to develop long-range fire control systems; at 8,000m it was thought that a 12in/305mm gun would generally hit the target, while medium- and small-calibre guns would rely on their high rate of fire to score regular hits. Director control was not trialled by the Marine Nationale until 1920, when a British system from Vickers was fitted in the battleship *Bretagne*. Because of this the 340mm turrets in the *Bretagne* class were designed with an elevation of only 12° for a maximum range of 14,500m. Modifications to a single turret of *Provence* were made in 1917 (i.e. within two years of her completion) to permit firing to 18,000m at 18° elevation, but modifications to her other turrets and those of her two sisters had to wait until after the end of the war.

In propulsion the French were also behind their competitors. Steam turbines had been adopted for the last pre-dreadnoughts of the *Danton* class, and also powered the more modern fleet torpedo boats. However, the early direct-drive turbines proved uneconomic at lower speeds and there were problems with astern turbines – with the *Normandie* class the French planned to revert to a mix of turbines on the centre shafts and triple-expansion engines on the outer shafts for cruising (cf. the US Navy above). The French were late in adopting oil-firing and the first, experimental geared turbine installation (in the destroyer *Enseigne Gabolde*) had to wait until after the Armistice.

Moreover, the propulsion machinery of submarines and flotilla craft was notoriously prone to failure. The latter ships were generally built by private shipyards to a specification which permitted considerable latitude with regard to the hull form and the propulsion machinery installed. Thus the most modern fleet torpedo boats of the *Bouclier* and *Bisson* classes had four different types of turbines installed: Parsons, Bréguet, Rateau and Zoelly. Two ships, *Bouclier* and *Casque*, had three shafts whereas the others units of the 800-tonne type had only two. This resulted in wide variations in operational performance; the slowest ship, *Commandant Bory*, managed only 24 knots in service, whereas the fastest, *Casque*, made 29 knots.[10] The adoption of machinery of widely differing design from a variety of manufacturers inevitably complicated maintenance because of the need for the naval dockyards to carry large numbers of different spares.

Italy

Italy was a relatively new country, unified only in 1861, and in its first naval battle, the Battle of Lissa in 1866, had been defeated by an Austrian fleet inferior in numbers. However, by the early 1900s Italy was confident enough to attempt to realise some of her colonial ambitions in North and East Africa, and successful operations in the central and eastern Mediterranean against Turkey in 1910–11 led to the annexation of Tripolitania together with the occupation of Rhodes and islands in the Dodecanese, which subsequently became Italian naval bases.

The Italian relationship with Austria–Hungary during this period was ambiguous. Since 1882 Italy had been a partner in a triple alliance with Germany and Austria–Hungary, and the Naval Convention of 1913 envisaged the collaboration of all three fleets in the Mediterranean under unified Austrian command. On the other hand, there were long-standing territorial disputes between Italy and the Austro-Hungarian Empire, which centred on Italian claims to the Trieste and Trentino regions in the north-east Adriatic, and Italian ships were designed specifically to counter those of Austria–Hungary. When Italy entered the war on 24 May 1915 it was on the side of the Allies, and after successfully bottling up the Austro-Hungarian Fleet in the Adriatic for the next three and a half years it was the Italian Navy that took the surrender of the latter in 1919.

Under Navy Minister Carlo Mirabello (1903–9) the Regia Marina developed coherent programmes which responded to Italian strategic requirements. However, the need to minimise the funding of major surface units in any given financial year, together with the relative inexperience of Italian shipyards, resulted in protracted building times, so that ships which were of modern design when laid down were often outdated on completion. Thus the first of the pre-dreadnought battleships of the *Vittorio Emanuele* class, which had a number of advanced and innovative features, was laid down in September 1901 but took seven years to complete. The Italians also laid down four excellent armoured cruisers in 1905–7, the last of which (*San Giorgio*) incorporated advanced features such as four-screw steam turbines, a gyroscopic compass, a liquid-based anti-roll system, and electric gun-mounting machinery, but by the time they were completed four/five years later they were completely outclassed by the new British and German battlecruisers. Nevertheless, by the time Italy joined the war on the side of the Allies five modern dreadnoughts mounting multiple 305mm (12in) guns in twin and triple turrets were in service, with a further ship close to completion, and by the time of the Washington Conference it could be argued that the Italian Navy was in a much better state than the French Marine Nationale.

Initially the Italians built small, fast scout cruisers (*esploratori*) comparable to those in the British Royal Navy for fleet work. However, by the outbreak of war they had veered towards the ideas of the British Admiral Fisher, and were building what were essentially large destroyers, designated *esploratori*

Leonardo da Vinci, one of six modern dreadnoughts completed by the Italian Navy from 1913. Armed with British 12in (305mm) guns, these impressive ships were instrumental in raising the status of Italy as a naval power to a point at which it was felt appropriate to accord her nominal parity with France in the Washington negotiations. (Leo van Ginderen collection)

leggeri, for this role. The three ships of the *Mirabello* class laid down in 1914–15 had a displacement of 1,750 tonnes, a speed of 35 knots, and were armed with eight single 102mm (4in) guns and two twin 450mm (17.7in) torpedo tubes. They were particularly successful, and were followed by the five ships of the even-larger *Leone* class, which, although ordered in 1917, could not be laid down until 1921 because of a shortage of steel.[11] These had eight 120mm (4.7in) guns in four twin-gun mountings, together with two triple banks of torpedo tubes. They displaced fully 2,200 tonnes, and clearly influenced the design of the first French *contre-torpilleurs* of the *Tigre* class (with which incidentally they shared their 'Big Cat' names[12]).

From 1912 onwards the Italians began the construction of a series of turbine-powered three-funnelled destroyers, beginning with the ten-ship *Indomito* class. With a displacement of 650–800 tonnes and a speed of 30 knots, these proved to be very successful ships. By the time of the Washington Conference no fewer than thirty had been completed, with a further six building, and the latest ships were armed with three/four 102mm guns and two twin 450mm torpedo tubes. In the immediate postwar period they were complemented by a series of larger, two-funnelled ships based on a Yarrow design. The four 900-tonne *Palestros*, launched 1919–20, were followed by the four 1,100-tonne *Curtatones*. Both types had a speed of 32 knots and an armament of four 102mm guns and four/ six 450mm torpedoes. These later destroyers were superior in every respect to the French 800-tonnes type.

The Regia Marina was always open to new ideas, but was hampered by limited funding and a weak military-industrial base. It was an Italian designer, Cuniberti, who was the earliest proponent of the 'all-big-gun' battleship –

During the Great War the Regia Marina embarked on the construction of large numbers of modern flotilla craft, some of which were based on British designs. This is the 800-ton *Confienza*, completed postwar and armed with four 102mm (4in) guns and four 450mm (17.7in) torpedoes.

a proposal judged over-ambitious by the Italian navy minister of the day.[13] Faced by the particular difficulties of blockading the Austro-Hungarian Fleet in the confined waters of the Adriatic, the Italians showed themselves capable of evolving innovative strategies and technologies on a smaller scale. The success of the *MAS*-type fast motor torpedo boat, of which three hundred were built, culminated in the sinking of the battleship *Szent Istvan* in open waters in June 1918. Underwater warfare also became something of a speciality. Small coastal submarines were built in numbers,[14] and the Italians developed automatic setting for moored mines. In October 1918 frogmen with self-propelled mines sank a second Austro-Hungarian dreadnought, the *Viribus Unitis*, in Pola Harbour.

Conclusion

The Washington Conference took place at a crossroads in naval affairs. Of the older, established navies the British Royal Navy was at the peak of its power but facing an uncertain future as postwar financial stringency tightened its grip, while the French Marine Nationale was at a low ebb and in serious need of renewal. The ambitious US naval construction programme of 1916 on the one hand threatened British naval supremacy, and on the other threatened to stoke up a new naval arms race with Japan, with each of these two powers vying to exert political and economic influence in the Western Pacific. Meanwhile Italy, another young, ambitious power, had taken advantage of France's deteriorating naval situation to build up her naval forces to a level which, by December 1921, gave her almost as many modern dreadnoughts and a superior force of modern flotilla craft. The proposals for establishing relative naval strengths and status at Washington would be based on a 'snap-shot' of the force levels prevailing at that time, taking into account not only ships in service but also those on the stocks. This would be at the root of the flaws inherent in the treaty, many of which would be exposed only later in the decade when an attempt was made to extend the treaty ratios agreed for capital ships and aircraft carriers to other types of ship.

Table 1.1: Dreadnought Battleships and Battlecruisers in Service on 12 November 1921

	GB	USA	Japan	France	Italy
12in gun battleships	–	8	1	4	5(6)
12in gun battlecruisers	2	–	–	–	–
13.4/13.5/14in gun battleships	12	11	4	3	–
13.4/13.5/14in gun battlecruisers	3	–	4	–	–
15in gun battleships	10	–	–	–	–
15in gun battlecruisers	5	–	–	–	–
16in gun battleships	–	1	2	–	–

Notes: One Italian dreadnought (*Leonardo da Vinci*) had been sunk in 1916 but subsequently salvaged; she was to have been rebuilt. Japanese 16in gun battleship *Mutsu* is counted as completed (disputed at Conference).

Table 1.2: Battleships & Battlecruisers Building or Projected on 12 November 1921

Great Britain
Battleships

4 N3	(LD 1922)	48,500t	9–18in (3 × III)	23 knots

Battlecruisers

4 G3	ord 1921	48,400t	9–16in (3 × III)	31 knots

USA
Battleships

3 Colorado	LD 1919-20	32,600t	8–16in (4 × II)	21 knots
6 South Dakota	LD 1920-21	43,000t	12–16in (4 × III)	23 knots

Battlecruisers

6 Lexington	LD 1920-21	43,500t	8–16in (4 × II)	33 knots

Japan
Battleships

2 Kaga	LD 1920	40,000t	10–16in (5 × II)	26 knots
4 Kii	2 ord 1921	42,500t	10–16in (5 × II)	30 knots

Battlecruisers

4 Amagi	LD 1920-21	41,000t	10–16in (5 × II)	30 knots
4 No.13	(LD 1922)	47,500t	8–18in (4 × II)	30 knots

France & Italy
None

Key: LD – laid down, (LD) – to be laid down, ord – ordered

CHAPTER 2

Postwar Projects 1918–1921

The material state and the status of the navies in question in the period leading up to Washington has been outlined in general terms in the previous chapter. This chapter aims to look in greater detail at some of the projects developed in the immediate postwar period. Many of those projects reflected the lessons learned during the war at sea 1914–18. They therefore not only informed and influenced both the discussion at Washington and its outcomes, but they also provide an indication of the thinking that would dominate naval development in the years which followed.

Rather than take each of the five navies in turn and describe in detail the various projects on the drawing board, the author has chosen to select certain key projects which reflect the thinking of the immediate postwar period regarding the established categories of warship: capital ships, aircraft carriers, cruisers, destroyers and submarines.

The G3 Battlecruisers: Britain

With the end of the First World War the Royal Navy was acutely aware that it would need new battleships to oppose the latest American and Japanese designs. These ships would need to incorporate the lessons both of Jutland and of postwar trials of shells and protection systems. They would also need to mount guns of larger calibre than the 15in weapons mounted in the battleships of the *Queen Elizabeth* and *Revenge* classes and the warbuilt battlecruisers.

The first step was to cancel the last three battlecruisers of the *Hood* class, with their 'pre-Jutland' protection systems, and to proceed with a series of studies. The Admiralty initially hoped to order three battleships and a single battlecruiser in 1920–21, and three battlecruisers and a battleship the following year. The designs are interesting because, unlike those of their US Navy counterparts, there was considerable interaction between them, particularly with regard to layout, and also because they were the most radical designs of the postwar era, and therefore influenced subsequent construction to an extent unmatched by the relatively conservative designs already adopted by the United States and Japan.

An initial report in 1920 by a committee headed by Vice-Admiral Phillimore suggested that Royal Navy requirements would be met by a battleship of 35,000 tons with either five twin turrets or four triple turrets and a speed of 23 knots, and a battlecruiser with four twin mountings and a speed of 33 knots. These ships would have been the equivalents of the *South Dakota* class battleships and the *Lexington* class battlecruisers projected for the US Navy, except that 35,000 tons was a spectacularly optimistic figure, particularly with regard to the battlecruisers, given that the American ships had a projected displacement in excess of 43,000 tons.[1]

The US Navy designs were all 16in-gun ships, but since the British 15in gun had similar hitting power to the American weapon, and both the Americans and the Japanese were rumoured to be considering larger-calibre weapons, the Royal Navy was inclined to move to the next level and to adopt the 18in gun as the basis for its new designs. A 40-calibre weapon was already in service aboard the light battlecruiser *Furious* and two monitors. It had proved satisfactory but too short for accuracy and penetration at long range; it was therefore decided to begin development of a new 45-calibre gun. The Royal Navy initially favoured the twin mounting – perceived to be simpler and more reliable – over the triple adopted for the latest US Navy battleships. However, it was clear that there would be space and weight advantages in adopting triple mountings, so an improvised triple mounting using 15in guns was trialled aboard the monitor *Lord Clive* to study the possible mutual interference of shell trajectories in salvo fire.

The adoption of the 18in gun brought with it a significant increase in the dimensions and displacement of the hull – initial estimates suggested a ship of perhaps 50,000 tons. This would have serious implications not only for cost, but also for infrastructure: hardly any of the existing docks could accommodate such a leviathan, and beam would have to be restricted to less than 110ft if the ship were to transit the Suez or Panama canals. Moreover a ship armed with 18in guns would, according to established design practice, require protection sufficient to resist shells of similar calibre. With engagements conducted at increasingly long range, this implied a vertical armour belt of 18in thickness (less if it were inclined), and deck armour of the maximum thickness compatible with stability, probably in the region of 8–9in.

Mindful of the need to minimise the size (and cost) of the new ships, a study was undertaken of three possible levels of protection: the highest level was protection against 18in shellfire throughout; the intermediate level was protection of the magazines against 18in shellfire and protection of the machinery spaces against 15in; and the lowest level was protection against 15in shellfire throughout.[2] The highest level was estimated to cost an additional 7,000 tons and 2 knots speed over the lowest, and the intermediate level 5,000 tons and 1 knot of speed.

Detailed studies were then undertaken to see what could be done, based on the docks available. Two baseline designs of June 1920 mounted four twin or three triple 18in guns and had a speed of 25/26 knots. They became the first of a series of sketch designs, which for the battleships advanced from the

HMS *Hood*: Midship Section   G3 Battlecruiser: Midship Section

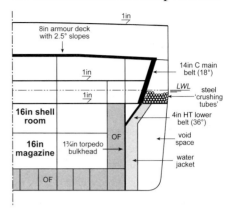

The pre-Jutland protection system of *Hood* features the traditional 'graduated armour' system which predated the dreadnought. The main 12in side belt of cemented plate over the magazines and machinery spaces is complemented by upper belts of 7in and 5in which extend to the upper deck. In theory the splinters of shells striking the upper belts would be kept out of the ship's vitals by the multiple lightly plated decks and inboard bulkheads, while shells passing over the ship's sides would strike the 2in plating on the upper deck at an oblique angle, making full penetration unlikely. As improved fire control made engagements at longer ranges possible, it became apparent that this system of lightly plated decks and internal bulkheads could be penetrated by plunging shell, resulting in the detonation of magazines and the disabling of machinery. Even before *Hood*'s completion it was recognised that her horizontal protection was totally inadequate, and that subsequent capital ship designs would have to be armoured on completely different principles, with heavy box protection over the magazines and machinery but little protection outside the 'citadel'. The G3 design exemplifies this new system of protection.

Nevertheless, *Hood* incorporated some advanced features which would be retained in the British postwar designs: these included an inclined main belt, intended to increase the theoretical thickness of the armour against shells with trajectories close to the horizontal, and to increase the angle of obliquity at which AP shell would strike at longer ranges, thereby reducing its chances of penetration, and an anti-torpedo bulge 10ft deep which featured outer void compartments and an inner compartment filled with sealed steel tubes to absorb the force of an underwater explosion before it reached the holding bulkhead. Both the inclined belt and the steel tubes were to be features of the G3 battlecruiser design, the tubes being used as a filler between the inclined belt and the (vertical) sides of the hull to stop uncontrolled flooding of this space; they were replaced in the anti-torpedo system by a liquid-loaded (water) compartment inboard of the void spaces. Because of concerns about the ship's stability in the damaged condition the outer void compartments were to have been fitted with a compressed-air system similar to those installed in submarines for blowing out tanks. Note the very different shape of the outer hull, the external bulge of *Hood* being superseded by an anti-torpedo system which was purely internal, as in the latest US Navy construction. In contrast to their American counterparts, however, the G3s persisted with the placing of the oil fuel tanks inboard of the torpedo bulkhead – in the US system oil fuel was used as the liquid in the outer impact-absorbing 'sandwich'.

letter 'L', and for the battlecruisers descended from the letter 'K', the figure '2' or '3' being appended to indicate twin or triple turrets.

The layout of these early designs was entirely conventional, with the machinery amidships and the turrets fore and aft. Both were judged to be too big, despite a novel attempt to reduce length by adopting a transom stern. The armoured belt of the battleship was felt to be too short, while the battlecruiser was altogether under-protected yet still failed to match the speed of the US Navy's *Lexington*s.

The next series of designs was much more radical: all had the machinery aft and the main guns forward and amidships. This had the effect of reducing the length of the citadel, thereby saving on both belt and deck armour. The centre turret or turrets were also amidships, at the widest point of the hull, so the magazines could be kept well away from the sides of the ship. The bridge and control spaces were located in a distinctive tower between the gun mountings, with heavy directors for the main/secondary batteries and the anti-aircraft main fire control position atop the tower. The funnel (or funnels in the case of the battlecruisers) and tripod mainmast were located on a low after superstructure, the sides of which were angled sharply inboard at its forward end in order to improve the arcs of the after turret (or turrets in the case of the four-turret designs). In the M2 and M3 battleship designs the engine rooms were – unusually – located forward of the boiler rooms in order to maximise the depth of the torpedo protection for the former.

The weight savings of this novel arrangement were substantial: almost 1,800 tons in the three-turret design, 1,500 tons in the four-turret design. The adoption of the triple turret over the twin saved a further 1,000 tons. Thus the total weight of protection in the four-turret L2 was 18,850 tons (37.1 per cent of displacement) while in the three-turret M3 it was 16,060 tons (31.4 per cent) for the same level of protection.

There were some drawbacks with the new layout. There were concerns regarding the safe firing arcs of the after turret, as experience with HMS *Furious* had revealed the blast effects of the 18in gun to be severe. The other major problem was the relatively small proportion of the waterline which was protected: flooding of the unarmoured ends of the ship could threaten

Table 2.1: Armour: 'L' versus 'M'

Design	Length of belt	Weight of armour	% of displacement
L2	470ft	18,850 tons	37.1%
L3	445ft	17,800 tons	36.3%
M2	440ft	17,310 tons	33.2%
M3	401ft	16,060 tons	31.4%

Note: Table from David K Brown, *The Grand Fleet*, p.174.

Design M2, one of the more striking British 18in battleship designs which preceded the Washington Conference. Length and weight were saved by locating the armament all forward and the machinery aft, but it was found that adopting three triple turrets (design M3) in place of the four twins saved 40ft in length and 1,800 tons in protection. (Drawn by Ian Johnston)

stability. This was exacerbated by the adoption of an inclined armour belt, which made possible the flooding of the outer hull at the sides of the citadel. The designers went on to effectively resolve the problem by building in an unusually high metacentric height, but it should be noted that the design would not have met the US Navy's criteria, which insisted on protection for a minimum proportion of the waterline.

Despite these drawbacks the advantages of the new, radical layout were considerable, and the M3 design was further developed as N3, which was finally adopted as the battleship for the new programme in November 1921, immediately prior to the Washington Conference. The final design was 50ft longer, but was otherwise similar.

The attempt to design a viable battlecruiser armed with 18in guns proved more problematic because of the need to accommodate machinery spaces approximately 100ft longer than those of the battleships but armoured on the same scale. The I3, which had a four-shaft propulsion plant with a conventional layout but was otherwise similar to the M3, would have been 915ft long, thereby precluding docking at either Portsmouth or Rosyth. This was deemed unacceptable so in the next design, H3, the number of turrets was reduced from three to two. This arrangement was disliked, and the final G3 design reverted to the M3 layout, but with a reduction in main gun calibre – initially from 18in to 16.5in, and subsequently to 16in. This was the design ordered in the run-up to the Washington Conference. Because of the greater size of the propulsion plant, the G3 featured a much longer after section than N3 and had two funnels. The G3s would, however, have been only 36ft longer than their battleship counterparts; they would have had a similar displacement, and their protection would have been on only a slightly reduced scale.

It is difficult to avoid the conclusion that these postwar designs provided ample justification for the Washington Conference. The attempt to build battleships and battlecruisers armed with guns of greater calibre than 16in, incorporating the latest thinking on protection, proved to be a far greater

exercise in escalation than the British Admiralty initially anticipated. The
N3 battleship, had it been built, would have been nearly 200ft longer than
the *Queen Elizabeth*s it was designed to succeed, and displacement would
have been almost double. Construction would have entailed a massive
investment of taxpayers' money both to build the ships and to provide the
necessary infrastructure to maintain them. In the postwar British economic
and political climate this level of funding was simply not possible.

Table 2.2: The G3 and N3: a Comparison

	G3 battlecruiser	N3 battleship
Displacement:	48,400 tons	48,500 tons
Dimensions:	856ft oa × 106ft	820ft oa × 106ft
	(261m × 32m)	(250m × 32m)
Machinery:	4-shaft geared turbines;	2-shaft geared turbines;
	160,000shp = 31–32 knots	60,000shp = 23 knots
Armament:	9–16in/45 (3 × III)	9–18in/45 (3 × III)
	16–6in/50 (8 × II)	16–6in/50 (8 × II)
	6–4.7in HA (6 × I)	6–4.7in HA (6 × I)
Protection:	belt: 14in/12in	belt: 15in/13½in
	deck: 8in/4in	deck: 8in/4in

Despite all the above these designs were extremely influential, and made
a considerable impact abroad. Key features of the N3 and G3, including the
all- forward main armament and the tower structure for the main fire control
directors, were subsequently adopted by the French, both for their fast
battleships of the *Dunkerque* class and for their successors of the *Richelieu*
class. The G3s would have also been the first post-dreadnought capital ships
to have their secondary battery not in casemates nor in single shielded upper-
deck mountings, but in power-operated twin turrets which protected the gun
crews against the elements and against the blast from the ship's own main
battery. This feature would be adopted for all capital ships designed after
1922.

A number of British commentators have suggested that had they been built,
the G3 battlecruisers could have held their own against any of the modern
battleships completed during the Second World War, and as far as gunnery
engagements go this is undoubtedly true. However, there were aspects of
battleship design which became more important during the 1930s which the
G3 failed to anticipate, and for which it was poorly adapted. Although the
anti-aircraft battery, comprising six single 4.7in HA (high-angle) guns and
four ten-barrelled (sic) 2-pdr pom-poms with elaborate fire control provision,

G3 Battlecruiser 1921 (GB)

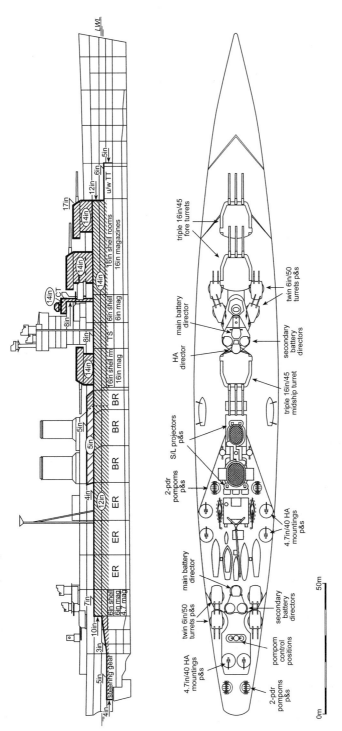

In the plan view, note the division of the secondary armament between the forward and after parts of the ship. Note also the disposition of the anti-aircraft battery, which had to be located on and around the after superstructure to keep it clear of the blast from the big guns.

was particularly advanced for its time, it had to be concentrated around the after superstructure because of the potential blast effect of the main guns. Any attempt to provide a substantial and well-balanced AA battery of the type considered necessary by the mid-1930s would have been frustrated by the layout. Significantly the next class of British battleships, the *King George V* class, would revert to a more conventional arrangement with two turrets forward and one aft, despite the consequent disadvantage of having to make space amidships for the catapult and aircraft hangars. The French took advantage of a modified G3 layout to locate the aircraft-handling facilities of their new battleships above the stern, but even they would have reverted to a more conventional main battery arrangement for the fourth unit of the *Richelieu* class, *Gascogne*. There was also protection for a greater proportion of the waterline in the later British battleships, and inclined internal armour was abandoned in favour of a more conventional deep vertical external belt in the *King George V* design of the mid-1930s.

The Aircraft Carrier Hermes: Britain

In late 1917, following the entry of the United States into the war, the Royal Navy constructor Stanley Goodall was seconded to the US Navy's Bureau of Construction and Repair (C&R).[3] He took with him a number of warship plans, including sketch designs for the latest British aircraft carriers. When addressing the General Board on the latest British operational thinking, he stated:

> Air fighting has become a feature of naval operations, and the tactical movements of a fleet before an engagement opens will, most probably, be governed by information obtained from air scouts. A series of fights between opposing aircraft will most likely be a preliminary to a fleet action. A fleet should, therefore be attended by reconnaissance and fighting machines ...

Jutland still loomed large in the Royal Navy's consciousness, and would continue to dominate its thinking throughout the 1920s and well into the

The aircraft carrier *Hermes* off Plymouth shortly after completion. In the final design the bow was enclosed and plated up to the flight deck. Note the raised wind-break on the flight deck. (David Hobbs collection)

Aircraft Carrier *Hermes* 1920 (GB)

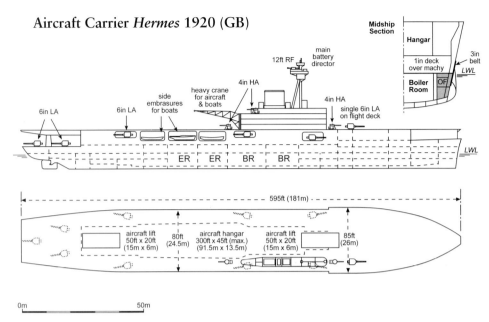

The drawings are based on plans dating from March 1920. They show a main armament of ten 6in guns: a single mounting forward of the island, six in embrasures along the sides of the hull, just beneath the flight deck, and three on the stern. They would shortly be replaced by the same number of 5.5in guns from the discarded cruiser *Birkenhead*. When completed only the six side-mounted guns would remain, the quarterdeck being cleared to accommodate seaplanes. The 4in HA guns were disposed at either end of the island superstructure. The hangar, like those of later British carriers, was enclosed, with workshops to the sides.

The completion of *Hermes* was delayed by the closure of Armstrong's Elswick yard and by subsequent changes to the design plans, which included plating up the bow to the flight deck and 'T'-shaped aircraft lifts. The incomplete hull was towed to Devonport dockyard, where *Hermes* would finally be completed in February 1924.

1930s. The prevailing view was that the Grand Fleet had failed to impose itself on the German High Seas Fleet largely because of inadequate intelligence regarding the latter's strength, location, and course during the various phases of the battle. Traditionally it had been the role of 'scout' cruisers to provide this information, but a combination of poor visibility, inadequate reporting and effective use of cruisers by the enemy to 'screen' their own force had frustrated this at Jutland. Although poor visibility (and poor weather) would similarly inhibit scouting aircraft, the latter had the advantage of operating in three dimensions, which meant that in good or fair conditions they could overfly an enemy fleet and more easily establish its strength, formation and course.

Aerial scouting was now seen as so important to the success of a major naval action that each side would attempt to prevent the other from acquiring this intelligence by contesting the airspace above its ships. Fighter aircraft would therefore be required to shoot down enemy reconnaissance aircraft before they could get in position to report, and to secure the airspace above the enemy fleet to ensure that friendly reconnaissance aircraft could perform their mission without interference.

It is in this context that the design of *Hermes*, begun in 1917, needs to be considered. She was the world's first 'through-deck' aircraft carrier to be designed from the keel up,[4] and her design was in every respect a response to the perceived operational needs of the Grand Fleet. Intended to complement the scout cruisers, she was intended to operate with them in the vanguard of the fleet, where she might be engaged by enemy cruisers tasked with a similar mission. She therefore needed to be armed to protect herself. Initially Admiral Beatty, C-in-C of the Grand Fleet, wanted eleven 6in guns, although this was later reduced to ten 5.5in and, in the final design, only six.

The main armament was not the only 'cruiser' aspect of the design. Although not built on a modified cruiser hull, as has been claimed by some, *Hermes* was built to cruiser standards: her hull was similar in length – though slightly broader in the beam – to the contemporary 'Elizabethans', she had the standard two-shaft light cruiser propulsion plant, which had an output of 40,000shp, and protection was also on a par with contemporary light cruisers, comprising a 3in (76mm) belt and 1in (25mm) deck over the magazines and machinery spaces.

Unlike the converted merchantman *Argus*, *Hermes* had a prominent island to starboard, featuring a single broad funnel and a heavy tripod with a fire control top equipped with both a director and a 12ft rangefinder.

There was a large enclosed hangar for some twenty aircraft with large rectangular lifts at either end. In the final design the latter would be replaced

An overhead of *Hermes* during the mid-1920s, with a battleship of the *Iron Duke* class in the background. The three aircraft with rounded wingtips are Fairey Flycatcher fighters. During construction the configuration of the lifts was changed to a 'T' shape, enabling aircraft to be transferred between the flight deck and the hangar deck with wings fully deployed. The fore and aft restraining wires which were a common feature of the early British carriers can just be made out on the centre section of the flight deck. As completed *Hermes* had all her low-angle 5.5in guns at gallery deck level, with four 4in HA guns fore and aft of the island. (David Hobbs collection)

by 'T'-shaped lifts better suited to the raising and striking down of aircraft with fully-deployed wings, and the lifts would be moved farther apart in order to accommodate a new system of longitudinal arrester wires. Proposals for a trainable catapult forward (to enable aircraft to be launched without the ship having to be turned into the wind) and for a trainable flying-off deck forward were ultimately rejected.

For her time *Hermes* was conceptually far in advance of any aircraft carrier contemplated abroad, and was particularly influential in some of the carrier designs (and conversions) of the 1920s. When completed she proved to be an excellent seaboat, with good handling qualities despite her large 'sail' area. However, even as she was being designed she was criticised by former naval aviators, now serving with the newly created Royal Air Force, as too small and too slow. Both criticisms were borne out by later experience, and by the 1930s *Hermes* was regarded very much as a 'second-line' carrier unable to accommodate or operate successfully the latest high-performance aircraft. *Hermes* therefore serves to exemplify one of the Royal Navy's key problems during the interwar period: without influential aviators in its ranks the navy was poorly placed to anticipate technical and tactical developments in aviation, and preferred to design ships in which seagoing qualities, protection and anti-aircraft capabilities took precedence over the size, capability and ease of operation of the air group.

Scout Cruisers for the Pacific Powers

As early as 1914 proposals for an eight–four battle fleet drafted for the Imperial Japanese Navy included three 'scout cruisers' of 6,000 tons armed with four single 20cm (8in) guns. This first project was postponed following the outbreak of war in Europe, due to a shortage of destroyers. However, the General Staff tasked the Navy Technical Department with drawing up a preliminary scout cruiser design, and Kure Naval Dockyard was charged with the development of a 20cm gun to replace the Vickers-derived 45-calibre Type 41. The plans which resulted were for a ship of 7,200 tons with a maximum speed of 36 knots, a 76mm (3in) non-cemented (NC) belt and an armoured deck of special steel over the magazines and machinery, and a range of 6,000–8,000nm at 14 knots. Armament was to have comprised four twin and four single 14cm/50-calibre guns of the type currently being fitted as secondary armament in the battleships of the *Fuso* and *Ise* classes,[5] together with four pairs of fixed 61cm torpedo tubes; it was envisaged that the 14cm guns might be replaced by a smaller number of 20cm.[6]

European influences (especially the Royal Navy) then pushed the IJN in the direction of smaller fleet cruisers armed with single 14cm guns. However, the US Naval Expansion Act of 1916, which included ten scout cruisers of 7,100 tons armed with 6in (15.2cm) guns, prompted the IJN to revive its own scout cruiser proposal, and in the summer of 1917 eight 5,500-ton cruisers were replaced in the building programme by six 3,500-ton fleet cruisers for flotilla work, and three 7,200-ton scout cruisers. A further three ships of the

Furutaka class 1921 (Jap)

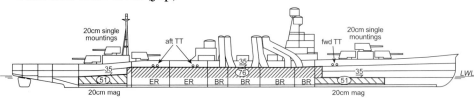

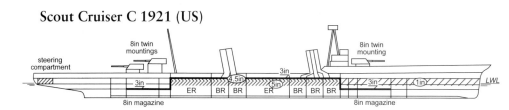

Scout Cruiser C 1921 (US)

Two different approaches to the same problem. Both designs were formulated in early/mid-1921, prior to the Washington Conference. The upper drawing is of the Japanese *Furutaka*, which was actually built. The six single 20cm (7.9in) guns are in enclosed 'semi-turrets' disposed in two 'pyramids' on the centre-line fore and aft to give maximum broadside fire. The 76mm (3in) non-cemented belt over the machinery spaces is topped by a 35mm deck, and the magazines are protected by armoured boxes with 51mm sides and 35mm crowns – the original design used imperial measurements, hence the slightly odd thicknesses. The seven boiler rooms are grouped together with the engine rooms aft. Note the heavyweight bridge structure with directors atop. The lower drawing is a schematic of design 1c of the series produced for the US Navy in the spring of 1921 (see table 3 for details). The six 8in guns are in twin turrets. There is a narrow 5in (127mm) belt over the machinery spaces, and the armoured deck is of 3in plating with 4.5in slopes at the sides. There is an armoured box over the steering gear, but the magazines (located well below the waterline) have only 3in crowns. Unusually, there is 1in protection on the ship's sides from the main belt to the bow to prevent the waterline forward from being torn up by penetrating hits. The machinery is arranged on the unit system, with two independent groups of boiler rooms, each serving an engine room.

The substantial weight of armour of the US design, combined with the weight of machinery required for 34.5 knots, pushed the displacement up to 11,250 tons, whereas the Japanese *Furutaka* had a designed displacement of only 7,500 tons (although this was largely exceeded on completion). In order to save weight the Japanese employed novel design/construction methods such as the undulating deck line and using side armour to provide longitudinal strength as well as protection. It should be noted that the total weight of the six semi-turrets was 345 tons as compared with 450 tons for the three twin turrets of their half-sisters of the *Aoba* class.

The *Furutaka* design looked backwards to the British 'Elizabethans', while the US Navy designs of spring 1921 anticipated more closely the 'treaty' cruiser, and the various alternatives considered prefigured the guns/protection/speed dilemma which was to haunt the constructors following the signing of the treaty in February 1922. Once the pattern of post-treaty construction became clear there were proposals to rearm the two *Furutaka*s with the new twin 20cm mounting, but construction was by that time too advanced, and reconstruction of these ships had to wait until 1936–37.

The cruiser *Kako*, sister to *Furutaka*, in 1930. Note the six single 'semi-turrets' for the 20cm guns. These would later be replaced by three twin turrets for the 20.3cm guns of the same type fitted in the later 'treaty' cruisers. (Leo van Ginderen collection)

latter type were added to the subsequent eight–six completion programme authorised in March 1918, and the design was recast as a ship of 8,000 tons with five or six twin 14cm mountings. Again the 20cm gun was specified as an alternative, but uncertainties regarding the relative desirability of mounting a larger number of quick-firing guns or a smaller number of heavy-calibre weapons reflected similar debates in the US Navy.

A new eight–eight completion programme authorised in August 1920 included twelve cruisers, of which eight were to be fleet types of 5,500 tons, and four were to be 8,000-ton scout cruisers. It was proposed to begin construction of two 8,000-ton cruisers immediately, but because of continued uncertainties surrounding the design the initial order was for four cruisers of 5,500 tons. A review of requirements was prompted by rumours of modifications to the armament of the US *Omaha* class. Moreover the IJN had also been much impressed by HMS *Hawkins* (armed with seven 7.5in guns), which became the flagship of the China Station in October 1919 and visited Japan the following year. The Japanese Naval Constructor Hiraga Yuzuru therefore proposed a new design for the scout cruiser in 1921, which featured six single 20cm guns all on the centre-line. This would give a main armament broadly comparable to that of *Hawkins* (and with twice the weight of broadside of *Omaha*, together with a heavier torpedo battery) and a speed of 35 knots (comparable to the US Navy ships and 5 knots faster than the British cruisers). Despite this the projected displacement was only 7,500 tons normal, a figure possible only because of the adoption of innovative design and construction techniques (see Chapter 6). Hiraga's proposal was approved by the Naval Staff and detailed planning for the new ships, which would become the *Furutaka* class, was well underway by the time the Washington Conference took place in November 1921.

Meanwhile, on the other side of the Pacific Ocean, the US Navy was considering the scout cruisers which would follow the *Omahas*. The relatively light armament of the latter ships was already attracting criticism, despite continued advocacy of multiple QF guns over slow-firing large-calibre guns in some quarters. The persistence with casemate-mounted guns in the *Omahas* not only weakened broadside fire but resulted in a ship which looked particularly dated when compared with the latest foreign types.

Large scout cruisers armed with 8in guns had been considered as early as 1917, when the USN planning section based in London proposed a number of ship-types similar (but marginally superior) to those currently under construction for the Royal Navy. In consequence the redesign of the battle scouts of 1916 was influenced by HMS *Hood*, and the British 'Elizabethans' set the standard for the next generation of scout cruisers. The planners recommended an armament of six 8in guns on the centre-line, a speed of 32.5 knots, a 3in belt over the machinery, and a substantial torpedo battery. Endurance was to be 10,000nm at 12 knots.

At the same time the Royal Navy's small fleet cruiser type was rejected as having no relevance to US Navy operations in the broad expanses of the Pacific. Sea lines of communication could be both attacked and defended by the large cruiser, and the threat posed by such ships would compel the enemy to use strong escorts for its mercantile fleet. It was further stated that:

> Units of this class will have complete tactical freedom except in the presence of enemy battlecruisers; and even those they will be able to escape by their speed. We consider such a class of intermediate fighting vessels a very important class in screening and scouting operations, as well as in preying on the enemy's communications.[7]

These arguments were accepted by the General Board, which in 1920 initiated a series of preliminary designs for 8in gun cruisers of around 10,000 tons displacement. In September 1920 the General Board requested ten of these large cruisers per year over a three-year programme for the fiscal years (FY)1922–24, but Congress baulked at the cost, and the figure was subsequently revised downwards to six ships per year during FY1923–25.

Six guns in twin splinter-proof mountings were initially proposed, but some members considered this too few on the displacement. By April 1921 thinking was moving in the direction of eight guns in four twin mountings, but as the board continued to insist on high speed to enable the ships to outrun enemy battlecruisers, it was already becoming apparent that these two qualities could only be achieved by a significant reduction in protection. Thus the basic scheme of January 1921, which had eight guns, a speed of 34.5 knots and protection comprising a 5in belt and a 3in deck over the machinery spaces,[8] came out at an unacceptable 12,000 tons displacement. The design was therefore progressively modified with reduced speed (design 'a'), reduced protection ('b'), reduced battery ('c') and all three reductions ('d') – see table 2.3. The only design which

Table 2.3: USN Cruiser Schemes 1921

	1	1a	1b	1c	1d
Displacement:	12,000t	10,750t	10,000t	11,250t	8,250t
Length:	635ft	610ft	600ft	625ft	560ft
Propulsion:	125,000shp	96,000shp	118,000shp	122,000shp	88,000shp
	34.5 knots	**33 knots**	34.5 knots	34.5 knots	**33 knots**
Armament:	8–8in	8–8in	8–8in	**6–8in**	**6–8in**
Belt:	5in	5in	**1.5in**	5in	**1.5in**
Deck:	3–4.5in	3–4.5in	**1–1.5in**	3–4.5in	**1–1.5in**

Notes: The reductions from the baseline requirements are in **bold** type.
Data from Friedman, *US Cruisers*, p.115.

was considered both acceptable and affordable was scheme '1b', which had the side belt reduced to 1.5in with a 1in armoured deck (even so, displacement was 10,750 tons normal). These preliminary US Navy designs prepared the ground for the limitations which were established at the Washington Conference, and provided the justification for the US Navy delegation's advocacy of such a high ceiling for surface ships below the capital ship category. They also anticipated the problems which would be experienced by all five navies post-Washington in designing an effective 'treaty' cruiser.

Flotilla Craft for the Marine Nationale

With the conclusion of the Great War the Marine Nationale at last had the opportunity to take stock of its current situation and to plan for the future. In a note dated 25 February 1919 Admiral de Bon, Chief of the Naval General Staff, pointed out to the minister that the Italian Navy, which was now France's greatest potential rival at sea, had completed or laid down twelve flotilla leaders and forty torpedo boats during 1914–18; the corresponding figure for the Marine Nationale was three fleet torpedo boats (to which should be added four torpedo boats building for Argentina, which had been requisitioned in August 1914, and twelve *Kaba*-class destroyers purchased directly from Japan in 1917 to compensate for the forced inactivity of the French shipbuilding yards). De Bon proposed that the new priority for construction be as follows: 'destroyers' (English terminology was used to denote the full range of flotilla craft), followed by light cruisers, and finally capital ships.

These suggestions were immediately approved by the new navy minister, Georges Leygues, who also approved a more detailed '*note sur les destroyers*' only a few days later, on 12 March, which attempted to define the missions and capabilities of the *contre-torpilleur* ('torpedo boat destroyer', as opposed to the *torpilleur d'escadre*, 'fleet torpedo boat').

The double role of the latter had been clearly set out in a study dating from 1914, which summarised the experience of the Russo-Japanese war together with the theories for the employment of flotilla craft that had been developed and refined in the build-up to the Great War. The primary function of the *torpilleur d'escadre* was to attack the enemy battle line with torpedoes; its secondary role was to disrupt by torpedo and gunfire the attacks of enemy flotilla craft against the French line.

The *contre-torpilleur* as defined in the note of March 1919, however, had a triple role, with a markedly different set of priorities. Its primary role was scouting and screening, followed by the protection of the battle line against enemy flotilla craft. Torpedo attacks against the enemy line of battle were relegated to third place, and were circumscribed by constraints on approaching the enemy ships too closely.

The qualities required for the first two roles were stated to be: high speed, endurance, a large radius of action, and a powerful armament. When scouting for the battle line the *contre-torpilleurs* would be expected to hold a contact and to be capable of engaging not only destroyers but small cruisers. This implied a speed and armament superior to current flotilla craft, light protection and a displacement of at least 2,000 tonnes.

The ability to engage small cruisers was necessary because of France's failure to build light cruisers capable of scouting for the battle line prior to or during the First World War. The Italians, in contrast, had completed three 3,500-tonne scout cruisers of the *Quarto* and *Bixio* classes in 1913–14, and the Marine Nationale would have been familiar with their capabilities from liaison duties with the Italian Fleet during the war. These ships had only light protection (a 38mm deck plus 100mm plating around the conning tower), and were relatively lightly armed with six 120mm (4.7in) and six 76mm (3in) guns. The *contre-torpilleurs* proposed by the Naval Staff would therefore be

The *contre-torpilleur Chacal*, one of a class of six 'super-destroyers' which made a considerable impact abroad. With a top speed in excess of 35 knots and a heavy gun armament of five 130mm guns, they completely outclassed foreign flotilla craft, from which they were designed to protect the fleet. Their primary role was scouting and screening, for which mission they normally operated in three-ship divisions. (Leo van Ginderen collection)

quite capable of holding their own against such ships, and their comparative lack of protection would have been compensated by a significant advantage in speed (35 knots as compared with only 26–28 knots for the Italian cruisers).

The small scout cruisers of the Regia Marina were followed by a series of *esploratori leggeri* ('light scouts'), which were essentially large destroyers with a displacement of 1,500–1,750 tons, armed with a mix of 152mm and 102mm guns, and with a maximum speed of 34–35 knots. The new French *contre-torpilleurs* would be expected to match these in size, power and speed.

The Naval Staff considered that torpedo attacks on the enemy battle line would no longer have to be launched at the close ranges accepted before and during the war. Torpedo technology had progressed to the point at which attacks could be launched at 12,000–15,000m. Whilst accepting that the percentage of hits obtained at such distances would be small, the solution was seen to lie in combining multiple torpedo firings with superior fire control. The French gave serious consideration to torpedo reloads but deemed them impractical under action conditions.[9]

Close combat was envisaged by the report as being most likely at night, when hostile forces might stumble into one another. In these conditions ramming might still be possible (ramming was also considered important for the effective prosecution of submarine contacts), so the bow would need to be reinforced. Both the scouting role and night combat would require propulsion machinery which was flexible and responsive.

In the context of the above considerations the following detailed recommendations were made:

Jaguar class 1921 (Fr)

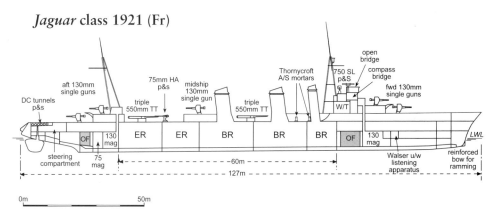

Inboard profile of the *contre-torpilleur Jaguar* as ordered in 1922. The preliminary design had been drawn up by the STCN in 1921, prior to the Washington Conference on the basis of the discussions outlined in the text. The initial batch of ships were completed with the 130mm gun, but the French Navy was still anxious to revert to its original proposal of 14cm (nominal calibre – in reality 138.6mm) guns, and went to the expense of ordering thirty of the 138.6 Mle 1923, developed for the following class, to re-equip the six *Jaguar*s. In the event, too much was attempted, even on the considerable displacement of these ships, and stability concerns forced the abandonment of the project. The four Thornycroft A/S mortars were also landed, and the planned director control tower failed to materialise. Note the extent to which the design is dominated by the length of the machinery spaces, required to produce the desired 35.5 knots.

- The hull was to be sufficiently robust to sustain high speeds in all weather without deformation. The bow was to be reinforced, with marked flare and high freeboard; and the anchors were to be carried in hawsepipes.
- There was a need for compromise between the weight of shell and the rate of fire; the largest practical calibre was considered to be 138.6mm. A main armament of four 138.6mm was proposed, disposed in single mountings superimposed fore and aft. All guns were to have shields to protect their crews from splinters and spray; and each gun was to be provided with 150 rounds, including some ready-use rounds stowed close to the gun for rapid response (an innovation attributed to British practice) and illuminating shell. Anti-aircraft protection was to be provided by one heavy 75mm HA gun plus four machine guns. There should be two triple centre-line mountings for 550mm long-range torpedoes with good forward arcs. Although not primarily anti-submarine vessels, eight 100kg depth charges were to be carried. And a study was proposed for laying mines in the path of the enemy battle line, ten mines being carried by each destroyer.
- The importance of centralised control and communications was emphasised. The bridge was to be protected against both sea and wind, the firing of torpedoes, depth-charging and minelaying were all to be controlled from the bridge, and the main W/T office was to be close to the bridge with direct communication. Fire control for the main guns was to comprise a director incorporating a rangefinder. Searchlight projectors were to be replaced in their traditional role of illuminating enemy ships at night by illuminating shell in order not to provide a target point for the opponent. A single 60cm projector was to be fitted for long-range signalling, plus a 30cm projector for signalling in formation.
- The ships were to be capable of 40 knots at full load displacement for six hours in order to ensure a comfortable 35 knots in normal service. Boilers and auxiliaries had to be robust and reliable (a rough weather trial was proposed) to enable these ships to accompany the battle line in all circumstances.
- The machinery spaces were to be protected by 5cm grilles with a height of three metres (one metre above and two below the waterline), with transverse end bulkheads of the same composition, and there was to be a protective deck of 4cm grilles over the same area. The bridge, torpedo tubes and guns were to have protective mattressing to absorb splinters. Paravanes against mines were to be carried. Comprehensive damage control arrangements were to include hand-operated steam pumps and powerful ventilators to disperse gases. The ship was to be divided into three sections for damage control purposes, with the central section comprising the machinery spaces. The ship was to be capable of steaming with either of the outer compartments flooded. Each of the three sections was to be fitted with two powerful independent pumps per compartment, with counter-flooding to be possible in the centre section.
- Smokescreens were to be generated by admitting oil directly into the funnels, and a winch for balloons was to be provided.

Some of the thinking encapsulated in these requirements was retrospective and analytical, reflecting on lessons based on hard wartime experience (cf. the observations on hull-form, the reliability of machinery, and on damage control). However, the document also shows an acute awareness of the tactical possibilities opened up by new technology (lightweight medium-calibre guns, long-range torpedoes, illuminating shell). Of particular note is the emphasis on superior battle control from a capacious, (relatively) comfortable bridge, with centralised director fire control and long-range torpedo sights. Such was the philosophy which was to underpin not only the *contre-torpilleur*, but also the new *torpilleur d'escadre*, the design of which would also incorporate many of the above features.

Unfortunately the concepts elaborated in the 1919 submission could not as yet be translated into orders for new ships. The parlous state of the French economy in the immediate postwar period, the disorganised state of the established shipyards and the naval infrastructure, and the need to develop the new weapons and machinery required for the proposed flotilla craft, imposed a hiatus on construction which the Marine Nationale could ill afford.

In 1919 the French tinkered with the idea of purchasing surplus 'Modified W' hulls offered by British shipbuilders, and in April 1920 contemplated

Table 2.4: Large Destroyers Under Construction 1918

	Scott class (GB)	S113 class (Ger)	Leone class (It)
Built:	1916–18	1916–18	1921–24
Displacement:	1,580t	2,060t	2,195t
Length:	333ft (101m)	105m	113m
Propulsion:	2 shaft geared	2 shaft geared	2 shaft geared
	turbines;	turbines;	turbines;
	40,000shp = 36 knots	45,000shp = 36 knots	42,000shp = 34 knots
Armament:	5–4.7in (120mm)	4–15cm	8–120mm
	6–21in (533mm) TT	4–60cm TT	6–450mm TT

Notes:

- The *Scott* class were large, powerful flotilla leaders ordered in the spring of 1916; they had one more gun than the Modified 'W' class destroyer building at the end of the war, a pattern which would be repeated in the French *contre-torpilleurs* and *torpilleurs d'escadre* of the postwar programme.

- The German S113 was also designed in 1916; it was to have been the first of a new heavily-gunned type, which however exhibited poor sea-keeping qualities. The sole unit completed was operated by the Marine Nationale for some years as the *Amiral Sénès*.

- The Italian *Leone* class was the last in a series of *esploratori leggeri*, large fast destroyers with a scouting role. Originally ordered 18 Jan 1917, these ships were not laid down until 1921 due to a shortage of steel.

ordering two ships of an intermediate *contre-torpilleur* type of 1,780 tonnes armed with five 100mm guns. However, the purchase of modern destroyers in Britain fell foul of an alarming fall of the franc against the pound sterling, while the *contre-torpilleur* proposal was rejected because the 100mm calibre was considered inadequate at a time when both the British and the Italians were moving to the 120mm/4.7in calibre. In the meantime successful trials were conducted with a new 130mm/40-calibre gun (Model 1919), which subsequently served as the basis for a larger 2,400-tonne design, and aggressive attempts were made to secure former German and Austro-Hungarian torpedo boats as war reparations.

The inadequacies of the 100mm gun were also an important factor in the design of the new *torpilleurs d'escadre*. The staff requirements for the new ships, as approved in April 1920, stipulated four single 100mm mountings plus two 75mm AA, but these were quickly followed by a recommendation that a larger calibre be adopted, either a new-model 120mm or the lightweight 130mm Model 1919. Without a 120mm gun on the drawing board there was little alternative to the 130mm, and installation of the latter aboard the *torpilleurs* was approved in June 1921. Design displacement was increased by 75 tonnes to accommodate the heavier mounting, but the latter would be largely responsible for the topweight and sea-keeping problems which would be experienced with the new ships.

Washington then intervened, and the Marine Nationale would have to await the 1922 programme drawn up in its wake before the new flotilla craft could be submitted for approval. The final characteristics of the six *contre-torpilleurs* of the *Jaguar* class and the twelve *torpilleurs d'escadre* of the *Bourrasque* class will be dealt with in Chapters 8 and 10 respectively.

Fleet Submarines for Japan

Up to 1918 Japan had viewed the submarine as useful primarily for defence of the homeland, and most of her early submarines were coastal types of American or British design with limited range and endurance. During the First World War interest turned to the larger patrol submarines being built in Europe, and plans were purchased from Italy, France and Britain, resulting in the Fiat-Laurenti F1 and F2 types, the Schneider-Laubeuf K1 to K4 series and the Vickers L1 to L3 series. No fewer than thirty-two of these boats were laid down from 1917 onwards. Later units had 53cm (21in) tubes in place of the earlier 45cm (17.7in), and all had a maximum range of 5,500–6,000nm. They could operate comfortably in waters dominated by the IJN surface fleet, but operations outside the confines of the Western Pacific would depend on the use of forward bases which had not been developed in the early postwar period and which would subsequently be prohibited by the Washington Treaty.

However, by the late-war period both the British and the Germans were building large submarines of 2,000 tons surfaced displacement, albeit for very different purposes. The Royal Navy, obsessed with the notion that the Germans were building fast U-boats for deployment against the Grand Fleet, attempted to counter these: first with the 'J' class, in which three twelve-cylinder four-stroke diesels (developed by Vickers from its standard eight-cylinder model) powered three shafts; then when these failed to deliver the necessary high speed, the navy embarked on the even larger fleet submarines of the 'K' class, which were 330ft (100m) long and were powered by steam turbines, their twin Yarrow boilers being provided with retractable funnels with watertight covers. The 'J' class had a designed speed of 19.5 knots on the surface, the steam-powered 'K's 24 knots.

At the same time the German Navy was embarking on the construction of submarines of comparable size to the British 'J' and 'K' classes, not for fleet work but for commerce raiding. Following the decision to abandon unrestricted U-boat warfare in March 1916, when it was feared that persistence with this policy would bring the United States into the war, the German Admiralty began the construction of a series of large submarine cruisers armed with 15cm (5.9in) guns and capable of conducting commerce warfare according to Prize Laws. The 'U-cruisers' of the *U-139* class (originally designated 'Project 46') had a surfaced displacement of 1,930 tons, and were powered by two powerful MAN six-cylinder four-stroke diesels rated at 1,650bhp. Because of their oceanic commerce-raiding mission, the design emphasis was not on high speed (a modest 15 knots on the surface), but on range and endurance. Capacious fuel bunkers held 450 tons of diesel fuel, giving them a maximum range of 17,500nm at 8 knots. Besides their two single 15cm deck guns, which were located fore and aft of the conning tower, the U-cruisers had four bow and two stern 50cm (19.7in) torpedo tubes for a total load-out of nineteen torpedoes, and a crew of sixty-six was complemented by a twenty-strong prize crew.

Three of these Project 46 boats had been completed by the end of the war, and they were duly allocated to France, the United States and Britain respectively as war reparations. Their successors, the Project 46A type, fitted with even more powerful MAN ten-cylinder four-stroke diesels rated at 3,000bhp, would have had a surfaced speed of 17.5 knots. However, only four had been launched by the time of the Armistice, and all units were subsequently broken up.

The Imperial Japanese Navy was attracted by the high tactical speed of the British fleet boats which, in theory at least, enabled them to operate in conjunction with the battle fleet, and which facilitated the interception of hostile surface units located by aircraft or friendly picket submarines on patrol. However, it was equally impressed by the endurance of the German U-cruisers, with their large number of torpedo reloads and their huge surface radius, and was quick to see the potential of such submarines in the open expanses of the Pacific Ocean. The IJN therefore embarked on a programme of large experimental submarines, which it was hoped would spawn effective production types. These new submarines were classified as *Kaigun-dai* (shortened to *Kaidai*), meaning 'large Admiralty type', and subsequent mainstream classes of fleet submarine would retain this 'KD' designation together with a number to denote the sequence.

The first boat, no.44 (KD1 type), was authorised as part of the 1919 programme and launched on 29 November 1921, during the Washington Conference. Her design was derived from the British fleet submarines of the 'J' and 'K' classes, but with diesels in place of the controversial steam plant of latter boats to provide the necessary endurance. The KD1 had a surfaced displacement of 1,500 tons, and the problem of providing sufficient power for high speed when running on the surface was resolved by fitting four Sulzer two-stroke diesels of 1,300bhp powering four shafts for a designed speed of 20 knots. Endurance was 20,000nm at 10 knots, which was considerably in excess of the figure for the German U-cruisers. There were six bow tubes and two stern tubes for 53cm (21in) torpedoes, of which twenty-four were carried. However, the 'fleet' mission of the KD1 was evidenced by the conventional gun armament, which comprised only a single 12cm (4.7in) gun complemented by a 8cm (3in) HA gun.

The second boat, no.51 (KD2 type), was authorised in 1920 and was laid down immediately after the conclusion of the Washington Conference. Her design was even more closely influenced by the large German U-boats, and she was powered by two Sulzer diesels built under licence and rated at 3,400bhp. These were by some margin the most powerful diesels yet installed in a submarine anywhere in the world. The Swiss Sulzer Works had pioneered two-stroke diesel technology, which delivered almost twice the power/weight ratio of diesels with the more conventional four-stroke cycle, and in 1917 signed a licence agreement with Japan under which Japanese shipyards were permitted to manufacture diesel engines designed and developed by Sulzer at their factory in Winterthur. The first fruits of this agreement was the 1,300bhp diesel fitted in the KD1, and which also powered the IJN's Schneider-Laubeuf boats of the 'K' series built from 1917 onwards. The model installed in the KD2 was an advanced engine designed postwar and which delivered almost three times the brake horsepower, allowing the new submarine to revert to a more conventional two-shaft machinery layout. On a similar displacement to her immediate predecessor, the KD2 was even faster, with a designed speed of 22 knots on the surface. Endurance, however, was only half that of the earlier boat: 10,000nm at 10 knots. Armament was identical to the KD1, except that only sixteen torpedoes were carried. The KD2 was to have been a production boat. A class of six was projected, but following the Washington Conference it was decided to proceed only with the first unit, and to cancel the remaining five in favour of a new, more advanced design.

Neither of these experimental submarines was particularly successful. The four-shaft propulsion system of the KD1 was a conspicuous failure and in 1932, barely eight years after her completion, *I-51* was re-engined with two

KD2 (Jap)

0m   30m

The KD2 was the IJN's second attempt to design a viable fleet submarine combining high speed, a powerful torpedo armament and good endurance. Powered by 3,400bhp Sulzer diesels, the single boat that was completed was designed for 22 knots on the surface. Five other projected boats of the KD2 type were cancelled in favour of a more advanced design, the KD3 (see Chapter 9).

larger diesels of Japanese design and manufacture driving two shafts. By that time she was being used as a training boat, continuing in this role until 1939; she was stricken in 1941. The 3,400bhp diesel engine which powered the KD2 seems to have been subject to frequent breakdowns. *I-52* took over the *I-51*'s training duties in 1940, and she too was deleted from active service in July 1942. However, these two experimental submarines effectively blazed a trail for the Imperial Japanese Navy, which during the 1920s and 1930s would focus its submarine construction on large fleet boats with high service speed, a large operational radius and a powerful armament of guns and torpedoes (see Chapter 9). With primary missions which included the reconnaissance of enemy bases, long-range 'strategic' scouting and the attrition of the enemy battle fleet from the moment it sortied from its bases to its arrival in the area designated for the decisive fleet action, these submarines were to become a crucial component of Japanese naval strategy in the Pacific.

Table 2.5: Fleet Submarines for the IJN: Some Comparisons

	'J' (GB)	KD1 (Jap)	Proj.46A (Ger)	KD2 (Jap)
Built:	1915–16	1921–24	LD 1918	1922–25
Displacement:	1200t	1500t	2115t	1500t
Length:	275ft (84m)	91m	98m	101m
Propulsion:	3 shafts;	4 shafts;	2 shafts;	2 shafts;
(surface)	3 Vickers diesels;	4 Sulzer diesels;	2 MAN diesels;	2 Sulzer diesels;
	3,600bhp = 19 knots	5,200bhp = 20 knots	6,000bhp = 17 knots	6,800bhp = 22 knots
Endurance:	5,000nm at 12 knots	20,000nm at 10 knots	20,000nm at 6 knots	10,000nm at 10 knots
Armament:	6–18in (457mm) TT	8–533mm TT	6–50cm TT	8–533mm TT
	1–3in (76mm)	1–12cm	2–15cm	1–12cm

CHAPTER 3

The Washington Treaty, 6 February 1922

The modern reader is struck by the essential simplicity of the Washington Treaty. Chapter I, which outlines the 'general provisions' of the treaty, contains only twenty short clauses, many of which comprise a single sentence. Chapter II is essentially an annex providing detailed lists of vessels to be retained or scrapped and the schedules for future replacement, together with some definitions of terms, while Chapter III sets out the terms for the operation of the treaty and for its eventual renewal. The wording is concise, and the treaty itself a model of clarity.[1]

Of the twenty clauses in Chapter I, two (Articles I and XX) are general statements, five are specifically concerned with capital ships, four with aircraft carriers and only two with warships beneath these categories. Six clauses are concerned with possible evasions of the treaty, while Article XIX sets out the rules for the development of bases in the Pacific agreed by the British Empire, France, the United States and Japan (see Introduction).

Capital Ships

Articles II to VI, which outline the rules for the retention and construction of capital ships, can reasonably be regarded as the focal point of the treaty, as it was the capital ship programmes of Great Britain, the United States and Japan during the immediate postwar period which provided the primary impetus for the Washington Conference.

Although there was general agreement on the need for a period of stability and on the parameters laid down for future ships, there was some disagreement over detail. Britain was concerned that the original proposals made by the United States failed to take into account the age of her current battle fleet; her most modern battleships had been completed in 1916–17 with an armament of eight 15in guns, whereas both the US Navy and the IJN had completed battleships armed with twelve 14in guns since that time, and battleships armed with eight 16in guns over the past year. This issue was resolved by permitting the British to build two new battleships within the prescribed limits to replace four super-dreadnoughts of pre-war vintage. In return the US Navy would be permitted

The Japanese insistence on the retention of the battleship *Mutsu*, paid for largely by public subscription and rushed to completion for the Washington Conference, had a wider impact than initially anticipated. The British insisted on being permitted to build two new battleships armed with 16in guns, and this then had to be balanced by allowing the United States to complete two more *Colorado*s (Article II). These decisions in turn impacted on treaty provisions which allowed the French and the Italians to modernise their elderly dreadnoughts and to lay down two modern capital ships before the end of the ten-year 'battleship holiday'.

to complete two further 16in-gun ships of the *Colorado* class currently under construction[2] and to dispose of two older 12in-gun dreadnoughts (Article II). Japan agreed to this clause on condition that it was permitted to retain the 16in-gun *Mutsu* (second of the *Nagato* class), which had been rushed to completion in time for the conference. France and Italy, with no capital ships of modern design currently under construction, were compensated by a clause in the 'replacement' section of Chapter II which would permit early replacement of some of their older dreadnought and pre-dreadnought battleships. This stipulated that new ships subject to the new limits could be laid down by France and Italy in 1927 and 1929, whereas the three major navies would have to wait until the initial ten-year period governed by the treaty had elapsed before laying down replacement construction for their existing capital ships.

Article IV established the quantitative limits for capital ships. The total displacement figures for each of the contracting powers were: 525,000 tons for the British Empire and the United States, 315,000 tons for Japan, and 175,000 tons for France and Italy – often expressed as a 5:3:1.75 ratio.[3] These figures were used to determine the lists of ships which could be retained (detailed in Chapter II of the treaty), and were to serve as a ceiling for future construction.

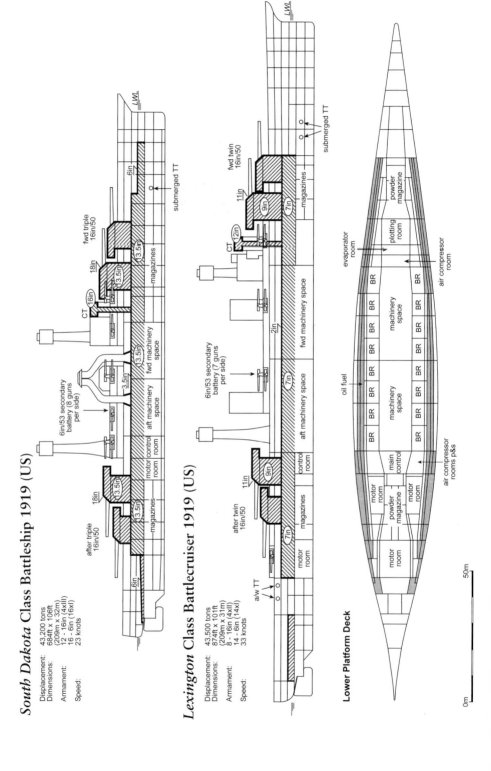

South Dakota Class Battleship 1919 (US)

Displacement: 43,200 tons
Dimensions: 684ft x 106ft
(209m x 32m)
Armament: 12 - 16in (4xIII)
16 - 6in (16xI)
Speed: 23 knots

CT 16in
18in
13.5in
13.5in
13.5in
fwd triple
16in/50
6in
magazines
submerged TT

6in/53 secondary
battery (8 guns
per side)

3.5in
3.5in
fwd machinery
space
aft machinery
space
motor control
room room

18in
13.5in
13.5in
magazines
after triple
16in/50
6in

LWL

Lexington Class Battlecruiser 1919 (US)

Displacement: 43,500 tons
Dimensions: 874ft x 101ft
(209m x 31m)
Armament: 8 - 16in (4xII)
14 - 6in (14xI)
Speed: 33 knots

CT 12in
9in
7in
fwd twin
16in/50
11in
magazines
submerged TT

6in/53 secondary
battery (7 guns
per side)

2in
7in
fwd machinery space
aft machinery space
control
room

11in
9in
7in
magazines
motor
room
after twin
16in/50

a/w TT

LWL

Lower Platform Deck

evaporator
room
powder
magazine
plotting
room
air compressor
room

oil fuel

BR BR BR
BR BR BR BR BR
machinery
space
machinery
space
BR BR BR BR BR
BR BR BR

main
control
motor
room
powder
magazine
motor
room
motor
room
air compressor
rooms p&s

0m
50m

Two of the more prominent casualties of the Washington Treaty were the battleships of the *South Dakota* class and the battlecruisers of the *Lexington* class. Authorised under the Naval Expansion Act of 1916, these twelve ships would have formed, together with the four battleships of the *Colorado* class, the core of the postwar US Navy. Had they been completed, their combined displacement would have approached the total tonnage allocation to the United States under the treaty.

The *South Dakota* marked the apogee of US Navy First World War battleship design. Compact and well-protected, with a main armament of twelve 16in guns in triple turrets, these ships would have taken the path already established by the *Tennessee* and *Colorado* designs to its ultimate conclusion. The *Lexingtons*, on the other hand, were essentially an outgrowth of the cruiser type – the original design was classified as a 'battle scout'. Overall length was some 30 per cent greater than the *South Dakotas*, while beam was slightly less. These ships had a powerful armament but only moderate protection, and were designed to sustain exceptionally high speeds in order to carry out their primary mission of strategic scouting for the US battle fleet; ship horsepower was three times that of the *South Dakotas*.

Both types featured turbo-electric propulsion, introduced in the battleship *New Mexico* and adopted for the *Tennessee* and *Colorado* classes. They had two long machinery compartments on the centre-line for the turbo-generators which supplied all electric power to the ship. Individual boiler rooms (twelve for the *South Dakotas*, sixteen for the *Lexingtons* in their final guise) were located outboard of these spaces (see drawing), providing a high degree of underwater subdivision. The turbo-generators provided power for four large electrical drive motors, coupled directly to each of the four shafts and housed in separate motor rooms located around the after magazines. Turbo-electric propulsion provided greater flexibility – and therefore greater fuel economy – than steam turbines, but it was heavy and space-intensive, and with the advent of more compact, lightweight steam turbine machinery during the 1930s it was abandoned by the US Navy for its later generation of battleships.

Five of the *South Dakotas* and four *Lexingtons* were laid down in 1920, the remaining three ships being laid down in early/mid-1921. However, although much equipment had been ordered, little progress had been made on the hulls by the time of the Washington Conference. Following the conference all six battleships were cancelled, their boilers being utilised to upgrade existing US battleships. Two of the six *Lexingtons* survived, however, as aircraft carriers – a project which had already been studied prior to the conference. Their length, and especially their high speed, made them prime candidates for carrier conversion, and they ultimately took on the same role as the battlecruisers: strategic scouting for the battle fleet.

As we have already seen, this agreement constituted a political defeat for Japan – which argued for a 10:7 ratio vis-à-vis the US Navy – and for France, which argued that its status as the world's second imperial power should have been recognised by an offer at least of parity with Japan, and which felt humiliated when offered only parity with Italy.

Articles V and VI determined the qualitative limits on new capital ship construction. Article V imposed an upper limit of 35,000 tons (35,560 metric tons) on new capital ship construction, and Article VI prohibited guns in excess of 16in (406mm). The latter provision was inevitable given that the United States and Japan were already building ships armed with 16in guns, and that this was also the calibre ultimately adopted for the British G3 battlecruisers.

The displacement limit of 35,000 tons standard, imposed as a necessary barrier to escalation, was a reasonable figure given the technology of the day.[4] The latest US battleships of the *Colorado* class had a displacement of 32,600 tons[5] and the Japanese *Nagato* 33,800 tons, so 35,000 tons standard in theory gave a small margin for an extra gun, a couple of knots speed, or a 'post-Jutland' protection system, all of which would have been attractive to the British negotiators. However, it clearly precluded the combination of a powerful main battery with high speed and heavy armour which characterised the latest British and Japanese designs. Even HMS *Hood*, with her eight 15in guns, 31 knots and 'pre-Jutland' protection system, largely exceeded this figure, weighing in at 41,200 tons (normal) when completed in May 1920. It also spelled the end of the battlecruisers of the *Lexington* class (43,500 tons), although it was already envisaged by the US Navy that the first two hulls, which were yet to be launched, would be completed as aircraft carriers.

The long-term implication was that the British and US fleets would comprise fifteen capital ships; Japan would have nine, and France and Italy would each have five. One cannot help but surmise that the British were still anxious to retain the traditional 'two-power standard', even though in future the viability of that policy would have to assume a friendly (or at least non-belligerent) United States. This would not have been possible had Japan secured the desired 10:7 ratio (11 IJN battleships + 5 French), nor if the French had secured parity with Japan (9 IJN battleships + 9 French).

Aircraft Carriers

The four clauses which deal with aircraft carriers – only one fewer than those concerned with capital ships – are an indication of how seriously this new class of vessel was taken by Britain, the United States and Japan. Although the aircraft carrier was still an experimental type, and was acknowledged as such in Article VIII of the treaty, its future possibilities both as a 'force multiplier' for one's own battle line and as a potential threat to the enemy battle line were a major concern. It was also clear that the large, fast hulls of battlecruisers currently building for the USA and Japan were prime candidates for conversion, given the resources already invested in their construction.[6]

Prior to the Washington Conference the British fleet requirement had been established as five carriers of 25,000 tons, so the British proposal for total tonnage in the aircraft carrier category at the conference was 125,000 tons. The United States, on the other hand, was interested only in the reconstruction of two of its 40,000-ton battlecruisers currently on the slipways, and made a counter-proposal of 80,000 tons. The USA further proposed that the tonnage allocation for the three smaller navies should conform to the 5:3:1.75 ratio initially proposed for capital ships, so that the total tonnage for Japan would be 48,000 tons, while the Italians and the French would have only 28,000 tons available.

The US proposals met with considerable opposition from all four of the other contracting powers. The British pointed out, with some justification, that a 40,000-ton limit on individual carriers was incompatible with the American proposal for a 35,000-ton limit on capital ships.[7] The French and the British both expressed a preference for 25,000 tons, which would permit the conversion of the capital ship hulls available to both navies.[8] However, the Americans were well aware from their own preliminary studies that this figure would be far too low to permit the planned battlecruiser conversions, and the 25,000-ton figure would have also been too low for the Japanese if they wished to undertake a similar conversion of the *Amagis*. In the end a compromise was reached whereby the displacement limit for individual carriers was set at 27,000 tons (Article IX), while American intentions were legitimised by permitting each signatory to convert two incomplete capital ship hulls with a maximum individual displacement of 33,000 tons.

The low ceilings on total displacement allocation also proved unacceptable. Italy pointed out that the proposed 28,000-ton limit proposed for Italy and France would permit the construction of only a single standard carrier – which would spend one-third of its time in refit – and demanded a minimum tonnage allocation of 54,000 tons. The British delegation supported the Italians, and protested that it was unfair to impose such low limits on carrier construction if there were no such limits on submarines, given that sea-based ASW aircraft might prove to be a necessary and effective countermeasure.[9] The Japanese strongly supported the British position, claiming that the proposed 48,000 tons was totally inadequate given Japan's geostrategic situation, which would increasingly require effective air defence; they wanted a mimimum of 81,000 tons (equivalent to three standard carriers), and if this were agreed would raise no objection to the ceiling for Britain and the United States being raised in line. The British therefore proposed new limits based on the Italian and Japanese demands: 135,000 tons (equivalent to five standard carriers) for the United States and Britain, 81,000 tons (three standard carriers) for Japan, and 54,000 tons (two standard carriers) for Italy and France. However France, which had also supported the initial Italian objection, assessed the Marine Nationale's needs as three carriers (two for European waters, and a third for the protection of the colonies), and combined its own preference for a 25,000-

ton individual displacement with a demand for an overall tonnage allocation of 75,000 tons. This demand received no support from the other powers, but led to a further compromise by which the Italian and French allocation was increased to 60,000 tons, thereby permitting the construction of three smaller carriers of 20,000 tons. Thus under Article VII of the treaty the total carrier tonnage allocated to Britain and the USA was 135,000 tons; the corresponding tonnage for the other three major navies was 81,000 tons for Japan, and 60,000 tons for France and Italy.[10]

The British, who were in the forefront of carrier development, were not unnaturally concerned that the Royal Navy would be stuck with its ragbag of cruiser, battleship and mercantile conversions as part of its own tonnage allocation while nations such as Japan and the United States would be able to build state-of-the-art ships within a structured programme. It was therefore agreed that all aircraft carrier tonnage in service or building on 12 November 1921 should be regarded as experimental, and could be replaced at any time without regard for the rules for replacement laid down for new construction (Article VIII).

At the time of the Washington Treaty there was a strong body of opinion which held that aircraft carriers, which for their primary scouting mission would be expected to operate independently and in advance of the battle fleet, would need to be able to defend themselves against enemy cruisers. Thus *Eagle* and *Hermes*, currently building for the Royal Navy, were to be armed with nine 6in and six/seven 5.5in guns respectively. Such an armament would have been adequate against the small 'fleet' cruisers of the period. However, with the prospect of larger ships armed with 8in guns it was inevitable that the rules for carrier gun batteries embodied in the treaty would have to conform with these developments. Largely at the prompting of the US Navy delegation, Article X stipulated that the maximum calibre should be 8in (203mm) and that the maximum number of guns above 6in (152mm) calibre should be ten.[11] No limit was placed on the number of anti-aircraft guns which could be carried, as these were regarded as purely defensive in nature.[12]

'Auxiliary' Warships

Although there was an attempt to regulate the construction of smaller surface warships such as cruisers and flotilla craft,[13] complete agreement on all issues proved beyond the capacity of the conference.

Neither the British nor the Americans were keen to see a low ceiling on the displacement and armament of individual cruisers, as the US Navy increasingly regarded 10,000 tons as a minimum figure for an effective scout cruiser with the necessary range to operate in the Western Pacific from bases on the West Coast and in Hawaii, and the Royal Navy not only wished to retain its influential *Hawkins* class cruisers, which were armed with 7.5in guns, but viewed ships of this size as essential to protect the sea lanes in the Far East. Japan, which was already committed to 8in-gun scout cruisers (see Chapter 2), was happy to go along with the United States, and France was faced with similar strategic problems to the British Empire.[14] Agreement on the maximum size and gun calibre for new cruisers was therefore obtained relatively easily. Article XI stated that no warship other than a capital ship or an aircraft carrier should have a displacement exceeding 10,000 tons (10,160 metric tons), and Article XII that no warship other than a capital ship should carry a gun in excess of 8in (203mm).

However, the British naval delegation was unwilling to accept any quantitative limit on cruiser construction which would involve parity with the United States given Britain's much more substantial overseas trade defence commitments,[15] while the United States was only prepared to negotiate an overall tonnage limit based on parity. Moreover, whereas the French, whose imperial commitments were on a similar scale to those of Britain, had been compelled to accept a fait accompli with regard to capital ship tonnage, they made it clear that the extension of the 5:3:1.75 ratio to 'auxiliary' categories was unacceptable. This created a fundamental impasse which left all the Washington co-signatories free to build as many cruisers as they wished, provided the limits on the displacement and main battery of individual ships were respected. Britain and France, with extensive empires to police, were quite happy with this decision at the time, but subsequently found that their respective governments were both unwilling and unable to fund these costly 'treaty' cruisers in the required numbers, and attempted to remedy this by proposing lower qualitative limits which would permit them to build more hulls. Failure to reach agreement on this issue at Washington therefore simply

The British 'Elizabethans', designed to hunt down German commerce raiders on the trade routes, made a big impression on the two Pacific navies, particularly the IJN. Their key characteristics – a displacement of 9,750 tons and an armament of seven 7.5in guns – undoubtedly influenced the Washington qualitative upper limits for 'auxiliary' vessels, even though the US Navy was already committed to building cruisers of this size and power for scouting operations in the Pacific (see Chapter 2). This is *Frobisher* during the 1920s.

postponed the inevitable acrimonious debate to Geneva in 1927 and London in 1930 (see Chapter 11).

The British were also unwilling to submit to any numerical constraints on destroyers while the submarine issue remained unresolved (see below). The French were equally determined to resist attempts to impose quantitative and qualitative limits on flotilla craft, particularly if the quantitative limits were to be based on the ratios agreed for capital ships. Torpedo-armed surface ships and submarines had traditionally been regarded by influential elements of the Marine Nationale as an essential defensive counter to Great Britain's superior battle fleet, and since the Anglo-Saxons were now forcing on the French a catastrophic statutory inferiority in capital ships, it was clear that the Marine Nationale would need carte blanche in the development and construction of both types. Preliminary designs for large, fast *contre-torpilleurs* were already on the drawing board (see Chapter 2). These ships, like the Italian *esploratori leggeri* which inspired them, were intended to fulfil the tactical scouting mission of small cruisers in the narrow waters of the Mediterranean. The disparity in types and requirements of the major navies with regard to flotilla craft militated against any agreement at the Washington Conference, and would provide a serious obstacle at the London Conference of 1930.

Evasions

No fewer than six clauses were devoted to possible evasions of the Washington Treaty. The British appear to have been primarily concerned about the possible conversion of mercantile vessels as commerce raiders.[16] The United States was concerned about the possibility that some of Britain's surplus modern dreadnoughts and super-dreadnoughts might be transferred at give-away prices to friendly powers, thereby upsetting the carefully negotiated strategic balance established by the Washington Treaty.[17]

Article XIII prohibited the reconversion of a ship designated for scrapping by the treaty into a vessel of war, and Article XIV outlawed the prior preparation of merchant vessels for conversion to vessels of war (i.e. for commerce raiding). Decks could, however, be stiffened for the mounting of guns not exceeding 6in calibre, thereby permitting armed (auxiliary) merchant cruisers to be used for convoy defence and the fitting-out of 'Q'-ships to protect fishing boats and coastal mercantile traffic.

Articles XV and XVI prohibited the construction of vessels exceeding the treaty limitations for another (non-contracting) power, and required full details of any warship built for a foreign power to be communicated to the other four contracting powers. Article XVII prohibited the requisitioning of any such ships while building in the event of war. During the First World War it had been the Royal Navy which had benefited most from such measures: the battleships *Agincourt*, *Erin* and *Canada*, all three requisitioned from foreign powers, had been present in the battle line at Jutland. However the advent of the Washington Treaty, with its strict limitations on overall capital ship tonnage, made it inevitable that this option would be closed down.

Article XVIII, which banned the transfer by gift or sale of vessels of war to another power, may have been prompted by the transfer of the German battlecruiser *Goeben* to Turkey in 1914, which fundamentally altered the balance of power in the Eastern Mediterranean. However, the large number of relatively modern British capital ships available for sale or transfer was undoubtedly the most immediate concern.

Bases in the Western Pacific

Article XIX prohibited the building of new bases or the fortification of existing bases in the Western Pacific.[18] The intention was to make the entire Western Pacific a demilitarised zone, thereby reducing the potential for conflict between the United States and Japan on the one hand, and the European imperial powers and Japan on the other, while at the same time outlawing further European (or Japanese) colonial adventures in what the United States was anxious to preserve as a free trade zone.

The effect of this article on subsequent naval construction for the concerned powers cannot be overstated. It effectively precluded the defence of the Philippines from forward bases in Manila or Guam by the US Navy, which was therefore compelled to develop its existing 'expeditionary fleet' strategy ('War Plan Orange') during the 1920s. In the short term this meant the build-up of Pearl Harbor (Hawaii) as a springboard for such an expedition plus a continuing commitment to ships whose primary qualities were range and endurance; the long-term implications included the development of specialised vessels for amphibious assault and the creation of a large fleet train of auxiliary vessels to provide logistic support for operations from advanced island bases. For the Imperial Japanese Navy a powerful strategic scouting force comprising large, long-range submarines would be required both to locate and shadow the US battle fleet as it trundled westwards across the Pacific and to take every opportunity to weaken it by attritional attacks. And for the British it meant the fortification of Singapore – selected over Australia because the Malacca Straits which it commanded were effectively the gateway to the Indian Ocean – as a forward base for its own expeditionary fleet, together with an emphasis on long-range cruisers and large patrol submarines to counter the Japanese threat.

Submarines

The most controversial issue discussed at the Washington Conference, and the one which generated the most heated debates, was that of the submarine. Great Britain had indicated in advance of the conference that it would propose the complete abolition of the submarine as a weapon of war. Britain had been brought almost to her knees in 1917 by the unrestricted U-boat campaign conducted by Germany, and was anxious that this situation should never be permitted to arise again. The Royal Navy was more than prepared to sacrifice its own increasingly potent submarine arm to ensure that its supremacy at sea was not threatened by the underwater threat posed by potential enemy powers.

Fear of the U-boat had constrained the use of the battle fleet in its traditional role of close blockade of enemy ports, and large numbers of destroyers and smaller surface units for convoy escort and anti-submarine operations had to be built in the latter part of the war at the expense of capital ship construction. Moreover, in the aftermath of the First World War German U-boat technology was available to all the victorious powers, with the French and the Japanese particularly anxious to acquire ex-German war prizes and access to former U-boat personnel, MAN diesels and German design teams.

The proposal to abolish the submarine elicited angry and determined opposition from France, which was strongly supported by Italy and Japan. The United States, which had a relatively small and short-ranged submarine arm and as the other major battleship power had a similar interest to the British in the primacy of 'sea control' forces, affected to remain neutral on this issue, and became the arbiter of the debate which took place during the conference. However, the US delegation was strongly of the opinion that if the submarine were retained as a weapon of war, overall tonnage allocations should be on the same ratio as that established for capital ships.

The French government, which had been made aware of the proposal to restrict her capital ship strength to one third that of the Royal Navy prior to the opening of the Washington Conference, issued a strong statement on 22 October 1921 justifying the position it was resolved to take. This *Déclaration du gouvernement français concernant les sous-marins* made the following points:

- The submarine was the only effective means of defending a country with a small number of capital ships against a country possessing a more powerful battle fleet.
- The submarine was incapable of giving a country control of the seas, and so could not be regarded as a weapon of domination.
- The inhumane and unlawful *use* of the submarine by *one* belligerent [author's italics] in the First World War was not a reason to condemn the submarine as a legitimate weapon of war.
- Because a relatively small number of submarines could be maintained at sea at any given time[19] swingeing restrictions on total submarine tonnage were unacceptable.
- The proposal for the ratio of submarine tonnage to be in line with that for capital ships was unreasonable because of the above (if anything reason dictated that submarine tonnage should be in *inverse* proportion to the number of capital ships!).
- Because of her extensive overseas security commitments France would need large ocean-going submarines, so any limit on the size of individual boats was unacceptable.

At the conference the French delegation insisted that the proposed limitation on capital ships could be accepted only if France were permitted

90,000 tons of submarines for self-defence. This figure was unacceptable to the British, who countered the French proposal with a derisory offer of 30,000 tons. This was rejected by the French, who also refused to sign up to an American compromise proposal to prohibit the use of submarines for commerce warfare (the Root Resolution). This effectively frustrated any agreement on submarines at the Washington Conference, although constant efforts were subsequently made by the British through the League of Nations to restrict or outlaw the use of submarines against merchant shipping, and the issue of individual and overall submarine tonnage would be revisited at the London Conference of 1930, when limitations were finally agreed – although the French were prepared to agree only qualitative, not quantitative limitations.

Chapter II of the Treaty

Chapter II was concerned with the rules relating to the execution of the treaty. Part I provided lists of the capital ships which might be retained by the contracting powers. The accompanying tables, which provide a compressed version of the treaty lists by grouping the ships in classes, reveal the extent to which Britain and France would need to 'build down' to their total tonnage allocation, while the total displacement of the ships to be retained by the United States and Japan was below their statutory allocation, allowing future expansion.

As the new definition of 'standard' displacement would be agreed only at the conference, the nominal displacement recorded for existing vessels was that submitted by the respective powers; these displacement figures, together with the total tonnage figures which were based on them, were in long tons for Britain and the USA, and in metric tons for the other three contracting powers.

Part II of Chapter II detailed the rules for the scrapping of capital ships which did not feature in the lists in Part I. It further stipulated that where replacement construction was permitted by the treaty (Articles II and III), the disabling of ships to be disposed of should have commenced by the time of the replacement vessel's completion, and should be completed within six months of that date, with final scrapping to take place within 18 months of the first date. This was designed to ensure that older ships could not be returned to service after they had been 'replaced'.

Part III established the rules for replacement under the treaty. No new capital ships other than those specifically permitted for Britain, France and Italy were to be laid down for ten years from 21 November 1921. Moreover, even from that date ships could be replaced only when their statutory lifespan of twenty years from completion had elapsed, and the full details of their replacements, to include displacement and dimensions, were to be communicated to each of the other contracting powers. Tables were produced for each country with detailed timetables for the replacement of existing ships (Section II – see accompanying table).

Table 3.1: The British Empire

Capital ships to be retained under the Washington Treaty:

	Built	Displ.	Main guns	Speed
15in-gun battleships and battlecruisers				
Hood	1916–20	41,200t	8–15in (4 × II)	31 knots
2 *Renown*	1915–16	26,500t	6–15in (3 × II)	30 knots
5 *Revenge*	1913–17	25,750t	8–15in (4 × II)	22 knots
5 *Queen Elizabeth*	1912–16	27,500t	8–15in (4 × II)	24 knots
13.5in-gun battleships and battlecruisers				
Tiger	1912–14	28,500t	8–13.5in (4 × II)	28 knots
4 *Iron Duke*	1912–14	25,000t	10–13.5in (5 × II)	21 knots
3 *King George V*	1911–13	23,000t	10–13.5in (5 × II)	21 knots
Thunderer	1910–12	22,500t	10–13.5in (5 × II)	21 knots
24 ships		**580,450 tons**		

Notes: All the displacements used in these calculations were 'normal', as the definition of 'standard' displacement was to be applied only on the conclusion of the treaty. Those for Britain and the United States were in 'long' tons (2,240lb); those for Japan, France and Italy were in metric tons.

On completion of the two new battleships authorised under Article II, the four oldest battleships of the *King George V* and *Thunderer* classes were to be disposed of, for a total displacement of 558,950 tons.

Table 3.2: The United States

Capital ships to be retained under the Washington Treaty:

	Built	Displ.	Main guns	Speed
16in-gun battleship				
Maryland	1917–21	32,600t	8–16in (4 × II)	21 knots
14in-gun battleships				
2 *Tennessee*	1916–21	32,300t	12–14in (4 × III)	21 knots
3 *New Mexico*	1915–19	32,000t	12–14in (4 × III)	21 knots
2 *Pennsylvania*	1913–16	31,400t	12–14in (4 × III)	21 knots
2 *Nevada*	1912–16	27,500t	10–14in (2 × III, 2 × II)	21 knots
2 *New York*	1911–14	27,000t	10–14in (5 × II)	21 knots
12in-gun battleships				
2 *Wyoming*	1910–12	26,000t	12–12in (6 × II)	21 knots
2 *Florida*	1909–11	21,825t	10–12in (5 × II)	21 knots
2 *Delaware*	1907–10	20,000t	10–12in (5 × II)	21 knots
18 ships		**500,650 tons**		

Note: On completion of the two battleships of the *Colorado* class authorised under Article II, the two oldest battleships of the *Delaware* class were to be disposed of, raising total displacement to 525,850 tons.

Table 3.3: Japan

Capital ships to be retained under the Washington Treaty:

	Built	Displ.	Main guns	Speed
16in (41cm)-gun battleships				
2 *Nagato*	1917–21	33,800t	8–16in (4 × II)	26 knots
14in (36cm)-gun battleships and battlecruisers				
2 *Ise*	1915–18	31,260t	12–14in (6 × II)	23 knots
2 *Fuso*	1912–17	30,600t	12–14in (6 × II)	22 knots
4 *Kongo*	1911–15	27,500t	8–14in (4 × II)	27 knots
10 ships		301,320mt		

Note: At the time of the Washington Conference the British and the Americans believed that *Nagato* and *Mutsu* had a top speed comparable to the *Ise* class.

Table 3.4: France

Capital ships to be retained under the Washington Treaty:

	Built	Displ.	Main guns	Speed
13.4in (340mm)-gun battleships				
3 *Bretagne*	1912–16	23,500t	10–13.4in (5 × II)	20 knots
12in (305mm)-gun battleships				
4 *Courbet*	1910–12	23,500t	12–12in (6 × II)	20 knots
3 *Danton*	1906–11	18,890t	4–12in (2 × II)	19 knots
			12–9.4in (6 × II)	
10 ships		221,170mt		

Note: Because none of its capital ship construction was recent, France would be permitted to lay down two new ships each of 35,000 tons before the end of the ten-year 'battleship holiday' imposed on the three major contracting powers: one in 1927 and one in 1929. These would replace three of the four early dreadnoughts of the *Courbet* class. (The military value of the elderly pre-dreadnoughts of the *Danton* class would have declined even further by this time.)

Table 3.5: Italy

Capital ships to be retained under the Washington Treaty:

	Built	Displ.	Main guns	Speed
12in (305mm)-gun battleships				
2 *Andrea Doria*	1912–16	22,700t	13–12in (3 × III, 2 × II)	22 knots
3 *Conte di Cavour*	1910–15	22,500t	13–12in (3 × III, 2 × II)	22 knots
Dante Alighieri	1909–13	19,500t	12–12in (4 × III)	22 knots
4 *Vittorio Emanuele*	1901–08	12,600t	2–12in (2 × I)	21 knots
			12–8in (6 × II)	
10 ships		**182,800mt**		

Notes: One unit of the *Cavour* class, *Leonardo da Vinci*, had been sunk in Taranto Harbour in 1916, but as she was refloated in 1919 and it was planned to refit her she was counted in Italy's Washington Treaty inventory.

As with France, Italy would be permitted to lay down the equivalent of two new ships each of 35,000 tons before the end of the ten-year 'battleship holiday' imposed on the three major contracting powers: one in 1927 and one in 1929. These would replace the early dreadnoughts *Dante Alighieri* and *Leonardo da Vinci*.

In the case of the loss or accidental destruction of capital ships or aircraft carriers, immediate replacement was permitted provided limitations on overall tonnage and qualitative restrictions were respected.

The reconstruction of existing capital ships and carriers was also permitted, provided such reconstruction was limited to providing defence against air and submarine attack. This meant that existing vessels could be fitted out with bulges (US: 'blisters') for anti-torpedo protection, and could have additional deck armour fitted for protection against aerial bombs, subject to a 3,000-ton maximum increase in displacement. Alterations to side armour and to the main armament were prohibited, except for France and Italy, who were permitted to rearm their existing battleships with 16in guns provided that the 3,000-ton limit was not exceeded.[20] This clause was intended to ensure that the agreed ratio of battleship strength remained constant, whilst permitting defence against threats not regulated by the treaty, such as aerial and submarine attack. The wording prohibiting alteration of 'the general type of mounting of the main armament' would subsequently be invoked by the British in an attempt to prevent the US Navy from increasing the angle of elevation of the main guns of its older battleships (see Chapter 5).

A British Admiralty sub-committee set up immediately after the conclusion of the Washington Conference noted that a strengthening of deck armour 'ostensibly for the purpose of protection against aircraft' would 'also provide protection against plunging shell',[21] and all three of the major navies would

Table 3.6: Replacement Capital Ship Construction: Britain and the United States

Year	Laid down USN / RN	Completed USN / RN	US ships to be scrapped (age)	RN ships to be scrapped (age)	Pre-Jutland ships USN / RN	Post-Jutland ships USN / RN
1922	- / A B	A B / -	*Delaware* (12) *North Dakota* (12)		15 / 21	3 / 1
1923–24		- / A B			15 / 21	3 / 1
1925				*Thunderer* (13) *King George V* (13) *Ajax* (12) *Centurion* (12)	15 / 17	3 / 3
1926–30					15 / 17	3 / 3
1931	C D				15 / 17	3 / 3
1932	E F				15 / 17	3 / 3
1933	G				15 / 17	3 / 3
1934	H I	C D	*Florida* (23) *Utah* (23) *Wyoming* (22)	*Iron Duke* (20) *Marlborough* (20) *Emperor of India* (20) *Benbow* (20)	12 / 13	5 / 5
1935	J	E F	*Arkansas* (23)	*Tiger* (21)	9 / 9	7 / 7

Year	Laid down USN / RN	Completed USN / RN	US ships to be scrapped (age)	RN ships to be scrapped (age)	Pre-Jutland ships USN / RN	Post-Jutland ships USN / RN
1936			Texas (21) New York (21)	Queen Elizabeth (20) Warspite (20) Barham (20)	7 / 7	8 / 8
1937	K L	G	Nevada (20) Oklahoma (20)	Malaya (20) Royal Sovereign (20)	5 / 5	10 / 10
1938	M	H I	Arizona (21) Pennsylvania (21)	Revenge (21) Resolution (21)	4 / 4	11 / 11
1939	N O P Q	J K L	Mississippi (21) New Mexico (21) Idaho (20)	Royal Oak (22) Valiant (23) Repulse (23)	2 / 2	13 / 13
1940		M	Tennessee (20)	Renown (24)	1 / 1	14 / 14
1941		N O	California (20) Maryland (20)	Ramillies (24) Hood (21)	0 / 0	15 / 15
1942		P Q	West Virginia (20) Colorado (20)	A (17) B (17)	0 / 0	15 / 15

Notes:
- A, B, C, D, etc., represent individual capital ships of 35,000 tons standard displacement, laid down and completed in the years specified (the dates assumed a building time of three years).
- A and B for Great Britain were the two new-build capital ships agreed at the conference (subsequently *Nelson* and *Rodney*).
- A and B for the USA were the recently launched *Colorado* and *West Virginia*.

Table 3.7: Replacement Capital Ship Construction: Japan

Year	Laid down	Completed	Ships to be scrapped (age)	Pre-Jutland ships	Post-Jutland ships
1922–30				8	2
1931	A			8	2
1932	B			8	2
1933	C			8	2
1934	D	A	*Kongo* (21)	7	3
1935	E	B	*Hiei* (21)	5	4
			Haruna (20)		
1936	F	C	*Kirishima* (21)	4	5
1937	G	D	*Fuso* (22)	3	6
1938	H	E	*Yamashiro* (21)	2	7
1939	I	F	*Ise* (22)	1	8
1940		G	*Hyuga* (22)	0	9
1941		H	*Nagato* (21)	0	9
1942		I	*Mutsu* (21)	0	9

Note: It was agreed that the IJN could retain the 16in-gun battleship *Mutsu*, which had been rushed to completion in time for the Washington Treaty. No other capital ship could be laid down or completed for Japan during the ten-year 'battleship holiday'.

take full advantage of this clause to reinforce the horizontal armour of their older battleships during the 1920s and 1930s, thereby enhancing their military capabilities against other capital ships in a way unforeseen by those who framed the treaty rules.

Part IV of Chapter II contained the definitions of key terminology used in the treaty. The 'Capital Ship' was any vessel of war except an aircraft carrier with a displacement exceeding 10,000 tons or carrying a gun with a calibre exceeding 8in. The 'Aircraft Carrier' was a vessel of war with a displacement exceeding 10,000 tons[22] 'designed for the specific and exclusive purpose of carrying aircraft … so constructed that aircraft can be launched therefrom and landed thereon'.

'Standard' Displacement

Last, but most certainly not least, there was a definition of 'standard displacement', which because of its implications for the design of ships in the post-treaty era, is reproduced verbatim:

The standard displacement of a ship is the displacement of the ship complete, fully manned, engined, and equipped ready for sea, including all armament and ammunition, equipment, outfit, provisions and fresh water for crew,

Table 3.8: Replacement Capital Ship Construction: France and Italy

Year	Laid down	Completed	French ships to be scrapped (age)	Italian ships to be scrapped (age)	Pre-Jutland ships Fr / It	Post-Jutland ships Fr / It
1922–26					7 / 6	0 / 0
1927	35,000t (Fr/It)				7 / 6	0 / 0
1928					7 / 6	0 / 0
1929	35,000t (Fr/It)				7 / 6	0 / 0
1930		35,000t (Fr)	Jean Bart (17) Courbet (17)		5 / 6	* / 0
1931	35,000t (Fr/It)	35,000t (It)		Dante Alighieri (19)	5 / 5	* / *
1932	35,000t (Fr) 45,000t (It)	35,000t (Fr)	France (18)		4 / 5	* / *
1933	35,000t (Fr) 25,000t (It)	35,000t (It)		Leonardo da Vinci (19)	4 / 4	* / *
1934		35,000t (Fr)	Paris (20) Bretagne (20)		2 / 4	* / *
1935		35,000t (Fr/It)	Provence (20)	Giulio Cesare (21)	1 / 3	* / *
1936		35,000t (Fr) 45,000t (It)	Lorraine (20)	Conte di Cavour (21) Caio Duilio (21)	0 / 1	* / *
1937		25,000t (It)		Andrea Doria (21)	0 / 0	* / *
1938–42					0 / 0	* / *

Notes:
- Because of the lack of recent construction both powers were permitted under the treaty to lay down replacement tonnage in 1927 and 1929, whereas the other contracting powers would have to wait until the end of the statutory ten-year period.
- Neither France nor Italy was happy with the theoretical allocation of only five capital ships of the maximum specification. Both powers therefore reserved the right to employ the capital ship tonnage allocation (*) however they wished, subject to treaty limits. They subsequently gave serious consideration to using their combined 1927 and 1929 tonnage allocations to build either three ships of 23,300 tons or four ships of 17,500 tons (see Chapter 5).

miscellaneous stores and implements of every description that are intended to be carried in war, but without fuel or reserve feed water on board.

Prior to the Washington Treaty the displacement of a ship had been calculated in different ways according to the operational practices of a particular navy. The term 'light' was generally used to denote the displacement of the ship without fuel or ammunition, and at the other end of the scale 'full load' or 'deep load' was the displacement with all ammunition, fuel and provisions embarked. However, most ships were designed around a 'normal' (or 'legend') displacement, a theoretical operational condition which meant different things in different navies.

At Washington it was acknowledged that overall tonnage limitations and a maximum agreed displacement for individual ships in the defined categories made little sense unless all ships were being measured in the same way, hence the proposal for a newly defined 'standard displacement', to which all the contracting powers would be expected to conform.

Logic would have suggested that either 'light' or 'full load' displacement would have provided an indisputably fair way of comparing ships of different navies. However, 'light' displacement would not include ammunition, which was an important component of a ship's military capabilities, while 'full load' displacement included fuel, which added nothing to a ship's fighting power. The US Navy, which built its ships for endurance because of the exceptionally great distances its battle fleet would have to cover before engaging an opponent, and which as part of the Four-Power Treaty had now agreed not to develop or fortify potential forward operating bases in the Western Pacific, pushed hard for the exclusion of fuel and reserve feed water from the definition of standard displacement. In this it would undoubtedly have received the support of the British, now faced potentially with a commitment to dispatch the fleet from European waters to defend their possessions in the Far East, and the French, who had similar geostrategic concerns.

There would be two major consequences resulting from the agreement on standard displacement. From this moment onwards a ship would have to be designed for two displacements: normal/legend displacement, which would be the displacement at which the ship would be expected to operate under normal conditions, and which would dictate draught and freeboard, stability, operational speed and endurance; and standard displacement, a purely abstract concept which involved simply totalling up the weights of all the components which made up the ship, together with all ammunition and provisions, in accordance with the treaty definition. This was a very serious constraint which was to plague ship design (especially the design of cruisers, which during the agreed hiatus in capital ship construction were the type most affected), and was to lead to some serious design errors and miscalculations; some ships emerged grossly overweight, others underweight, with unfortunate consequences in both cases (see Chapter 6).

On the other hand, the inclusion of ammunition and provisions for the crew in the definition of standard displacement was to become the focus of numerous attempts to circumvent treaty regulations not merely by the two major miscreants, Italy and Japan, but also by Britain, the United States and France. When calculating 'Washington' displacement, it was not uncommon to include a notional (declared) figure for ammunition stowage, perhaps 100 rounds per gun, whereas magazine space might be provided in the design for a (wartime) expansion of up to 150 rounds per gun. In a similar vein, peacetime complements were traditionally lower than those embarked in time of war, enabling the designers to shave off weight allocated to provisions and drinking water, often to an unacceptably low figure.

In the 'treaty' cruiser, where these design practices were most marked, the result was a steady increase in the weight of armour which could be fitted into the maximum 10,000 tons permitted, often without any evolution in propulsion machinery and despite limited possibilities for weight-saving by improved construction practices in the shipyards (see Chapter 6).

Chapter III

Chapter III, entitled 'Miscellaneous Provisions', outlined the modus operandi of the Washington Treaty. Article XXI (the numbering followed on from the twenty articles which made up Chapter I) stipulated that should the national security of any of the contracting powers be materially affected by a change in circumstances, a new conference would be convened, and that a new conference would in any case be convened after eight years to review the provisions of the treaty in the light of 'possible technical and scientific developments'.

Article XXII permitted a contracting power to suspend its obligations under the treaty should it become engaged in hostilities, provided that the other powers were formally notified, and stipulated that the other contracting powers should consult with a view to agreeing possible temporary modifications to the treaty.

Under Article XXIII the treaty would remain in force for an initial period of fifteen years (until 31 December 1936), and would continue in force beyond that date unless two years' prior notice was given by any one of the five contracting powers. Such notice was to be communicated in writing to the government of the United States, which would then transmit this notification to the other powers. The withdrawal of any one power from the treaty would effectively terminate the treaty for all, although any notice of termination would trigger a further conference within one year.

The final clause, Article XXIV, urged ratification of the treaty by the constitutional parliaments 'as soon as possible', the ratifications to be deposited with the US government in Washington, which would transmit to each of the contracting powers a certified copy of the *procès-verbal*. The treaty itself, of which there were parallel 'authentic' versions in English and French (but not in Japanese or Italian), was also to be deposited in the archives of the US government, with duly certified copies transmitted to the governments of the remaining contracting powers.

CHAPTER 4

Winners and Losers

The USA

The United States attained most of its objectives at Washington: nominal parity with the world's premier naval power, the British Empire; the termination of a financially unsustainable naval arms race at a point which favoured the US Navy; an end to the Anglo-Japanese Alliance, together with a statutory margin of superiority (a ratio of 10:6) over the Imperial Japanese Navy in the crucial capital ship category; and a set of ancillary treaties backed by all the major European powers which would hopefully restrain Japanese expansionism on the Asian mainland. The only major concession was the agreement not to build new military bases (nor to fortify existing ones) in the Philippines or on Guam. This would make the defence of the latter territories against an attack by Japan more difficult, and would imply the despatch of a large expeditionary fleet supported by an array of auxiliary vessels across the broad expanses of the Pacific in the event of conflict.

The United States was a colonial power only by default, not by intention or inclination; Guam had been inherited and the Philippines purchased cheaply following the successful outcome of the war against Spain in 1898. The United States, unlike its co-signatories of the Washington Treaty, was also a nation rich in natural resources. It required only markets overseas for its manufactured goods, hence its espousal of free trade as the first principle of international relations. The great European colonial empires, on the other hand, were predicated on the need not just for markets but for the raw materials from which to produce their manufactured goods. It was the scramble for colonies in Africa and Asia which at the turn of the century had become the focus of European rivalry, whereas it was the conflict between imperialism (which implied exclusive or protected markets) and the principle of free trade which would continue to create tensions between the United States and the other powers, particularly Japan. During the 1930s an increasingly isolationist United States would attempt to resolve the strategic problem presented by the defence of the Philippines by preparing to grant that nation full independence, with its own armed forces. This would enable US security to be focused on the Alaska/Hawaii/Panama triangle favoured by the Republican administration of President Herbert Hoover.

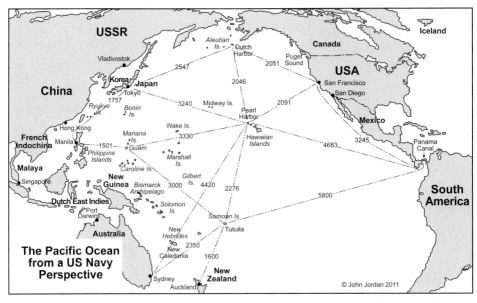

The map illustrates the immense distances involved in naval operations in the Pacific: 5,000 miles or more from the West Coast of the United States to the Western Pacific, 3,000 miles from Pearl Harbor. In the period which followed the Great War the US Navy planned to develop Guam as a forward naval base. Guam could protect US interests both in the Philippines and in China, and has been compared to 'a lancet pointed to Japan's side'.[1] Under the terms of the Washington Treaty, the USA renounced its right to develop and fortify Guam in return for Japanese acceptance of a 5:3 ratio in capital ships. The US Navy now had to accept that any military expedition to the Western Pacific would have to be conducted by large warships with great endurance, and these would have to be supported by a 'fleet train' of supporting vessels and large floating docks. Successive Republican administrations, the natural instincts of which were isolationist, would focus America's defence on a Pearl Harbor/Alaska/Panama 'strategic triangle' which was essentially defensive in its orientation. Britain was compelled to choose between Australia and Singapore for its own forward defensive base, and opted for the latter primarily because it guarded the gateway to the Indian Ocean. This, however, left Hong Kong, halfway between Singapore and the Japanese home islands, out on a limb. Although the intention of Article XIX of the treaty was to make the Western Pacific a 'zone of peace', it also had the effect of making Japan the dominant military power in the region.

Britain

The British came home from Washington shaken, but having nevertheless secured an end to a naval arms race the country simply could not afford, as well as a network of treaties which on the face of it appeared to guarantee the international stability necessary for the security of the British Empire. However, numerous concessions had had to be made from what was essentially a position of economic and political weakness. The Washington Treaty marked an end to British naval supremacy, leaving Britain with less leverage when dealing with other powers. The Anglo-Japanese Alliance was dead, which meant that the Imperial Japanese Navy, built largely with British expertise and assistance, would no longer be able to 'mind the shop' in South-east Asia on Britain's behalf. On the contrary, with Britain's decision to align herself more closely with the United States, Japan became a potential threat to her possessions in South-east Asia and to the dominions of Australia and New Zealand. These territories could now be defended only by the despatch of a large expeditionary fleet to Singapore, which would have to be further developed (at considerable expense) as a major base. However, whereas the expeditionary fleet envisaged by US policy would be the main US Fleet based on Pearl Harbor, any such British fleet would have to be transferred from the British Isles or from the Mediterranean, and such a transfer could take place only if there were a stable political situation in Europe. The 5:5:3 ratio (for Britain–USA–Japan) agreed at Washington made it impossible for Britain to have material superiority in both European waters and the Far East, and the growing crisis in Europe during the late 1930s would compel Britain to back-track on its assurances to the South Pacific dominions. By May 1939, *the* fleet to be dispatched had become *a* fleet, and the journey time had been extended from forty days to ninety days – by September the Chiefs of Staff were informing the military authorities in Malaya that it could be six months!

The British delegation also failed to secure the total abolition of submarines it had set out to achieve. In this they were unable to convince the French, who were adamant that they needed submarines to compensate for their inferiority in capital ships, or the Americans and Japanese, who were interested in developing submersibles based on the German 'cruiser' models for strategic scouting in the broad expanses of the Pacific. The British also lost their fight to preserve the G3 battlecruiser programme, these ships being so far beyond the new limits on displacement as to be unacceptable to the other contracting powers. However, they did secure permission to build two new 16in-gun battleships within the new limits, to counterbalance the Japanese and American 16in-gun ships already building.

Intransigent French resistance to other proposals at the Conference also indirectly benefited the Royal Navy. The United States failed in its efforts to extend the ratio agreed for capital ships to other categories. This meant that there was no legal restriction on the size of the force of cruisers that Britain could keep in service to police her large empire – the current requirement, set on the advice of Admiral John Jellicoe following his tour of the Empire in 1919–20, was for seventy. Unfortunately for the Royal Navy, the high level at which the qualitative limits were set for this type of vessel (10,000 tons with 8in guns) would ensure that the new 'treaty' cruisers were unaffordable in the numbers required. This would drive the British to seek a reduction in those limits at both Geneva 1927 and London 1930; it would also compel Britain to accept quantitative limits which effectively restricted the Royal Navy to fifty cruisers at the latter conference to secure an agreement with the United States and Japan.

Japan

Although Japan had ambitions to become a great power, and had made immense strides in that direction during the early part of the century, her industrial infrastructure was not yet fully developed, and her people were regarded by the European imperial powers and by the United States as racial inferiors. Despite her powerful modern navy, Japan therefore lacked the necessary economic and political 'clout' to secure a favourable outcome at the Washington Conference. Moreover, the IJN delegation to the Washington Conference was divided by personal and political antagonisms. The experienced navy minister, Kato Tomosaburo, who headed the delegation, held to the view that an arms race with the United States was not in Japan's interest, and was inclined to accept the 6:10 ratio in capital ships offered in return for concessions on the basing of foreign warships close to Japan. However, this ran counter to the views of the 'Young Turk' element in the IJN, who opposed any constraint on the development of the navy and who regarded a 7:10 ratio as the minimum compatible with Japan's security. The insistence on this 7:10 ratio by the younger Kato Kanji, president of the Staff College and chief naval aide at Washington, split the Japanese delegation and ensured that the treaty would never be accepted by the increasingly influential nationalist faction of the IJN.

Some concessions were obtained by Japan, notably the completion of the 16-inch battleship *Mutsu*, and the non-fortification of naval bases in the Western Pacific, which gave the IJN uncontested naval superiority in East Asian waters. However, the new imperial defence policy drafted in 1922 and published in 1923 would establish the United States as the most likely hypothetical enemy for the army and the navy, and both services would come to regard war as inevitable given US economic expansion in China and anti-Japanese agitation on the US West Coast. Japan would eventually abandon the treaty in 1936, the first of the five contracting powers so to do.

France and Italy

The Italians were quite happy with the outcomes of the conference. The wheeling and dealing on the Pacific theatre, which were fundamental to the key political negotiations for the other major powers, were peripheral to Italian interests, and Italy was flattered by the offer of parity in capital ships with France,[2] an offer which constituted a recognition of her recent efforts to build a powerful modern fleet. Italy now had the naval means to support her long-standing colonial ambitions in North Africa, which would ultimately bring her into conflict with Britain and France.

The French, on the other hand, were devastated. The Marine Nationale could not be renewed during the Great War because the workforce in the dockyards had been redirected into the manufacture of guns and munitions for the French Army (see Chapter 1). By 1918 the Marine Nationale comprised a large and obsolescent fleet of predominantly pre-dreadnought vintage, fit only for the scrapyard. This was the status quo with which the unholy Anglo-Saxon alliance of Britain and the United States confronted the French at Washington. The resulting treaty placed France well below Japan in the permitted tonnage of capital ships (a ratio of nine ships to five), and on a par with the Italian Fleet. This was seen as incompatible with French security obligations. The French Empire stretched from the West Indies to the south-west Pacific, via Africa, the Indian Ocean and South-east Asia, and was second only to the British Empire in scale and importance. French Indochina was even closer to Japan than Malaya and Singapore (and in 1941–42, ironically, would become the platform for the invasion of both). Moreover, France was traditionally a major European power, straddling both the Atlantic Ocean and the Mediterranean. Italy, by contrast, was a relatively new country whose navy needed to operate only in neighbouring waters.

When the French delegation returned to France with the treaty, there was considerable anger at the humiliation inflicted by 'perfidious Albion' and its American cousins, and much heated debate took place in the French Parliament before the Washington Treaty was reluctantly ratified in 1923. This made the French even more determined to fend off the inevitable attempts by the other major powers to extend the ratios agreed for capital ships to other categories, particularly cruisers and submarines. The latter types would increasingly take on the role of the defence of French trade and the empire.

In truth France's humiliation was a result of economic exhaustion in the wake of the Great War. When the Marine Nationale finally embarked on its programme of renewal it found that it could neither afford all the ships it wanted – of the twenty-one treaty cruisers requested post-Washington only seven were built – nor find the shipbuilding or military-industrial capacity to deliver them within the contracted time.

Conclusion

Such then were the successes and disappointments which the delegations took away with them in unequal measure from the conference to their respective countries. The following chapters will consider in detail the effects of the Washington Treaty on the subsequent development of the five navies in terms both of their strategic posture and of the ships they chose to design and build within the constraints of the treaty.

CHAPTER 5

Capital Ships 1922–1930

After Washington the only capital ships which could be laid down before 1931 (1927 in the case of France and Italy) were the two new treaty battleships which Great Britain was permitted to build as compensation for recent American and Japanese construction. The Japanese 16in-gun battleship *Mutsu*, sister-ship to the *Nagato*, was already complete, and the US Navy's *Colorado* and *West Virginia* had both been launched before the signing of the treaty and would enter service during 1923.

The British Nelson *class*

Despite its support for a displacement limit of 43,000 tons for individual capital ships, the Royal Navy accepted that it was likely that the lower figure of 35,000 tons proposed by the United States would prevail, and the director of naval construction (DNC) was duly instructed to prepare sketch designs for battlecruisers at this reduced displacement while the conference was proceeding. By 30 November designs designated F2 and F3 had been submitted. Both had three turrets grouped together forward of the bridge tower: F2 had twin 15in turrets, a speed of just under 30 knots and a 13in armour belt, whilst in the triple-turret F3 speed was reduced to 28.5 knots and the armour belt to 12in; both types had the thick 7in armoured deck of the G3 (see drawings).

However, as the conference proceeded and it became clear that both the Americans and the Japanese would have at least two battleships armed with 16in guns, Royal Navy thinking veered towards a 16in-gun battleship with a maximum speed of 23 knots.[1] Three further sketch designs were prepared: O3 with three triple 16in turrets all forward of the bridge as in the battlecruiser designs, and P3 and Q3, which were essentially scaled-down versions of the 18in-gun M3/N3 designs with three triple 15in turrets, the third of which was abaft the bridge. The O3 design, which traded armour weight (by compressing the citadel) for the larger-calibre gun, was adopted and became the basis of the *Nelson* class. The two ships were approved on 6 February 1922 (the date the Washington Treaty was signed), the legend design was approved on 11 September of the same year, and the contracts were signed on 1 January 1923, three days after the keels had been laid.

Table 5.1: *Nelson* class: Characteristics (as completed)

Displacement	33,500 tons standard; 38,000 tons full load
Dimensions	710ft oa × 106ft × 30ft (216m × 32m × 9m)
Machinery	8 Admiralty 3-drum boilers; 2-shaft geared turbines; 45,000shp = 23 knots
Armament	9–16in/45 (3 × III); 12–6in/50 (6 × II); 6–4.7in/40 (6 × I) HA, 2–24.5in u/w TT (10 torpedoes)
Protection	belt 13–14in, deck 3¾–6¼in, turrets 16in faces, CT 14in max.
Complement	1,315 (1,360 as flag)

Nelson and *Rodney* had all the revolutionary features (and the defects) of their drawing-board predecessors. The main armament was concentrated amidships, the second of the three triple turrets being raised in the superfiring position, with the first and third turrets ('A' and 'X' in Royal Navy parlance) at forecastle deck level. The bridge tower, atop which the fire control directors for the main, secondary and anti-aircraft guns were mounted, was also derived from the earlier sketch designs. The low after deckhouse with the single funnel and tripod mainmast carried the anti-aircraft weaponry, and there were three twin 6in turrets (a reduction from the four of the earlier designs) on either beam, the centre turret on either side being superimposed.

The main armour belt, which was inclined at 18°, was 14in thick over the main magazines and 13in thick over the machinery spaces, which were arranged as in the M3 and N3 designs with the engine rooms forward of the boiler rooms in order to maximise the depth of the anti-torpedo protection system. At Jutland there had been instances of the main belt armour being pushed in at the plate joins when struck by heavy shell. This weakness was resolved in the new battleships by using the largest possible armour plates and 'keyed' joints backed up by heavy bars. There was 6¼in armour on ½in deck plating above the magazines, and 3¾in armour on ½in deck plating above the machinery spaces. Firing tests against the old battleship *Superb* suggested that the magazines were safe against any shell at all battle ranges, and that there was only a slight risk of large-calibre shells penetrating the machinery spaces.

The torpedo protection system was virtually identical to that of the G3, with an outer air-filled space, an inner water-filled space, and a torpedo bulkhead comprising two riveted plates of ¾in HT steel. The system was designed to resist a 750lb charge comparable to that of the ship's own large-diameter 24.5in torpedoes.[2] A full-scale section built to test the system was subjected to a 1,000lb charge, which caused extensive damage to the outer plating but only slight leakage through the bulkhead.

The water protection weighed 2,870 tons, and was not declared under Washington; it also increased the ship's draught by nearly 2ft (0.6m), reduced

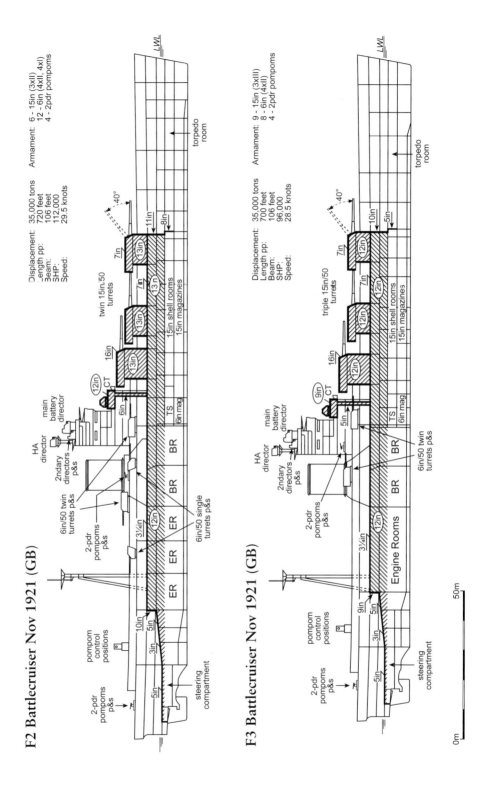

F2 Battlecruiser Nov 1921 (GB)

Armament: 6 - 15in (3xII)
12 - 6in (4xII, 4xI)
4 - 2pdr pompoms

Displacement: 35,000 tons
Length pp: 720 feet
Beam: 106 feet
SHP: 112,000
Speed: 29.5 knots

torpedo room

twin 15in/50 turrets

15in shell rooms
15in magazines

main battery director

HA director

2ndary directors p&s

6in/50 twin turrets p&s

6in/50 single turrets p&s

2-pdr pompoms p&s

pompom control positions

2-pdr pompoms p&s

steering compartment

11in
8in
7in
13in
13in
13in
13in
16in
6in
CT 12in
TS
6in mag
ER ER ER ER
BR BR
3¼in
12in
10in
5in
3in
5in
5in

40°

LWL

F3 Battlecruiser Nov 1921 (GB)

Armament: 9 - 15in (3xIII)
8 - 6in (4xII)
4 - 2pdr pompoms

Displacement: 35,000 tons
Length pp: 700 feet
Beam: 106 feet
SHP: 96,000
Speed: 28.5 knots

torpedo room

triple 15in/50 turrets

15in shell rooms
15in magazines

main battery director

HA director

2ndary directors p&s

6in/50 twin turrets p&s

2-pdr pompoms p&s

pompom control positions

2-pdr pompoms p&s

steering compartment

10in
5in
5in
7in
12in
12in
12in
12in
12in
16in
5in
CT 9in
TS
6in mag
Engine Rooms
BR BR
3¼in
12in
9in
5in
3in
5in

40°

LWL

0m   50m

F2 and F3 were the two 35,000-ton battlecruiser designs prepared during the early days of the Washington Conference and presented to the Admiralty Board on 30 November 1921. Compared to the 48,000-ton G3s there were reductions in gun calibre, in speed and in the weight of protection – although armour thickness was broadly maintained, particularly in the six-gun F2. The surviving sketch plans suggest that unhappy compromises were inevitable. The single broad funnel is very close to the tower, the arrangement of the secondary turrets and forward pom-poms around the tower is cramped, and the 4.7in HA guns and the after set of fire control directors have been suppressed altogether. The rationale for this appears to be the suppression of the secondary magazines aft to make room for the battlecruiser machinery. They would be reinstated in the *Nelsons*, which had less powerful battleship machinery on two shafts.

Nelson (GB)

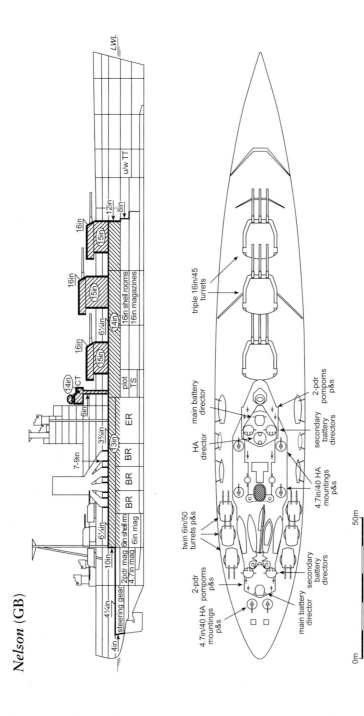

The design for the *Nelson* class was essentially a scaled-down version of the G3 battlecruisers (see Chapter 2), with the engine rooms forward of the boiler rooms as in the parallel N3 battleship design. Note the exceptionally short and heavily protected citadel made possible by adopting an all-forward main armament. The *Nelsons* had a major influence abroad; the French fast battleships of the 1930s had essentially the same layout, and the 'tower' bridge structure was widely adopted.

A dramatic view of the battleship *Nelson* during the early part of her career. She had many of the revolutionary features of the G3 battlecruiser design, but the Royal Navy's decision to retain the original heavy armament and protection at the expense of high speed was questionable. These ships nevertheless remained the world's most powerful battleships throughout the interwar period. (Royal Naval Museum)

An aerial view of of *Nelson* dating from March 1937, with recognition markings atop 'B' and 'X' turrets. (Royal Naval Museum)

speed by one third of a knot, and increased fuel consumption, so was not embarked during peacetime operations. It is disingenuous to claim, as some writers have, that the water protection did not have to be declared because the Washington definition of 'standard' displacement excluded all liquids. The only liquids specifically excluded from the definition were fuel oil and reserve feed water, for reasons which have already been discussed in Chapter 3; other liquids such as drinking and washing water, and the water already in the boilers and condensers were not excluded. Water for protection never entered into the specifics of the definition. However, as it would have been an essential element of the protection system in wartime (and therefore contributed to the 'military' qualities of the ship) it should strictly have counted towards the 35,000-ton limit. Presumably the British felt this omission justified as the water was performing the same function as heavy oil fuel, which was excluded from standard displacement, in the comparable US Navy systems. The Royal Navy preferred to locate the fuel bunkers inboard of the torpedo bulkhead, in part due to concerns about combustion resulting from the explosion of the torpedo warhead (which were subsequently found to be unjustified), but also to reduce the likelihood of the fuel being contaminated by seawater in the event of the extensive damage to the light outer skin of the bulge or hull which would result from a torpedo strike.

The potential drawbacks of these ships' protection systems have been noted previously in Chapter 2. They included an unusually short armoured belt (approximately 58 per cent of the length between perpendiculars), which had to be compensated for by an exceptionally large metacentric height of 9.4ft at deep load[3] in order to preserve stability in a damaged condition. During the Second World War Nelson was to suffer severe damage from mines and a torpedo, all of which caused extensive flooding to the unarmoured bow section.

In order to save weight, a new high-tensile steel (Ducol or 'D' quality steel) was used in the construction of the hull. It permitted the use of thinner plates with overall savings estimated at 1,500–2,000 tons. The weight of components and fittings was also strictly supervised during construction, and both ships turned out underweight (Nelson: 33,580 tons standard; Rodney: 33,785 tons). This may have contributed to the relatively high roll accelerations experienced in service, which impaired gunnery. It may also have been partially responsible for the unexpected level of structural damage when the big guns were fired in earnest.

The 16in turrets were the first triple mountings in service with the Royal Navy, and numerous problems were experienced. British experience at Jutland prompted the adoption of flash-proof hoists for the charges, which were exposed only as they crossed the handing room and while entering the gun, and the large number of safety locks introduced for the transit from magazine to gun made the loading process extremely slow. The three guns in each turret had to be loaded together but, in order to minimise dispersion, the centre gun fired in a different salvo to the outer guns, so the firing cycle during gunnery trials was in excess of one minute. These initial problems appear to have been partially resolved during the 1930s, but the triple 16in Mk I never approached the impressive firing cycle of the twin 15in Mk I mounting (one round every 25 seconds)

The change from a heavyweight shell with a low muzzle velocity to a relatively lightweight shell with high muzzle velocity proved equally problematic. The short-bodied, long-headed projectile was found to strip the rifling of the gun, causing rapid barrel wear and a dramatic fall-off in accuracy after the first few rounds.[4] The problem was partially resolved by reverting to a smaller explosive charge and by modifying the rifling of the barrel.

The secondary battery of 6in/50-calibre guns, mounted in six power-operated turrets, was only lightly protected (1in plating), and was relocated aft in order to minimise blast damage from the main guns. There was some criticism that the decision to group the turrets together could result in all the secondary guns on one side of the ship being put out of action by a single heavy shell. The new Mk XXII gun was designed as a dual-purpose weapon with a maximum elevation of 60°. However, it failed to attain its designed firing cycle of 7–8rpm, and the Mk XVIII mounting proved too slow in elevation and training for the gun to be effective in the anti-aircraft role.

The fire control director layout duplicated that of the G3. Directors for the main guns, each equipped with a 15ft-base rangefinder, were located atop

Table 5.2: *Nelson* Class: Breakdown of Weights (designed)

	Weight	% of displ.
Hull	14,250t	41%
Machinery	2,550t	6.5%
Protection	10,250t	29.5%
Armament	6,900t	20%
Equipment	1,050t	3%
Standard displacement	**35,000tW**	**100%**
Oil fuel	4,000t	
Reserve feedwater	245t	
Armament	+474t	
Equipment	+155t	
Water in buoyancy space	2,870t	
Extra deep load displacement	**42,744t**	

Notes:
• Weights are in long tons.
• The major weight savings over the G3s were: hull (4,350t), machinery (3,450t), and protection (4,190t).

the bridge tower and abaft the mainmast; the four secondary directors, which incorporated 12ft rangefinders, were disposed on either side of the main directors. Stabilised director sights and general improvements in postwar fire control technology went some way towards compensating for the quick roll of the ships.

The 4.7in/40-calibre HA gun, which could elevate to 90°, was an adequate weapon for its day, but the positions available on the after deckhouse and the stern did not meet the recommendations of the AA Gunnery Committee that at least four guns should be capable of bearing on any point in the sky. No more than three could fire on either beam, and forward arcs were obstructed by the bridge tower, so that the guns were incapable of tracking aircraft flying across the bow. Nevertheless the provision of well-sited director control for AA fire was in advance of any other navy of the period; the control position was at the highest point of the ship, and comprised two-sided HA directors with an axial 12ft-base rangefinder, and an HA calculating position equipped with an Evershed bearing indicator and a Dumaresq rate instrument at the level of the main gunnery director platform. Development of the 2-pdr multiple pom-poms, on the other hand, was protracted, and single 2-pdr guns were fitted in their place on completion. The first eight-barrelled mounting was fitted only in 1931, and it was 1935–36 before the second was installed.

Despite the impression they created abroad,[5] history was not kind to the *Nelsons*. Although in 1939 they were still the core of the British Home Fleet based at Scapa Flow, they were far too slow to catch any of the new generation of German battleships. When the *Bismarck* sortied in May 1941, the force dispatched to deal with her comprised the elderly 30-knot battlecruiser *Hood* and the brand-new 28-knot *Prince of Wales*, and *Rodney* had to be summoned from convoy protection duty to deliver the *coup de grâce* to an already crippled vessel. The hitting power of these ships remained undiminished, but their maximum service speed of just over 20 knots meant that they were too slow to operate effectively with the modern battleships or even the older battlecruisers, let alone a fast carrier task force, and they spent the latter part of the war on convoy escort and shore bombardment duties, like their US Navy counterparts. With the benefit of hindsight it is arguable that the Royal Navy would have had better value from the 15in-gun battlecruisers for which sketch designs were prepared in November 1921, and which were subsequently rejected in favour of the slow, heavily armoured 23-knot battleship.

Modernising the Battle Fleets

The ten-year building 'holiday' decreed at Washington made it imperative that existing capital ships be brought up to modern standards. This was regarded as a particular priority by the British, the core of whose battle fleet was six to seven years old when the Washington Treaty was signed in February 1922. During the intervening seven-year period the US Navy had commissioned no fewer than ten modern battleships, and the Japanese six. It was therefore largely at British insistence that the proviso in Section I, Part III of the treaty, permitting the fitting of bulges and anti-air deck protection within a 3,000-ton limit, was included. No sooner was the ink dry on the treaty than the British Admiralty appointed a sub-committee to consider possible improvements in the protection of its existing battleships and battlecruisers.

The report of this sub-committee in May 1922 identified underwater protection as the priority in the near term, although it was felt that deck armour could subsequently become the priority with the development of effective bomber aircraft. The Naval Staff was duly instructed to draw up a modernisation programme for the battleships of the *Queen Elizabeth* class and later. It was considered that older ships were unlikely to remain in service during the 1930s, when capital ship construction could again be resumed. The ten battleships of the *Queen Elizabeth* and *Revenge* classes, together with the three modern battlecruisers and the two new-build 35,000-ton ships, made up the fifteen-ship fleet decreed by the Washington Treaty, on which future planning would be based.

Naturally the Admiralty wanted both bulges and deck armour, but it was becoming increasingly clear that the necessary funding would not be available for both, so providing protection against air- and submarine-launched torpedoes was considered the priority. The cost of bulging was estimated at £200,000 per ship, whereas the fitting of additional deck armour would have cost £350,000, and six of the more modern ships (*Hood*, *Repulse* and four of the 'R' class) were already bulged, leaving only seven to be modified. Moreover, the topweight involved in fitting additional deck armour would have been so great that ships would need to have been bulged first in order to retain sufficient draught and stability.

The sub-committee had suggested that the 3,000-ton limit would in any case only provide deck armour sufficient to resist a 550lb (250kg) bomb, and that a concentrated attack by bomber aircraft might cripple battleships by destroying the ever-more-crucial fire control systems located in unprotected positions high in the ship, and also might render manoeuvring in close formation dangerous. It therefore proposed that existing anti-aircraft guns be replaced by a battery of four 4in HA guns backed up by two multiple pom-poms, directed by the latest high altitude control systems (HACS). With equipment such as this the sub-committee felt that there was no reason to believe that air attack would disable or cause the loss of a capital ship while underway.

The ships to be bulged would have to be docked, and the only dock suitable for the purpose was at Portsmouth Naval Dockyard. This would be occupied until 1924 with the refits of the battleship *Royal Sovereign* and the battlecruiser *Renown* authorised prior to Washington, so a refit programme beginning in that same year for the five battleships of the *Queen Elizabeth* class was drawn up, with docking scheduled at eight-month intervals. Financial restrictions on the navy's budget meant that money was not forthcoming for

The modifications made to four of the five *Queen Elizabeth*s during the 1920s were less radical and significantly less costly than those extended to the US Navy's older battleships or the IJN's *Kongo* class. The principal improvements concerned underwater protection and high-angle anti-aircraft capabilities. The new bulge and the trunked funnel are particularly prominent in this photo of *Queen Elizabeth* taken in 1930.

even this limited modernisation programme, which in the event was delayed and delivered piecemeal (see table).

The bulges fitted in the *Queen Elizabeth*s comprised an upper bulge extending 3ft from the ship's side over the armour belt, divided by transverse bulkheads into compartments 16ft long, and a lower bulge 6ft from the ship's side beneath the belt, divided by transverse bulkheads into compartments 20ft long. The space between the outer plating of the bulge and the inner torpedo bulkhead was divided into three longitudinal compartments: the bulge itself, the double bottom and the wing compartments. Outboard of the machinery spaces the double bottom and wing compartments were filled with fuel oil, which became the liquid component of the underwater protection system. It was envisaged that these bunkers would be the last to be used, in which case the oil would be replaced by seawater. Abreast the main magazines forward and aft, where the depth of protection was less than amidships, there was an air–water–air 'sandwich'. The water protection alone in this system weighed 815 tons.

The maximum depth of the anti-torpedo protection amidships was now 16ft, comparable to that of the new 35,000-ton ships, and like the latter was designed to resist a 750lb warhead. On completion in 1915–16 the *Queen Elizabeth*s had been overweight, a condition aggravated by wartime additions. The prominent bulges therefore had the welcome effect of restoring buoyancy and stability, at the expense of slightly reduced speed and higher roll accelerations.

Queen Elizabeth (GB)

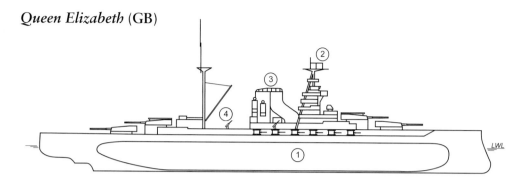

Four of the five ships of the *Queen Elizabeth* class (all except *Barham*) were given major refits during the period 1924–30. The key modifications were:

1. Deep bulges incorporating a liquid-layer underwater protection system.
2. Revised fire control arrangements with a modified foretop and additional platforms around the forward tripod mast.
3. The trunking back of the fore-funnel to clear smoke from the bridge and foretop.
4. A new anti-aircraft armament comprising four single 4in/45-calibre HA guns.

Queen Elizabeth after modifications

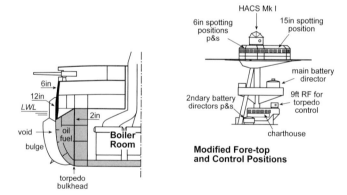

Table 5.3: Queen Elizabeth Class Modernisation

Name of ship	Date of mod.
Warspite	1924–26
Queen Elizabeth	1926–27
Malaya	1927–29
Valiant	1929–30
Barham	1931–34

Note: The modernisation of *Barham*, which followed the London Conference of 1930, included a horizontal protection upgrade.

There was no problem in fitting the four 4in HA guns, but the location of the HACS was less straightforward, as it was considered imperative to have the best possible sky arcs. The solution was a new enlarged foretop with the 15in-gun control position at its forward end, and the HACS located at its after end between the twin 6in control positions, which were connected by a passageway. There was a new platform for the 15in director directly beneath the foretop, with an enclosed torpedo fire control position equipped with a 9ft rangefinder below. It was feared that the enlarged bridge structure would create a backdraught drawing funnel gases onto the bridge, so a proposal from the DNC for the fore-funnel to be trunked back onto the second was approved by the Board of Admiralty.

Modifications to the 'R'-class battleship *Royal Oak* (refit 1922–24) were similar to those applied to the *Queen Elizabeth* class. The other four ships had been fitted with bulges before Washington,[6] so received only the 4in HA guns and HACS. A 1922 proposal to place the magazines beneath the shell rooms for additional protection did not proceed, in part because stowage and rate of fire would have been reduced, in part on grounds of cost, but primarily because it was decided that such a modification was not permissible under treaty rules.

The major reconstruction of the battlecruiser *Renown*, which had been planned before the Washington Conference, and for which specific permission was granted by the treaty itself, took place between 1923 and 1926. It was even more radical than that of her sister-ship *Repulse*, which had been bulged and fitted with the 9in armour belt from the ex-Chilean battleship *Almirante*

The battleships of the 'R' class had already been bulged – *Royal Oak* was the last to be so fitted in 1922–24 – and were otherwise little modified during the 1920s. This is *Resolution* at Malta, probably during the early 1930s. Note the clinker screen on the funnel and the catapult for a spotter aircraft on the stern. (Leo van Ginderen collection)

Cochrane (completed as the Royal Navy carrier *Eagle*) during 1918–21. Besides a newly ordered 9in main armour belt, the upper 6in belt of the *Repulse* was omitted in favour of a heavy armoured deck 4in thick above the magazines and 2½in thick over the machinery. The redesigned bulge was lighter than that fitted in *Repulse*, the steel crushing tubes being omitted. The cost of rebuilding *Renown* was £750,000 – a quarter of what the same ship had cost to build only six years earlier. At a time when large sums were required to build the new generation of treaty cruisers, this can have served only to reinforce Treasury concerns about the Admiralty's proposals for wholesale modernisation of the battle fleet.

Of the remaining modern battlecruisers *Repulse*, which had already undergone her major postwar reconstruction, received only the standard AA modifications. *Hood*, which was less than two years old at the conclusion of the Washington Conference, had received her full AA outfit on completion and was to remain virtually unmodified until the Second World War.

Modernising the US Navy's Older Battleships

Following the completion of the *Colorado* and *West Virginia* in 1923, the US Navy would have eighteen battleships in service. Of these only the two 14in-gun ships of the *Tennessee* class and the three new 16in-gun ships of the *Colorado* class, known as the 'Big Five', had a modern underwater protection system and main guns which elevated above 15°. The other thirteen ships would all need major work to bring them up to standard; following the conclusion of the Washington Conference, the US Navy immediately commissioned studies for the reconstruction of these ships. There was a marked reluctance on the part of Congress to fund a full-scale modernisation of the battle fleet in the wake of what it regarded as a successful naval arms limitation conference. However, it soon became apparent that other Washington powers, notably Britain and Japan, were drawing up modernisation programmes for their older ships, and there were concerns that the elderly US dreadnoughts which remained in the post-Washington inventory would be no match for their foreign counterparts.

One of the less obvious benefits of the Washington Treaty for the US Navy was that there were now incomplete hulls and discarded ships available for weapons tests; the elderly dreadnought *South Carolina* was used to test bulges, the *North Dakota* was employed as a radio-controlled target ship, and the *Washington*, which was complete up to the armoured deck, was used for underwater explosions. Another important side-effect of the treaty was that there was a mass of *matériel* ordered for the battleships and battlecruisers that had been cancelled, and which was therefore available for reconstruction of the older battleships. In particular there were complete sets of modern oil-fired boilers for the equivalent of five new battleships and three battlecruisers, together with a large quantity of armour plating.

Table 5.4: US Navy Battleship Modernisation

Name of ship	Propulsion	Fuel	Date of mod.
Florida	turbines	coal	1924–26
Utah	turbines	coal	1926–28
Wyoming	turbines	coal	1925–27
Arkansas	turbines	coal	1925–27
New York	VTE	coal	1925–27
Texas	VTE	coal	1925–27
Nevada	turbines	oil	1927–29
Oklahoma	VTE	oil	1927–29
Pennsylvania	turbines	oil	1928–31
Arizona	turbines	oil	1928–31
New Mexico	turbo-electric	oil	1931–33
Mississippi	turbines	oil	1931–33
Idaho	turbines	oil	1931–33

For the purpose of modernisation the eighteen US battleships were divided into three groups: the six coal-burners completed between 1911 and 1914, the seven relatively modern oil-burners completed from 1916 to 1919, and the so-called 'Big Five'. The immediate priority was the modernisation of the elderly coal-burners, which experienced a series of engineering breakdowns during the 1923/24 'Winter Maneuvers'. These ships were inferior in many respects to the British *Iron Duke* class, which in the view of the Royal Navy were not worth modernising due to their impending obsolescence. Besides their unreliable propulsion machinery, the US ships had no underwater protection system, their horizontal protection was inadequate by postwar standards, their main guns could elevate to only 15°, and their casemate-mounted secondary 5in batteries were wet. The US Navy intended to address all these deficiencies in its modernisation programme, although the proposal to increase the elevation of the main guns had to be abandoned in the face of opposition from the British (of which more later).

The six older units were duly taken in hand from 1924 to 1928. The original twelve/fourteen coal-burning boilers were replaced by four/six new oil-fired boilers originally ordered for the cancelled battleships of the 1916 programme. This made it possible to reduce the width of the boiler rooms and to provide a corresponding increase in the depth of the underwater protection system, and only a single funnel was now required to accommodate the boiler uptakes. Anti-torpedo bulges were fitted, although these had the effect of making the ships even wetter and stiffer than before.

Horizontal protection against plunging shell was improved by adding 3½in of armour above the magazines fore and aft, ¾–1¼in plating above the machinery spaces, and 1¾in plating on the roofs of the turrets and the conning tower. However, this 'compound' armour, which comprised the original plus new additional plating, was acknowledged to be less effective at resisting shell than single sheets of the same nominal thickness.

The mainmast was reduced to a short tripod or pole mast to permit the fitting of a catapult for fighter/spotter floatplanes atop the upper turret amidships, and in the last two ships of the series the original cage foremast was replaced by a heavy tripod. Taken together with the reduction to a single funnel, this resulted in a major change in the external appearance of these ships. The opportunity was also taken to relocate part of the secondary battery of 5in guns from hull casemates to the upper deck, and the HA battery was doubled to eight single 3in HA guns.

These extensive modernisations, which took around two years per ship, were labour-intensive and costly. Whether they represented good value for money is open to discussion. Even after modernisation, these elderly vessels were never really regarded as first-line units by the US Navy. They were never part of the prestigious battle force based at Pearl Harbor, serving first with the embryonic scouting force and then, when this was modernised and rebuilt around treaty cruisers and aircraft carriers, with the Training Squadron.

The Gun Elevation Controversy

The gun elevation issue began as a misunderstanding, fanned by misleading reports in the press on both sides of the Atlantic, and later escalated into a full-blown political row which threatened the post-Washington cordiality of Anglo-American relations.

In early 1923 Congress allocated the sum of $6.5m for the purpose of increasing the elevation of the main guns of the thirteen older US Navy battleships from 15° to 30°. The measure was passed following evidence from the secretary of the navy before the Committee on Naval Affairs in which he stated that the guns of the British battle fleet had recently had their elevation similarly increased. This erroneous information, which appears to have originated with the US naval attaché based in London,[7] was categorically denied by the British government through their ambassador, and the acting US secretary of the navy was subsequently compelled to withdraw the statement and issue a formal apology on 23 March. The request for funding from Congress was simultaneously withdrawn and deferred.

The US Navy was most unhappy, and put forward a strongly argued case: i) that this measure was necessary in order to bring gun elevations into line with those of the British Fleet, and ii) that none of the steps necessary to increase the elevation of the guns involved the change in the 'general type of mounting' prohibited under the treaty (Part III, Section I (d) 2). Recourse was even made to the wording of the parallel French-language version of the treaty, and much was made of the phrase *'tout changement dans son plan général d'installation*', which was interpreted as referring to the 'layout of the armament' rather than the 'type of mounting'.[8]

Meanwhile, the British were taking their own legal advice on the wording of the treaty, and on 14 February 1924 submitted a formal complaint via their chargé d'affaires in the United States, Henry Chilton. In the view of the British the wording of point 2 could not be taken in isolation, but should be read in the context of the entire paragraph (d), which made it clear that: 'nothing which amounts to "reconstruction" [of existing capital ships] may take place unless its object is to provide means of defence against air and submarine attack.' The proposed increase in gun elevation was therefore 'not permissible under the terms of the treaty'.

There was an additional British concern, framed to appeal to the US administration and Congress, namely that such a move on the part of the US Navy was escalatory, and would compel the British and Japanese navies to take similar action, resulting in considerable expenditure without in any way materially affecting the relative position of the three fleets. This, it pointed out, was 'inconsistent with the objects of the Naval Treaty and the hopes which its conclusion inspired'.

The US Navy was not prepared to concede, and produced further technical (and emotive) arguments to argue its case. On 6 March 1924 Secretary of the Navy Edwin Denby submitted to the State Department a letter in which it was argued that in the event of a battle between the current US and British battle fleets, at a range of 23,000 yards the US Navy would have only ten ships in action against twenty on the British side. (Full tables of ships and ranges, which are reproduced here, were provided in support of this.) It was conceded that this figure would increase to eighteen ships vs. twenty at 22,000 yards, and that above 25,000 yards the US Fleet would have the advantage, but it was pointed out that since the British ships were generally faster than their US counterparts they could effectively choose the range, as they had done at the Battle of the Falkland Islands in 1914. Denby suggested that this 'very great superiority of the British capital-ship fleet at vital and presumably decisive ranges'(!) served to undermine the concept of 'parity' embodied in the treaty and, in an appeal to patriotic sentiment, he concluded by stating his belief that 'our national interests require a navy second to no other.'

It was left to the US Secretary of State Charles Evans Hughes, the chief architect of the Washington Treaty, to arbitrate on these overheated arguments, and he did so in his customary unflustered way. Whilst he tended to agree with the US Navy that an increase in gun elevation did not constitute 'reconstruction' in the treaty definition of that term, he questioned whether the expense of modifying the eight ships with inferior range to the British battle fleet was justified, given that these ships would probably be replaced by new construction within ten to twelve years. He also expressed his concern that it would 'tend to evoke the competition which it has been the policy of this Government to mitigate'.[9]

Table 5.5a: Range Tables Accompanying Secretary of Navy's Memo

Name of ship	Range (yds)	Name of ship	Range (yds)
Nelson	34,300	West Virginia	34,500
Rodney	34,300	Colorado	34,500
Hood	30,300	Maryland	34,500
Royal Sovereign	24,300	California	35,000
Royal Oak	24,300	Tennessee	35,700
Resolution	24,300	Idaho	24,000
Ramillies	24,300	Mississippi	24,000
Revenge	24,300	New Mexico	24,000
Queen Elizabeth	24,300	Pennsylvania	21,000
Warspite	24,300	Arizona	20,900
Valiant	24,300	Nevada	21,000
Barham	24,300	Oklahoma	21,000
Malaya	24,300	Texas	21,000
Renown	23,800	New York	21,000
Repulse	23,800	Arkansas	24,350
Benbow	23,800	Wyoming	23,500
Emperor of India	23,800	Utah	21,600
Iron Duke	23,800	Florida	22,000
Marlborough	23,800		
Tiger	23,800		

Note: The table appears to assume that *Renown* and *Repulse* were fitted with 13.5in guns.

Table 5.5b: Number of Ships in Action at 'Moderate' and 'Decisive' Ranges

Range in Yards	British Ships	US Ships
24,000	13	10
23,000	20	10
22,000	20	12
21,000	20	18

The US Navy would subsequently abandon its plan to modify the oldest group of battleships, but would insist on the upgrading of the middle group to enable them to fight in the line of battle with the latest ships of the 'Big Five' group.

The Japanese cleverly avoided this Anglo-American squabble by being deliberately evasive about their own intentions. When consulted by the Americans at an early stage in the proceedings, the Japanese government expressed the view that any attempt to clarify the meaning of the wording of this part of the treaty would probably result in disagreement and bad feeling. At the same time the IJN was preparing to increase the gun elevation of the four *Kongos* from 20/25° to 33°, thereby bringing these ships up to the standard of the six battleships of the *Fuso*, *Ise* and *Nagato* classes, all of which completed with guns capable of 30° elevation.

As for the French and the Italians, it was recognised from the outset that point 2 of paragraph (d) had no relevance to their elderly dreadnoughts, which could legitimately be rearmed with guns up to 16in in calibre in any type of mounting they cared to adopt. In the event the Marine Nationale settled for an increase in elevation for their existing 12in (305mm) and 13.4in (340mm) guns, and neither the British nor the Americans saw fit to raise this as an issue.

The Modernisation of the US Battle Fleet: Phase 2

The next group of US Navy battleships to be modernised was that derived from the *Nevada*. Completed from 1916 onwards, they were oil-burners from the outset, and their 'all-or-nothing' protection systems effectively anticipated the 'post-Jutland' schemes adopted by the British for their influential postwar capital ship designs. However, they lacked an underwater protection system, director fire control and a modern anti-aircraft capability.

Taken in hand from 1927, the four ships of the *Nevada* and *Pennsylvania* classes underwent refits similar to those extended to their predecessors. New, more powerful boilers were fitted which were more economical on space than the ones they replaced (six in place of twelve), and this again made possible an increase in the depth of the underwater protection. Bulges of improved design were also fitted (see drawing), and these seem to have led to fewer sea-keeping problems than the ones fitted in the earlier ships. Although these were the first battleships in the world to have a 3in armoured deck over the vitals, even this was now considered inadequate and was boosted over the magazines by additional 1¾–2in plating.

In the face of continuing British opposition, which ended only after an informal agreement on battleship modernisation at the London Conference of 1930, the elevation of the main guns of these ships was doubled, from 15° to 30°. A new deckhouse similar to that of the most recent US battleships was constructed at forecastle deck level to house part of the secondary battery, and atop the deckhouse eight 5in/25-calibre HA guns of a new model were fitted.

Unlike their predecessors these ships had only a single funnel when first completed, but they now received heavy tripods fore and aft equipped with director fire control for the main and secondary batteries. There was no midship turret on these ships, so the aircraft catapult was fitted atop the

Nevada (US)

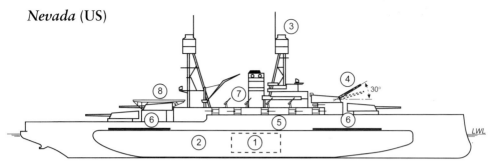

Four of the seven ships of the oil-burning 'middle group' of US battleships (see text) were given a comprehensive modernisation during the period 1927–31. The key modifications were:

1. Six modern oil-fired boilers in place of the original twelve.
2. Deep bulges incorporating a liquid-layer underwater protection system.
3. Revised fire control arrangements, the original cage masts being replaced by heavy tripods.
4. Increasing the maximum angle of elevation of the main guns from 15° to 30°.
5. A new deckhouse to house the secondary battery of 5in/51-calibre anti-destroyer guns.
6. An additional 1¾–2in of deck protection above the magazines.
7. A new anti-aircraft armament comprising eight single 5in/25-calibre HA guns.
8. A catapult for floatplanes atop no.3 turret.

Nevada before and after reconstruction

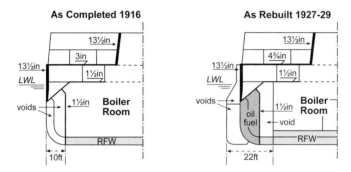

superimposed turret aft, with new articulated handling cranes to serve the boats and the catapult. A second catapult, together with a handling crane, was located on the quarterdeck to permit four aircraft (two fighters and two spotters) to be carried.

The last three ships of the middle group, the *New Mexico* class, were not scheduled for modernisation until after the London Conference of 1930, and the 'Big Five' also remained essentially unmodified throughout this period.

The US battleship *Pennsylvania* following reconstruction. The heavy tripod masts carrying the spotting and fire control tops which replaced the original cage masts are particularly prominent in this striking view, which dates from 1934. There is a trainable catapult on the quarterdeck and a second atop turret no.3.

The US battleship *Tennessee*, showing off the 30° elevation of her main guns while at anchor in 1925. The battleships completed at the end of the Great War for the US Navy, and known as the 'Big Five', had turbo-electric propulsion and a modern underwater protection system featuring a liquid–air 'sandwich'. Because of this they were a low priority for reconstruction, and entered the Second World War largely unmodified. (US Navy, Leo van Ginderen collection)

Battlecruisers to Battleships: The Japanese *Kongo* Class

Although six of the IJN's ten capital ships were of recent construction, Japanese ship design was essentially stuck at the early-war super-dreadnought stage. The latest two ships, *Nagato* and *Mutsu*, were inspired by the British *Queen Elizabeth* class. Like the latter they had a pre-Jutland protection system, with multiple thinly-plated decks. Although the *Nagato*s had a British-style anti-torpedo bulge with a curved inner bulkhead, this continued to be complemented by bulky torpedo nets as late as 1926, when they were finally removed.

Modifications to Japanese battleships during the early and mid-1920s were restricted to the fitting of additional platforms for the plethora of minor fire control aids favoured by the IJN, and the fitting of prominent cowls to the fore-funnel on various ships to keep smoke clear of the latter,[10] together with some additional 8cm HA guns. This enabled the limited funds available to the navy to be concentrated on the new generation of treaty cruisers and the development of long-range submarines for strategic scouting.

The first Japanese ships to benefit from a more extensive upgrade were the battlecruisers of the *Kongo* class, which by the mid-1920s were more than ten years old. The IJN decided that these ships would undergo a comprehensive modernisation which included new boilers, anti-torpedo bulges, a major increase in the thickness of horizontal protection, and improvements in the main artillery and associated fire control systems. *Haruna*, which suffered an explosion in no.1 turret during 1920, was taken in hand early; reconstruction began in 1924. *Kirishima* followed in 1927, and *Kongo* and *Hiei* began long refits in 1929.

The anti-torpedo bulges fitted increased the beam of the ship by three metres. Like the early British models, with which the Japanese would have been familiar from their close contact with the Royal Navy before 1921, they comprised an outer void compartment and an inner compartment filled

Despite their relative modernity, all the Japanese battleships were subjected to modernisations during the 1920s which focused on fire control and the provision of additional control platforms built around the foremast. The latter were subject to smoke interference, so in the two *Nagato*s the fore-funnel was trunked back into a distinctive 'S' shape.

Three of the four *Kongo*s underwent a major reconstruction during the 1920s. They entered
refit as battlecruisers, and emerged as battleships, two knots of speed having been sacrificed to
upgrade their horizontal and underwater protection. At the same time the angle of elevation of
the main guns was increased from 20° (25° for *Kongo*) to 33°.

with steel crushing tubes. Horizontal protection was substantially reinforced
so that there was now 120mm over the magazines and 80mm over the
machinery spaces, and additional plating was applied to the turret roofs. The
total weight of armour was now 10,480 tonnes, as compared with only 6,650
tonnes prior to modernisation.[11]

Although the original thirty-six coal-fired boilers were replaced by sixteen
modern units, the Japanese were reluctant to increase their dependency on
oil, which would have to be purchased from abroad, and six of the new
boilers continued to burn coal. As with the early US Navy coal-burning
battleships there were significant space and weight savings: the weight of the
propulsion machinery decreased from 4,825 tonnes to 4,005 tonnes, thereby

Table 5.6: The Modernisation of the *Kongo* Class

Name of ship	Date of mod.
Haruna	1924–28
Kirishima	1927–30
Kongo	1929–31

Note: *Hiei* began reconstruction in 1929, but this was halted in April 1930 following the
London Conference, when it was agreed she would become a gunnery training ship.

The IJN fast battleship *Haruna* following her conversion during the mid-1920s. The original fore-funnel has been suppressed, and the second enlarged and heightened. Note the multiple platforms around the tripod foremast, many of which were associated with improved fire control.

providing some compensation for the additional 3,830 tonnes of armour and the weight of the bulges. The power of the propulsion machinery remained the same, however, and this effectively meant that top speed declined from a designed 27.5 knots to less than 26 knots. These ships therefore made the transition from the 'battlecruiser' to the 'battleship' category; they now had a maximum speed comparable to that of the *Nagato* class, with which they could have formed a 'fast wing' of the battle fleet.[12]

Kongo (Jap)

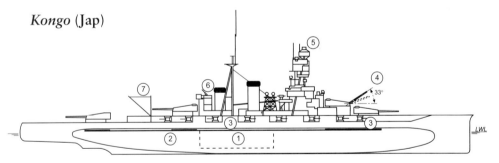

Three of the four former battlecruisers of the *Kongo* class received a comprehensive modernisation during the period 1927–31 – the modernisation of *Hiei* was halted and abandoned following the London Conference of 1930. The key modifications were:

1. Sixteen modern oil/coal-fired boilers in place of the original thirty-six coal-fired boilers, and the suppression of the fore-funnel (speed was reduced from 27.5 knots to less than 26 knots).
2. Bulges incorporating an underwater protection system based on steel crushing tubes.
3. A new armoured deck 120mm thick above the magazines and 80mm above the machinery.
4. Increasing the maximum angle of elevation of the main guns from 20/25° to 33°.
5. Revised fire control arrangements with an enlarged bridge structure and multiple platforms around the tripod foremast.
6. A new anti-aircraft armament comprising four/six single 8cm/40-calibre HA guns.
7. Stowage arrangements for small floatplanes atop the after deckhouse, together with a handling crane.

The reduction in the number of boilers made possible the suppression of the fore-funnel. This in turn enabled the forward superstructure to be built up around the original tripod foremast. The fire control systems for the main and secondary batteries were upgraded, and new HA control positions for four/six single 8cm/40 HA guns were installed to port and starboard. The searchlight arrangements and boat stowage were also modified.

The elevation of the main guns was increased from 20° (25° in *Kongo*) to 33°, the maximum which could be attained without a radical rebuilding of the turrets. The secondary casemate battery remained unmodified, but the four underwater torpedo tubes were removed to enable the bulges to be fitted. Following this refit two or three reconnaissance floatplanes were carried abaft no.3 turret, but these were intended to be launched from the water in favourable conditions; the Japanese were slow to develop a viable catapult, and the aircraft were handled by a light crane mounted to starboard.

When these ships emerged from refit their official Washington displacement was given as 29,330 tons, representing an increase of 3,010 tons. Whether this was an honest representation of their new displacement is open to question. If we subtract the 807-tonne saving on propulsion machinery from the 3,830 tonnes of additional armour we are already close to the 3,000-ton treaty limit imposed on anti-aircraft and anti-submarine improvements. Even if the weight of the bulges, complete with steel crushing tubes, was included in the figure for protection, it still seems unlikely that the massively built-up foremast with its multiple platforms and elaborate fire control arrangements would not have taken these ships well above the 3,000-ton (3048-tonne) margin. If the Japanese broke the rules it seems likely that the customary interference by the Naval General Staff, with its persistent demands for additional items of equipment which might enhance the ships' fighting capabilities, was largely responsible.

Modernising the French Dreadnoughts

As part of a comprehensive review of the French fleet in the aftermath of the First World War, a report published in 1920 noted the following deficiencies in the French dreadnoughts in comparison with their foreign contemporaries:

- No director fire control for the main guns
- Insufficient angle of elevation for the main guns (12°)
- Weak protection against torpedoes
- Inadequate horizontal protection
- Negligible anti-aircraft capabilities
- Retention of coal-firing for boilers
- Organisation of crew, lighting and internal communications outdated

Some of these inadequacies were by no means unique to the Marine Nationale. Only the latest British and American ships had an effective underwater

The six French dreadnoughts (*France* was lost in 1922) were so dated in terms of their design that a radical reconstruction would have been uneconomic. The principal modifications made during the 1920s concerned the provision of director fire control for long-range firing, and a corresponding increase in the elevation of the main guns. Their appearance following modification was dramatically changed, with a heavy tripod foremast to carry the new fire control apparatus replacing the former pole mast. In the three ships of the *Courbet* class (the name-ship is seen here) the first two funnels were trunked together. (Leo van Ginderen collection)

protection system, and only the more modern US Navy ships with the 'all-or-nothing' protection system had horizontal armour of the requisite thickness. Coal-firing was an issue for both the US Navy and Japan, and AA capabilities were universally recognised to be inadequate against the new threat of air attack. The French ships pre-dated the British *Queen Elizabeth* class and the American *Nevada*, and therefore suffered from the same limitations as the oldest capital ships retained by those two navies after Washington.

However the *Courbet* and *Bretagne* classes also suffered from being obsolescent in conception even when they were designed, with many features derived from the pre-dreadnought battleships that they replaced on the building ways (see Chapter 1). In attempting to modernise their own dreadnoughts the French were therefore working with particularly unpromising material. The Marine Nationale made little attempt to fight for completion of the battleships of the *Normandie* class at the Washington Conference simply because it recognised the extent to which the design had been rendered obsolescent by developments abroad.

Table 5.7: French Battleship Modernisations

Name of ship	1st mod.	2nd mod.
Paris	1922–23	1927–29
Courbet	1923–24	1927–31
Jean Bart	1923–25	1929–31
Bretagne	1919–20	1924–25
Lorraine	1921–22	1924–26
Provence	1922–23	1925–27

Note: The battleship *France* was lost in 1922 and therefore received no modernisation.

A drastic rebuilding of the existing ships, even though permitted by the terms of the treaty,[13] was out of the question. The financial outlay involved in such a programme would have been prohibitive, and would have placed major constraints on the ability of the Marine Nationale to embark on the large programme of cruisers, flotilla craft and submarines it had defined as its priority following the conclusion of the Washington Conference. Modernisation of the *Courbet* and *Bretagne* classes was therefore piecemeal, and focused on improving their fighting capabilities without resorting to major reconstruction.

The first modernisation of the three ships of the *Bretagne* class was already well underway when the Washington Conference opened in

Courbet (Fr)

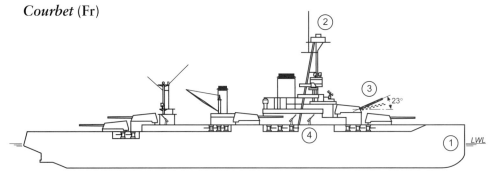

The elderly French dreadnoughts of the *Courbet* class received a less comprehensive modernisation than many of their counterparts abroad. Modifications carried out during refits from 1922–25 and subsequently 1927–31 included:

1. Removal of the heavy bow armour, which had been responsible for sea-keeping problems.
2. Revised fire control arrangements, incorporating director fire control; the original fore-funnels were combined into a single broad funnel, and a tripod fitted in place of the original pole foremast to support the fire control apparatus.
3. Increasing the maximum angle of elevation of the main guns from 12° to 23°.
4. A new anti-aircraft armament comprising four single 75mm/50-calibre HA guns.

November 1921, with the first ship, *Bretagne*, having been taken in hand at Toulon Naval Dockyard in 1919. The main modifications related to the effective range of the main artillery. A new heavy tripod foremast was fitted with a British Vickers director control system (the other two ships received a French model designed and built by Laurant-Paquelier), and the elevation of the main guns was increased from 12° to 18°, giving a theoretical maximum range of 18,000m. The bridge structure was enlarged and the fore-funnel heightened. The four foremost 138.6mm casemate guns, which had proved to be so wet in even light sea conditions as to make them unusable, were removed, and 2m rangefinders for the secondary battery were fitted in the enlarged bridge wings. A new high-angle battery of four single 75mm guns was also fitted.

This first modernisation was completed in 1923. A similar but more substantial refit was extended to the three surviving units of the *Courbet* class[14] immediately after the conclusion of the Washington Conference. Fitting a new tripod foremast in these ships required the trunking together of the first two funnels,[15] and the elevation of the main guns was raised from 12° to 23°. The new HA battery was identical to that of the *Bretagne*s. In an attempt to improve the poor sea-keeping of these ships the bow was stripped of its heavy armour. New oil-fired boilers replaced the original coal-firing units in one of the five boilers rooms.

These refits were completed in 1925, by which time the *Bretagne* class were undergoing their second modernisation. They too had their bow armour removed, and boiler room no.6 received new oil-fired boilers. The elevation of the main guns was further increased to 23° and new shell was provided for a maximum range of 26,600m, and new rangefinders were fitted. The arm of the port-side crane was extended to enable it to handle seaplanes, although as yet no catapult was fitted. These latter modifications were duly extended to the *Courbet* class, which also received a Saint Chamond-Granat director of French design, during refits from 1927 to 1931.

The elderly machinery of all six ships was by this time causing trouble. *Bretagne* had to undergo a further major refit in 1927–28 at Toulon, in which her boilers were rebuilt. At the same time her original Vickers director fire control system was replaced by the new French model. And *Lorraine* was taken in hand at Brest Naval Dockyard in 1929–31, when the coal-firing boilers in boiler room no.5 were replaced by new oil-fired types.

The Regia Marina Opts Out

The Italian Regia Marina, faced with similar problems to the French in bringing its elderly dreadnoughts up to an acceptable standard, opted for minimal (and inexpensive) modifications to improve their operational capabilities.

The *Dante Alighieri*, Italy's first dreadnought, had her pole foremast replaced at refit during 1923 by a more substantial tripod to accommodate the observation fore-top for the main guns, and had the forward pair of

The Italian dreadnoughts received even less care and attention than their French counterparts, and were largely unmodified by the late 1920s. This is *Andrea Doria* during the mid-1920s. Note the triplex rangefinder atop the conning tower and the fixed aircraft catapult on the port side of the bow; the ship is otherwise in her original configuration. (Erminio Bagnasco collection)

funnels heightened to keep smoke clear of the bridge, but remained otherwise unmodified until she was prematurely discarded in 1928.

In the two surviving ships of the *Cavour* class, which, as completed, had inward-facing tripod masts, the foremast was replaced in 1925 by a new quadruped mast between the funnel and the bridge structure, the vertical strut of the original mast serving as a derrick post. A fixed catapult was also installed on the port side of the forecastle together with a folding crane to handle a single reconnaissance Macchi M18 seaplane. The two ships of the *Duilio* class also received a fixed catapult for a seaplane in 1925–26, but remained otherwise unmodified. The third ship of the *Cavour* class, *Leonardo da Vinci*, which had been raised in September 1919 following her loss to a magazine explosion in 1916, was never rebuilt, and was sold for scrap in March 1923.

During the late 1920s the Regia Marina gave serious consideration to scrapping its elderly dreadnoughts altogether and concentrating resources on the new generation of cruisers, fast flotilla craft and submarines. In the event the ships were retained for two key reasons: one tactical, the other political. It was argued that the light forces currently favoured would still need heavy ships to fall back on if the opposing fleet included heavy ships, and if the latter were used in an aggressive manner. An even more important consideration was Italy's status as a major naval power: at Washington the British/US proposal to give Italy parity with France had rested primarily on her fleet of dreadnoughts, which almost matched that of the Marine Nationale – six versus seven if the *Leonardo da Vinci* was included. Given the Regia Marina's decision not to build aircraft carriers, it was feared that a future arms limitation conference would look on Italy's unused carrier tonnage allocation and her failure to maintain in service or to replace the capital ships she was permitted as sufficient justification for downgrading her status, and that this would then make the Regia Marina subject to further limits on construction in all other categories of warship. The Marine Nationale, on the other hand, clearly had no intention of consigning its own elderly dreadnoughts to the scrapyard, despite their limited military value, and was on the point of commissioning its first aircraft carrier, with two more purpose-built ships in its long-term plan.

It was therefore decided that a core battle fleet would be retained, but would comprise only three capital ships, of which one would normally be in refit. In 1928 the oldest of the Italian dreadnoughts, *Dante Alighieri*, was paid off, the *Cesare* became a training ship, and the *Cavour* was placed in reserve, leaving only the two *Duilio*s in service.

'Cruiser Killers' and Small Battleships

In 1926 the French began studies for the new battleships that they would be permitted to lay down from 1927 to replace the *Courbet* class. It was recognised that a completely new design would be required, incorporating a modern geared-turbine propulsion system, improved horizontal and underwater protection, and an effective modern fire control system which would make it possible to engage other ships at long range.

In theory the French were permitted to build two ships of 35,000 tons armed with 16in (406mm) guns, but both the French and the Italians had insisted on keeping their options open when the replacement schedules were negotiated at Washington (see Chapter 3), and the construction of 35,000-ton ships was not seriously considered at this time.[16] In part this was because the French simply could not have built or maintained ships of this size without a considerable investment in infrastructure: the existing slipways, fitting-out basins and docking facilities at the naval dockyards would have required major modifications to accommodate the hulls. However, the Naval Staff was also anxious to use the total 70,000-ton allocation in a more imaginative way. French naval thinking of the period was shifting away from the traditional concept of relatively slow, heavily armed and well-protected ships fighting in a battle line in favour of a fleet of fast, lightly armoured, hard-hitting vessels capable of 'hit-and-run' raids. The Western Mediterranean was seen as ideally suited to such operations and the Italian Regia Marina, to judge from its latest building programmes, appeared to have reached similar conclusions.

The Marine Nationale was particularly concerned about the threat to the sea lines of communication with the North African colonies posed by the new Italian 10,000-ton cruisers of the *Trento* class (see Chapter 6), which had been laid down in 1925 and had a designed speed of 35 knots. Thus in 1926 Admiral Salaün, Chief of the French Naval Staff (CEMG), requested the study of a *croiseur de combat* ('battle cruiser') of 17,500 tons capable of hunting

Table 5.8: French and Italian Small Battleship Projects 1928–29

	'Protected Cruiser' (Fr)	Small Battleship (It)
Displacement:	23,333 tons standard	23,000 tons standard
Dimensions:	196m × 28m × 8.5m	190m × 26m × 8m
	(643ft × 92ft × 28ft)	(620ft × 85ft × 25ft)
Machinery:	6 small tube boilers;	6 small tube boilers;
	4-shaft geared turbines;	4-shaft geared turbines;
	100,000shp = 29 knots	90,000shp = 28–29 knots
Armament:	10–305mm (1 × IV, 2 × III)	6–381mm (3 × II)
	8–138.6mm (4 × II)	8–120mm (4 × II)
	16–100mm HA (8 × II)	12–100mm HA (6 × II)
		4/8–533mm TT (2 × II/IV)

Notes:
- The machinery figures are 'guesstimates' based on the drawings and contemporary French/Italian practice.
- No data for protection thicknesses are available.

down and overpowering fast 10,000-ton cruisers. Specifications included eight 305mm/55-calibre (12in) guns, a speed of 35 knots, and protection sufficient to resist shells of 203mm (8in) calibre. The main armament was to be capable of engaging targets out to a maximum range of 43,000m, and was to be disposed in two quadruple turrets forward, both to assist pursuit and to reduce the length of the armoured citadel.[17] Besides being able to hunt down treaty cruisers, the new ships would be able to attack merchant shipping defended by slow battleships, and could act as a strategic scouting force for a combined Allied fleet.

The figure of 17,500 tons is significant, in that for every battleship of 35,000 tons that France was permitted under the Washington Treaty two of these smaller units could be built. Thus the 70,000 tons allocated for new construction in 1927 and 1929 would permit a class of four *croiseurs de combat*. This would still leave 105,000 tons of France's capital ship allocation for the construction of either three battleships of 35,000 tons or, more probably, four ships of 26,250 tons.

The *Service Technique des Constructions Navales* (STCN) studies for these ships remained on the drawing board. Neither Italy nor France laid down a new battleship in 1927 or 1928, and in December 1928 publication of the details of the new German *Panzerschiff Deutschland* effectively rendered the earlier French studies obsolete. It had previously been considered unthinkable that the Germans, who were working under the even more stringent constraints of the Treaty of Versailles, could design a ship with the displacement of a cruiser and the armament of a battleship.

23,690t 'Protected Cruiser' (Fr)

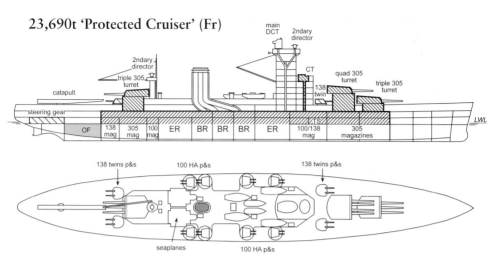

The French and the Italians had reserved their positions at Washington on their use of the 70,000-ton allocation permitted before the expiry of the ten-year 'battleship holiday'. Both came to similar conclusions, developing designs for small battleships of 23,000 tons standard. The results, despite national preferences with regard to external appearance and the French adoption of the 12in (305mm) calibre for the main battery, which anticipated the lower limits proposed by the British, were remarkably close. The Italian design was derived from the treaty cruiser *Pola*, the French anticipated that of the fast battleship *Dunkerque*. Note that in the French ship the engine rooms were separated by the boiler rooms to enable the single funnel to be placed well clear of the director tower. The internal layout of the Italian ship is conjectural, based on the ship's external appearance, as are the figures for armour thickness. Protection details are also missing from the French proposal, but the weight and disposition of armour would probably have been comparable.

23,000t Battleship (It)

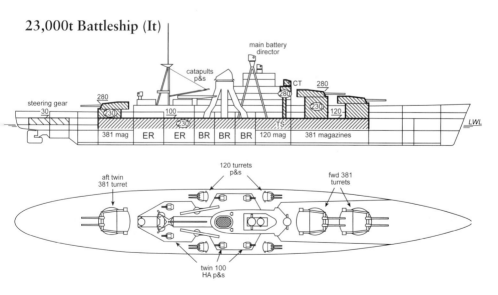

Although the projected *croiseur de combat* would have the speed and the hitting power to hunt down such a ship, its protection would be totally inadequate against 28cm (11in) shell.

This led the Marine Nationale to reassess the mathematics of its situation, the *Conseil Supérieur* having stipulated in December 1927 that the displacement of any new ship should be a precise fraction of 175,000 tons. During 1928 the new Chief of Staff, Admiral Violette, ordered the study of a battleship of 29,600 tons with a speed of 27 knots (six ships). Studies of a battleship of 35,000 tons (five ships) were also undertaken, but in March 1929 the STCN reported that whilst a ship of 215m length with a speed of 25 knots was technically feasible, infrastructure remained a problem. The latter conclusion led the *Conseil Supérieur* to advise the French government to back a British proposal to reduce the maximum individual displacement permitted for new capital ships at the upcoming London Conference (the figure of 25,000 tons and 12in guns was touted prior to the conference). The 23,690-tonne design illustrated here almost certainly dates from this period.

The Italians were likewise permitted by the Washington Treaty to lay down new capital ships in 1927 and 1929, and gave equally serious consideration to the issue. Of the five contracting powers Italy was arguably the only one to seriously consider the possibility that the treaty cruiser might become the primary surface unit in a modern conflict dominated by air power and fast naval strike forces, and when Italy's first treaty cruisers of the *Trento* class were designed, it was as fighting ships rather than strategic scouts for the battle fleet. Although fast and more heavily armoured than their French counterparts, they were not as well protected as the Regia Marina would have liked, and in the mid-1920s the Deputy Chief of Naval Staff, Rear-Admiral Romeo Bernotti, who enjoyed a growing reputation within the navy as a strategist and tactician, proposed building cruisers of 15,000 tons, asserting that three such powerful vessels would defeat six treaty cruisers of the 10,000-ton type.

This line of argument was rejected principally because it effectively pre-empted a resolution of the capital ship problem; cruisers of 15,000 tons were classified as capital ships under the Washington Treaty, so building even three would reduce Italy's tonnage allocation from 175,000 tons to 130,000 tons, whereas any number of 10,000-ton ships could be built without impinging on the tonnage available for capital ships.

Having rejected the 'super-cruiser' proposal, the Italians returned, like the French, to considering how its initial new capital ship allocation of 70,000 tons might best be used. The existing dreadnoughts of the Regia Marina, like those of the Marine Nationale, displaced around 23,000 tonnes (normal), and the Italians were by no means convinced that the 35,000-ton battleship armed with 16in/406mm guns offered the best solution to operations in the confined waters of the Mediterranean. British experience with the design of the *Nelsons* suggested that a combination of heavy guns and heavy protection precluded the high tactical speed favoured by the Italians for new battleships, which would have to be capable of intervention in support of light forces based on cruisers and flotilla craft operating at well over thirty knots. There were also problems relating to military-industrial infrastructure similar to those which featured in the French deliberations (see above). Finally, there was the issue of numbers: given that new battleships designed for high tactical speed could not operate with the existing dreadnoughts, three ships would be needed to guarantee two in service at any given time – the minimum required for the 'support' role. Since only 70,000 tons was available under the Washington Treaty this implied a ship of around 23,000 tons standard displacement, for which studies were duly requested.

The constructors department came up with a 190m ship with a main battery of six 381mm (15in)[18] guns and a secondary battery of eight 152mm (6in) or 120mm (4.7in) guns in twin power-operated turrets. The layout was conventional, with two turrets forward and one aft. Four-shaft geared steam turbines would have driven the ships at 28–29 knots, giving them a margin of 6 knots or more over existing foreign battleships and a speed sufficient for intervention in support of smaller surface units; endurance would have been on a par with the *Trento* class cruisers. Few details are available of the protection system, but it has been suggested that the belt would have been around 230mm (9in) with a 100–120mm (4–4.7in) armoured deck; there would also have been a modern underwater protection system.

In the event it had to be accepted that in a period of financial stringency there was insufficient funding available for these ships and for the major programme of cruisers which was currently underway (the first of the 10,000-ton cruisers of the *Zara* and *Bolzano* classes were already on the slipways). Moreover, the French had yet to commit themselves to a new capital ship design, and Italy was reluctant to be the first of the major powers to embark on new construction, particularly in light of the latest British proposals to reduce the individual displacement of capital ships to a maximum of 25,000 tons. The Regia Marina therefore decided to keep a watching brief, and to embark on alternative studies for ships of 35,000 tons to cover all possible eventualities.

The major theoretical problem with the Italian 'small battleship' proposal, as with the French battleship studies of the same period, is that the resulting ship would have fallen between two stools. The main battery was powerful enough to take on the elderly French super-dreadnoughts of the *Bretagne* class, but the main belt would have been inadequate against the 340mm shell of the latter ships; the relatively high speed of the Italian ships would enable them to outrun and outmanoeuvre France's older battleships, but the reduction in armour which bought the high tactical speed made it unwise to stand slugging it out in a line of battle with them. The 23,000-ton battleship, had it been built, could easily have defeated a treaty cruiser in combat, but was not quite fast enough to catch or to maintain contact with such ships. The Italian battleship replacement problem, like that of the French, would await resolution.

CHAPTER 6

The Treaty Cruiser

Having effectively stifled the development of a new generation of ever-larger and more powerful capital ships, the Washington Treaty spawned a new monster, the 'treaty cruiser'. The latter was so christened because had it not been for the Washington Conference it seems highly unlikely that all five of the major naval powers would have allowed their thinking to converge in such a way as to produce large cruisers of comparable size, hitting power and cost.

The Japanese were committed to a programme of scout cruisers of 7,500-ton displacement armed with 20cm guns. The British were completing the large 'trade defence' cruisers of the *Hawkins* class, armed with 7.5in guns, and the first two of these had emerged from the shipyards with a displacement of about 9,600 tons standard. However, this figure was some 850 tons higher than the designed displacement, and could probably have been reduced with the more stringent hull design and building practices that characterised the postwar cruisers. Certainly the British could have produced an effective trade defence design on a smaller displacement, as they were to demonstrate with the 8,200-ton 'B'-type cruiser design of 1925. Both the French and the Italians seem to have been perfectly happy with small fast cruisers armed with 120–155mm guns to scout for their battle fleets in the confined waters of the Mediterranean – although by 1920 the French were contemplating a larger cruiser for overseas deployment. The 'blame' for the 8in gun, 10,000-ton treaty cruiser therefore has to fall principally on the Americans, who ironically were to build some of the worst examples of the type.

With the imposition of a ten-year 'battleship holiday', it was perhaps inevitable that the five contracting powers would look to the largest and most powerful type they were permitted to build, the treaty cruiser, as the new capital ship. All five powers immediately requested studies for the design and construction of 10,000-ton cruisers, and previous fleet structures were adjusted – or discarded altogether – in order to accommodate the new ships strategically and tactically. For the US Navy they would be, as anticipated, long-range strategic scouts for the wide expanses of the Western Pacific. For the IJN they initially performed a similar role, but would subsequently be allocated an additional 'advanced strike' mission. For the British, they were essentially trade defence ships, but would also be required to counter the Japanese and US Navy ships in possible oceanic fleet engagements. However, for the French and the Italians, whose slow and ageing battleships were fundamentally unsuited to combat operations in the confined (and increasingly air-dominated) waters of the Mediterranean, these ships were to become the backbone of fast surface strike forces, operating in tactical divisions of three or four ships like the capital ships they effectively superseded.

Shortly after the closure of the Washington Conference the IJN, which had already embarked on its programme of four 7,500-ton scout cruisers, announced its intention to follow these with eight treaty cruisers of 10,000 tons. The British Naval Staff responded with a request for seventeen such ships, on the grounds that eight were required for fleet operations (any expeditionary fleet to the Far East would need to match Japanese capabilities), and nine for trade defence (in case the Japanese detached their cruisers for commerce raiding). This would be but the first stage in a much larger replacement programme for the small warbuilt 'fleet' cruisers, which lacked the necessary range and endurance for deployment outside home waters. By the end of 1923 the Admiralty was proposing a long-term programme of forty-eight cruisers:[1] eight to be laid down over each of three consecutive years beginning with the 1924–25 programme, then four per year over the following six years.

The French Marine Nationale responded to the new category with unbounded enthusiasm, seeing the absence of any quantitative limit on cruiser tonnage as an opportunity to challenge the Anglo-Saxon supremacy in capital ships. The Marine Nationale was on the point of placing orders in its 1922 fleet-renewal programme for an 8,000-ton light cruiser armed with 155mm (6.1in) guns – which could form the basis of a 10,000-ton design armed with 203mm (8in) guns – and a staff requirement drawn up on 6 July 1922 proposed no fewer than twenty-one of the new ships. These were to be as fast as possible, in order to outrun contemporary British and Japanese battlecruisers (of which the *Hood* was fastest at 31 knots), and were to have as their primary missions strategic scouting for the battle fleet, the support of light surface forces and submarines in a major fleet encounter, and trade defence. Commerce raiding was not included in the list of possible missions for fear of the impact it might have on the British, but it was almost certainly discussed as a possible mission and was equally certainly suspected by the British.

The Italians were determined to match any French programme ship for ship, and began studies for new 10,000-ton cruisers armed with 203mm guns as soon as the Washington Conference ended. The primary emphasis for the new ships would be on high speed, but since the Italians envisaged that the new ships would, in the absence of any new capital ship construction, become the backbone of the fleet, they also wanted them to be sufficiently well protected to defeat any ship they could not outrun in combat. With France the most likely future opponent, a key mission for the new cruisers would be to threaten French sea lines of communication with her colonies in North Africa.

The US Navy, which was largely responsible for the treaty cruiser, was nevertheless slow to commit itself to new construction. Discussions about fleet requirements in the wake of the Washington Conference led to a policy statement adopted in December 1922 which called for the completion of the ten scout cruisers of the *Omaha* class, some of which had had their construction suspended in the lead-up to the Washington Conference, and for the construction of sixteen new treaty ships armed with 8in guns to replace all older cruisers in the fleet. Future construction was to be sufficient to maintain parity with Britain as well as the 5:3 ratio with Japan. The General Board called for eight ships in the FY1924 programme, but Congress was unwilling to provide the necessary funding, and the first pair of ships was authorised only in late 1924 for FY1925. Moreover, the design process was protracted, and was marked by serious differences of opinion between the General Board and the various bureaux representing the engineering, ordnance, and ship design communities. By the time the first ship, *Pensacola*, was laid down in October 1926, work had already begun on an alternative design with a radically different hull configuration and armament layout (the *Northampton* class).

By way of contrast, Britain had nine treaty cruisers (*Kent* and *London* classes, two of the 'County' classes of cruisers) under construction by April 1926, six months before the first of the American cruisers was laid down, and five of these had been launched during the previous month. The first two 7,500-ton scout cruisers (*Furutaka* class) had been completed for the Imperial Japanese Navy; the remaining two (*Aoba* class – completed to a revised design) were fitting out, and the first four treaty cruisers (*Myoko* class) had been laid down: one pair in

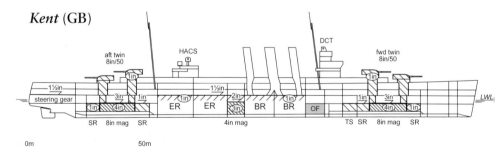

Kent (GB)

Arguably the most successful and well-balanced of the first generation of treaty cruisers, the British 'Counties' had a deep, broad-beamed flush-deck hull which made them stable gunnery platforms and comfortable for the men that served in them. Protection was primarily focused on the magazines, which were virtually immune to 6in shell, although the 1in side plating over the machinery spaces was acknowledged to be inadequate, and was beefed up considerably when the *Kent*s were modernised in the late 1930s.

Cornwall, seen here shortly after completion, was one of the first (*Kent*) group of 'Counties' ordered for the Royal Navy. Note the anti-torpedo bulge at the waterline; this was suppressed in the next two classes, resulting in an increase in maximum speed of three-quarters of a knot. (Leo van Ginderen collection)

One of four cruisers of the *London* class, the second group of 'Counties', *Devonshire* is seen here at Malta in 1935. The weight saved by omitting the bulge and the protection for the midship 4in magazine was used for a catapult and aircraft crane abaft the third funnel. (Leo van Ginderen collection)

Table 6.1: The First Generation of Treaty Cruisers: Breakdown of Weights as Designed

	Kent (GB)	Duquesne (Fr)	Trento (It)	Myoko (Jap)	Pensacola (USA)
Hull + fittings:	5,400t (54%)	4,708t (47%)	4,955t (49.5%)	4,094t (36%)	4,930t (50%)
Machinery:	1,850t (18.5%)	2,235t (22.4%)	2,256t (22.5%)	2,648t (25.5%)	1,935t (20%)
Protection:	1,025t (10.3%)	452t (4.5%)	874t (8.8%)	2,001t (19.3%)	1,090t (11%)
Armament:	1,050t (10.5%)	1,314t (13.1%)	1,194t (11.9%)	1,285t (12.4%)	1,425t (14.5%)
Equipment/provisions:	675t (6.7%)	1,291t (13%)	726t (7.3%)	357t (3.4%)	420t (4.5%)
Washington Displ.:	10,000tW	10,000tW	10,005tW	10,385tW	9,800tW

Notes:
- Weights are in long tons; displacements are in tons standard (tW).
- The figures for *Pensacola* are approximate, as they have had to be based on the breakdown of weights as completed, and have had to be modified to take account of the US practice of including horizontal protection in the hull weight. In the event standard displacement on completion was 9,100 tons, with most of the savings coming from the use of welding by the shipyards (i.e. hull + fittings).
- The 'Armament' figure for *Kent* does not include aircraft, which were not provided for in the original calculation.
- The figure for 'Equipment/provisions' for *Duquesne* probably embraced items included under other categories by other navies.

1924 and the other in 1925. The French had also laid down their first two ships (*Duquesne* and *Tourville*) in 1924–25, and these were followed closely onto the slipways by their Italian counterparts *Trento* and *Trieste*.

Design Issues

All five of the major powers found that it was more difficult to design an effective 8in-gun cruiser on 10,000 tons than had been anticipated. Quite aside from the difficult technical issues of designing ships of a completely new type to a fixed (and abstract) maximum displacement, the respective Naval Staffs had to draw up and review their requirements while casting frequent glances over their shoulders to check what everybody else appeared to be doing. As each new ship took on average three years to build, successive classes had to be designed and ordered before their predecessors had been completed (or even launched), so modifications had to be made on a theoretical basis without the benefit of trials and operational service. The British, with the 'Elizabethans', the Japanese (*Furutaka*) and the French (*Duguay-Trouin*) at least had an existing design that could be scaled up – although in the event the British opted for a completely new design for the *Kent* class; the Americans and the Italians were designing from scratch.

All five powers opted to adopt the maximum 8in calibre permitted, although this decision did not meet with universal approval. There were those – in the US Navy in particular – who considered the 8in gun a 'mongrel' weapon which had neither the weight and power to engage armoured warships nor the high rate of fire necessary to deal with destroyers and small cruisers; they considered that the 6in QF gun was the weapon of choice. These views were reinforced by British experience with the single 7.5in mounting of the 'Elizabethans', which proved cumbersome in service. Power-operated multi-gun turrets with electrical loading systems were seen as the partial answer to the problem,[2] but there would be a huge cost in the weight of such mountings. By way of example, the single 7.5in Mk VI open-backed mounting of the *Hawkins* weighed 46 tons, whereas the twin 8in Mk I power-operated mounting of the *Kent* class was 205 tons (more than twice the weight per gun!).

Once the 8in calibre had been adopted, the key design issues were how many guns (and rounds per gun) the ships should carry, and whether twin or triple turrets should be adopted.[3] The Royal Navy had traditionally favoured the twin over the triple, in part because of the simpler layout of the turret, but also because of the dispersion problem inherent in firing three guns together in the same salvo, and considered eight guns provided the most effective salvo fire. The French, Japanese and Italians also favoured the twin turret. The IJN was anxious to maximise firepower and opted for ten guns in five twin turrets, and it was clear from the outset that the longer hull implicit in this decision would be pushing at the 10,000-ton boundary even before the protection issue reared its ugly head.[4] The US Navy, on the other hand, had favoured the triple turret ever since the battleship *Nevada* of 1912 as a means of accommodating the maximum gun battery on the shortest possible hull. One of the earlier US Navy treaty cruiser sketch designs was for a fast, 35-knot cruiser mounting no fewer than twelve 8in guns in four triple turrets. Although virtually unprotected, this ship did provide the basis for the final *Pensacola* design, which featured two twin and two triple turrets for ten guns, and which was by some margin the shortest of the treaty cruisers.

Speed was to become a key issue for the early treaty cruiser designs. The US Navy's scout cruisers of the *Omaha* class of 1916, which were in many respects scaled-up destroyers in conception, had been designed for a maximum speed of 35 knots. The IJN responded with the 7,500-ton scout cruisers of the *Furutaka* and *Aoba* classes, which were designed for the same speed. However, unlike the *Omaha*s and unlike the latest IJN fleet cruisers of the *Kuma*, *Nagara* and *Sendai* classes, which were designed to operate as flagships for the destroyer flotillas and therefore had a similar high speed, the *Furutaka* and *Aoba* types were armed with 20cm (8in) guns. With the end of the Anglo-Japanese Alliance these ships and their larger treaty successors posed a potential threat to British and French commerce in the Far East.

French enthusiasm for high-speed cruisers was in part a reaction to the Japanese threat in the Far East, but also constituted a warning shot across the bows of the British, whose paranoia regarding fast French commerce-raiding cruisers was never far from the surface. Had the British known that the high speed of the French ships was ostensibly to enable them to outrun IJN *and* British battlecruisers they would hardly have been reassured. The French Naval General Staff was just as concerned as its British and American counterparts when it saw just how little protection could be bought for a 34-knot ship armed with eight 8in guns, but news that the new Italian cruisers would have a similar speed effectively ended any argument.

The US Navy was anxious to match the speed of the new Japanese scout and treaty cruisers, and was equally conscious of the need to be able to outrun the British and Japanese battlecruisers. However, when it became clear that a 35-knot ship armed with twelve 8in guns might find itself quickly disabled by even destroyer shell, both armament and speed were sacrificed in the pursuit of a modest level of protection. It should also be noted that the US Navy constructors justified a slight reduction in speed by pointing to the notorious failure of their Japanese counterparts to produce ships within their designed weight parameters, and the probability therefore that an IJN cruiser designed for 35 knots would not exceed 32 knots in service.

The British looked upon these developments with some alarm. The 'Elizabethan' class, which had turned out not far short of 10,000 tons standard, but was a well-balanced design with a powerful armament and good protection, had been designed for 30 knots (they achieved only 28–29 knots in service due to overweight). A ship with a speed of 34–35 knots would require double the horsepower, and so twice the weight of machinery. Add in 8in guns in twin power-operated turrets and a modern AA battery and it immediately became apparent that there would be little weight available for protection. Yet the Admiralty could not altogether disregard developments abroad. The new ships would have to have a sea speed comparable to the treaty cruisers planned by the Japanese and the French, or they would be tactically outflanked. It therefore requested a series of alternative designs with a common speed of 33 knots, and then (predictably) pronounced itself unhappy with all of them because of their inadequate protection.

Hull Form and Propulsion

The selection of the hull form which might best deliver the required military characteristics was an issue that taxed the designers to the limit. High speed pointed to a long, narrow hull form with a high length-to-beam ratio. This also favoured the accommodation of an additional turret on the centre-line, and it is therefore unsurprising that the Japanese treaty cruisers provided the most extreme example, with a length (pp – between perpendiculars) to beam ratio of about 10:1 (the corresponding figure for the more conservative British 'Counties' was just over 9:1).

In order to power the new ships at their designed speed all five navies opted for four-shaft geared steam turbines using small-tube boilers operating at pressures between 18kg/cm² and 21kg/cm² (250–300lb/in²). While the need to keep machinery weight to a minimum again favoured the long hull – which was more efficient at high speed – these ships were less efficient at cruise speed, and had to carry large quantities of oil fuel to provide the required endurance. This solution was in effect encouraged by the Washington Treaty definition of standard displacement, which excluded fuel oil and reserve feed water, but it posed the additional problem of how to accommodate this quantity of fuel oil in a ship in which exceptionally large magazine and machinery spaces were competing for volume with a complement bloated by the need to man the main guns and the AA batteries, increasingly complex fire control systems and a large propulsion plant. One solution adopted by the US Navy designers, faced with a General Board requirement for an operational range of 10,000nm at 15 knots, was to locate fuel bunkers alongside the forward magazines. As oil fuel was still generally regarded as potentially combustible and therefore hazardous this arrangement was viewed with some concern, but it had to be accepted because the only alternative, moving the bunkers to the bow and stern of the ship, would have resulted in unacceptable stresses on the hull.

Hull volume was an important issue for the designers of all five nations, and all except the French opted initially for a flush-deck hull in order to maximise internal volume. The French retained the hull form of the new light cruisers of the *Duguay-Trouin* class, which had a raised forecastle with marked sheer and flare to enable them to operate at high speed even with a strong head sea. Both the *Duguay-Trouins* and the *Duquesnes* proved to be good seaboats, despite their relatively light construction, at the expense of somewhat cramped accommodation.

Duquesne (Fr)

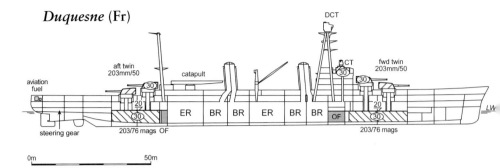

Trento (It)

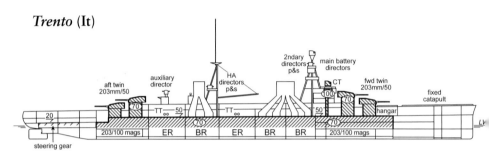

The treaty cruisers developed by France and Italy were designed primarily for high speed, as evidenced by the length of the machinery spaces. In contrast to the British and Japanese ships their machinery was arranged on the 'unit' principle, with boiler rooms alternating with engine rooms. For protection the French ships relied primarily on tight subdivision, with light 30mm plating only on the magazines, the gunhouses and the conning tower. The Italians, on the other hand, opted for an armoured box with 70mm sides and a 50mm deck over the machinery and magazines, and also managed to protect the turrets. Displacement as completed exceeded treaty limits by a considerable margin.

The British opted for a flush-deck hull form with high freeboard throughout, which constituted a marked departure in practice from earlier light cruiser designs (including the 'Elizabethans'), and which gave them the appearance of cruise liners rather than cruisers, particularly once the short funnels with which they were completed were heightened by 15ft (4.5m).[5] The hull form of the 'Counties' was also broader and deeper than that of their contemporaries, giving them a long slow roll. They were not only stable gunnery platforms, but were popular in the fleet because of their spacious, relatively comfortable accommodation.

The Americans, Japanese and Italians all adopted flush-deck designs with maximum freeboard at the bow and minimum freeboard aft. The Americans opted for a hull form with relatively low freeboard amidships and marked sheer towards the bow. This saved hull weight but at the expense of sea-keeping, and the *Pensacolas* proved to be very wet. The US Navy was so concerned about the design compromises that had to be made in these ships

Two of the French Navy's early treaty cruisers at Toulon during the early 1930s. The ship on the left is either *Duquesne* or *Tourville*; the cruiser on the right is *Suffren*. The two early ships were virtually unprotected, whereas the later *Suffren* had a narrow 50mm waterline belt over her machinery. She can be identified here by the twin aircraft catapults abaft the second funnel.

and their possible effect on platform performance, that it quickly embarked on an alternative design, the *Northampton* class, which featured one turret fewer and a 'straight' hull with a raised forecastle – it was thought this would have much-improved sea-keeping characteristics.

The Italians opted for a constant sheer-line from the stern to the bow, which provided higher freeboard amidships at the cost of some discontinuity

The Italian cruiser *Trento* shortly after completion. Note the continuous sheer from stern to bow and the heavy quadruped foremast designed to carry the main gunnery directors. With their first treaty cruisers the Italians managed to achieve both extreme high speed and moderate protection, although the 10,000-ton Washington limit was exceeded in the process. (Leo van Ginderen collection)

in the internal decks. The Japanese, ever the innovators, persisted with the 'wavy deck line' introduced in the 7,500-ton scout cruisers. The hull was divided into three key sections: bow, centre section and stern. The height of the bow was then determined by sea-keeping requirements, the freeboard of the midships section was determined by overall stability considerations, and freeboard at the stern was reduced to a minimum to save weight. These three sections were then joined together by straight (or slightly curved) lines that imparted an undulating or wavelike appearance to the upper deck, and this was reflected in the lines of the internal decks. In theory this 'horizontal deck type', devised by the IJN's chief constructor, Rear-Amiral Hiraga Yuzuru, made the horizontal members continuous and therefore stronger, and also reduced structural weight, albeit at the expense of more complicated construction.

Protection

Protection was a major issue for all five navies. It was traditional for ships above destroyer size to be protected against shells of the calibre of their own main guns. The light fleet cruisers built for the Royal Navy prior to and during the First World War generally had a 3in (75mm) armoured belt and a light protective deck about 1in (25mm) thick over their magazine and machinery spaces. This level of protection had been sufficient to keep out destroyer projectiles and the 10.5cm (4.1in) shells of German cruisers, and was partially effective against 15cm (5.9in) HE shell. However, even this level of protection proved difficult to provide in a 35-knot cruiser armed with eight or more 8in guns and fitted with modern director fire control, a powerful AA battery and aircraft – all within the maximum available displacement of 10,000 tons standard.

The weight and penetrative capability of 8in shell was of a completely different order to even 6in shell,[6] so protection against semi armour-piercing 8in (203mm) SAP shell at any range was out of the question. Given that these cruisers could not be protected against the shells of their own kind, three key questions imposed themselves. If engaged by other treaty cruisers, how could the inevitable action damage best be contained? Given that complete protection was impossible, which were the priority areas of the ship to receive the limited weight of protection available, and what was the most economical way of utilising it? And finally, given that the ships could not be armoured against 8in shell, to what extent could protection be provided against the 4in, 5in and 6in shell of flotilla craft and small cruisers.

The French, who adhered strictly to treaty displacement limits for the *Duquesne* class, found that the weight available in their calculations was sufficient only for a small amount of light plating. The emphasis was therefore on survivability rather than protection, and the hull was tightly subdivided by transverse bulkheads. The boilers were disposed side by side in pairs in order to minimise the length of each boiler room.[7] The sixteen transverse bulkheads were continuous from the keel to the upper deck, and were watertight up to the main deck. Each of the seventeen compartments thus created had its own pumps and ventilation. The transverse bulkheads fore and aft of the engine rooms were reinforced to 20mm by sheets of 60kg HT steel in an effort to restrict flooding to three adjacent compartments in the event of torpedo or mine damage. The unit machinery arrangement, with alternating boiler rooms and engine rooms, was adopted to further enhance the survivability of the ship (the *Duguay-Trouin*s from which the *Duquesne* class was derived had their boiler rooms grouped together); even after a torpedo hit this ensured that at least two boilers and one set of turbines would be available to get the ship home.

Tactically, it was envisaged that these ships would fight at relatively long range using director fire control (the director for the main guns was located high above the waterline, atop a substantial tripod foremast). The threat from destroyer shell therefore received less consideration than it did in the British Royal Navy and the US Navy. The Marine Nationale was building a new type of super-destroyer, the *contre-torpilleur* (see Chapter 8), precisely to see off destroyer attacks, and therefore had at its disposition an additional layer of fleet defence which was intended to reduce the exposure of their treaty cruisers to close combat. It was thought that protection against the handful of destroyer shells which might be expected to strike home – and which were generally fuzed to burst on contact with a ship's external plating – could be provided by locating the magazines well inboard beneath the waterline and providing them with light 30mm plating. Plating of 30mm thickness was also provided for the main turrets and the conning tower, from which it was envisaged that the ship would be fought in action.

Both the British and the Americans were anxious to provide complete protection of the vitals against destroyer fire, and also some immunity from 6in cruiser shell. The potential 'citadel' of the treaty cruisers was exceptionally long due to the high-power propulsion plants, and magazines which had to accommodate not only the separate shells and charges of the main battery but the fixed ammunition for the HA battery. An armoured belt which completely covered the ships' vitals would necessarily be narrow, covering just the waterline: it would have insufficient thickness to keep out 6in shell and (because of the long range at which these ships were designed to engage their opponents) would have to be covered throughout its length by a protective deck, which would be extremely costly in weight.

British priorities post-Jutland lay firmly with the protection of the magazines, which were given 4in sides of cemented armour with 3in NC crowns and end bulkheads, providing complete immunity against 6in shell and partial immunity against 8in shell; the shell rooms had only 1in sides and crowns.[8] Local protection for the magazines and shell rooms was attractive because it reduced the width of the deck area which needed to be covered; the disadvantage was that it left the waterline in this area unprotected and therefore vulnerable to flooding. The cost in weight of even this level of protection was 745 tons – nearly twice the total weight of protection in the French *Duquesne* class.

The British Admiralty had originally demanded 33 knots, but when it saw how little protection could be worked into a ship of this speed, it had to accept a reduction in power from 100,000shp to 80,000shp (maximum speed was now 31.5 knots) in order to provide a light belt of 1in plating at the waterline over the machinery spaces, topped by a 1½in protective deck. This provided at least some protection for the machinery and for waterline buoyancy against destroyer shell. There remained, however, no protection – beyond 1in 'splinter plating' – for the 8in turrets and trunks, which could therefore be penetrated by a direct hit at any range.

The Americans came to similar conclusions to the British, but prioritised waterline buoyancy and machinery over magazines, despite the latter having been raised clear of the hull (ostensibly to protect against underwater explosions) to such an extent that their crowns were now above the waterline. The *Pensacola*s had a thicker 2½in belt over their machinery and 4in sides for their magazines, and their 8in turrets also had 2½in faces. Horizontal protection, however, comprised only 1in plating over the machinery and 1¾in over the magazines, which could easily have been penetrated by plunging 6in shell.

The Japanese, whilst acknowledging that it was not possible to guarantee protection against 8in shell, felt that immunity to 6in shell at most battle ranges was attainable using the advanced design/ construction techniques developed for the experimental light cruiser *Yubari* (completed in 1923). In the latter design the side and deck armour contributed to the longitudinal strength of the hull. This system had the effect of minimising hull weight while maximising protection. In *Yubari*

Pensacola (US)

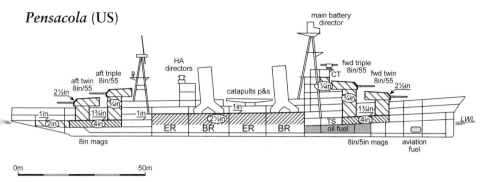

Northampton (US)

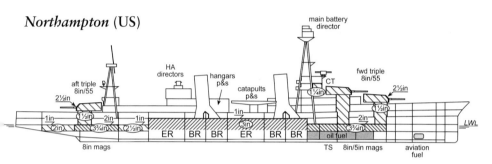

The US Navy's initial *Pensacola* design was unusual in adopting a mix of twin (nos.1 and 4) and triple (nos.2 and 3) turrets in order to match the ten guns of the IJN's ships without the extreme hull length (and therefore weight) implicit in a twin-turret layout. The *Pensacolas* were exceptionally compact, with relatively short machinery spaces, and the large main-gun turrets were quite close to the ends of the ship compared to their foreign contemporaries; they were also wet amidships. In the *Northampton* class a forecastle deck was adopted for improved sea-keeping, and a reduction from four to three (triple) turrets permitted the large boiler rooms of the first ships to be subdivided. The *Pensacolas* had a protection system similar to that of the British 'Counties', except that the belt over the machinery was heavier at the expense of the armour over the magazines. In the *Northampton* class the armoured box over the forward magazines was extended aft to cover a new plotting room located forward of the machinery spaces.

the weight of the longitudinal and transverse members per metre of cross section was 7.6 tons/m as against 11 tons/m for the contemporary light cruisers of the *Tenryu* class. Hull weight as a proportion of displacement fell from 36.5 per cent to only 31 per cent, a remarkably low figure for a ship of this type. Japanese confidence in the system was such that the internal vertical armour of the *Yubari* became an external sloped belt in both the *Furutaka/ Aoba* types and in the treaty cruisers of the *Myoko* class.[9]

In the *Furutaka/Aoba* classes a 76mm non-cemented armour belt protected the waterline between the fore and after magazines, and was topped by a 35mm deck. The magazines themselves, located internally beneath the waterline, were within armoured boxes with 51mm sides and 35mm crowns. The total weight of armour was almost 1,200 tons, greater than in any of the Western treaty cruisers.

Pensacola, the first of the US Navy's treaty cruisers, seen here in 1935. With her low freeboard amidships and her pronounced roll, *Pensacola* was not a successful design and was quickly superseded by the *Northampton* class. (Leo van Ginderen collection)

Louisville and her sisters of the *Northampton* class differed from the *Pensacola* type in having a raised forecastle and only three triple turrets. They were better seaboats as a result, but like the *Pensacola*s they completed at well below their designed weight. This margin was utilised to provide a much higher level of protection in the later US treaty cruisers. Note the elaborate and well-developed aviation arrangements. (Leo van Ginderen collection)

The Japanese *Aoba*, seen here shortly after her completion in 1927. Although strictly a 'pre-treaty' design, with a nominal displacement of 7,500 tons, *Aoba* and her sister *Kinugasa* had many of the features of Japan's first treaty cruisers of the *Myoko* class, and would be included in Japan's quota for 'category (a)' cruisers in the London Treaty of 1930. Note the distinctive 'wavy line' of the upper deck. (Leo van Ginderen collection)

For the much larger *Myoko* class the IJN went a stage further, providing a complete external belt 123m in length which was 3.5m high abeam the machinery spaces and 2m high abeam the magazines, and which was inclined at 12°. The thickness of the side belt was a uniform 102mm, and it was covered, as in the *Furutaka/Aoba* classes, by a 35mm deck. There was also 25mm protection for the turrets, barbettes and turret trunks, which were further reinforced at their base. The intention was to give complete protection of the ship's vitals against 6in shellfire, and indirect protection against 8in shell.

The *Furutaka/Aoba* classes had only a small anti-torpedo bulge, but a much more substantial version was devised for the *Myoko* class. The latter ships were given a two-compartment bulge 2.5m deep backed by a curved torpedo bulkhead comprising two 29mm HT steel plates. The underwater protection system was based on that fitted in the battleships of the *Nagato* class. The inner compartment of the bulge was to be filled with sealed steel tubes on the British pattern, but as the additional 200 tons would have had to be declared under Washington this modification would only be made in time of war.[10] Tests on the hull of the uncompleted battleship *Tosa* suggested that the underwater protection system of the *Myokos* would be effective against the contact explosion of a 200kg warhead. This was adequate to cope with US Navy 18in torpedoes (the warhead for a Mk 7 was 148kg), but not the new 21in models (211kg for the Mk 8). Nevertheless, the IJN would persist with the anti-torpedo bulge in their next class of treaty cruisers, presumably on the grounds that aircraft would continue to be armed with the smaller weapon.

Myoko (Jap)

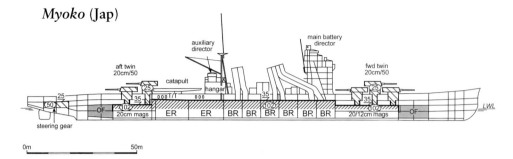

The four ships of the Japanese *Myoko* class were an enlargement of the 7,500-ton scout cruisers of the *Furutaka* and *Aoba* classes (see Chapter 2), and were the only treaty cruisers to feature five turrets. They had a long, narrow hull optimised for high speed, the distinctive 'wavy deck line' peculiar to IJN ships of the period, and an innovative longitudinal construction system in which armour was an integral part of the hull structure. There was a continuous 102mm (4in) non-cemented armoured belt covering not only the machinery spaces but the magazines fore and aft. Note the six fixed torpedo tubes to port and starboard above the engine rooms.

Myoko: Protection

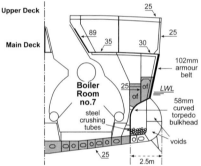

The protection system adopted for the *Myoko* class was a scaled-down battleship model, with a 102mm non-cemented (NC) belt inclined at 12° and an underwater protection system comprising a two-compartment bulge with a curved internal torpedo bulkhead comprising a double thickness of 29mm steel. The steel crushing tubes for the inner compartment would have been embarked only in wartime. The lack of depth of the bulge meant that its effectiveness was questionable against anything other than aerial torpedoes.

A feature of the Japanese treaty cruisers which subsequently attracted widespread criticism was the adoption of centre-line bulkheads for the engine and boiler rooms. In theory these made for tighter compartmentation of the machinery spaces and prevented flooding across the full beam of the ship in the event of one or more torpedo hits. In practice the centre-line bulkhead meant that a torpedo hit on one side tended to quickly destabilise the ship, and without rapid counter-flooding the latter would capsize. This was to be the fate of a number of IJN cruisers struck by submarine or aerial torpedoes during the Second World War.

Of the Western navies only the British opted to provide an anti-torpedo bulge for their treaty cruisers. An external bulge was incorporated in the *Kent* class, but it was quickly realised that such underwater protection systems lacked the necessary depth to be effective against ever-larger and more powerful torpedoes, and it was suppressed in the *London* class which followed. A further factor in the Royal Navy's decision to abandon anti-

This close-up of the midships section of the Japanese cruiser *Myoko*, taken from the US cruiser *Augusta* in 1936, shows clearly the features which were 'added on' during the design process, and which were in part responsible for the ship's overweight problem. The raised deckhouse at the base of the bridge structure replaced the accommodation spaces displaced by the torpedo tubes and reloads, and atop the deckhouse there were additional 12cm HA guns to port and starboard. (US Navy)

torpedo bulges was their negative effect on powering; the *London*s thereby gained 0.75 knots in maximum speed.

The Italians, unlike the other Western navies, attempted to follow the Japanese in attempting to provide armour over the entire length of the ship's vitals. The centre section of the *Trento* class, comprising the full length of the machinery spaces and the magazines, constituted an armoured box constructed on the longitudinal principle, while the unarmoured bow and stern sections had traditional transverse construction. Unlike the Japanese, however, the Italians seem not to have had any clear idea regarding resistance against particular calibres of shell (perhaps because the French, their most likely opponents, had confused the issue by the adoption of 'intermediate' 130mm and 138.6mm calibres, neither of which was yet in service, for their new *contre-torpilleurs*). Nor was any distinction made, as in the British and US navies, between magazines and machinery spaces. The consequence was a uniform side belt of 70mm thickness, topped by a 50mm deck. The turrets had 100mm faces, and there was 100mm plating for the conning tower.

The scale of protection of the *Trento*s was markedly superior to what the French achieved with the *Duquesne* class, and would have provided immunity against destroyer shell at the longer battle ranges envisaged. However, the declared weight of protection of 888 tonnes (8.8 per cent of standard displacement) was less than that achieved by the British in the *Kent* class (1,025 tons/10.3 per cent), even when differences in practice in the allocation of weights are taken into account. Despite this, *Trento* and *Trieste* were around 350 tonnes overweight on completion,[11] whereas their French counterparts were completed within the 10,160-tonne treaty limit.

Air Defence

During the First World War, cruisers operating with the fleet did not have to worry about air attack. Warbuilt ships generally had a pair of high-angle (HA) guns of around 3in (76mm) calibre to deal with Zeppelins and to frighten off reconnaissance planes, but the flimsy wood-and-canvas conventional aircraft of the day presented little or no threat to ships at sea. However, by the early 1920s more capable aircraft were coming into service, and they were being taken to sea in aircraft carriers (see Chapter 7). Fleet cruisers would need to play their part in chasing away or shooting down enemy spotter and reconnaissance aircraft, and in the longer term ships might be subjected to sustained attack by aircraft armed with bombs or torpedoes.

All the new treaty cruisers were designed to accommodate a modern battery of anti-aircraft guns from the outset, the guns being sited amidships on the port and starboard sides with the best possible arcs. The French opted initially for the relatively lightweight 75mm gun, the British and the Italians for the medium 4in/100mm gun, and the Japanese and the Americans for heavyweight 12cm and 5in guns respectively. The development of modern high-angle fire control systems for future installation was set in train, and these would generally be installed from about 1930. The British and the Americans opted for a standard battery of four HA guns, the Japanese (initially) six, the French eight (double the number fitted in the light cruisers of the *Duguay-Trouin* class), and the Italians no fewer than sixteen guns in twin mountings. The French ships also had eight 37mm Mod.1925 guns for close-range defence on completion, while the Italian ships had four 40mm/39-calibre Vickers AA guns plus light machine guns mounted in the mast platforms.

The close attention paid to anti-aircraft defence by the French and Italian navies reflected operating conditions in the confined waters of the Mediterranean. The geostrategic position of Italy was such that aircraft operating from its mainland bases could potentially dominate these waters, and the proximity of the main French naval base of Toulon to Italy presented in turn a potential aerial threat to Italian shipping.

The British had given the aerial threat considerable thought, and the four 4in HA mountings initially fitted in the 'Counties' told only part of the story, being but a single element in a three-tier 'layered' anti-aircraft defence, which would be complete only in the early 1930s. The 8in Mk I gun mounting, unlike the main gun mountings of the other treaty cruisers, was designed for long-range AA fire; the original specifications called for a gun which could elevate to at least 65°, and the final design achieved an impressive 70°. A high-angle control system (HACS Mk I) was under development, and would be fitted from about 1930; the ships were designed, like the battleships of the *Nelson* class, to be fitted with two multiple 2-pdr pom-poms for close-range fire. It was envisaged that the main 8in guns and the 4in HA guns would put up a layered barrage using time-fuzed shells through which groups of level- or torpedo bombers would have to fly in formation before being engaged directly at close range by the 2-pdr pom-poms. Unfortunately development of the latter weapon was considerably delayed due to funding problems, and the first mounting was installed only from 1930 onwards.

The Imperial Japanese Navy, which had traditionally clung to the coat tails of the British in technological developments, modified its second group of treaty cruisers (*Takao* class) to conform to British air defence philosophy. A new twin 20cm gun mounting with a 70° elevation (the 'E' model[12]) was developed, and the number of 12cm HA guns reduced from six to four accordingly.

In addition to their time-fuzed HE anti-aircraft ammunition, the medium HA guns mounted in the treaty cruisers were provided with illuminating shell. Searchlight projectors for target illumination in low visibility continued to be fitted, but had the disadvantage of revealing the position of the illuminating ship, so starshell from the medium guns, which could keep up a sustained and regular fire, was the preferred option. Indeed the US Navy initially considered mounting four single 5in/51-calibre LA/starshell guns on the *Pensacola*s, with anti-aircraft fire being provided by a battery of close-range 37mm guns. Although unsuited to the anti-aircraft role because the barrel length made it less manoeuvrable, the 5in/51-calibre was the standard anti-destroyer weapon of US battleships of the period, and was considered for the new cruisers largely because of concerns regarding the slow rate of fire of the main 8in battery. Although the short 5in/25-calibre HA gun was finally adopted because of delays in the development of the 37mm weapon, the decision to double the size of the 5in battery during the early/mid-1930s was influenced by anti-surface considerations, which weighed almost as heavily as the increase in anti-aircraft capability.

Where the US Navy would score over its competitors, despite the initial confusion regarding the choice of a suitable AA gun, was in the development of effective anti-aircraft fire control systems. With the advantage of later completion than the French, British and Japanese ships, the two *Pensacola*s went to sea with the Mk 19 director, a tachimetric (or 'predictive') system which was the ancestor of the very successful Mk 37 which equipped most US warships during the Second World War, and which proved to be superior in every respect to the British HACS.

Table 6.2: The First Generation of Treaty Cruisers: Characteristics (as completed)

	Kent class (GB)	*Duquesne* class (Fr)	*Trento* class (It)
Built:	7 ships 1924–28	2 ships 1924–28	2 ships 1925–29
Displacement:	9,750tW	10,000tW	10,005tW
Dimensions:	630ft × 66ft (192m × 20.8m)	191m × 19m	197m × 20.6m
Machinery:	4-shaft geared turbines; 80,000shp = 31.5 knots	4-shaft geared turbines; 120,000shp = 34 knots	4-shaft geared turbines; 120,000shp = 35 knots
Armament:	8– 8in/50 (4 × II) 4–4in/45 (4 × I) HA 8–21in TT (2 × IV)	8–203mm/50 (4 × II) 8–76mm/60 (8 × I) HA 6–550mm TT (2 × III)	8–203mm/50 (4 × II) 16–100mm/47 (8 × II) HA 8–533mm TT (8 × I)
Protection:	mach: 1in belt, 1½in deck mags: 4in sides, 3in crowns turrets: none	mach: none mags: 30mm sides, 20mm deck turrets: 30mm CT: 30mm	mach and mags: 70mm belt, 50mm deck turrets 100mm faces CT: 100mm

	Myoko class (Jap)	*Pensacola* class (US)	*Northampton* class (US)
Built:	4 ships 1924–29	2 ships 1926–30	6 ships 1928–31
Displacement:	11,500tW	9,100tW	9,010tW
Dimensions:	204m × 19m	586ft × 65ft (179m × 19.9m)	600ft × 66ft (177m × 20.1m)
Machinery:	4-shaft geared turbines; 130,000shp = 35 knots	4-shaft geared turbines; 107,000shp =32.5 knots	4-shaft geared turbines; 107,000shp = 32.5 knots

Armament:	10–20cm/50 (5 × II)	10–8in/55 (2 × III, 2 × II)	9–8in/55 (3 × III)
	6–12cm/45 (6 × I) HA	4–5in/25 (4 × I) HA	4–5in/25 (4 × I) HA
	12–61cm TT (12 × I)	6–21in TT (2 × III)	6–21in TT (2 × III)
Protection:	mach and mags: 102mm belt,	mach: 2½in belt, 1in deck	mach: 3in belt, 1in deck
	35mm deck	mags: 4in sides, 1¾in crowns	mags: 3¾in sides, 2in crowns
	turrets: 25mm	turrets: 2½in faces	turrets: 2½in faces
		CT: 1¼in	CT: 1¼in

Notes:

- The seven *Kents* (GB) were followed by four similar ships of the *London* class and two ships of the *Dorsetshire* class.
- The two *Duquesnes* (Fr) were followed by the improved *Suffren* and *Colbert*, which were slower but had some protection.
- The two *Trentos* (It) were followed by the improved *Bolzano*, laid down in 1930.
- The four *Myokos* (Jap) were followed by four modified ships of the *Takao* class.

Table 6.3: Treaty Cruiser Torpedoes: Performance Data

	Mk VII (GB)	Mk 11 (US)	Type 8 no.2 (Jap)	Mod.1923 (Fr)	SI 260 (It)
Diameter:	21in (533mm)	21in (533mm)	61cm	550mm	533mm
Weight:	4,106lb (1862kg)	3,511lb (1593kg)	2362kg	2120kg	1,550kg
Warhead:	740lb (336kg)	500lb (227kg)	346kg	310kg	260kg
Propulsion:	oxygen-enriched air	wet heater	compressed-air radial	Brotherhood alcohol-fuelled	Brotherhood
Range:	16,000yds at 33 knots	15,000yds at 27 knots	20,000m at 27 knots	20,000m at 29 knots	10,000m at 26 knots
		10,000yds at 34 knots	15,000m at 32 knots	14,000m at 35 knots	4,000m at 42 knots
		6,000yds at 46 knots	10,000m at 38 knots		

Torpedoes

For the British, trade defence was envisaged as being the primary role of their new treaty cruisers, whilst strategic scouting was the key mission for the Japanese and the Americans. For the French it was a mix of both, while raids on French communications in the Mediterranean figured largely in Italian calculations. All five navies, however, recognised that these ships would be employed as a component of the battle fleet in a major fleet action (hence the British requirement for a high rate of fire for their 8in guns, and the US Navy's preoccupation with anti-destroyer capabilities), and all five Naval Staffs initially insisted that their ships be armed with torpedoes fired from above-water tubes.

In this they faced opposition from those who felt that the small number of torpedoes these ships might fire in a single salvo would be unlikely to hit fast-moving targets at the longer engagement ranges envisaged. There were also concerns that large numbers of torpedo warheads – containing increasingly large quantities of high explosive – would be exposed to gunfire in the most vulnerable part of the ship. Whilst this risk could be more readily tolerated in small fleet cruisers designed to operate with the destroyer flotillas, the treaty cruisers were large, high-value units and losses would be less acceptable.

Another practical issue was the launching of torpedoes from ships of this size. Traditionally torpedoes launched from small cruisers and flotilla craft had been fired from fixed or trainable tubes mounted on the upper deck, while capital ships were given fixed underwater tubes, in part because of the vulnerability of the tubes if located topsides, but also because high freeboard made it difficult to launch torpedoes at the required angle of entry. Trainable tubes had the clear advantage of being able to launch torpedoes over an arc of 90–120° or greater if located on the deck edge, whereas fixed tubes could be fired only with the target broadside on and were therefore best suited to launch from a line of battle against an opposing battle line.

Clearly for cruisers of this size, operating in all probability in loose divisions and manoeuvring for position at high speed, trainable tubes were the preferred solution. However, the flush-deck hull-form adopted by four of the five navies for their first generation of treaty cruisers presented difficulties. The French, who adopted a raised-forecastle design, could locate their triple trainable tubes amidships, and the US Navy's *Pensacola* had such low freeboard amidships that triple trainable tubes could be mounted abeam the second funnel without a problem. However, the British, who had otherwise made fewer mistakes than the other navies with the design of their treaty cruisers, made a serious miscalculation in positioning their own quadruple torpedo mountings on the upper deck, immediately abaft the third funnel. The freeboard at this point was fully 27ft (8.2m), and during trials it was found that the Mk V torpedo could not withstand the force of entry into the water from this height. Further trials and costly modifications were required before the torpedoes were fully operational.[13]

The Japanese and the Italians, whose flush-deck ships had relatively high freeboard, would have experienced the same problems as the British had they opted for trainable tubes on the weather deck. Instead both decided in favour of fixed above-water tubes located at the level of the main deck (and therefore some three metres closer to the waterline). This installation was not a feature of the original design for the *Myoko* class, and was strenuously opposed by Chief Constructor Hiraga, who had already been compelled by the Naval General Staff to incorporate fixed torpedo tubes at main deck level in the *Furutaka* design. Hiraga feared that detonation of the torpedo warheads by shell hits or by spreading fires would result in the loss of the ship, and these fears appeared to be confirmed in tests on the hull of the uncompleted battleship *Tosa* in June 1924.[14]

The Italian *Trento* and *Trieste* were fitted with four pairs of fixed torpedo tubes located port and starboard above the forward and after engine rooms respectively, and there was a torpedo magazine for four reloads adjacent to the shell room of no.2 turret. The torpedo armament of the Japanese *Myoko*s, however, was of a totally different order to that of the Western treaty cruisers. Twelve fixed tubes, grouped in threes, were provided in a single large torpedo room directly above the engine rooms at main deck level, and it was envisaged that no fewer than twenty-four torpedoes (twelve in the tubes plus twelve reloads) would be carried in peacetime and thirty-six in wartime.

The deck space occupied by the fixed tubes and their reload facilities in the *Myoko* design was such that there was now insufficient internal volume for crew accommodation, and a deckhouse had to be built out to the ship's sides at the base of the forward superstructure to compensate, atop which two additional 12cm HA guns were to be mounted (the original complement was four). The Navy Technical Department, which had the large torpedo armament imposed on it by the Naval General Staff in Hiraga's absence, advised that these modifications would cost 500 tons, increasing the planned (trial) displacement from 11,850 tons[15] to 12,350 tons and breaking the treaty limit. However, the General Staff insisted on going ahead regardless of treaty obligations, which they seem to have viewed as being 'somebody else's problem' (presumably the same politicians who had conceded the 5:3 treaty ratio).

What the General Staff could not have known at that time was that due to a serious miscalculation of weights, which was fast becoming endemic in the IJN design process, a further 1,000 tons would accrue during construction of the *Myoko*s, so that on completion normal displacement was 13,338 tons and the ships were 12 per cent overweight (and 1,500 tons over treaty limits). Lacroix and Wells, in their authoritative book on IJN cruiser design,[16] have argued a strong case for the unintentional nature of this massive further breach of treaty limits. The *Furutaka/Aoba* classes also emerged from the shipyards 11 per cent overweight compared with initial calculations, and these ships as designed were well under the treaty limits. They and their treaty cruiser successors paid the price in terms of deeper draught, the near-submerging of their armour belts, and reductions in longitudinal strength, maximum speed and endurance.

The performance of the torpedoes themselves was a key factor in their subsequent retention (Great Britain, France), further development (Japan) or abandonment (USA, Italy). The tactical justification for their installation in the early treaty cruisers was their potential utility in a fleet action. However, these decisions were being made at a time when battle ranges were growing exponentially due to the advent of director fire control and aerial spotting. The 8in/203mm guns with which these ships were armed had maximum theoretical ranges of around 30,000m, and although it was unlikely that many hits would be achieved at these longer ranges, a daylight range of engagement of 18,000m was felt to be well within capabilities. Indeed, lesser ranges of engagement would probably expose the ships to frequent hits by the quick-firing 6in guns of smaller fleet light cruisers.

In the quest for a torpedo with an effective 'daylight' range, both the Japanese and the French developed large-diameter models in the postwar period, with the Marine Nationale moving to 550mm and the IJN to 61cm. The British Admiralty pursued the alternative route of advanced propulsion and pushed for development of the Type E torpedo, which was fuelled by oxygen, and the US Navy also considered oxygen propulsion as a solution to the lack of reach of its current Mk 8. British trials with oxygen-fuelled torpedoes led to the abandonment of the project following numerous accidents but the IJN was subsequently to show greater determination in tackling these technical problems, and the combination of a large-diameter torpedo body with oxygen propulsion was eventually to produce the most effective long-range torpedo of the Second World War: the Type 93 'Long Lance', which could run for 40,000m at 36 knots.

Of the five major navies only the IJN continued to believe that the torpedo had a major role to play in long-range daylight engagements involving large cruisers. When subsequently modernised, their 'A'-type cruisers would be fitted with multiple quadruple trainable tubes with a substantial reload capacity. The British and the French retained their own trainable tubes primarily for night action, when battles would most likely be fought at ranges below 6,000m. The Americans, on the other hand, became disenchanted with the idea of torpedoes aboard cruisers, feeling that their limited utility was outweighed by the potential hazard they posed, particularly in a confused night action dominated by quick-firing weapons. The second generation of US treaty cruisers was completed without torpedo tubes, and they were subsequently removed from the earlier types. The Italians, whose *Trento* class were equipped with torpedoes of modest performance, fired from fixed tubes fundamentally unsuited to the rapid-response demands of low-visibility encounters, seem to have come to similar conclusions, as the tubes were suppressed in their own second-generation ships of the *Zara* class.

Aircraft

With the advent of aircraft which could be launched from ships, strategic scouting was no longer restricted to visual range. A cruiser equipped with floatplanes, particularly when operating in the open expanses of the Atlantic, the Pacific or the Indian Ocean, could conduct aerial reconnaissance to determine the position and heading of an enemy squadron or fleet, and to provide advance warning of any threat to its own security or that of a convoy it might be charged with protecting. The attraction of on-board reconnaissance aircraft for IJN and US Navy cruisers when scouting in advance of their respective battle fleets was self-evident, as it was for French and British cruisers deployed on trade-protection duties. Of the five contracting powers the Italians were the only nation not to take up their option to build aircraft carriers to operate with the fleet, so they also came to regard on-board aircraft as important for reconnaissance.

The British and the Americans were also keen to use cruiser floatplanes for spotting purposes. Both navies were quick to appreciate that battle ranges would continue to increase, but that even with modern director control effective fire beyond 18,000–20,000m would be possible only with aerial spotting to supplement the spotting glasses mounted in the foretop. Ships would in any case obtain fewer hits at long range because plunging shell was far less likely to strike than shells fired at angles closer to horizontal, making the accurate spotting of salvoes even more important.

Numerous technical problems presented themselves, some of which were never to be satisfactorily resolved. The low-performance aircraft of the First World War, particularly the diminutive fighters, had proved capable of launch from simple platforms mounted atop the turrets of battleships. The larger, faster two- and three-seater models now envisaged for the reconnaissance and spotting roles would require some sort of power-assisted launch, so trainable or fixed catapults using either compressed air or gunpowder had to be developed.[17]

The French had a trainable Penhoët compressed-air model available for installation aboard the light cruiser *Primauguet* from 1 April 1927. With an overall length of 20.27m, it could launch aircraft with a maximum weight of 1,600kg at 93km/h. This experimental model served as the basis for a gunpowder-powered catapult with a 2,500kg capacity intended for *Duquesne* and *Tourville* but which was not ready for installation until the end of 1929. In the interim the FBA 17 and Cams 37A reconnaissance floatplanes were launched from the water. Once the catapult was installed these large, ungainly models were replaced by the purpose-built Gourdou-Leseurre GL.810, a modern metal-hulled two-seat monoplane with a range of 300nm. Two aircraft were carried: one atop the catapult, which was located high on the centre-line between the second funnel and the mainmast, the other between the two funnels.

IJN developments followed a similar pattern to the French. A 19.4m catapult powered by compressed air, with a launch capacity of 2,000kg, was fitted experimentally in the *Kinugasa* during 1928, and subsequently installed as the Kure Type No.1 in the *Myoko* class shortly after completion. A gunpowder-powered successor was also trialled in the *Aoba* during 1929 and adopted as the Kure Type No.2 for the second series of treaty cruisers (*Takao* class) in 1930. In the *Myoko* class a single catapult was mounted on the starboard side of a 'flight deck' immediately forward of no.4 turret, and a small hangar was provided beneath the tripod mainmast. However, the Type 15 seaplane initially embarked was too heavy to be launched from the catapult and had to be lowered onto the water for take-off, and it was only with the Type 90 No.2 two-seat reconnaissance floatplane adopted in 1931 that a true catapult-launch capability was achieved.

The British Royal Navy opted, like the French, for a high centre-line position abaft the funnels for their own trainable catapult, but required an even greater launch capacity of 6,000–8,000lb (2,700–3,600kg) for the large Fairey IIIF three-seat spotter-reconnaissance aircraft. This implied an even longer catapult beam, and there was limited centre-line space available in the *Kent*s even after the secondary fire control position was moved 14ft (4.3m) aft, so the heavy catapults developed for the Royal Navy were hinged, sliding or extendable. The EIIH ('E' for extending, 'H' for heavy) catapult developed for the 'Counties' was available for installation only from 1931. When fully extended it had an overall length of 76ft (23.2m), but this could be reduced to 46ft (14m) for stowage. It could launch an 8,000lb (3,600kg) aircraft at 57 knots, or a 7,000lb (3,200kg) aircraft at 60 knots. However, the FIIIF was to prove unsuitable for deployment aboard cruisers, and the smaller two-seat Hawker Osprey was carried in its place from 1933, thereby negating the advantages of the heavier catapult.

The Italians adopted a totally different solution to the other four major navies for their *Trento* class. Engineer-Major Luigi Gagnotto designed a catapult using compressed air which was set into the forecastle and extended from just forward of no.1 gun turret to the bow. Similar in principle and in configuration to the catapults (or 'accelerators') developed for aircraft carriers and submarines during the 1930s, that aboard the *Trento*s employed rails some 32m in length. A further novel feature of the Italian ships was that the aircraft were stowed in a hangar 13.7m long and 3.8m high located directly beneath the forecastle deck immediately forward of no.1 turret. They were raised onto the catapult by a collapsible derrick, and had to be assembled prior to launch. The aircraft carried from completion was the Piaggio P6 bis, which had an all-up weight of 1,850kg and a range of 240nm, but the P6 was soon replaced by the lighter but more capable Macchi M41. A total of three aircraft (two broken down in the hangar plus one fully assembled on the catapult) could be carried, but the more usual complement was two.

Of the five major navies it was the US Navy that placed the greatest emphasis on aviation facilities and capabilities in its treaty cruisers, and these were highly developed even in their earliest types. The US Navy had experimented with powered catapults as early as 1912, and all its treaty cruisers were equipped from the outset with two trainable catapults 68ft (20.7m) in length. These were mounted on the deck edge amidships between the funnels; additional aircraft were stowed to port and starboard of the second funnel on trolleys which enabled them to be manoeuvred directly onto the catapults. In the *Northampton* class large hangars were provided abeam the second funnel with additional stowage positions atop the hangars, the catapult pedestals being raised accordingly to bring the catapult beam in line with the hangar roofs. This gave the ships a theoretical capacity of six reconnaissance floatplanes, although this was reduced to four when the hangar roofs had to be used to accommodate the additional 5in/25-calibre gun mountings during the 1930s. In 1933 the British Director of Naval Air Department (DNAD) is reported to have commented very favourably on the 'excellent arrangements for rapidly handling aircraft in American 8in gun cruisers'.[18] The US Navy was fortunate in having a proven two-seat reconnaissance aircraft available for shipboard use. The Vought Corsair O2U was an all-metal biplane which in 1927 had set four world records for speed and altitude. It had an all-up weight of 1,670kg and a range of 450nm. Three were purchased in 1929 by the Japanese, who developed their own Type 90 No.2 model from the Corsair.

Launching was not the only issue with operating aircraft from cruisers. Once it had been launched and had conducted its reconnaissance (or spotting) mission the aircraft had to be recovered. This involved landing on the sea in close proximity to the mother ship, taxiing alongside, and being hoisted aboard by crane. While performing this lengthy and painstaking manoeuvre the ship would have to reduce speed or stop altogether, and during the time it took to hoist the aircraft aboard and secure it, the ship would be a sitting duck for a submarine or even for fast-moving surface vessels operating in close proximity.[19] Some navies fitted their floatplanes with wheels so that they could land ashore or on accompanying aircraft carriers, while the French experimented (unsuccessfully) during the late 1930s with German Kiwull and Hein mat systems in which a length of ribbed canvas was trailed from the stern of the ship, and the aircraft taxied onto it to be hoisted over the stern while the ship was underway.

Moreover, landing an aircraft on the water was dependent on sea and wind conditions. The British, for whom the Atlantic was a major theatre of operations, conducted a study of available weather data in 1934 which suggested that no aircraft of the size which could be operated from a cruiser could come down in the open sea with a wind of Force 4 or above, which meant that aircraft could only be recovered for 50 per cent of the year.

Other issues were the vulnerability of aircraft – stowed either on the catapults or on the open deck – to damage either from the elements or from the blast of the cruiser's main guns, and the potential fire hazard posed by aviation fuel. The US Navy, which was committed to naval aviation, adopted prominent blast-proof hangars aboard its treaty cruisers from the *Northampton* class onwards. The British, on the other hand, who were faced with more difficult operating conditions but were ambivalent about the value of operating aircraft from cruisers, did not adopt hangars until the mid-1930s, while the Japanese abandoned their own small hangars and the French continued to stow aircraft on catapults and open decks.

The flammable aviation fuel was stowed in multiple drums or tanks well away from the midships area where the aircraft launch facilities were located. The Americans located their aviation tanks close to the bow beneath the waterline, with external fuel lines running along the outside of the hull. The French, on the other hand, opted for a position high in the stern; fire-prevention measures included the replacement of used fuel by inert CO_2 gas, and the facility to pump the contents of the tank rapidly into the sea.

There was also considerable institutional resistance to aircraft among naval traditionalists who felt that aviation facilities aboard cruisers had a negative impact on their fighting qualities. A British admiral commanding the battlecruiser *Hood* went so far as to complain that it spoilt the look of his quarterdeck![20] Opponents claimed (with some justification) that aircraft interfered with the operation of the guns, introduced a further fire hazard to the vulnerable midships section, and put the ship at a tactical disadvantage when attempting to launch or recover aircraft. Nevertheless, aircraft continued to feature in the designs of the new treaty cruisers and their successors built during the 1930s. It was only during the latter part of the Second World War, when aircraft carriers began to enter service in numbers, that aviation facilities in cruisers were removed, generally with a view to increasing anti-aircraft capabilities.

Taking Stock

It quickly became apparent to the British Admiralty that the ambitious cruiser construction programme it had proposed would not be fully funded. Whereas the Admiralty had proposed eight ships to be ordered on each of three successive years, followed by four ships over the next six years, funding was obtained for only five ships in the 1924–25 Estimates and four in the 1925–26 Estimates. In the event the Dominion of Australia agreed to purchase an additional two *Kent* class cruisers, boosting the figure for the first year to seven ships, but it was clear that this rate of construction was unsustainable and unaffordable in the longer term. A more modest proposal of three ships per year over four years (1926–29) was submitted, and of these twelve cruisers no fewer than seven were to be of a smaller 8,000-ton type in an attempt to ensure affordability. Even this modest programme had to be abandoned in the face of financial retrenchment, and only four ships (two 10,000-ton and two 8,000-ton) were to be completed.

York (GB)

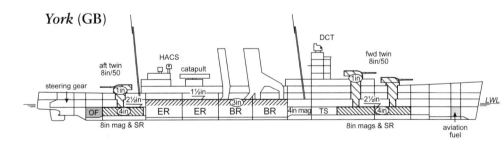

York was to have been the first in a series of 8,200-ton 'B'-type cruisers designed to provide a trade defence capability at lower cost than the 10,000-ton 'Counties'. In order to compensate for the reduced number of main guns she was given more substantial protection: a 3in armour belt 8ft deep covered the machinery spaces, and the shell rooms were given the same level of protection as the magazines.

The cruisers *York* and *Exeter* were an attempt by the Royal Navy to produce a smaller, more affordable 8in-gun cruiser capable of trade protection. Accommodation was more cramped than in the 'Counties', due to the cut-down hull aft, and in order to attain the required speed they needed propulsion machinery with a similar power output, but their machinery spaces were markedly better protected. *Exeter*, ordered a year after *York* and seen here shortly after completion, incorporated a number of modifications, which included vertical funnels and a new streamlined bridge structure. (Leo van Ginderen collection)

The 'B'-type cruisers[21] *York* and *Exeter* had their origins in a series of sketch designs presented to the Board of Admiralty for discussion by the director of naval construction in August 1925. All are believed to have had a main armament of six 8in guns and a displacement of 8,200 tons, but the Admiralty was insistent that they should otherwise be fitted out as per the *Kents*, with enhanced protection to compensate for the likelihood they would be outgunned by hostile cruisers in their primary trade defence mission. Reducing the main armament by two guns purchased a main belt 3in thick over the machinery spaces, but it proved impossible to obtain a corresponding reduction in the power of the machinery due to the less fine lines of the shorter hull, and 80,000shp was still required to provide the designed speed of 32 knots. In part compensation for the reduced armament it was envisaged that two aircraft catapults would be fitted, but the proposed catapult atop 'B' turret had to be abandoned on weight grounds. There was concern also regarding the weight implications of the proposed armoured director control tower (DCT), but this was eventually approved, albeit with protective plating of reduced thickness.

The first ship was ordered as HMS *York* in the 1926 programme; however, the proposed order for two further ships in the 1927 programme was reduced to one through lack of funds, and *Exeter* was the only other 'B'-type cruiser to be completed. This led the Admiralty to push for a quantitative limit on further 8in cruiser construction, and for a qualitative limit of 7,500 tons plus

Table 6.4: Treaty Cruisers: Intermediate Types

	York/Exeter (GB)	Foch/Dupleix (Fr)
Built:	2 ships 1927–31	2 ships 1928–33
Displacement:	8,250tW	10,000tW
Dimensions:	575ft × 57ft (192m × 20.8m)	194m × 19m
Machinery:	4-shaft geared turbines;	3-shaft geared turbines;
	80,000shp = 32.5 knots	90,000shp = 32 knots
Armament:	6–8in/50 (3 × II)	8–203mm/50 (4 × II)
	4–4in/45 (4 × I) HA	8–90mm/50 (4 × II) HA
	6–21in TT (2 × III)	6–550mm TT (2 × III)
Protection:	mach: 3in belt, 1½in deck	mach: 60mm b/head, 30mm deck
	mags: 4in sides, 2½in crowns	mags: 60mm sides, 30mm crowns
	turrets: none	turrets: 30mm
		CT: 30mm

Note: Armament and Protection data are for *Dupleix*; *Foch* had her 90mm guns in single mountings, and vertical protection for the sides and magazines was 54mm.

a 6in gun calibre on subsequent cruisers. These proposals were discussed at a hastily arranged conference in Geneva in 1927, but led only to a bitter row between Britain and the United States (see Chapter 11). The US opposed any reduction in main gun calibre or displacement, and was unwilling to accept anything other than parity with regard to smaller cruisers. Geneva was a total failure, and changes in the treaty rules would have to wait until the London Conference of 1930, when the same arguments would again be wheeled out.

The IJN duly proceeded with its planned programme of eight 10,000-ton treaty cruisers. The four ships of the *Takao* class were to have been repeats of the *Myoko* class, but the General Staff, with a constant eye on developments abroad, wanted improvements. The influence of the British *Kent*s was apparent in the new 20cm twin mountings, which had 70° elevation, in the heavier protection accorded to the crowns of the magazines (47mm vs. 35mm), and in the use of high-tensile Ducol steel for protective plating, as well as the influence of the US Navy's *Pensacola* class in the adoption of twin catapults for two two-seat spotter/observation floatplanes plus a three-seat reconnaissance floatplane with a range of 300nm.

The other major differences were a modified torpedo armament and a massive new bridge structure purpose-designed to accommodate enlarged command spaces and the latest fire control equipment. In place of the twelve fixed torpedo tubes of the *Myoko* class there were four trainable twin mountings housed in a superstructure deck amidships, with a further two sets of reloads stowed on rails at the same level. It was estimated that the second broadside could be fired within three minutes of the first, and the third within eight minutes. The Type 90 61cm torpedo under development would be faster than the Type 8, with a heavier warhead (390kg TNT). Even more significantly it would have a range of 15,000m at 35 knots and 10,000m at 42 knots, thereby keeping alive the prospect of launching torpedoes at likely combat ranges. As a safety measure, the IJN adopted the French procedure of stowing torpedo warheads in lockers of Ducol steel when not in the tubes.

The new bridge structure was the result of a joint study by the Naval Technical Department, the General Staff and the Bureau of Military Affairs, with considerable input from the various sections of the former (Gunnery, Torpedo, Navigation, Transmission, Electric and Optical). It was in every respect a superstructure 'designed by committee', with no fewer than ten levels, and with three times the volume of that fitted in the *Myoko*s. Even with the use of aluminium alloy and electric welding it weighed 160 tons – almost fifty tons more than the bridge structure of the earlier design. Despite the reduction from six to four HA guns and from twelve to eight torpedo tubes, together with other weight-saving measures such as the adoption of more modern shipyard construction techniques, the *Takao*s would have the same overweight problem as the *Myoko* class, and the reduction in metacentric height which resulted meant that 450–600 tons of liquid ballast had to be embarked in the light condition.

As soon as the design for the *Duquesne* class had been finalised the French looked forward to the next series of treaty cruisers, which were to be ordered at the modest (and achievable) rate of one per year. The French Naval General Staff was already concerned that the level of protection obtained in the *Duquesne*s appeared to be significantly less than that of their foreign contemporaries. The complete lack of protection over the machinery spaces was a particular concern, as a torpedo hit or a near-miss by even a relatively small bomb would cause major damage to the hull plating, resulting in extensive flooding. The Naval Staff also wanted protection against direct hits by 140mm (i.e. destroyer – and IJN light cruiser) shell.

The Japanese cruiser *Atago* on full-power trials in Sukumo Bay, 13 Feb 1932. Note the size of the bridge structure compared with the preceding *Myoko* class. (Fukui Shizuo collection)

Suffren (Fr)

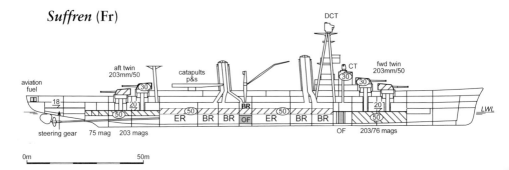

Foch (Fr)

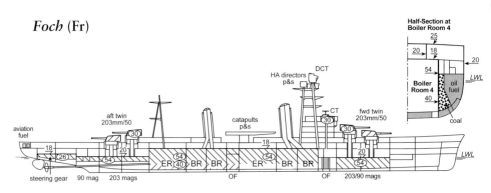

To follow the fast but virtually unprotected *Duquesne* class the Marine Nationale built four ships with reduced speed and a moderate level of protection. The first pair had a narrow 50mm belt over the machinery spaces, together with coal bunkers abreast the after boiler and engine rooms. The second pair, *Foch* and *Dupleix*, had a novel protection scheme based on an internal armoured caisson over the machinery spaces.

The technical department of the Marine Nationale, the STCN, expressed the view that this level of protection was possible only if maximum speed were reduced by 2 knots. *Suffren* and her three successors therefore sacrificed a quarter of their power (i.e. two boilers, one set of turbines and one shaft), bringing them closer in performance to the British 'Counties'. This reduction in power and speed bought them a 50mm armour belt 2.5m deep over their machinery spaces, and an increased thickness of armour for the magazine boxes (although the sides of the latter were still only 50mm in the first two ships, and therefore vulnerable to 6in/152mm cruiser shell).

Battleships before the British *Queen Elizabeth* class and the US Navy's *Nevada* class were fuelled by coal, and lateral coal bunkers were an important element in the ships' protection systems. In the *Suffren* and her near-sister *Colbert* the two after boiler rooms were retained, but because each now contained only a single boiler they were narrower, as was the after engine room, which now housed only a single set of turbines for the centre-line shaft. The constructors managed to squeeze in a fifth boiler room amidships for two small coal-burning boilers, and located coal bunkers abeam the after machinery spaces for protection. The beauty of the system was that under Washington fuel was not counted in standard displacement, so provided

For their middle generation of treaty cruisers the French adopted internal protection for the machinery spaces in the form of an armoured box or 'caisson'. This unusual expedient meant that the waterline of the ship remained totally unprotected, even against destroyer shellfire. This is *Dupleix* as completed. Note the temporary open duplex three-metre rangefinder above the bridge; this would shortly be replaced by the standard five-metre stereo model in an enclosed housing. (Courtesy of Robert Dumas)

the French could claim that this (protective) coal would be burned as fuel – an additional 2,000nm cruising radius was claimed – the 640 tons that it weighed did not need to be included in standard displacement.

By June 1927, when design modifications to the third ship in the series were considered, it was becoming apparent to the French that they were adhering more closely to the Washington treaty rules than some of their competitors; in particular, the Italians seemed to have managed to get high speed *and* protection for the *Trento*s. The STCN submitted a note with observations about probable methods of calculating Washington displacement practised by other navies, and suggested that a less narrow interpretation concerning fresh and boiler feed water, provisions and munitions could save 250 tonnes. If these weight savings were to be reinvested in propulsion machinery the department was of the opinion that maximum speed could be raised again to 34 knots. However, any change in the propulsion machinery would have resulted in delays, so the Naval Staff opted instead for additional protection.

The protection system adopted for *Foch* and *Dupleix* was radically different in conception from that of other treaty cruisers. The conventional external armoured belt was abandoned in favour of a protective internal caisson over the machinery spaces. In the first ship, *Foch*, the longitudinal bulkheads abreast the machinery were reinforced to 54mm to a height of 5.5–6.1m, and the protective box was completed by an 18mm deck. The upper deck amidships was reinforced to 25mm and the side plating to 20mm. In theory destroyer shell would be detonated by the 25mm plating of the upper deck or the 20mm shell plating, and the thicker internal plating over the ship's vitals would keep out the resulting splinters. The protective boxes over the magazines were similarly reinforced, with 54mm sides and 20mm crowns. It was calculated that this level of protection would give immunity against 140mm shell beyond 14,000m. The primary disadvantage of internal armour was that it could not protect waterline buoyancy; however, it was calculated that the ship could still survive the flooding of four compartments on the same side, while the reinforced internal bulkheads actually made counter-flooding more effective.

In the second of the pair, *Dupleix*, weight savings of 185 tonnes were made by a further paring down of the figure for provisions, by adopting twin mountings in place of singles for the 90mm HA guns, and by more extensive use of aluminium alloy and welding for the superstructures and fittings. This permitted reinforcement of the vertical internal plating to 60mm and the deck and magazine crowns to 30mm. It was calculated that this would give immunity against 155mm shell beyond 18,000m.[22]

Now that the French were becoming more comfortable with 'interpreting' the treaty they saw little point in persisting with the artifice of coal-burning. In *Foch* and *Dupleix* the small coal-burning boilers were removed and replaced by diesel fuel bunkers for the generators; the layer of coal protection, however, was retained, but was not counted in the standard displacement because, like the water protection of the British *Nelson*s and the steel crushing tubes of the IJN *Myoko*s, its embarkation was deemed 'optional'. All five of the contracting powers were to become adept at interpreting the wording of the treaty for their own purposes, and the moral justification employed was similar to that of modern athletes who take performance-boosting drugs – not to have done so would have been to present an unfair advantage to their competitors, who were undoubtedly up to the same tricks.[23]

The Second Generation of Treaty Cruisers

From 1927–28, following the failure of the Geneva Conference, there was a major reassessment of the qualities required in the 10,000-ton cruiser. All the ships laid down from this time, with the sole exception of the Italian *Bolzano*, which was intended to complete a fast three-ship division with *Trento* and *Trieste*, were slower and much more heavily armoured. The Japanese, who mistakenly believed that they could build fast, heavily armed and heavily armoured ships within the 10,000-ton limit, were generally quite happy with the *Myoko*s and the *Takao*s (although they had yet to face up to the realisation that these ships were all grossly overweight). The other four major navies, however, were less happy with the level of protection in their early ships.

Modern cruisers armed with 6in/155mm guns were now entering service with the US Navy (*Omaha* class) and the Marine Nationale (*Duguay-Trouin* class), and 6in/152mm cruisers were also being considered by Britain and Italy. Although protection against direct hits by 8in shell was still thought to be out of the question, it was thought possible to provide complete protection at most battle ranges against 6in shell, and a degree of (indirect) protection against 8in shell at some cost in speed. By the late 1920s more advanced boilers using higher-temperature steam conditions were becoming available, and these could be combined with lightweight turbines to provide a much-improved power-to-weight ratio within a much-reduced hull volume, so that maximum speeds in excess of 30 knots were possible in even a relatively heavily armoured ship.

The British Admiralty, which had had strong reservations about the treaty cruiser from the outset, was the first to break ranks. In 1927, with thirteen 10,000-ton cruisers plus the 8,200-ton *York* building, it accepted a design for a ship which sacrificed two boilers and 2 knots of speed for a substantially thicker armour belt and some protection for the turret trunks. The first ship should have been ordered under the 1927 programme, but was deferred to the 1928 programme, then again postponed until the 1929 programme when two ships, to have been named *Surrey* and *Northumberland,* were to have been ordered. By this time further modifications had been made to the design, which featured a short deep belt comprising 5¾in armour on 1in plating and a 2¾in deck, protective boxes with 5¾in sides and 3in crowns over the magazines, and 1in plating on the turrets and turret trunks. The total weight of armour was in excess of 1,600 tons, an improvement of almost 60 per cent on the *Kents*. In the event funds were not forthcoming for even this modest programme of two ships, such was the deterioration in Britain's finances. The orders were postponed, and *Surrey* and *Northumberland* were cancelled in January 1930, just prior to the London Conference, in what was intended politically as a statement of intent.

The French continued to pursue their policy of small incremental improvements in protection from the *Suffren* (1926 programme) to the *Dupleix* (1929 programme), the overall weight of protection rising from 760 tonnes in the former to 1,550 tonnes in the latter. However the Italians, who had initially opted for the super-fast *Trento* design, now changed tack with a radically new design which sacrificed speed for armour on a scale hitherto considered out of the question for a 10,000-ton cruiser.

Surrey (GB)

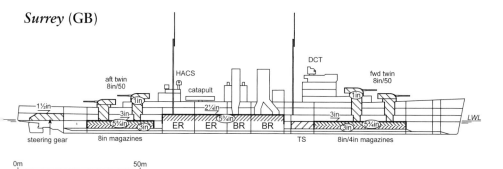

The *Surrey* class, which was to have been authorised under the 1928–29 Estimates, was essentially an enlarged version of the 'B'-type cruiser *Exeter*, with four turrets but only three-quarters the horsepower, maximum speed being reduced to 29–30 knots. The contraction of the machinery spaces permitted a thick external armoured belt. The magazines were given a similar level of protection, but there was only splinter protection for the main gun turrets and ammunition trunks.

The Italian Zara Class

The impetus for the new design came from the Naval Staff, which, faced with the terminal obsolescence of its elderly dreadnought battleships, wanted ships that could fight as the backbone of the fleet. The only logical way to achieve this was to build a cruiser sufficiently well armoured to take on its own kind in combat. Initial staff requirements were therefore for a ship armed with eight 203mm guns with a speed of 32 knots, and with an armour belt 200mm thick plus good deck protection.

The four cruisers of the *Zara* class were in many respects the mini-battleships the Regia Marina had long aspired to build: heavily armoured and well-armed, with a good turn of speed. However, in order to obtain these qualities the Italians consciously violated treaty limits on displacement; even as designed these ships displaced well in excess of 11,500 tons standard. This is *Fiume* shortly after her completion. (Leo van Ginderen collection)

The third and fourth ships of the *Zara* class, *Gorizia* and *Pola*, are seen here during the late 1930s. Note the multi-tiered bridge structure, with the director for the main battery of 203mm guns at its summit and the directors for the secondary guns to port and starboard just below. (Leo van Ginderen collection)

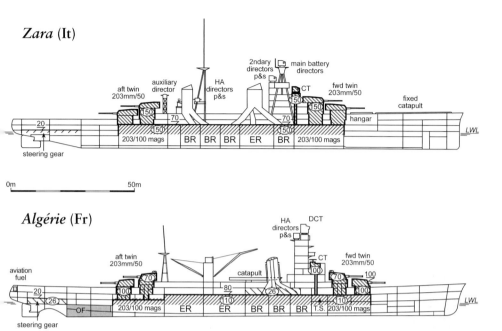

Zara (It)

Algérie (Fr)

Both of these designs broke away completely from the early treaty cruisers built by France and Italy, which had been designed primarily for high speed. In their pursuit of qualitative superiority over contemporary foreign types the Italians were prepared to break through the 10,000-ton treaty ceiling. The result was a mini-capital ship, with a maximum thickness of 150mm of armour on the sides and on the faces of the turrets, and a 70mm deck over the machinery spaces and the magazines. Careful design, and the adoption of a lightweight two-shaft propulsion plant derived from the light cruisers of the 'Condottieri' type, provided sufficient weight savings to permit a total armour weight of 2,700 metric tons, a figure unequalled by any foreign-built treaty cruiser. Note the compactness of the armoured citadel compared with the *Trentos*.

The design of *Algérie* was equally radical in its approach to providing an adequate level of protection, but the French constructors managed to keep displacement just within the 10,000-ton margin. Weight was saved by eliminating the forecastle deck of the earlier ships, by the adoption of more advanced high-pressure steam machinery and by grouping the boiler rooms together, as well as extensive use of welding and aluminium alloy. This provided a heavy armoured belt over the magazines and machinery spaces, and substantial protection for the turrets and conning tower. The total weight of protection was 2,035 tonnes.

Clearly these requirements were impossible to achieve on 10,000 tons, but the Italian constructors set about their task in their customary innovatory way. Hull scantlings were made as light as was technically feasible; a split-level hull configuration with a raised forecastle replaced the flush-deck hull of the earlier ships, and armour was used to provide longitudinal strength, so that the overall weight of the hull was 28 per cent less than in the *Trentos*. Lightweight machinery on only two shafts, derived from the propulsion plant of the new light cruisers of the 'Condottieri' type, was adopted, thereby saving around 900 tonnes. Now that it was envisaged that these ships would fight in the battle line (in fact Italian thinking of the time suggested that they might well *constitute* the battle line), the theoretical utility of torpedo tubes declined, so these could be omitted. Finally, the proposed armour belt of

200mm was pared down to 150mm, tapering to 100mm below the waterline, with a 70mm deck.

Even with these measures the ships as designed came out at around 11,500 tons standard, 1,500 tons above treaty weight. Although this was comparable to the standard displacement of the IJN's treaty cruisers as completed, the Japanese were as yet unaware of the full extent of their breach of the treaty, whereas the Italians were aware of this from the outset.[24]

The four cruisers of the *Zara* class, authorised under the 1928–30 programmes, were mini-capital ships in every respect (the Regia Marina classified them at one point as 'armoured cruisers'). Even the turrets, barbettes and turret trunks were armoured on a comparable scale to the hull: the turrets had 150mm faces and 120mm sides, and the barbettes and turret trunks had 130–150mm of armour above the upper deck and 120–140mm between the upper deck and the main deck. These figures put even the Japanese cruisers in the shade, and make the level of protection accorded to the ostensibly heavily armoured British *Surrey*s appear grossly inadequate. The total weight of protection in the *Zara*s was 2,700 tonnes (26.5 per cent of their declared 10,160 metric tons displacement, but about 23 per cent of standard displacement as completed).[25]

The French Algérie

The French felt compelled to respond to these developments. Initially it was envisaged that a linear successor to the *Dupleix* with an incremental increase in the thickness of protection, designated C4, would be built. However, there were reservations about the effectiveness and desirability of the internal armoured caisson, and it was decided to return to a conventional external armoured belt. There was also a feeling that the *Suffren* design, with its awkward three-shaft propulsion layout and the resulting discontinuity in the longitudinal internal bulkheads, had been taken as far as it could. France's seventh treaty cruiser, which would later be named *Algérie*, would therefore be a new design from the keel up, incorporating the latest thinking and taking advantage of the latest developments in technology.

The earlier ships were elegant ships with a raised forecastle, tripod masts and twin, raked, widely-spaced funnels. *Algérie* marked a complete break with this style of architecture. The forecastle deck was deleted for a saving of 80 tonnes (albeit at the cost of inferior sea-keeping). The heavy tripod foremast of the earlier ships was replaced by a modern tower structure, atop which were located the main and secondary fire control directors. Developments in superheated steam propulsion technology[26] permitted a reduction from eight boilers in four boiler rooms to five boilers in three boiler rooms, and the three boiler rooms were adjacent, permitting the exhaust uptakes to be led up into a single, broad raked funnel and reducing the length of the ship which would need to be protected. These modifications bought a weight saving of 275 tonnes over the C4 design despite the adoption of a four-shaft layout (the overall figure of 1,335 tonnes was comparable to the machinery weight of the two-shaft *Zara*s, although horsepower was only 84,000shp in *Algérie* as compared with 95,000shp in the latter).

Algérie is seen here at Villefranche during the mid-1930s. Note the contrast in build with the other two French treaty cruisers present, *Foch* and *Tourville*. The two four-funnelled *contre-torpilleurs* belong to the *Vauquelin* class (see Chapter 8); the third is is *Cassard*, and the other ship is either *Chevalier Paul* or *Tartu*. (Stephen Dent collection)

The main belt was 110mm thick, and was topped by an armoured deck with a thickness of 80mm over the magazines, shell rooms and machinery spaces. Moreover it proved possible to provide 70–100mm armour plating for the conning tower and the main turrets. In *Algérie* the total weight devoted to protection attained 2,035 tonnes, or 20 per cent of standard displacement. Unusually for a cruiser, there was also a well-designed underwater protection system comprising a liquid–air 'sandwich' with a maximum depth of 4.35m (see drawing).

For the first time in a major French warship welding was employed extensively in the construction of the hull. Riveting was however retained for the vertical and horizontal armour and the main strength elements of the hull girder, as well as for the internal partitions, which were of light duralumin alloy. Further weight was saved by mounting only a single catapult (the ships of the *Suffren* type had two), although this was compensated by increasing

The protection system of the French *Algérie* was unusual in incorporating a multi-layered underwater protection system with alternating void and liquid-loaded compartments. Note the unusual hull-form with its pronounced 'tumble-home', adopted in order to maximise the depth of the protection system below the waterline.

Algérie: Protection

the anti-aircraft armament from four twin 90mm guns in the *Dupleix* to six twin 100mm in the *Algérie*, with point defence now being provided by a new quadruple 13.2mm Hotchkiss machine gun in both types.

Authorised in 1930 *Algérie* appears to have been a successful design, and served as flagship of the French Mediterranean Squadron during the late 1930s. She showed what could be achieved with modern technology and careful design while keeping broadly within the 10,000-ton treaty limit.

The US Navy's New Orleans *Class*

By early 1929 the US Navy, having been largely responsible for the conceptual origins of the 10,000-ton treaty cruiser, was lagging some way behind its major competitors in the construction stakes. Britain had completed no fewer than eleven treaty ships, and had a further four under construction, while Japan had eight ships (including the *Furutaka/Aoba* classes) in service or fitting out, with the four *Takaos* on the stocks. By way of contrast, the first US treaty cruiser was not due to enter service until the end of the year, and the other seven which were under construction had yet to be launched.

The 1929 programme was intended to change all that. Five ships were to be authorised in each of the three fiscal years FY1929–31, so that by 1935 no fewer than twenty-one treaty cruisers would be in service. Initially it was envisaged that these ships would show few changes from the *Northampton* design currently building, thereby ensuring rapid production at moderate cost. However, the lack of protection in the early ships had attracted widespread

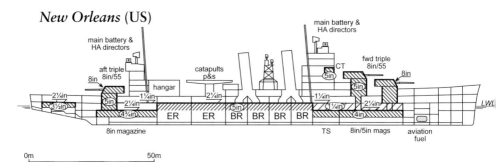

New Orleans (US)

The US Navy's *New Orleans* class retained the 32.5-knot maximum speed of the *Pensacola* and *Northampton* classes, but was radically redesigned with an emphasis on heavy protection in the knowledge that the earlier ships had emerged from the shipyards 900 tons underweight. Further weight savings were achieved by grouping the boiler rooms together, giving these ships two closely spaced funnels. By a combination of these measures the designers were able to provide a thick side belt, together with substantial protection for the turrets and ammunition trunks. The magazines, which in the earlier ships had been raised clear of the double bottom to protect them against underwater explosions, were again lowered so that their crowns were beneath the waterline. This gave the *New Orleans* class an 'immune zone' against 8in shell of 12,000–24,000 yards for the magazines, and of 15,000–24,000 yards for the machinery and plotting room. Note the disparity in the thickness of the side protection for the forward and after magazines; abeam and above the forward magazines there was 50lb (1.25in) 'ballistic plating' on the outer shell, with plating of similar thickness on the deck above (US 2nd Deck).

criticism – they were described in the press as 'tinclads' and 'eggshells armed with hammers' – and when the first to be completed, *Pensacola*, turned out 900 tons underweight the design of the new ships was radically remodelled.

At first it was envisaged that these changes would apply only from the second series of the FY1930 progamme, but as three of the five ships of the FY1929 programme were to be built in navy yards, it was decided that the modifications could be extended to these ships with minimal delay and minimal additional cost. Contracts for the remaining two ships had already been signed with their private builders, so these were completed to the original design but with additional armour 'bolted on', and became the *Portland* class.

There was still little hope of protecting the ships against 8in shellfire at all battle ranges, but for the first time an 'immune zone' rather than a specific thickness of armour was defined: the ships were to have an immune zone against 8in shell of 12,000–24,000 yards for the magazines, and of 15,000–24,000 yards for the machinery and plotting room ('transmitting station' in Royal

Table 6.5: Treaty Cruisers: Armoured Types

	Surrey class (GB)	*New Orleans* class (US)
Built:	(2 ships: cancelled)	5 ships 1931–34
Displacement:	10,000tW	10,136tW
Dimensions:	600ft × 64ft (183m × 19.5m)	588ft × 62ft (179m × 18.8m)
Machinery:	4-shaft geared turbines;	4-shaft geared turbines;
	60,000shp = 30 knots	107,000shp = 32.5 knots
Armament:	8–8in/50 (4 × II)	9–8in/55 (3 × III)
	4–4in/45 (4 × I) HA	8–5in/25 (8 × I) HA
	8–21in TT (2 × IV)	
Protection:	mach: 5¾in belt, 2¼in deck	mach: 5in belt, 2¼in deck
	mags: 5¾in sides, 3in crowns	mags: 4/4¾in sides, 2¼in crowns
	turrets: 1in	turrets: 8in faces
		CT: 5in

	Zara class (It)	*Algérie* (Fr)
Built:	4 ships 1929–32	1931–34
Displacement:	11,680tW	10,000tW
Dimensions:	183m × 20.6m	186m × 20m
Machinery:	4-shaft geared turbines;	4-shaft geared turbines;
	95,000shp = 32 knots	84,000shp = 31 knots
Armament:	8–203mm/50 (4 × II)	8–203mm/50 (4 × II)
	16–100mm/47 (8 × II) HA	12–100mm/45 (6 × II) HA
		6–550mm TT (2 × III)
Protection:	mach and mags: 150mm belt,	mach and mags: 110mm belt,
	70mm deck	80mm deck
	turrets: 150mm faces	turrets: 100mm faces
	CT: 150mm	CT: 100mm

Note: Two ships of the *Portland* class (US), authorised at the same time as the *New Orleans* class, were completed to a modified *Northampton* design with heavier protection.

New Orleans was the first of a series of heavily protected treaty cruisers laid down for the US Navy from 1931 onwards. The unit machinery arrangement of earlier types was abandoned in favour of a traditional in-line layout, with the boiler rooms forward of the engine rooms. This saved hull length and weight, and enabled the ships to be sufficiently well armoured to have substantial 'immune zones' against 6in and even 8in shell. It had the additional benefit of freeing up centre-line space amidships for aircraft and catapults, which are prominent in this 1935 view. Note the large double hangar aft. (USNHC NH71787)

Navy parlance). Both the magazines and the plotting room were to be below the waterline. Initially there was acceptance that it was not practical to protect the gunhouses against 8in shellfire, although it subsequently proved possible to provide substantial protection for the turrets, barbettes and turret trunks.

In order to reduce the length of the armoured citadel the unit machinery layout was abandoned in favour of grouping the four boiler rooms together. The close spacing of the funnels which resulted helped to simplify the aircraft arrangements, with the large double hangar being moved aft and used as the base for the after control positions. It also permitted the enhanced anti-aircraft battery of eight 5in/25-calibre guns to be grouped together abeam the funnels and the bridge structure, thereby simplifying ammunition supply. The bridge structure was remodelled as a simple tower, the heavy tripods of the earlier ships being replaced by light pole masts. Torpedo tubes were omitted altogether (they would shortly be removed from the earlier ships).

With these revised arrangements it proved possible to provide a side belt of 5in on ¾in STS steel plating with a 2¼in deck over the machinery, while the boxes enclosing the magazines had 4in sides (4¾in aft) and 2¼in crowns. Furthermore the newly-armoured turrets had 8in faces, and there was 5in protection for the barbettes and turret trunks. The 1,500 tons of protection accounted for 15 per cent of displacement, although the design was now so tight that fuel bunkerage had to be reduced by 25 per cent, and the ships could not be fitted as fleet flagships as originally intended. In fact, despite extensive use of welding these ships turned out slightly overweight.

In the event only two ships of the FY1930 programme were authorised, with a third ship deferred and the remaining two cancelled following the London Conference. However the *New Orleans* class, as it subsequently became known, provided the design baseline for all the pre-war and many of the warbuilt US large cruiser types.

Table 6.6: Treaty Cruiser Authorisations 1922–30

Estimates	Britain	USA	Japan	France	Italy
1922			2 *Furutaka* (1922–26)		
1923			2 *Aoba* (1924–27)		2 *Trento* (1925–29)
1924	7 *Kent* (1924–28)		4 *Myoko* (1924–29)	2 *Duquesne* (1924–28)	
1925	4 *London* (1926–29)	2 *Pensacola* (1926–30)		*Suffren* (1926–30)	
1926	2 *Dorsetshire* (1927–30) *York* (1927–30)	3 *Northampton* (1928–31)		*Colbert* (1927–31)	
1927	*Exeter* (1928–31)	3 *Northampton* (1928–31)	4 *Takao* (1927–32)	*Foch* (1928–31)	
1928	(2 *Surrey*: cancelled)			*Dupleix* (1929–33)	2 *Zara* (1929–31)
1929		2 *Portland* (1930–33) 3 *New Orleans* (1930–34)			1 *Zara* (1930–32) *Bolzano* (1930–33)
1930		2 *New Orleans* (1931–34)		*Algérie* (1931–34)	1 *Zara* (1931–32)
Total	15 ships	15 ships	12 ships	7 ships	7 ships

Notes:
- Although counted as treaty cruisers because of their main armament of 8in guns, the basic design for the four ships of the *Furutaka* class was completed prior to the Washington Conference, and their designed displacement was only 7,500 tons.
- Construction dates are in brackets (first laid down – last completed). Most of these ships took around three years to build. Note, however, the relatively short building times being achieved by the Italians during the late 1920s and early 1930s.
- The ships authorised from around 1928 onwards were much more heavily armoured than the early types with the sole exception of the Italian *Bolzano* (intended to form a three-ship division with the two ships of the *Trento* class).

Some Conclusions

By the time the London Conference began on 22 January 1930 the British had completed eleven treaty cruisers, and had four more in advanced stages of completion; the Japanese had eight 8in cruisers in service with a further four building; the French had completed two and had four more under construction; the Italians were in a similar situation, with two ships completed, two building and a further two on order; and the Americans, who were late in starting their own treaty cruiser programmes, had only just completed their first, *Salt Lake City*, but had a further seven ships at an advanced stage of construction, a further five on order, with orders for ten more to follow within the next two years (see accompanying table). Apart from the British 'Counties' few of the treaty cruisers had been in service for more than a year. It would therefore be some time before the strengths and weaknesses of the designs would be fully known.

Having started with the same overall parameters, the five navies quickly settled into design and construction patterns which followed their natural inclinations and predilections. The British opted for a practical, well-balanced ship with modest speed performance and well-protected magazines. The Japanese wanted ships that would outperform the treaty cruisers of the other major powers in every respect, and was prepared to take political and technical risks in order to achieve this. The French, having resolved never again to go down the road of the *flotte d'échantillons* – 'patchwork fleet', a fleet comprising a succession of experimental 'one-off' types – proceeded to build a succession of cruisers all with incremental technical improvements – the two *Duquesne*s were the only uniform class! The Italians were innovative as always, but their lack of combat experience in open waters showed in the emphasis on theoretical platform performance under ideal conditions. The Americans, on the other hand, wanted ships which could operate and fight far from their home bases, and were keen to settle on an effective design which could be built quickly, in large numbers and at relatively low cost.

The trend for the later ships, as we have seen, was towards protection – at the expense of around 2 knots in speed. Whilst it proved impossible to provide complete immunity against 8in shell on 10,000 tons, protection against direct hits by 6in/155mm shell was within the designers' capabilities, and this became more important with the proliferation of fast, modern cruisers armed with guns of this calibre towards the end of the decade, and the prospect that the 6in-gun type would become the standard cruiser after the London Conference. For the first generation of treaty cruisers it proved possible to provide only modest protection for turrets, barbettes and turret trunks, but the US Navy's *New Orleans* class, the Italian *Zara*s and the French *Algérie* incorporated enhanced protection for the main battery.

The extent to which the considerable design effort directed towards providing increased thickness of armour in the later treaty cruisers ultimately proved worthwhile is questionable.[27] The night actions of Matapan and Savo Island notwithstanding, most of the treaty cruisers lost during the Second World War were sunk by bomb or torpedo, against which even thick side belts and armoured magazine boxes provided little protection.

CHAPTER 7

The Development of the Aircraft Carrier

The limitations on aircraft carrier size agreed at the Washington Conference were quite different in character from those established for capital ships in that the limits for capital ships were based on current and projected force levels, whereas the limits on the size and armament of individual aircraft carriers and on total tonnage were drawn up with a view to future developments. The only navy of the five taking part in the conference with aircraft carriers already in service was the Royal Navy, which had converted the incomplete liner *Conte Rosso* in 1917–18 as HMS *Argus*, and had fitted separate flying-off and landing-on decks to the light battlecruiser *Furious* in 1917–18.[1]

Argus was the world's first genuine aircraft carrier, having both a full-length flight deck and a capacious hangar served by two lifts. However, she was too slow to keep pace with the battle fleet, and could therefore be regarded only as a first step. *Furious* was faster, having a maximum speed of 31.5 knots, but her first conversion was a failure, and served only to convince the navy of the necessity for a flight deck extending from the forward part of the ship to the stern. In 1918 the Royal Navy therefore embarked on the construction of two new 'through-deck' carriers, one of which was the purpose-built *Hermes*, the other a conversion of the incomplete Chilean battleship *Almirante Cochrane*, which subsequently became HMS *Eagle*. *Hermes* (see also Chapter 2) was derived from the cruiser type; she had a hull of similar overall dimensions to the 'Elizabethans' with protection to match, and a speed of 25 knots. Following her launch in September 1919 construction was suspended pending trials with *Eagle*, which was building at the same shipyard (Armstrong on the Tyne). The latter vessel, being based on a battleship hull, was larger, slower and better protected. Trials of a proposed 'island' superstructure to starboard were conducted during 1920, when the ship was still incomplete, and *Eagle* was still under construction at Portsmouth when the Washington Conference convened. Neither ship would enter service for a further two years.

The Imperial Japanese Navy, with technical assistance from the Royal Navy, laid down the experimental carrier *Hosho* in 1919. She was slightly

Table 7.1: Aircraft Carriers in Service or Building in December 1921

	Argus (GB)	Hermes (GB)	Eagle (GB)	Hosho (Jap)	Langley (US)
Built:	conv. 1916–18	1918–24	conv. 1918–23	1919–22	conv. 1920–22
Displacement:	14,450tW	10,850tW	22,600tW	7,470tW	10,290tW
Dimensions:	566ft × 68ft (173m × 20.7m)	598ft × 70ft (182m × 21.4m)	668ft × 94ft (204m × 28.7m)	168m × 18m	542ft × 65ft (165m × 19.9m)
Machinery:	4-shaft geared turbines; 20,000shp = 20 knots	2-shaft geared turbines; 40,000shp = 25 knots	4-shaft geared turbines; 50,000shp = 22.5 knots	2-shaft geared turbines; 40,000shp = 25 knots	2-shaft turbo-electric; 6,500hp = 15.5 knots
Armament:	6–4in/45 HA (6 × I)	6–5.5in/50 (6 × I) 4–4in/45 HA (4 × I)	9–6in/45 (9 × I) 4–4in/45 HA (4 × I)	4–14cm/50 (4 × I) 2–8cm/40 HA (2 × I)	4–5in/51(4 × I)
Protection:	none	belt 3in, deck 1in	belt 4½in, deck 1½in	none	none
Aircraft:	20	15	21	15 (+6)	36

Note: *Langley*'s aircraft were carried broken down in the former holds, and were assembled just prior to launch.

A Fairey IIIF three-seat spotter-reconnaissance aircraft overflies HMS *Eagle*. The carrier is in China
Station colours, with a white hull and buff upperworks. *Eagle* was the only two-funnel carrier
completed for the Royal Navy; the 16,500-ton design which was never built would have had twin
funnels but no island. Note the sharply tapered flight deck at the bow, which was also a feature
of HMS *Hermes*. (Courtesy of David Hobbs)

smaller than *Hermes* with a narrow 168m flight deck, but was similar in
conception and had an identical speed of 25 knots and a capacity of fifteen
aircraft;[2] she would be completed in December 1922. The US Navy was
even farther behind, having begun the conversion of the collier *Jupiter*,
previously a trials ship for turbo-electric propulsion, only in 1920 (she
became USS *Langley*). Moreover, the conversion was probably the least
satisfactory of all; there was no hangar as such, the aircraft being stowed
broken down in the former coal holds of the ship, then lifted by crane for
assembly and transfer to the flight deck via a single large elevator. The flight
deck was built atop a light girder structure, and maximum speed was only
15.5 knots.

Technical and Tactical Issues

At the time of the Washington Conference naval aviation was in its infancy,
and there were many technical and tactical questions to be addressed; these
would exercise all three of the major navies throughout the 1920s and well
into the 1930s, while the French Marine Nationale was also a committed
participant in the early stages.

In tactical terms the major discussion centred on how (and where) aircraft carriers would be operated in relation to the fleet. The British initially envisaged that slower carriers carrying spotter aircraft, fighters and torpedo planes would accompany the battle fleet, while those carrying reconnaissance and fighter aircraft and attached to the battlecruiser/scouting force would operate in a more exposed position in the van. The Americans and the Japanese were primarily interested in reconnaissance for their respective fleets, so they also favoured operating their carriers in advanced (and exposed) positions.

The advanced scouting role raised two issues: tactical speed and anti-surface firepower. The aircraft carrier would ideally be faster than any accompanying heavy ships to facilitate the manoeuvres necessary for effective air operations;[3] and carriers operating in the van of the fleet would be vulnerable to enemy scouting cruisers, and would therefore need high tactical speed to extricate themselves from the danger area.

Similar considerations applied to the armament of aircraft carriers. The early British fleet carriers were armed with either 6in or 5.5in guns to enable them to defend themselves against enemy cruisers and destroyers; an armament of six to ten guns of this calibre was considered more than adequate to counter the fleet cruisers of the day. However, the advent of the treaty cruiser armed with 8in guns posed a new problem: aircraft carriers operating in the van of the fleet for scouting and reconnaissance would be a primary target for such ships. The treaty rules therefore had to include provision for arming these ships with 8in guns.[4]

The restriction on total tonnage to the equivalent of five carriers for the two major navies effectively killed off the concept of specialised carriers operating specialised aircraft – a concept which was a prominent feature of British postwar discussions 1919–20,[5] and ensured that carriers designed during the treaty period would be multi-purpose vessels intended to operate large numbers of aircraft (hence the double and even three-tier hangars favoured by the British and the Japanese). In the case of the British, whose Royal Naval Air Service was subsumed under the newly created Royal Air Force towards the end of the Great War, they also favoured the development of multi-purpose aircraft. Attempts were made during the 1920s to merge both the fighter/reconnaissance (F/R) and the spotter/reconnaissance (S/R) categories, and the latter was succeeded during the 1930s by the TSR (Fairey Swordfish), a three-seat aircraft designed for torpedo attack, spotting and (contested) reconnaissance. The Americans and the Japanese, on the other hand, kept the categories separate but preferred to delegate the 'spotting' function to their cruisers and battleships, which operated specialised two-seat floatplanes from trainable catapults. This enabled both the Pacific navies to base their carrier air groups around fighters, reconnaissance aircraft (later superseded by dive-bombers), and torpedo attack planes. It also had the effect of 'freeing' their carriers from the battle line in a way that was thought neither possible nor desirable in the Royal Navy, and it prepared the tactical ground for the carrier-on-carrier battles which would quickly become a feature of the Pacific War.

There remained serious issues to be resolved regarding the ideal configuration of the aircraft carrier. The pilots of the day all initially favoured a flush deck without superstructures of any kind. Aircraft of the period were lightly built, with relatively slow landing speeds, and were particularly vulnerable to air turbulence from protrusions above flight deck level. They were also affected by turbulence caused by hot funnel gases, and discharging these in a way that minimised their effect on air operations presented serious problems, particularly in ships designed for high speed.

The issue of funnels and superstructures was by no means easily resolved, in part because of technical difficulties but also because of disagreements between the 'ship' and 'aviation' communities, with the former insisting on a raised bridge from which the ship could be more effectively conned and signal flags flown, and on which fire control directors with all-round vision could be mounted. Although the aviation community initially favoured the flush deck it later became aware of the benefits of a raised platform for supervising deck movement and take-off/landing operations.

The British began with a flush deck in *Argus*, then considered both twin and single 'island' superstructures, opting for the latter in *Eagle* and *Hermes*, and subsequently reverted to a flush deck with a retractable bridge for the second reconstruction of *Furious*. *Courageous* and *Glorious*, on the other hand, would be rebuilt as 'funnel' carriers, with only a small bridge forward of a large single funnel, and this arrangement was repeated in the 1930s-built *Ark Royal*. Finally, the full island superstructure of the early *Hermes*, but with an elliptical funnel designed for optimum air flow, was reinstated for the armoured carriers of the late 1930s.

The US Navy went through similar phases. *Langley*, like HMS *Argus*, was flush-decked with a pair of hinged funnels which could be lowered during flight operations, but the converted *Lexington* and *Saratoga* would have a single massive funnel which took the exhaust gases well clear of the flight deck, with a separate bridge structure to starboard. There was then a reversion to a flush-deck configuration with hinged funnels for the purpose-built *Ranger*, followed by a further change of direction for the late-1930s carriers of the *Yorktown* class, which had their large vertical funnel incorporated in a full island superstructure.

The Japanese *Hosho* was completed with a small island-type bridge to starboard and hinged funnels, but in 1924 the bridge was removed and operations controlled from a platform beside the flight deck. Likewise the converted *Akagi* and *Kaga* were completed with a flush-deck configuration, the funnel gases being discharged via large side-mounted vents. Although a small bridge was reinstated in later carriers (and in *Akagi* and *Kaga* following their 1930s reconstruction), only four warbuilt IJN carriers – two of them mercantile conversions – were built with above-deck funnels, and these were canted outwards to keep funnel gases away from the flight deck.

There was broader agreement on the most suitable configuration for the flight deck, hangar and lifts, but even here there were important differences.

The painfully slow tempo of early air operations from carriers[6] led to divergent practices in launching and recovering aircraft. Both the British and the Japanese adopted multiple flying-off decks for their early post-Washington conversions, although the relatively short lower flying-off decks had to be abandoned in the 1930s as aircraft became larger and heavier and therefore required a longer take-off run. Lift size and configuration was often tailored to the aircraft of the period, with the British initially favouring 'aircraft-shaped' lifts and subsequently narrow rectangular lifts designed for biplane aircraft with folding wings.[7] The Americans and Japanese initially had lifts of different sizes to accommodate different aircraft, as did the French, but this was found to hinder flight operations, and during the 1930s there was a shift, particularly in the US Navy, towards broadly rectangular lifts of greater dimensions which could handle all current or projected future aircraft.

The position of the lifts was often a matter of intense discussion, as it affected the speed with which aircraft could be struck down in the hangar following landing on. This was a less significant issue for the US Navy, which operated large deck parks and tended to use the hangar primarily for maintenance, than for the British and the Japanese, who used hangars for both maintenance and stowage, and whose air complements were governed by hangar size.

In the period which followed the First World War the operation of wheeled aircraft from ships was still in its infancy, and the early British carriers and the USS *Langley* were all equipped to launch and recover seaplanes. Virtually all the postwar naval aircraft were designed with an alternative wheel or float undercarriage, which enabled them to be recovered by cruisers and battleships if necessary, as well as by the parent carrier. The early British carriers had hangars which were open at their after end so that seaplanes could be lifted aboard by heavy cranes located above a low quarterdeck, and this practice was copied by the French Marine Nationale.

The early longitudinal arrester wires developed by the British were primarily intended to prevent the lightweight wood-and-canvas aircraft being blown over the side as they landed on. However, as aircraft became heavier and faster the transverse arrester wire systems favoured by the French and US navies were increasingly adopted; these were intended to slow the aircraft to a halt using a relatively short length of deck. Aircraft parked at the forward end of the flight deck could then be protected by a 'crash barrier' in the form of a net strung across the deck, which provided back-up in the event of an aircraft failing to pick up the transverse cables with its 'tailhook'.

Trainable catapults were considered for the early British carriers to enable reconnaissance aircraft to be launched without the need for the ship to turn into the wind, and fixed athwartships catapults at hangar-deck level were adopted for the US Navy carriers built during the 1930s for similar reasons. The heavier aircraft developed during the late 1920s and the 1930s also needed to develop a higher speed at take-off – this required either a longer flight deck or power assistance. Carrier dimensions therefore became important not simply because of the size and balance of the air complement which might be accommodated, but from an operational point of view. Smaller carriers would need catapults (or 'accelerators' in British parlance) to launch these aircraft, while flight deck catapults aboard larger carriers effectively permitted a larger deck park aft.

Despite the concessions made to flight operations all three major navies placed considerable emphasis on 'ship' characteristics in the aircraft carriers built or converted during the 1920s. Even *Lexington* and *Saratoga*, in contrast to later US Navy carriers, had enclosed hangars, and in construction terms the flight deck was the 'strength' deck. This influenced other considerations such as the size of lifts, because large openings weakened the hull girder; aircraft lifts and their associated mechanisms were also heavy, and were located high in the ship, with implications for stability. With the carriers built during the 1930s the US Navy would move to open hangars served by three large lifts. However, for the British, lift size would continue to be influenced by structural and topweight considerations.

Royal Navy Carriers of the 1920s

At the time of the Washington Conference HMS *Argus* had been in service for three years; the battleship conversion *Eagle* was well on the way to completion,

Furious was the first of the three British light battlecruisers to undergo a full carrier conversion. Like her half-sisters *Courageous* and *Glorious* she had two superimposed aircraft hangars, the upper one exiting onto a short flying-off deck forward capable of launching fighters. However, she was given a completely flush upper flight deck, the funnel gases being led aft through large-diameter horizontal trunks and exhausting at the stern – see the blackened area around the flight deck aft. In this view from 1926–27, shortly after conversion, she retains the fore-and-aft retaining gear intended to prevent aircraft from being blown over the side. Note the 'humps' fore and aft, and the raised wind-breaks around the forward of the two Blackburn Blackburn spotter-reconnaissance aircraft. (Courtesy of David Hobbs)

An excellent close-up of the forward end of the flight deck, showing a Fairey Flycatcher fighter aircraft warming up behind the raised wind-break on the lower flying-off deck. The control position to starboard is for navigation; the one to port is for air operations. Just abaft this is the port-side fire control position, fitted with a director and two rangefinders – also a feature of the contemporary 16,500-ton carrier design.

and the purpose-built *Hermes* was also fitting out. It was 1923 before *Eagle* entered service and a further year before *Hermes*, whose construction had been suspended pending the initial trials with *Eagle*, was completed.

Both ships had a similar configuration: the flight deck was tapered at its forward end and carried right to the bow; the hangar was open at the stern, with heavy cranes provided to lift seaplanes aboard; there was a prominent but narrow island superstructure to starboard, with a single funnel in *Hermes* and a distinctive twin-funnel arrangement in *Eagle*; both ships had massive tripod masts with large foretops to provide director control for an anti-surface battery of six single 5.5in and nine 6in guns respectively; and there was an HA battery of four single 4in guns as in the Royal Navy's modernised battleships and treaty cruisers. As completed the larger *Eagle* could operate around twenty aircraft, including the large four-seat spotters projected, while *Hermes* had an air complement of fifteen to twenty single- and two-seat aircraft.

A second major conversion for the ex-light battlecruiser *Furious* had been approved in July 1920, and the final design submitted to the board in October 1921. She was not taken in hand for conversion until some months after the conference ended, and was then in dockyard hands for more than three years. The reconstruction of *Furious* saw her emerge as a totally different type of ship. It had been accepted at a comparatively early stage of her redesign that the ideal carrier would have a completely flush deck, like *Argus*. However *Furious*, which as a light battlecruiser had been designed for a speed of 31.5 knots, produced six times the volume of funnel gases. The novel solution proposed (and in the event adopted) was for the uptake trunking to be led through large horizontal vents down both sides of the ship beneath flight deck level, with the hot exhaust gases being discharged over the stern.

In order to compensate for the reduced width of the hangar, a second (lower) hangar was provided beneath the first. In theory one of the two lifts would serve the upper hangar, where the heavier aircraft would be stowed, and the other the lower hangar, which would be home to the smaller fighters. Initially the lower hangar was to have had a clear height of only 13ft, but this was later increased to 15ft to secure greater flexibility in aircraft stowage, the height of the upper hangar being reduced from 17ft to 15ft to compensate.[8] The upper hangar deck was extended forward to the bow in the form of a 'flying-off deck', while the upper flight deck above it was rounded off at its forward end to improve airflow. It was envisaged that the heavier spotters and torpedo planes would be launched from the upper flight deck, while the fighters would be launched from the 130ft flying-off deck below. At the forward end of the upper flight deck there were two parallel control positions: one to starboard for navigation, and one to port for air control. These two positions were connected beneath the flight deck and between them, on the centre-line, there was a retractable charthouse.

The double-hangar arrangement made possible a designed complement of ten spotters, fifteen torpedo planes and twenty fighters.[9] This was equivalent to the air complements of *Eagle* and *Hermes* combined, so the double hangar became an attractive proposition in a post-Washington Royal Navy which needed to embark the maximum number of aircraft on a limited number of carriers. However, the horizontal funnel vents were not a success. The spaces around them became so hot at anything approaching full power that they became uninhabitable, and smoke hung low around the after end of the ship, particularly when the expeller fans were in use. Early trials with *Furious* served to confirm the move to a large conventional funnel in *Glorious* and *Courageous*, whose reconstruction had already begun.

It had been decided even before the Washington Conference that a second 'light battlecruiser' would undergo conversion to an aircraft carrier, and *Glorious* was duly selected in July 1921, with her conversion to duplicate that of *Furious*. The Washington Treaty led the Navy to reconsider this programme. The ten-year 'battleship holiday' agreed at the conference would in theory release funding for carriers – either new-build or conversions of existing ships – and there was now a 135,000-ton treaty allocation to be built up to. Even if both of the light battlecruisers were to be converted, there would still be

Furious (GB)

Profile

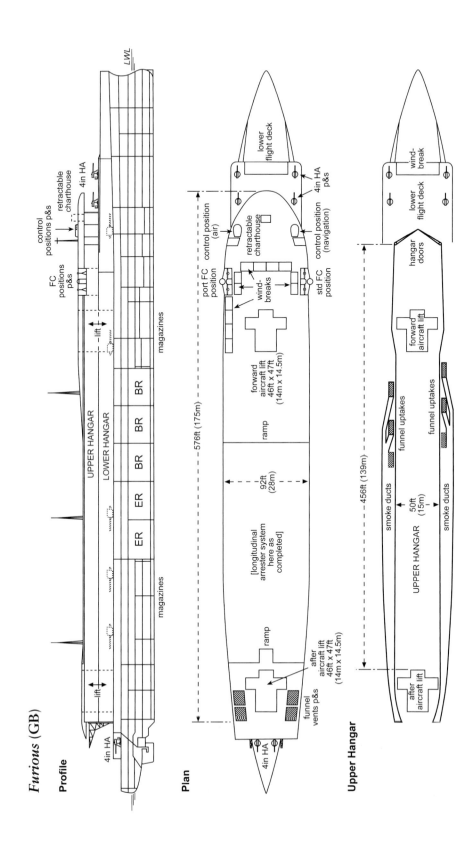

control positions p&s

retractable charthouse

4in HA

FC positions p&s

UPPER HANGAR

LOWER HANGAR

| ER | ER | BR | BR | BR |

magazines

lift

magazines

lift

4in HA

LWL

Plan

lower flight deck

4in HA p&s

port FC position

control position (air)

retractable charthouse

control position (navigation)

std FC position

wind-breaks

forward aircraft lift 46ft x 47ft (14m x 14.5m)

ramp

92ft (28m)

576ft (175m)

[longitudinal arrester system here as completed]

ramp

after aircraft lift 46ft x 47ft (14m x 14.5m)

funnel vents p&s

4in HA

Upper Hangar

lower flight deck

wind-break

hangar doors

forward aircraft lift

funnel uptakes

smoke ducts

funnel uptakes

UPPER HANGAR

50ft (15m)

smoke ducts

456ft (139m)

after aircraft lift

Lower Hangar

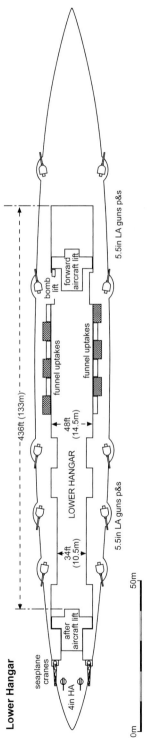

0m

50m

seaplane cranes

4in HA

after aircraft lift

5.5in LA guns p&s

34ft (10.5m)

LOWER HANGAR

funnel uptakes

funnel uptakes

48ft (14.5m)

bomb lift

forward aircraft lift

5.5in LA guns p&s

436ft (133m)

Formerly one of three 'light battlecruisers', *Furious* underwent a partial conversion in 1917, with separate flying-off and flying-on decks, and was taken in hand shortly after the Washington Conference for conversion to a fully fledged aircraft carrier. In contrast to *Hermes* and *Eagle* she had a completely flush deck, the ship being conned from twin positions on either side of the upper flight deck forward with a retractable charthouse between. There were two hangars and two flight decks, the lower flight deck being used as a take-off deck for fighters.

The exhaust gases from the machinery were vented over the stern via horizontal trunking which extended for 375ft (115m) on either side of the hangar (see Upper Hangar drawing), an arrangement which influenced the conversion of the IJN carrier *Kaga*. Although it occupied space which could otherwise have been used for workshops and accommodation, it was the impact of the low-angle armament of 5.5in guns on the dimensions of the lower hangar which reduced the number of aircraft that could be accommodated.

20,500 tons remaining. This could be used either to convert two large light cruisers of the 'Elizabethan' class, or to build new carriers, which would take advantage of this tonnage plus the additional 14,000 tons which could be made available by scrapping *Argus*. The larger carriers could also be complemented by ships below 10,000 tons, which were not subject to treaty restrictions.

The decision to convert both *Glorious* and *Courageous* was quickly taken; it was clear that both the United States and Japan would use their own tonnage allocation under the treaty to complete two of the large, fast battlecruisers each had on the stocks as aircraft carriers. The IJN ships would each displace 27,000 tons (total 54,000 tons) and their US Navy counterparts 33,000 tons (total 66,000 tons), so at 67,500 tons total displacement the three smaller British ships only just matched them. At the same time it was decided to undertake studies for new-build ships, and in 1923 the controller asked the director of naval construction to draw up proposals for carriers of 10,000 tons (Scheme A), 16,500 tons (Scheme B) and 25,000 tons (Scheme C).

Scheme A was a cruiser-sized carrier based loosely on *Hermes*, but with a flush deck for flying-on and a catapult for launch. With a maximum speed of only 24 knots, it would have been used for trade protection duties in the North Sea, the Mediterranean and, in the event of a war in the Far East, in the Formosa Straits. Although not subject to treaty limitations, such a carrier would have been a luxury in the prevailing financial climate, however, so the design

16,500-ton Carrier Design 1923 (GB)

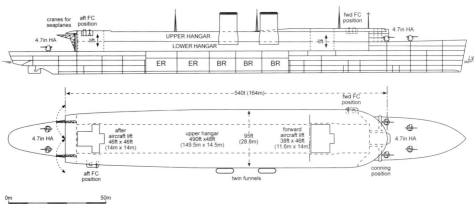

The sketch designs for the proposed new-build 16,500-ton carrier show a composite ship bringing together all the various strands of Royal Navy thinking of the period: the two superimposed hangars; the open ends of the ship, on which six 4.7in HA guns were to be mounted; and the open after end of the hangar, with a low quarterdeck served by cranes for seaplane operations. The configuration of the forward lift and the twin funnels are reminiscent of HMS *Eagle*, but the ship would have been a 'funnel carrier' without an island superstructure, the ship controls being beneath the forward end of the flight deck as in *Furious*, with fire control positions for the HA guns *en echelon* to port and to starboard. The hump in the flight deck forward was also a feature of the light battlecruiser conversions, and was intended to bring aircraft to a halt after landing – there was no transverse arrestor gear.

was shelved to be reconsidered at a later date as a possible 'mobilisation' type.

The 'fleet' carriers of Schemes B and C were designed for high speed and maximum aircraft capacity. On 16,500 tons it was found possible to combine a maximum speed of 34.5 knots and a double hangar with an aircraft capacity not far short of *Furious*, the horizontal exhaust trunking being replaced by two vertical side-mounted funnels to starboard. Armament was limited to an HA battery of six single 4.7in guns. The 25,000 tons design benefited from superior protection and had an anti-cruiser armament of six 8in guns in twin mountings, but the latter impinged on hangar space to such an extent that the air complement was only slightly larger than that of *Furious*. With aircraft capacity and overall tonnage both at a premium it was decided that the 16,500-ton scheme showed more promise, and in November 1923 it was authorised by the Board of Admiralty, with a view to building four new ships to replace *Argus*, *Eagle* and *Hermes* (the latter pair had yet to be completed!) and use up the remaining Washington tonnage allocation.[10] Despite a change of government in January 1924, work on the design proceeded until October, when it was recognised that the future size of aircraft would mean a larger ship, probably of 19,000–20,000 tons. Although originally included in the 1925–26 programme, the first of the new carriers was subsequently deferred, first to 1929 and then, with a deteriorating economic situation, to 1932. It was eventually ordered to a completely new design in 1934, becoming *Ark Royal*.

Table 7.2: British Fleet Carriers 1922–30

	Furious	Type B (1924)	*Courageous*
Built:	conv. 1922–25	(not built)	conv. 1924–30
Displacement:	22,450tW	16,500tW	22,500tW
Dimensions:	786ft × 90ft	765ft × 80ft	787ft × 91ft
	(240m × 27.5m)	(233m × 24m)	(240m × 27.5m)
Machinery:	4-shaft geared turbines;	4-shaft geared turbines;	4-shaft geared turbines;
	90,000shp = 30 knots	120,000shp = 34.5 knots	90,000shp = 30 knots
Armament:	10–5.5in/50 (10 × I)	6–4.7in/40 HA (6 × I)	16–4.7in/40 HA (16 × I)
	6–4in/45 HA (6 × I)		
Protection:	belt 3in, deck 1in	belt 2in, deck 1in	belt 3in, deck 1in
Aircraft:	36	32	52

Glorious *and* Courageous

The reconstruction of *Glorious* and *Courageous* was approved in 1922. Initially they were to have been rebuilt on the lines of *Furious*, but the armament issue was reopened to consider whether they should be armed with 8in guns as permitted by the treaty. Various alternative armaments were proposed, which included 8in guns in two twin turrets, 6in guns in twin or single mountings, and 5.5in guns as in *Furious*. Nothing less than an 8in gun was thought to be worthwhile, given that modern cruisers would be armed with this weapon, but it was found that 8in guns could not be mounted in sufficient numbers without seriously encroaching on hangar space. After much discussion it was finally decided in March 1924 that the ships would have no anti-surface guns whatsoever, featuring instead a large battery of eighteen single 4.7in HA guns, four of which would eventually be replaced by the multiple 2-pdr pom-pom mounting then under development.[11] The 4.7in gun used cased ammunition – a great advantage in a lightly armoured ship – and there was a four-corner fire control system. The 4.7in/40-calibre QF Mk VIII was also in theory an effective anti-destroyer weapon; however, it seems to have been accepted that the carriers would now have to rely on accompanying cruisers and their own high speed for protection against enemy treaty cruisers. With hindsight the decision seems remarkably prescient: carriers designed from the early 1930s onwards had only anti-aircraft batteries, and the 8in power-operated turrets incorporated in the IJN and US Navy post-Washington battlecruiser conversions at such great cost had all been removed by the early stages of the Pacific War (earlier in the case of the Japanese ships). However, at the time the Admiralty's decision did not meet with universal acceptance, and was regarded by some as a 'second-best' option which increased the ships' vulnerability to other surface units.[12]

The carrier *Courageous* at Malta in 1929. Note the open after end of the lower hangar and the aircraft handling cranes stowed against the after wall of the upper hangar. All the early British carriers were designed to operate seaplanes, lowering the aircraft for launch from the low quarterdeck. When seaplane operations were abandoned in the 1930s the quarterdeck was raised one deck. The palisades ranged along the flight deck amidships were to prevent aircraft being blown over the side on landing. (Leo van Ginderen collection)

Courageous (GB)

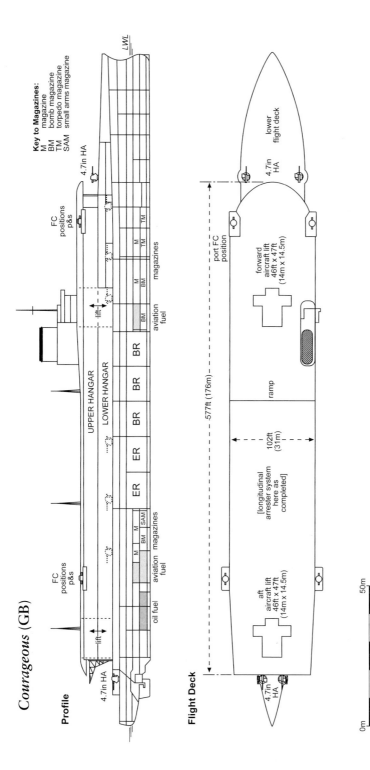

Profile

Key to Magazines:
M   magazine
BM bomb magazine
TM torpedo magazine
SAM small arms magazine

4.7in HA

FC positions p&s

magazines

| M | M | SAM |
| BM | | |

aviation magazines
fuel

M		M		M
	BM		TM	
				TM

aviation fuel

oil fuel

LWL

UPPER HANGAR
LOWER HANGAR

| ER | ER | BR | BR | BR |

lift

4.7in HA

FC positions p&s

Flight Deck

lower flight deck

4.7in HA

forward aircraft lift
46ft x 47ft
(14m x 14.5m)

port FC position

ramp

← 102ft (31m) →

[longitudinal arrester system here as completed]

← 577ft (176m) →

aft aircraft lift
46ft x 47ft
(14m x 14.5m)

4.7in HA

0m   50m

The other two 'light battlecruisers', *Courageous* and *Glorious*, were completed to a different design to their near-sister *Furious*. They retained the double hangar and the lower flying-off deck forward, but abandoned the horizontal funnel vents in favour of a large vertical funnel to starboard with an integral bridge. This, together with the abandonment of anti-cruiser guns in favour of a large HA battery, enabled them to carry more aircraft: fifty-two instead of thirty-six.

The decision to abandon the flush deck of *Furious* in favour of a short island incorporating a large single funnel was equally controversial. The Air Council (the RAF equivalent of the Board of Admiralty) was opposed to it, and there were those on the Naval Staff who pointed out that should the island be a failure, the navy would not be permitted to modify the ships under the provisions of the Washington Treaty. However, weight savings from suppressing the longitudinal ducts and their associated expeller fans amounted to almost 200 tons, and the increase in hangar volume and workshop space made possible a 25–30 per cent increase in the size of the air complement. Other improvements included raising the height of the hangars from 15ft to 16ft (to allow for future aircraft developments), and a significant increase in bomb and aviation fuel stowage. A catapult for launching reconnaissance and ASW aircraft in harbour was also considered, but experience with *Furious* suggested this was unnecessary, and after lengthy and detailed studies to determine the best location for the catapult the idea was abandoned.

Glorious and *Courageous* were taken in hand for conversion during 1924. *Courageous* re-entered service in mid-1928, but work on *Glorious* was delayed and she was completed only in early 1930.[13] The flight deck configuration was broadly similar to that of *Furious*, with a short flying-off deck forward at upper hangar deck level and two cruciform lifts. The air complement initially specified comprised: three flights of fleet spotter or reconnaissance aircraft, two flights of torpedo attack aircraft, and four flights of fleet fighters. Each flight was of six aircraft except for one flight of fighters being four aircraft, giving a total of fifty-two aircraft.

Lexington *and* Saratoga

In the United States, postwar studies for aircraft carriers had begun in earnest in 1920, when the Preliminary Studies Bureau was asked to work out cost estimates for carriers displacing 10,000 tons, 20,000 tons and 30,000 tons with speeds of 25 knots or 31–35 knots. The disparity in speed reflected British thinking of the period: the 25-knot carriers were intended to work with the battle fleet, while the faster ships would accompany the new battlecruisers in the scouting force. The lower-end 10,000-ton type would be based on the scout cruisers of the *Omaha* class, and would have been comparable to the British *Hermes*. However, the studies seemed to favour the larger type, which could accommodate an air group of seventy-two aircraft and a useful battery of both anti-surface and anti-aircraft guns.

In establishing requirements for the air group a clear distinction was made between aircraft fully assembled (i.e. ready for launch), partially assembled (i.e. with wings folded) and disassembled (carried broken down as reserve aircraft). The characteristics of November 1920 (for a carrier to be authorised in FY1922) called for twenty-four torpedo aircraft (of which sixteen would be fully assembled) and forty-eight fighters (sixteen fully assembled), with stowage for reserve aircraft equivalent to 50 per cent of the air group. This philosophy was to be reflected in the deep girders beneath the flight deck on all US carriers – the broken-down aircraft being stowed between them. It would also influence the shape of the aircraft lifts on the 1920s carriers: a large 'T'-shaped lift at the forward end of the hangar for fully deployed aircraft, complemented by a smaller rectangular lift aft or amidships for aircraft with folded wings.

Ideally the carrier needed to be fast enough to outrun all opposition. However, as an insurance policy the General Board initially wanted a large anti-surface battery of sixteen 6in guns disposed in two groups with director control on either side of the ship. It also wanted eight 5in/25-calibre HA guns to provide barrage fire against enemy bombers, with a minimum of four guns able to fire on any bearing. However, it was quickly pointed out that it would be impossible to accommodate this number of guns without unacceptable interference with air operations.

By early 1921 studies for the large carrier were being based on the battlecruiser design, and displacement had increased to 35,000 tons. The turbo-electric propulsion machinery, which could deliver 180,000shp for a speed of 33–34 knots, was so large that it was impossible to provide an effective anti-torpedo protection system beyond the internal compartmentation. The other major issue was the disposal of funnel gases. Initially it was proposed that these be vented through the side of the ship as in *Furious*, which would have been disastrous as the US battlecruisers produced twice the volume of gases. In the event a broad slim funnel to starboard was adopted, with a separate bridge structure forward, atop which the fire control installations were mounted.

Although 80ft wide in the initial design, the hangar occupied only the after part of the ship, the decks beneath the flight deck forward being given over to accommodation. Beneath the after end of the hangar was a hold for disassembled aircraft. The carrier was expected to provide maintenance facilities for battleship and cruiser floatplanes, so there was a low-power electrical flywheel catapult forward to enable these to be launched without the need for the carrier to turn into the wind.

As had been predicted, it proved impossible to accommodate the large anti-surface battery the board wanted. However, there were six 6in guns in the twin power-operated turrets adopted for the *Omaha*s: one on the flight deck forward of the bridge, and the other two located on either side of the flight deck aft. There were also to be six 21in fixed torpedo tubes, mounted on the upper deck close to the stern. The HA battery was increased to twelve single 5in guns, disposed in groups of three to cover the four corners of the ship. Displacement was by now 39,000 tons normal, and the ship was so close to the dimensions of the battlecruisers that it was suggested that it would be far cheaper to adapt existing hulls already on the stocks.

In July 1921 the General Board determined the navy's requirements as three fleet carriers, to be built as a matter of priority. During the same month the United States sent out invitations to attend the Washington Conference, so the navy thought it wise to initiate a study for the conversion of the *Lexington*-class battlecruisers, which might well be primary candidates for cancellation under any new arms limitation treaty. The study established that the battlecruiser conversion would have superior anti-torpedo protection and larger magazines. However, it would have narrower lines aft, so that hangar capacity would be reduced by some 16 per cent. The ship would also be slightly heavier at 40,000 tons normal (roughly equivalent to 36,000 tons at the new Washington 'standard' displacement). This was of some concern once it was decided to propose a 35,000-ton limit on capital ships in advance of the conference, but the only real possibility for weight-saving lay in a reduction in the size of the propulsion plant, and this was deemed unacceptable given the premium accorded to high speed for the new carriers.

As the limit on converted capital ships agreed at Washington was 33,000 tons, the US Navy seized on the extra provision for the modernisation of capital ships against the underwater and aerial threat (deck armour, AA guns and bulges up to a maximum of 3,000 tons) to justify the 36,000-ton displacement of *Lexington* and *Saratoga*. This was certainly contrary to the spirit of the treaty, as the relevant clause was intended to provide for the reconstruction of capital ships completed prior to the Washington Conference, not of capital ships reconstructed as carriers after the signing of the treaty (for which the 33,000-ton exception had been specifically made). Nevertheless, the US Navy felt that the wording of the treaty was sufficiently imprecise as to justify its position; the new carriers were officially to be declared to displace 33,000 tons with a footnote stating: 'does not include weight allowance under Ch. II pt.3 Sec.1 art.(d) of Washington Treaty for providing means of defense against air and submarine attack'. Moreover, in the interests of legality, this additional weight was itemised and even subdivided under the 'air' and 'submarine' defence categories.

The sketch design was submitted in April 1922. In the wake of the Washington Conference it had been decided that the ships would need to accommodate an anti-cruiser armament of eight 8in guns in twin mountings. If these had been located at hangar deck level fore and aft – both the British and the Japanese opted to mount guns at the bow and the stern of their capital ship conversions – a full-length flight deck would have been out of the question; and had they been mounted to the sides of the flight deck like the twin 6in mountings in the early design, the width of the flight deck and hangar would have been reduced to only 60ft (trials with *Langley* had indicated that 84ft was a minimum requirement). It was therefore decided to mount the guns on the flight deck to starboard, with the forward pair of turrets forward of the bridge, and the after pair abaft the large funnel. This impinged to a certain extent on flight deck operations, and undoubtedly increased air turbulence over the deck for planes landing on, but it was by far the most practical solution. The major downside was the even greater

The carrier *Lexington* early in her career, with a full deck-load of aircraft. With their huge flight decks and relatively small hangars, *Lexington* and her sister *Saratoga* operated permanent deck parks. The disparity between the number of aircraft operated by British and American carriers was so great that the Royal Navy refused to believe the reported figures. Note the powerful battery of 8in guns in twin turrets fore and aft of the island and the flywheel catapult to starboard.

Langley, converted from a US Navy collier, was never intended to be more than an experimental carrier. She had a continuous flight deck but no hangar, the aircraft being broken down in holds and assembled on the former upper deck before being raised for take-off using the single large central lift. During the mid-1920s, under the direction of Captain (later Rear-Admiral) Joseph M Reeves, *Langley* was used to develop the key operational procedures which would make possible the 'pulsed' air strikes, using a full deck-load of aircraft, favoured by the US Navy. (Leo van Ginderen collection)

Lexington (US)

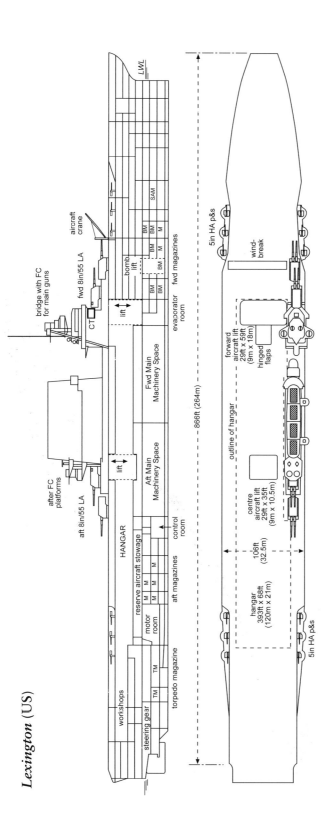

bridge with FC for main guns

aircraft crane

after FC platforms

fwd 8in/55 LA

aft 8in/55 LA

bomb lift

lift

SAM

BM
BM M
BM M
BM
BM M
BM

HANGAR

reserve aircraft stowage

M M
M M M
M M

control room

motor room

aft magazines

Fwd Main Machinery Space

Aft Main Machinery Space

evaporator room

fwd magazines

CT

lift

torpedo magazine

TM
TM

workshops

steering gear

LWL

866ft (264m)

outline of hangar

forward aircraft lift 29ft x 59ft (9m x 18m)

wind-break

hinged flaps

centre aircraft lift 29ft x 35ft (9m x 10.5m)

hangar 393ft x 68ft (120m x 21m)

106ft (32.5m)

5in HA p&s

5in HA p&s

0m

50m

Lexington and *Saratoga* were by some margin the largest (and heaviest) aircraft carriers built during the interwar period. The power of their turbo-electric machinery (twice that of the British light battlecruiser conversions) necessitated the adoption of a massive funnel to starboard which relied on its height to keep the hot funnel gases clear of the flight deck. A separate bridge structure incorporating ship and fire control facilities was mounted forward of the funnel, and

the eight 8in anti-cruiser guns permitted by the treaty were also mounted in twin turrets fore and aft on the starboard side of the flight deck. Despite their 890ft (270m) flight decks there was only a single, relatively short internal hangar, and there were only two aircraft lifts, of which the after one was relatively small. This impelled the US Navy towards operating with large deck parks.

concentration of weight on the starboard side of the ship, which had to be compensated by permanent ballast to port.

In addition to the 8in battery there were twelve 5in/25-calibre HA guns, disposed in groups of three to cover the four 'corners' of the ship. The initial plans also showed four single above-water torpedo tubes, which were not fitted on completion. Even on 36,000 tons the design was now very tight, and some weight savings were made by reducing the height of the 5–7in armour belt. An electrically powered flywheel catapult was fitted to starboard, but it was no longer useful once the carriers moved away from the battle line in the early 1930s, and was removed during 1934.

Work on *Lexington* and *Saratoga* proceeded very slowly; Congress proved reluctant to release the necessary funds and costs escalated. Doubts were expressed not only about whether the ships represented good value for money, but also about whether this was the best use of the limited tonnage available for the construction of aircraft carriers (66,000 tons was nearly half the US Navy's allocation under the Washington Treaty). The relatively small internal hangar attracted particular criticism. However, the combination of a small hangar, a large flight deck and a large air complement (seventy-two aircraft as in the FY1922 Characteristics), served to promote operational doctrine which increasingly diverged from British (and Japanese) practice. Flight deck stowage was transformed into a virtue, and paved the way for larger aerial strike groups and faster flight deck cycles. Instead of the laborious procedure of striking down aircraft in the hangar as they landed on, US Navy carriers parked them at the forward end of the flight deck, and then wheeled them aft to be refuelled and rearmed ready for the next strike.

Table 7.3: The US Navy and IJN Battlecruiser Conversions

	Lexington (US)	*Akagi* (Jap)	*Kaga* (Jap)
Built:	1920–27	1920–27	1920–28
Displacement:	33,000tW	26,900tW	26,900tW
Dimensions:	888ft × 105ft	261m × 29m	239m × 30m
	(271m × 32.1m)		
Machinery:	4-shaft turbo-electric;	4-shaft geared turbines;	4-shaft geared turbines;
	180,000shp = 33 knots	131,000shp = 31 knots	91,000shp = 28 knots
Armament:	8–8in/55 (4 × II)	10–20cm/50 (2 × II, 6 × I)	10–20cm/50 (2 × II, 6 × I)
	12–5in/25 HA (12 × I)	12–12cm/45 HA (6 × II)	12–12cm/45 HA (6 × II)
Protection:	belt 7in, deck 1¼in	belt 150mm, deck 60mm	belt 150mm, deck 40mm
Aircraft:	90	60	60

Note: The displacement recorded for the *Lexington* is the official declared displacement. In fact both these ships were completed to a displacement of 36,000tW, of which 3,000 tons was declared to be for anti-submarine and anti-aircraft protection.

The hangar was used only for additional stowage and for maintenance. The size of the air group was determined by flight deck area, not by hangar capacity as in the British and Japanese navies: US carriers, as they developed, therefore operated larger air groups, and they learned to operate them more efficiently.[14]

Early criticism of *Lexington* and *Saratoga* was answered during Fleet Problem IX of 1929, when *Saratoga* showed the value of her large flight deck by launching a multi-plane strike against the Panama Canal.[15] Operational techniques developed during the mid-1920s with *Langley* meant that the seventy-plane strike was launched in only eighteen minutes, with recovery taking fifty minutes – a remarkable achievement for the period.

The IJN's Akagi *and* Kaga

Under the terms of the Washington Treaty Japan was permitted a total of 81,000 tons of aircraft carriers. As one of the two signatories with over-sized capital ships already under construction, she also had the option of rebuilding two of these hulls up to a maximum individual displacement of 33,000 tons.

As we have seen, there were some in the US Navy who questioned the wisdom of investing such a large proportion of their 135,000-ton carrier allocation in two 33,000-ton ships. However, even the conversion of *Lexington* and *Saratoga* would still leave 69,000 tons, which could be used in a number of ways; the IJN did not have the same flexibility. If its own capital ship conversions displaced 33,000 tons, the 81,000 tonnage allocation would permit the future construction of only a single small carrier of 15,000 tons. However, if displacement could be kept to 27,000 tons, there would be sufficient tonnage available for a further new-build carrier of 27,000 tons – the maximum permitted by the treaty – or two carriers of 13,500 tons.

The two hulls initially selected for conversion were the battlecruisers *Amagi* and *Akagi*, which had been laid down in December 1920 at the Yokosuka and Kure naval dockyards respectively, and were close to launch when work on them was formally suspended in February 1922 at the conclusion of the Washington Conference. The battlecruisers were selected in preference to the fast battleships *Tosa* and *Kaga*, which had been launched in November–December 1921, primarily because of their superior speed. The final decisions on their conversion were not taken until the treaty was ratified in mid-August 1923, and only two weeks later the IJN's plans were thrown into disarray by the Tokyo earthquake, which caused substantial damage to the Yokosuka yard. The hull of *Amagi* was severely strained and her reconstruction had to be abandoned. In her place the IJN selected the incomplete battleship *Kaga* for conversion.[16]

This decision created problems for the Japanese constructors, as the *Kaga* was some 20m shorter than *Akagi*. She also had less powerful propulsion machinery, being designed as a fast battleship rather than a battlecruiser. New plans had to be drafted for her conversion, and her reconstruction was

Akagi (Jap)

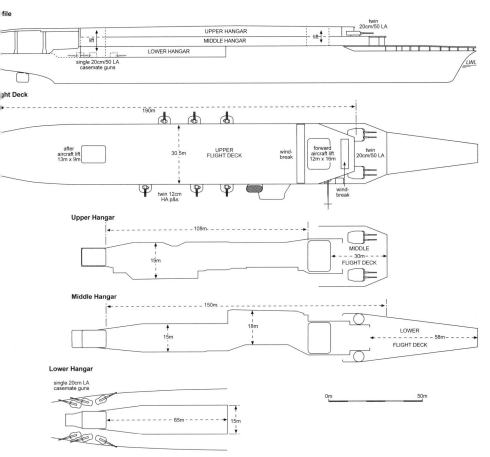

The two conversions of capital ship hulls on which the IJN embarked after Washington bore a much closer resemblance to those of the British former 'light battlecruisers' than to the US Navy's *Lexington* and *Saratoga*. *Akagi* and *Kaga* as converted featured the multiple-hangar, multiple-flight-deck layout of the British ships, adding a third 'flying-off' deck and a third, shorter hangar aft. The twin trainable 20cm turrets forward impacted adversely on flying operations, and were removed during a major reconstruction in the 1930s which saw both ships emerge with a single, full-length flight deck and a small island for ship and fire control.

subsequently delayed by the damage sustained at the Yokosuka yard, which would be responsible for rebuilding the ship.

The close contacts with the Royal Navy maintained up to the time of the Washington Conference are evidenced by the similarities between the two Japanese carriers and HMS *Furious*, whose second reconstruction had been authorised in July 1920, the final design being submitted for approval in October 1921. These similarities are apparent in: the overall flush-deck configuration with 'open' bow and stern, the ship control spaces being

Akagi on her full-power trial on 17 June 1927. Note the huge volumes of smoke produced by the former battlecruiser. After extensive model trials the IJN opted for a large downward-facing vent with a smaller vertical funnel abaft it. (Fukui Shizuo collection)

located directly beneath the forward end of the flight deck; the adoption of separate flying-off decks in addition to the main landing-on deck; the double hangar with the lifts at either end; the British-style longitudinal arrester gear; and the horizontal funnel trunking adopted for *Kaga*.

However, *Akagi* and *Kaga* as reconstructed were by no means carbon copies of *Furious*; the Japanese showed their customary talent for adaptation and innovation. In place of the single lower 'flying-off' deck of the British light battlecruiser conversions there were two: a short, 17/23m deck which extended forward from the upper hangar, and from which small fighter aircraft could be taken off; and a more substantial lower flying-off deck some 58m in length extending from the forward end of the lower hangar to the bow, from which heavy bombers and torpedo planes could be launched. Beneath the two main hangars there was a third, shorter hangar for disassembled aircraft, which was served by the after lift.[17]

The other major departure from the British conversions was that in the wake of Washington the IJN, like the US Navy, considered it essential that these major surface units, operating in the van of the fleet, would need to protect themselves against treaty cruisers. A further motivation for keeping displacement within the 27,000-ton figure was therefore to enable the ships to accommodate the maximum permitted battery of ten 8in/20cm guns. Fitting these in without major interference with air operations was to prove a major challenge. In the event it was decided to mount twin turrets on either side of the short upper flying-off deck forward, the remaining six guns being mounted singly in casemates aft. The casemates were at the original main deck level, and were therefore very close to the waterline and of questionable value in combat. Nevertheless, the importance accorded to these anti-surface weapons by the IJN is evidenced by the fact that when *Kaga* was modernised during the mid-1930s and her multiple flying-off decks replaced by a single full-length flight deck, the 20cm guns formerly mounted in the twin turrets

This well-known aerial view of *Kaga* as first completed shows to advantage the multiple flying-off decks forward with the two twin 20cm mountings at upper hangar level. As in *Akagi* there was a large aircraft lift forward serving the upper two hangars, and a smaller lift serving all three hangars aft. The aircraft lined up on the lower flying-off deck forward are A1N (Type 3) fighters; those on the upper flight deck are B1M (Type 13) torpedo bombers. (Fukui Shizuo collection)

A close-up of *Kaga*'s stern during fitting out, showing the massive exhaust trunking alongside the upper hangar. Note the three starboard 20cm guns in casemates aft, and the sponsons for the twin 12.7cm HA guns. (Fukui Shizuo collection)

were relocated to new casemates forward of the original six so that the battery remained at ten.

The high-angle anti-aircraft armament comprised six twin 12cm/45-calibre guns, and these were mounted on sponsons just below the level of the flight deck amidships; there were no torpedo tubes. Although much has been made of the differences between *Akagi* and *Kaga* as first completed, the extent of these differences, particularly with regard to aviation facilities, has been overstated. Both ships were designed to operate sixty aircraft, and hangar volume was virtually identical. Although the hull of *Kaga* was some 20m shorter and the main hangar structure began at about the same point at its forward end, its after end was some 20m closer to the stern than in *Akagi*. The upper hangars did not extend to the ships' sides, and appear to have been unaffected by the funnel uptake arrangements, having a width of 15–18m in both ships. *Kaga*, which was commissioned two years later than her half-sister due to the damage sustained by the Yokosuka yard, had a slightly longer upper flying-off deck, and the length of the forward lift was increased by one metre to take account of larger aircraft. *Akagi* had an upper flight deck of 190m which was given a slight incline fore and aft, whereas *Kaga*'s flight deck was 170m and flat (the width of the flight deck was identical – approximately 30m in both ships).

The major difference between the two ships was in the disposal of funnel gases. For *Kaga*, which had virtually the same power output as the British light battlecruisers (91,000shp), the IJN adopted the same solution as for *Furious*: long horizontal funnel trunking on both sides of the ship which vented the hot gases downwards close to the stern. This had precisely the same adverse effects as the British experienced with *Furious*: it disturbed the air flow over the deck for aircraft landing on, and it made the accommodation for NCOs and deck officers virtually uninhabitable because of the high temperatures in the after section of the ship. The conspicuous failure of this arrangement was largely responsible for the early modernisation of *Kaga*, which took place within five years of her entry into service.

Had the same solution been adopted for *Akagi* it would have been an even greater disaster, as installed horsepower (131,000shp) was almost 50 per cent greater than *Kaga*. However, the IJN opted for the novel solution of a large downward-facing exhaust vent amidships to starboard, complemented by a smaller uptake at its after end. Such was the concern that the mouth of the larger vent might be submerged in the event of action damage that there were removable plates in the upper part to provide emergency venting of the exhausts. The larger vent also incorporated a cooling system which used seawater to reduce the temperature of the exhaust gases.[18] The downward-facing vents proved relatively successful, and were repeated in later IJN carrier designs.

Although both *Akagi* and *Kaga* were officially declared to displace 26,900 tons standard, as had been intended when their reconstruction was authorised, the customary combination of late additions and modifications ensured that displacement was closer to 30,000 tons by the time they entered service with the Japanese fleet. Had the IJN possessed the same degree of legal acumen as the US Navy, it could have used a similar subterfuge to justify the overweight, and claimed the 3,000-ton weight allowance permitted under Chapter II of the Washington Treaty to provide defence against air and submarine attack in capital ship conversions. However, by this time the Japanese were already making breaches of Washington Treaty limits something of a habit (the *Myoko* class cruisers had already run their trials); later Japanese carrier designs would likewise have an official 'declared' displacement well below the actual figure.

The French Béarn

The Marine Nationale had shown an early interest in naval aviation, and before the First World War had set up a commission which recommended taking wheeled torpedo bombers to sea, carried by a vessel with fore and aft decks (essentially similar to HMS *Furious* as first converted in 1917). The old cruiser *Foudre* was duly converted, receiving a hangar and crane in 1911–12 and a short flying-off deck in 1913–14, and was subsequently used for trials with a variety of seaplanes. These trials were effectively cut short by the outbreak of war, and from the end of 1914 *Foudre* would serve as a repair ship for the French Mediterranean Squadron, the hangar being converted into workshops. However, the concept of the *transport d'hydravions* (seaplane carrier) was by now established in French tactical thinking.

The French Fleet Air Arm (Aviation d'Escadre) was created on 1 October 1918, just over a month before the Armistice, with a view to reviving this early interest and matching developments on the other side of the Channel. The postwar Marine Nationale vacillated between a 'mobile base' for seaplanes and an aircraft carrier able to operate with the fleet. It was eventually to pursue both options.

Contacts between the Marine Nationale and the Royal Navy were close in the immediate aftermath of the war, and a French commission visited HMS *Argus* to observe aircraft handling and flying operations in 1920. Out of this visit came a proposal for the conversion of one of the incomplete battleships of the *Normandie* class. This was duly incorporated in a new building programme designated Project 171, which also proposed the abandonment of the battleship in favour of the construction of fast light cruisers and flotilla craft. The conversion was initially to have been based on *Argus*, and staff requirements included:

- embarkation of the maximum number of land-based aircraft, and the ability to operate seaplanes in harbour;
- a continuous wooden flight deck at least 150m long, with maximum possible width and no obstructions;

- a hangar connected to the flight deck by two lifts, of which the larger should be 20m by 12m;
- an access bay 20m wide for seaplanes at the after end of the hangar.

The hull of *Béarn*, which had been launched without ceremony to clear the slipway on 15 April 1920 and was complete up to the lower armoured deck, was selected for trials. Initial modifications involved a wooden platform 43m by 9m with an access ramp constructed directly on top of the lower armoured deck. The improvised arrester system used for the trials was based on transverse cables raised on circular pieces of cork and weighted with bags of sand. Successful take-offs and landings at Toulon during late 1920 led to initial studies by the STCN for a full conversion. However, there was still some hesitation about whether it would be better to complete the ship as a battleship or a carrier, and no final decision was made.

The Washington Conference then intervened. According to its provisions France was allocated 60,000 tons of carrier construction. The Marine Nationale therefore decided to proceed with the proposed conversion of *Béarn,* and this decision was formalised in the 1922 naval programme. The converted battleship was nevertheless regarded essentially as an experimental design, the intention being to complete two purpose-built 30,000-ton 'aircraft-carrying cruisers' (*croiseurs porte-avions*) at a later date. This latter project was subsequently accorded low priority, since Germany was not permitted to build carriers and Italy considered them unnecessary for operations in the confined waters of the Mediterranean. In a period of financial stringency money spent on these ships would reduce the number of conventional cruisers, flotilla craft and submarines which could be built, and it was only during the 1930s that the Marine Nationale would again contemplate the construction of fast, purpose-built carriers of new design.

The French commission which had visited HMS *Argus* in 1920 had also been shown around the incomplete *Eagle*. Given that the latter ship was based on a super-dreadnought battleship hull of similar vintage and similar dimensions to the *Normandie* class, it is unsurprising that, as completed, *Béarn* resembled *Eagle* more closely than *Argus*. She had an armoured hull with a similar level of protection; the flight deck was tapered at the bow and angled downwards at the stern; there was an island with a single broad funnel; and there was a powerful anti-surface battery of eight single 155mm (6.1in) guns in casemates, disposed at the four 'corners' of the ship and complemented by 75mm HA guns and single 37mm light AA weapons mounted on sponsons beneath the flight deck.

There were some important differences between *Béarn* and *Eagle*, however. *Béarn* had a double hangar served by three electrically powered lifts, of which the after lift was by some margin the largest and the forward lift the smallest. The size of the lifts reflected aircraft stowage in the hangar: the height of the upper hangar at its forward end was significantly reduced by a gallery deck

Béarn (Fr)

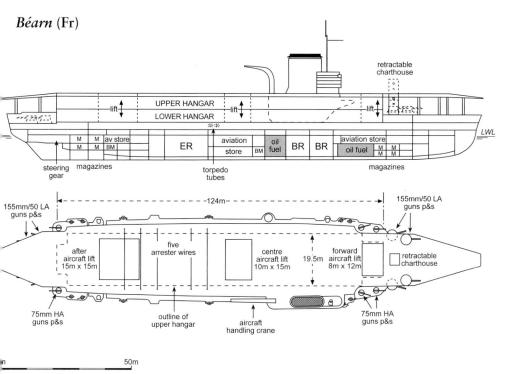

The French carrier *Béarn* was formerly a super-dreadnought battleship of the *Normandie* class whose construction had been suspended during the First World War. The resulting conversion was similar to that of the British *Eagle*, but with two hangars, the lower of which was constructed atop the original main deck. Aviation facilities were generally well designed, and there were some interesting innovations such as athwartships arrester wires with hydraulic braking and air cooling for the funnel gases.

directly beneath the flight deck which provided accommodation for the flight crew, so the smaller fighters were stowed at this end of the hangar deck, while the larger torpedo bombers and reconnaissance aircraft were stowed at the after end. As in the British carriers steel fire curtains divided both hangars into separate areas.

The double hangar was clearly influenced by the British light battlecruiser conversions, and 'cross-pollination' between the two navies was also apparent in the configuration of the short island superstructure, which closely resembled that of *Courageous* and *Glorious*, and in the retractable charthouse, which was a feature of *Furious*. One significant innovation by the French was a special vented chamber at the base of the funnel which admitted cold air to be mixed with the hot funnel gases; it was anticipated that this would reduce air turbulence over the after end of the flight deck.

The air complement was closely influenced by British practice, as were air operations. The designed air group comprised a twelve-plane squadron of reconnaissance aircraft, a twelve-plane squadron of torpedo attack aircraft, and an eight-plane squadron of fighters. Aircraft could be taken off in

Béarn during the early 1930s. Taking off from the flight deck is a Levasseur PL.7, one of a series of large (4,000kg) three-seater aircraft intended to perform in the scouting, spotting and torpedo attack roles. Note the battery of 155mm LA guns in casemates and the prominent *cul de lampe* ('lamp base') beneath the island which provided air cooling for the hot funnel gases before they were discharged over the flight deck. (Courtesy of Robert Dumas)

squadron-sized groups from the after end of the flight deck, but were landed individually and struck down immediately on landing (a process which, as in the Royal Navy, took around six/seven minutes per aircraft). When the centre and after lifts were lowered the openings were closed by heavy hinged doors to permit continued flight operations, while the forward lift had three levels; this was a complex solution which slowed the operation of the lifts – the after lift had an operating cycle of five minutes, the other two three minutes.

The flight deck itself was of African teak 70mm thick on a base of 28mm steel. The Marine Nationale was in the vanguard when it came to developing an effective arrester system using transverse cables and drums with hydraulic braking mechanisms. Prototypes were installed from 1928, and a workable operational system from Schneider was subsequently installed in 1932.

Béarn ran trials from 1 September 1926, and entered service with the fleet in May 1928. Although on a par with the carriers in service with other navies when first completed, she quickly became obsolescent, in part because of the extent to which her aviation facilities were too specifically tailored to the aircraft and naval air operations of the day, but principally because she was simply too slow to accompany a modern battle fleet. Her dated propulsion machinery, which incorporated triple-expansion engines on the outer shafts and Parsons direct-drive turbines on the inner shafts,[19] produced a maximum of 21.5 knots on trials – 2 knots slower than her British counterpart *Eagle*. This did not give her an adequate margin over even the elderly French dreadnoughts with which she operated during the 1920s and early 1930s. Once France started building fast battleships capable of 30 knots during the 1930s it was clear that *Béarn* would have to be superseded by new, more capable carriers operating high-performance aircraft.

Table 7.4: French Aircraft Carriers of the 1920s

	Béarn (Fr)	*Commandant Teste* (Fr)
Built:	conv. 1922–25	1927–32
Displacement:	22,150tW	10,000tW
Dimensions:	181m × 27.7m	167m × 27m
Machinery:	4-shaft VTE/turbines;	2-shaft geared turbines;
	40,000hp = 21 knots	23,230shp = 21 knots
Armament:	8–155mm/50 (8 × I)	12–100mm (12 × I) HA
	6–75mm HA (6 × I)	8–37mm (8 × I)
	4–550mm TT (4 × I)	
Protection:	belt 83mm, deck 28mm	mach: 50mm sides
		mags: 50mm sides, 20mm deck
Aircraft:	32	24 seaplanes and floatplanes

The 'Mobile Aviation Base'

With the decision to complete the hull of the battleship *Béarn* as an aircraft carrier, attention turned to that other strand of French naval aviation thinking, the *centre mobile*, or mobile aviation base. Although the Marine Nationale would have preferred a second fleet carrier with similar missions to those defined for *Béarn*, it was accepted that in the absence of a suitable hull for conversion this would be an expensive solution. The Naval General Staff was therefore prepared to accept a *transport d'aviation*, which would be cheaper to build and could be completed more quickly. Such a ship could serve as a mobile base for seaplane squadrons deployed overseas, and in wartime would have an auxiliary function, serving as a repair and replenishment vessel to support other warships equipped with aircraft.

Initial requirements were for a ship equipped with two catapults capable of launching a 2,500kg aircraft (such a catapult was already under development for the new 10,000-ton cruisers), an air complement of nine scout seaplanes and six float fighters, a speed of 17 knots, and an armament of four single 75mm HA guns. It was thought that an ocean liner might prove suitable for conversion. However, this solution implied a displacement above 10,000 tons, which would then have to be counted as part of the 60,000-ton allowance allocated to France by the terms of the Washington Treaty. Other possibilities were therefore considered, including:

- the conversion of a freighter (judged too slow);
- the conversion of an elderly armoured cruiser;
- a purpose-built ship with a speed of 18–20 knots and nine seaplanes.

The purpose-built option was preferred, and in September 1924 the Naval Staff proposed that two such ships should feature in the new *Statut Naval*, and that the STCN should begin technical studies. In November of the same year the design team came up with a draft proposal for a 16-knot ship able to accommodate twelve 2,400kg scout seaplanes. The armament was to be four 138.6mm guns in casemates and four 75mm HA guns. Operational radius was a mere 2,000nm – i.e. sufficient for transit to the French colonies in North Africa and the Middle East. The ship would have a dual role as a mobile seaplane base, providing repair and maintenance facilities together with accommodation for the crews, and as a seaplane transport for a specific attack mission. The first unit was duly included in the 1925 Estimates but construction was delayed, and the *Commandant Teste* was not laid down until September 1927.

Commandant Teste (Fr)

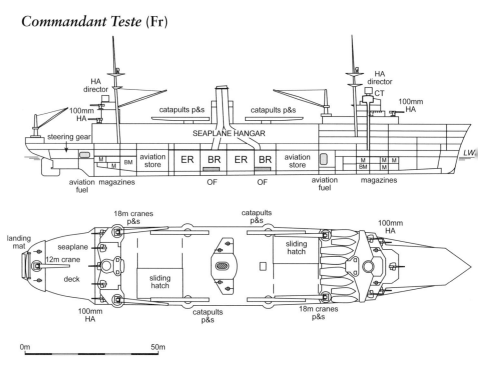

A cheaper (but less flexible) alternative to the fleet carrier was the *transport d'aviation*, a mobile base which could launch and maintain a variety of seaplanes from sheltered anchorages. The *Commandant Teste* had a large double hangar, divided by the funnel uptakes, which could accommodate heavy (five-tonne) torpedo bombers, reconnaissance aircraft and float fighters. The fighters and reconnaissance aircraft were lifted through large sliding hatches onto the upper deck by one of four twelve-tonne cranes ready for catapult launch, while the torpedo bombers were wheeled out on twin rail tracks onto the low quarterdeck and lowered into the water. A Hein mat, comprising a rectangle of ribbed canvas 12m long by 8m wide, was fitted during the 1930s to enable the aircraft to be recovered over the stern with the ship underway, but was unsuccessful and had to be abandoned.

Designed as a cheap alternative to the fleet carrier, *Commandant Teste* was effectively a mobile seaplane base. The twin seaplane hangars and the canvas landing mat (in stowed position) are prominent in this stern view. Note the powerful HA armament and the heavy cranes for lifting the seaplanes and floatplanes aboard. (Jean Moulin collection)

Numerous changes were made as the design evolved. It was by now envisaged that the air complement would comprise: ten huge Farman Goliath torpedo bombers, of which eight would be housed in the hangar and two would be carried broken down in crates in the hold; and twelve fighter/reconnaissance floatplanes, of which four would be readied on the catapults, four would be in the hangar, and four in crates in the hold. When employed as a transport, the ship would carry twelve Goliath, twelve reconnaissance floatplanes, and thirty-six aero engines. By the time the project was passed to the Naval Staff for approval in March 1926, speed had been increased to 20 knots by the adoption of superheated boilers and lightweight turbines, and a uniform armament of 100mm/45-calibre dual-purpose guns, backed up by single 37mm AA guns, had replaced the original mix of anti-surface and HA weapons.

The massive box hangar, located atop a conventional but unarmoured 'cruiser'-type hull measured 80m by 26.5m, was three decks (7m) high, and was divided into two by a longitudinal partition which incorporated the exhaust uptakes for the funnel and the ventilation trunking for the machinery rooms. The aircraft were lifted by one of four large twelve-tonne cranes onto the upper deck via two large sliding hatches in the roof of the hangar. The reconnaissance aircraft were launched by one of the four catapults, which were powered by compressed air. The larger torpedo planes were generally wheeled out for assembly onto the short quarterdeck and lowered into the water for launch by the seven-tonne stern crane.

It was felt that the *transport d'aviation* as a type had certain advantages over the *Béarn*: it could operate large, long-range torpedo bombers; by keeping displacement to 10,000 tons it escaped the Washington Treaty constraints; and cost was relatively low. On the other hand there were clear limitations in the ways in which the ship could be employed. Operations in adverse weather conditions were impossible (they were in any case marginal with fleet carriers, given the aircraft and the technology of the day) and the ship could not operate at sea with the battle fleet due to her lack of stability.

uss **Ranger**

Even as the plans for the conversion of *Lexington* and *Saratoga* were proceeding, the US General Board was setting in motion studies for new purpose-built carriers. Following the completion of the converted battlecruisers there would be 69,000 tons available for new construction[20] and the board was anxious to have the maximum possible number of effective aircraft at sea. The figure of 69,000 tons suggested the following options: three carriers of 23,000 tons, four of 17,250 tons or five of 13,800 tons, and studies were undertaken of all of these types together with a study for a carrier of 27,000 tons, the maximum permitted under Washington. At the same time extensive trials were conducted aboard *Langley* with a view to determining the best configuration for the new ship.

The era of close co-operation with the Royal Navy had ended soon after the First World War, so although the US Navy was aware of the broad thrust of British carrier developments post-Washington, it did not have the benefit of the first-hand experience acquired during trials with *Argus*, *Eagle* and *Hermes*. Early experience with *Langley* resulted in a strong preference for a flush deck, although the usual concerns were expressed regarding the disposal of funnel gases, particularly after the extent of the problems with HMS *Furious* was reported in late 1925 by the assistant naval attaché in London. A consensus on armament also proved difficult to arrive at; early sketches showed 8in turrets, while as late as 1926 an armament of four twin 6in turrets was a feature of even the smaller designs. Anti-surface weapons would finally be abandoned in favour of a purely anti-aircraft battery of twelve 5in/25-calibre HA guns, backed by heavy machine guns for use against dive-bombers.

The perceived vulnerability of the carriers, which could not be armoured on anything like the same scale as *Lexington* and *Saratoga*, and whose flight decks would now be exposed to the new aerial tactic of dive-bombing,

Ranger (US)

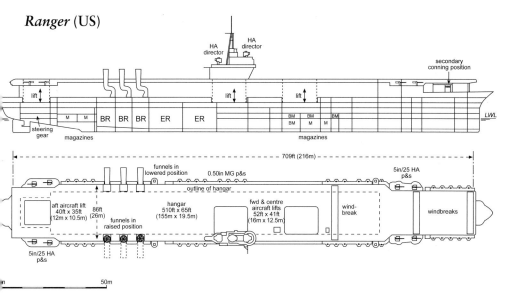

In contrast to the US Navy's two large battlecruiser conversions, *Ranger* was designed from the keel up to provide the optimum 'aviation' characteristics on the minimum displacement. As originally designed she had a completely flush deck, with six hinged funnels aft which were lowered during air operations, although a small bridge structure with ship and fire control facilities was added while she was building. Her single hangar had 25 per cent greater floor area than that of *Lexington*, the width of the flight deck was maximised by giving the relatively small hull an unusual degree of flare, and there were three large rectangular lifts. *Ranger* introduced the concept of the 'open hangar' to the US Navy, and there were originally to have been cross-deck catapults at hangar-deck level fore and aft of the first lift, to enable single reconnaissance aircraft or fighters to be launched without impacting on the deck park and without the ship having to turn into the wind.

appears to have been a major factor in the decision to built five small ships rather than three or four larger ones. It was estimated that five carriers of 13,000 tons would have 15–20 per cent greater flight deck area than three carriers of 23,000 tons, and at only 20 per cent greater cost. Moreover, the loss of a single carrier would have a smaller impact on overall force levels. Carrier vulnerability meant that the major emphasis would be on the ability to launch the largest possible deck-load of aircraft at the earliest possible opportunity, with a view to taking out enemy carriers before the latter had the opportunity to strike back. *Ranger* and her projected sisters were envisaged as being 'one-shot' ships which would in all probability not survive the initial round – the 'air superiority' phase – of the decisive battle.

The other major issue concerned speed. The fleet favoured a 32.5-knot carrier which could keep pace with its cruiser escort when operating in the long-range scouting role. However, the large steam propulsion plant required for 32.5 knots was found to reduce aircraft capacity by 25 per cent as compared with a relatively slow ship of 29 knots. Halving the installed horsepower reduced the volume of exhaust gases by the same amount, thereby facilitating

Ranger was the first US Navy carrier to be designed from the keel up. She had a spacious 'open' hangar, together with three large lifts for the rapid transfer of aircraft between hangar and flight deck. Note the full flight deck load of aircraft in this 1939 view, taken in Hampton Roads. (Leo van Ginderen collection)

the flush deck favoured by the 'aviators'. Characteristics for the new ship were duly submitted in 1927, and the first of the new carriers was included in the FY1929–33 five-year programme, with funding to be authorised in FY1929.

USS *Ranger*, although ultimately not a successful design, was arguably the first carrier in the world to be designed with a primary focus on air operations, with ship characteristics coming second by a substantial margin, and she incorporated a number of influential new features. There was a capacious single open hangar with provision for cross-deck catapults, and a 'gallery' around the flight deck to facilitate the mounting of large numbers of light machine guns, and which also provided access points for fire and refuelling hoses. The hangar was longer and almost as wide as that of the much-larger *Lexington*s (510ft by 65ft vs. 393ft by 68ft), and supported a broad rectangular flight deck whose width was maximised by adopting unusually flared sides to the hull. There were three large lifts of rectangular configuration, of which two were at the forward end of the hangar. In addition to *Ranger*'s air complement

Table 7.5: The US Navy and IJN Carrier Designs of the Late 1920s

	Ranger (US)	*Ryujo* (Jap)
Built:	1931–34	1929–33
Displacement:	13,800tW (designed)	7,600tW (designed)
Dimensions:	769ft × 110ft	180m × 20.3m
	(234m × 33.4m)	
Machinery:	2-shaft geared turbines;	2-shaft geared turbines;
	53,500shp = 29 knots	65,000shp = 29 knots
Armament:	8–5in/25 HA (8 × I)	12–12.7cm/40 HA (6 × II)
Protection:	none	none
Aircraft:	72	36

of seventy-two aircraft, there was stowage for no fewer than forty assembled fuselages between the deep girders which supported the flight deck, and wings for these aircraft were stowed in a special compartment at hangar-deck level for ease of access. A two-level 'ready room' for the air crews was provided on the starboard side of the hangar, and this was complemented by a large space dedicated to aviation intelligence and equipped with an air plot.

Ironically, in view of the sacrifices made to provide a flush deck, an island superstructure housing the ship and air control spaces was provided at a relatively late stage while the ship was under construction – the primary justification for which was the impossibility of providing effective fire control below flight deck level. However, the six hinged funnels of the original design were retained, three on either side of the flight deck aft. The island had to be counterbalanced by permanent ballast to port, which effectively increased displacement.

Ranger was laid down only in late 1931, and by the time she was completed in 1934 other modifications had been made to the original design. The hangar-deck catapults were suppressed to save money, and torpedo stowage was also eliminated,[21] so that *Ranger* operated an extra squadron of scouts in place of the torpedo bombers of other US carriers. Her low speed, lack of underwater protection, and her inability to conduct air operations comfortably in the broad Pacific swells led to her relegation to second-line duties during the early stages of the Second World War, and she was subsequently employed as a training carrier. Nevertheless *Ranger* blazed a trail for later, more successful US carrier designs such as the *Yorktown* and *Essex* classes.

The Japanese Ryujo

Pending a decision on how to use its remaining 27,200-ton Washington allocation the IJN was keen to investigate the feasibility of aircraft carriers below 10,000 tons, which thereby avoided treaty limits. Japan's first carrier, *Hosho*, weighed in at only 9,500 tons normal (hence around 8,000 tons standard), and although she had her limitations in terms of tactical speed and aircraft capacity, it was felt that an effective ship displacing less than 10,000 tons was by no means impossible to achieve.

The initial design for a new carrier to be built under the 1927 programme was for a ship of 8,000 tons standard with a cruiser-type hull some 12m longer than *Hosho* but with a substantially broader flight deck. The propulsion plant was half that of a treaty cruiser, and produced 65,000shp on two shafts for a maximum speed of 29 knots. There was no armour protection for the hull, but there was a powerful HA battery of twelve guns in twin mountings. When the ship was designed these were almost certainly to have been the 12cm/45-calibre model fitted in *Akagi* and *Kaga* and contemporary treaty cruisers, but the 12cm/45-calibre was replaced at a relatively late stage in the design by the new and more capable (but heavier) 12.7cm/40-calibre.

As first designed *Ryujo* had a single hangar, served, as in *Akagi* and *Kaga*, by a large lift (for bomber and torpedo planes) forward and a much smaller

Ryujo (Jap)

Conjectural View of Original Design with Single Hangar

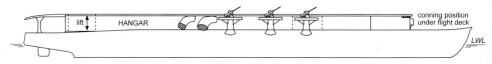

***Ryujo* as Completed**

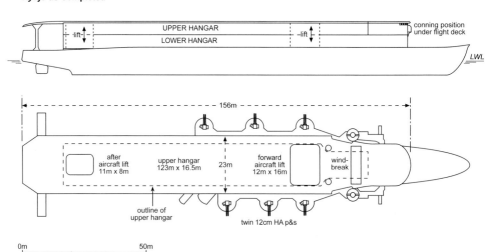

Ryujo was an attempt to build a viable aircraft carrier under 10,000 tons, and might have been more successful had the original single-hangar design been adopted. However, the incorporation of a second hangar above the first increased overall displacement and topweight to such an extent that the ship's stability was seriously affected, and major modifications had to be made during the mid-1930s. The long-term lesson learned from *Ryujo* was that a carrier of this size was not a realistic proposition for fleet work.

lift for fighters aft. This would have given her an air complement of eighteen to twenty-four aircraft. However, following the London Treaty, under which *Ryujo* would have to be included in Japan's overall carrier allocation, the Naval General Staff wanted this figure increased, and pressured the constructors into incorporating a second hangar above the first, for a theoretical maximum of forty-eight aircraft. The adverse consequences of the redesign were wholly predictable. Not only did the new hangar structure increase overall displacement but the additional weight was high in the ship, and the topweight problem was further exacerbated by the need to raise the AA guns, their supporting sponsons, and the funnel trunking and exhausts to match the increased freeboard.

Despite the pressure to maximise the air complement, there was a corresponding pressure to keep weight to a minimum in order to maximise the

Ryujo was an attempt by the IJN to design an effective aircraft carrier displacing less than 10,000 tons, and which would therefore not be counted against its carrier tonnage allocation under Washington. Note the low bow, the height of which was increased in a later reconstruction. The ship was conned from a position beneath the forward end of the flight deck. (Fukui Shizuo collection)

tonnage remaining for new carrier construction. Weight-saving measures such as welding were beginning to be adopted by the Japanese naval yards, and the standard displacement of *Ryujo* as completed was only 8,130 tons, although the implications for seaworthiness and stability were serious. Shortly after her completion in 1933, *Ryujo* had to be taken in hand for major modifications, which included hull strengthening, permanent keel ballast, the removal of two twin 12.7cm mountings, and the addition of bulges to compensate for the increase in weight – standard displacement was subsequently 10,600 tons. Even so the low bow shipped large quantities of water during the Great Storm off Honshu in 1935, and was raised one deck level the following year.

The failure of *Ryujo* ensured that there would be no repeat design. However, it was already becoming apparent during the early 1930s, when the ship was still under construction, that she was too small to operate the latest aircraft. By 1940 the after aircraft lift could handle only the Nakajima B5N 'Kate' torpedo bomber, which had fully folding wings; even the relatively small 'Zero' fighter could use only the forward lift. Moreover, the flight deck was too small to accommodate an effective deck-load of aircraft and was very lively, making air operations in adverse weather conditions extremely hazardous. *Ryujo*'s natural successors, *Soryu* and *Hiryu*, would be larger, more capable ships.

Italy the 'Unsinkable Aircraft Carrier'

Of the five major naval powers Italy was the only country not to build an aircraft carrier during the interwar period. It is not easy to untangle the conflicting accounts of the debates which resulted in this decision. The memoirs of Italian admirals who served during the period (published since the Second World War) are unreliable: loss of memory and 'revisionism' are common, with numerous attempts to blame the opposition of Mussolini and the Regia Aeronautica (established in 1923 to take responsibility for all aircraft, and comparable to the British RAF) for the navy's failure to develop a carrier force. However, any study of the strategic arguments and policy statements of the period leads inevitably to the conclusion that, regardless of 'political' pressures, the Regia Marina itself was never sufficiently convinced of the need for carriers and preferred to spend its limited funding on battleships and cruisers.

During the First World War Italy, like the other major world navies, had experimented with seaplane carriers and floatplanes launched from warships. However, an admirals' 'think tank' set up postwar to consider the future shape of the navy reported in 1921 that it saw no need for aircraft carriers given Italy's geostrategic position astride the Mediterranean, and that the navy's aviation requirements could best be served by aircraft flying from mainland bases, from Italian islands in the Western Mediterranean and the Dodecanese, and from North Africa.

There was no serious proposal to convert the hull of the super-dreadnought battleship *Francesco Caracciolo*, which was launched in May 1920, only to be sold in October of the same year to a shipping company which subsequently decided to have her broken up. And although from time to time the carrier

Bonfiglietti Carrier Design 1928 (It)

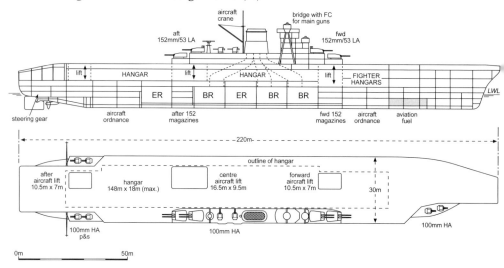

In the face of determined opposition from the Italian Air Force, the Regia Marina undertook a number of carrier studies during the interwar period. The most developed of these was a design put forward by General Genio Navale (Naval Constructors Corps) Filippo Bonfiglietti in 1928. With an air complement of forty, the carrier would have had the following characteristics: length 220m, beam 30m, and standard displacement 15,240 tonnes. Two-shaft lightweight machinery similar to that of the cruisers of the 'Condottieri' type would have delivered 70,000shp for a top speed of 29 knots. Despite an agreement made in December 1927 that a carrier for the navy would be deferred for economic reasons but not cancelled – it was to be rescheduled for the 1931–32 Estimates – the Italian Air Force finally secured the cancellation of the project, having objected to the positioning of the main guns and the appointment of a non-aviator as captain of the ship.

question was debated, there was never sufficient support from within the navy for any proposal to get off the ground. 'Paper' designs included the Rota hybrid 12,500-ton carrier/cruiser design of 1925, which in conception anticipated the US Navy's flying-deck cruiser of 1930–31 (see Chapter 11), and the more conventional Bonfiglietti design (see accompanying drawing), which in many respects prefigured the French and German carrier designs of the mid-1930s. These efforts ultimately came to nothing, however, leaving the Regia Marina without any direct experience of carrier air operations when war was declared on France and Britain in 1940.

Conclusion

The Washington Treaty gave an undoubted impetus to the development of the aircraft carrier as a first-line naval unit. It was the only warship category other than the capital ship to have its characteristics clearly defined. However, in contrast to the capital ship, not only could the aircraft carrier continue to be built, but the overall tonnage allocation for the latter was effectively a blank page, to be divided up according to the preferences of the contracting powers. Moreover, the halt called on the construction of large numbers of capital ships that had been laid down in the two years prior to the Washington Conference, many of which were designed for high speed, meant that there was no shortage of suitable candidates for conversion.

This first post-Washington generation of carriers did not enter service until 1928–30, and subsequently conducted air operations which were still essentially experimental, using metal-and-canvas biplane aircraft which were only one stage on from their wartime predecessors. The first purpose-built carriers, the Japanese *Ryujo* and the US Navy's *Ranger*, were laid down only at the end of the decade and would not enter service until 1933–34. Both would prove to be too small to be satisfactory ships, but they marked an important step in the development of more effective classes of carrier built for the IJN and the US Navy during the next decade.

Of the five contracting powers, only the Royal Navy came close to taking up its carrier tonnage allocation by 1930, with almost 115,000 tons in service out of a permitted 135,000 tons. The corresponding figure for the US Navy was 76,300 tons (including the converted collier *Langley*); the Japanese had 53,800 tons out of 81,000 tons in service, the French only 22,150 tons out of 60,000 tons, while the Italians had no carriers in service or even projected. The US Navy and the IJN were actively pursuing smaller designs, while British thinking was moving towards a fast carrier of moderate displacement (effectively a purpose-built version of *Glorious* and *Courageous*); the latter, however, was subject to on-going delays due to a crisis in funding. As for the French, an increasing focus on Mediterranean operations centred around a new generation of fast cruisers and flotilla craft meant that the Marine Nationale lost interest in the aircraft carrier around this time, and its tactical thinking became virtually a mirror-image of that of its most likely opponent in this theatre, the Italian Regia Marina.

CHAPTER 8

Esploratori, Contre-Torpilleurs, 'Condottieri'

The French Vice-Admiral Raoul Castex, in his influential book *Théories Stratégiques*, observed: '... it is certain that light, fast units, with a moderate radius of action, will find better employment there [in the Mediterranean] than in other theatres, given the short distances to negotiate and the proximity of numerous bases; it is the ideal operational area for the flotillas ...'[1]

Although large flotilla leaders (*conducteurs de flotilles*) patterned on British models were considered by the French in the aftermath of the Great War (see Chapter 2), the six *contre-torpilleurs* ordered under the 1922 naval programme were intended not to lead the destroyer flotillas, but to operate rather in the manner of the British fleet cruisers of the First World War: in support of the fleet, with tactical scouting and screening and anti-destroyer work as their primary missions.[2] Subsidiary missions included the defence of French maritime communications (by intervention rather than escort) and high-speed strikes against enemy communications. When completed these ships were organised tactically to fight in divisions of three ships apiece.

The Mediterranean was the primary operational theatre for which the *contre-torpilleurs* were designed. The emphasis was on speed and hitting power; endurance and staying power were less important. Since the cruiser as a type was traditionally associated with range and endurance, it is unsurprising that the French should have opted for a large, fast destroyer with powerful guns and long-range torpedoes for employment in the confined waters of the Western Mediterranean, where the ships would never be operating far from their operational bases in North Africa or metropolitan France.

Although in theory a division of *contre-torpilleurs* could comfortably deal with an isolated fleet cruiser, the most likely opponents of these ships, at least during the 1920s, were the Italian *esploratori leggeri* (light scouts). The latest type, the *Leone* class, had originally been ordered in 1917, but their construction had been delayed by a lack of steel and other materials. Three ships out of the five were duly re-ordered in 1920, and these were laid down during 1921–22. The *Leone*s were large destroyer-type ships with a normal

The *esploratori leggeri* of the *Leone* class had been ordered in 1917, but their construction had been delayed for lack of steel. Their design influenced the French *Jaguars*, which they almost equalled in displacement. Armed with eight 120mm guns in twin mountings and two triple banks of 450mm torpedo tubes, they were capable of 34 knots when first completed. This is *Tigre* in 1925. (Leo van Ginderen collection)

displacement of 2,195 tons, a main armament comprising eight 120mm guns in modern twin mountings and two triple banks of 450mm torpedo tubes, and had a designed speed of 34 knots.

The Early Contre-Torpilleurs

The first *contre-torpilleurs* built for the Marine Nationale were the six *Jaguars* authorised under the post-Washington 1922 programme alongside the three light cruisers of the *Duguay-Trouin* class and the twelve *torpilleurs d'escadre* (destroyers, literally 'fleet torpedo boats') of the *Bourrasque* class.

The *Jaguars* had much in common with the *Bourrasques* (see Chapter 10), particularly in terms of weaponry. However, they were significantly larger, with a length overall of 127m (vs. 106m) and a standard displacement of 2,160 tonnes (vs. 1,500 tonnes). They were also significantly faster, being designed for a speed of 35.5 knots – 2.5 knots in excess of the maximum speed of their destroyer counterparts.

Longitudinal construction was used for the hull (a 'first' for French flotilla craft), and the hull was tightly subdivided by eleven watertight transverse bulkheads. In order to secure high speed the hull form was unusually fine, with a length to beam ratio of almost 11:1. The raised forecastle, which was also a feature of contemporary French cruiser designs, meant that the *Jaguars* were much better seaboats than French flotilla craft of Great War vintage.

The five Guyot du Temple small water-tube boilers, rated at a conservative 18kg/cm^2, were grouped together on the centre-line in three boiler rooms with the engine rooms abaft them (see drawing of the *Jaguar* in Chapter 2). This was reflected in their funnel arrangement, with a slim fore-funnel serving the single forward boiler room, and two broader funnels serving the second and third (double) boiler rooms. All six ships attained their designed speed

Table 8.1: The Early Italian *Esploratori* and French *Contre-torpilleurs*

	Leone (It)	Jaguar (Fr)	Guépard/Valmy (Fr)	Navigatori (It)
Built:	3 ships 1921–24	6 ships 1922–27	6 ships 1927–31	12 ships 1927–31
Displacement:	1,525tW	2,125tW	2,440tW	1,630tW
Dimensions:	113m × 10.3m	127m × 11.3m	130m × 11.7m	107m × 10.2m
Machinery:	2-shaft geared turbines;	2-shaft geared turbines;	2-shaft geared turbines;	2-shaft geared turbines;
	42,000shp = 34 knots	50,000shp = 35.5 knots	64,000shp = 35.5 knots	50,000shp = 38 knots
Armament:	8–120mm/45 (4 × II)	5–130mm/40 (5 × I)	5–138.6mm/40 (5 × I)	6–120mm/45 (3 × II)
	2–76mm/40 (2 × I) HA	2–75mm/50 (2 × I) HA	4–37mm (4 × I) AA	2–40mm (2 × I) AA
	6–450mm TT (2 × III)	6–550mm TT (2 × III)	6–550mm TT (2 × III)	6–533mm TT (2 × III)
	(60 mines)	12 DC	16 DC	(86 mines)

on trials, and *Tigre* managed an impressive 36.7 knots, albeit for a short period with some forcing of the machinery. The boilers proved very reliable; however, the geared turbines suffered from heavy wear during the ships' first years in service, when they were used extensively to test the *contre-torpilleur* concept in exercises both in the Mediterranean and the Atlantic, and were subject to frequent repair and replacement during the 1930s.

The long hull, necessary to accommodate the powerful machinery, was utilised to accommodate an additional main gun, so there were five single 130mm mountings as compared with only four in the *torpilleurs d'escadre*. There were also two single 75mm HA guns and two triple banks of tubes for the new 550mm Model 1919D torpedo which, with its range of 6,000m at 35 knots, was vastly superior in performance to the older 450mm models and could match any torpedo in service with foreign navies of the period. Other novel features included 200kg depth charges stowed in twin tunnels in the stern, launched using a continuous chain mechanism powered by an electric motor. These were to be complemented by four Thornycroft Model 1918 240mm anti-submarine mortars, capable of firing a 100kg depth charge every 40–60 seconds, and by Ginocchio Model 1917 towed A/S torpedoes. Multiple reloads for the depth charge racks and A/S mortars were stowed in a capacious below-decks magazine aft.

On the face of it this was a very impressive weapon-load for a ship of this size. The 130mm calibre effectively outgunned the Italian *esploratori leggeri*, the latest of which were armed with a 120mm/50-calibre model; the torpedoes outperformed their 450mm Italian counterparts by a wide margin, and the comprehensive anti-submarine outfit was a major advance on anything fitted hitherto.

However, none of these systems was to meet expectations in service. The 130mm/40-calibre Model 1919 was derived from pre-war ideas and was rushed into development after the First World War. Its 32.5kg HE shell could in theory penetrate 20cm of armour at 3,500m and 8.8cm of armour at 16,600m, but the low initial velocity of the gun meant that it was inaccurate at longer ranges. It also had a slow rate of fire due to the traditional Welin screw breech and the use of separate ammunition. During development it was decided to increase the elevation of the gun to 36° by raising the trunnions 1.5m, which made the gun difficult to load and further slowed the rate of fire.

The problem was compounded by the behaviour of the ships in a seaway. Despite the provision of 40m bilge keels the concentration of weight high in the ship gave the *Jaguar*s a pronounced and rapid roll (25° with a roll period of 8–10 seconds with a beam sea), and they heeled badly in high winds or under helm (20° at 35 knots with only 5–6° of rudder). This made them poor gunnery platforms. The guns were initially given only light wind-shields, and a more substantial 'wrap-around' shield had to be installed shortly after completion to protect the crews from spray and splinters; this cost an additional 2.5 tonnes in topweight.

When the ships were first conceived there were ambitious plans to fit them with a light director providing automatic correction of elevation and centralised firing of the guns. However, the complexity of the system resulted in prolonged development (as it did for the cruisers – see Chapter 6), and installation had to be abandoned when it was realised just how overweight the ships were. Fire control on completion was provided by a single coincidence rangefinder with a 3m base located atop the bridge, and full director control (training only) had to wait until 1931. In service it was found that a degree of accuracy was possible only if the guns were fired at the mid-point of the ship's roll, which served to reduce further the rate of fire.

A projected centralised torpedo fire control system was also delayed. Firing data for the torpedoes was provided by the main rangefinder and its associated mechanical computer, but firing orders had to be relayed from the bridge using a system of lights, and settings had to be made locally. ASW capabilities were hampered from the outset by the absence of an effective submarine detection system. It was initially envisaged that this would be provided by a Walser listening device comprising passive acoustic hydrophones derived from a model developed during the First World War, but when tested on *Panthère* this proved useless when the ship was underway, as water disturbance and noise from the ship's own machinery effectively obliterated any signal. When the ships turned out overweight it was the anti-submarine provision which bore the brunt of the weight-saving measures. All reserve depth charges were disembarked from 1928, the Ginocchio A/S torpedoes (which had in any case experienced depth-keeping problems) in 1929, and the Thornycroft mortars in 1932, although the seatings were retained for a possible improved variant.

It was proposed while the *Jaguar*s were building that the 130mm Model 1919 be replaced by the more powerful 136.8mm Model 1923 adopted for the next series of *contre-torpilleurs*, but this would have resulted in unacceptable delays in completion. As it was, these ships took five years to build, in part because of the novelty of their construction and the technical sophistication of the new weapons and propulsion machinery to be installed, but also because the French shipyards and the industrial infrastructure which served them was still recovering from the Great War. From 1925 thirty 138.6mm guns were purchased with a view to replacing the original 130mm mountings soon after completion, but the additional 10 tons of topweight proved prohibitive given the overweight condition of the ships.

The designed operational radius of the *Jaguar*s was a mere 3,000–3,500nm at 15 knots, and 700nm at their top speed of 35 knots, figures which reflected the relatively low demands of the Western Mediterranean theatre and Naval Staff calculations of (straight-line) transits between metropolitan France and the North African colonies. However, the high fuel consumption of the main turbines meant that even these modest figures were not attained. Trials suggested that a radius of 3,300nm was possible at a lower cruise speed of 13 knots, but only 600nm at 35 knots.

The next series of *contre-torpilleurs* were ordered under the 1925 and 1926 tranches. The six ships of the *Guépard* (1925) and *Valmy* (1926) classes were virtually identical, and were built to a modified design. They were slightly larger than the *Jaguar*s, with a length overall of 130m and a displacement of 2,475 tonnes standard. This enabled them to carry the heavier 138.6mm Model 1923 gun in place of the 130mm Model 1919. The armament as designed was otherwise as per the *Jaguar*s, except that the two 75mm HA guns were replaced by four single 37mm guns of a new model.

Larger size implied greater horsepower, and the *Guépard/Valmy* class had four larger-capacity Yarrow-Loire boilers of more advanced design operating at 20kg/cm², for a total horsepower of 64,000shp. Machinery layout was on the unit system: the two boiler rooms, each housing two boilers in line, were separated by the forward engine room, creating two independent propulsion units. The ships could therefore in theory survive the flooding of two adjacent compartments amidships. Externally this arrangement of the machinery was characterised by the two pairs of slim funnels, a distinctive feature of these ships and the next two series of *contre-torpilleurs*, which were grouped together by the Marine Nationale under the nickname '*quatre-tuyaux*' ('four-pipes').

The 138.6mm Model 1923 was significantly more powerful than the 130mm Model 1919, firing a 40kg (vs. 32kg) shell out to a theoretical range of 18,200m. However, the low initial velocity of the 40-calibre gun still made for inaccuracy at longer ranges, and fire control provision was only on a par with the earlier ships. In theory the firing cycle was five to six rounds per minute (vs. 4–5rpm for the 130mm Model 1919) but again this was rarely attained in service. The *Guépard/Valmy* design, like the *Jaguar*, proved to be a lively gunnery platform, and the Model 1923 retained the complex screw breech of the Model 1919.[3]

Guépard/Valmy (Fr)

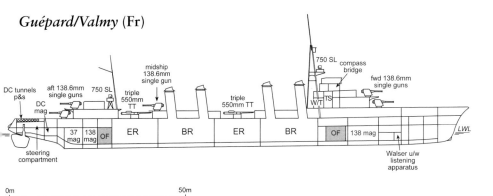

The principal differences between the *Guépard/Valmy* series and their predecessors of the *Jaguar* class (for drawing see Chapter 2), were the heavier 138.6mm guns and the unit layout of the propulsion machinery. There were four larger boilers, each of which was vented through a single funnel, giving these ships and the two six-ship classes which followed them their distinctive appearance.

Verdun shortly after completion. The six ships of the *Guépard* class, ordered as two sub-groups of three, were the first of a series of eighteen four-funnelled *contre-torpilleurs* built for the Marine Nationale. Compared with the preceding *Jaguar* class, they had the more powerful 138.6mm gun and the machinery was in a unit arrangement reflected in the paired funnels. Note the traditional 'cruiser' stern. (Courtesy of Robert Dumas)

The 'Navigatori'

Clearly the Italian Regia Marina could not let these developments go unanswered. By 1926 there were twelve French *contre-torpilleurs* on order, and the first six were nearing completion. The Italians therefore embarked on the construction of a matching group of twelve light scouts.

The *esploratori leggeri* of the 'Navigatori' class were, like their lineal predecessors of the *Mirabello* and *Leone* classes, enlarged destroyers. Although smaller than their French counterparts, they had a number of features in common: they differed from contemporary destroyers building for the Regia Marina in having an additional (twin) gun mounting, and in having a higher designed speed to fit them for their role as fleet scouts. They almost matched the *Jaguar*s in armament, the lighter weight of the 120mm shell (23kg vs. 32kg

'Navigatori' (It)

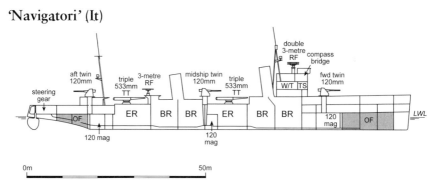

The twelve *esploratori leggeri* of the 'Navigatori' type were essentially enlarged destroyers with a heavy gun and torpedo armament and exceptionally high speed. There were six 120mm guns in a new twin mounting and two triple banks of 533mm tubes, and the designed speed was 38 knots. In contrast to the standard Italian destroyer types (see Chapter 10), there was a unit arrangement of the machinery, with each pair of boiler rooms paired with a single engine room.

for the French 130mm Model 1919) being compensated by the provision of three twin mountings. Moreover the 120mm/50-calibre gun was a new model with a horizontal sliding breech block and a designed firing cycle of 6–7rpm. It had a range of 18,200m at 35° elevation, and the gun was highly regarded in the Regia Marina, which fitted it in all subsequent classes of destroyer up to and including the 'Soldati' class of 1936–40. There was also a modern light AA armament, two triple banks of 533mm torpedo tubes, and the traditional *esploratori* minelaying capability, with a capacity of between 86 and 104 mines, depending on type.

Even more impressive was the speed of the ships when first completed. Designed for a top speed of 38 knots with 50,000shp, all ships largely exceeded this figure on trials: *Antonio Pigafetta* attained 41.6 knots with 65,000shp, and *Alvise da Mosto* is reported to have touched 45 knots with 71,000shp for a short period. As with the *Trento*-class cruisers these trials were frequently undertaken at light displacement and with considerable forcing of the machinery. Nevertheless, speeds of 35 knots and above seem to have been comfortably sustained in service during the early years, before machinery wear, hull fouling and weight additions took their toll.

However, other aspects of their performance suggested that the 'Navigatori' were too small for their intended missions. Their low freeboard made them wet, they rolled badly in heavy weather and their reserve of stability was small. In an effort to reduce these problems the bridge was lowered and the funnels shortened during the 1930s; a pole mast replaced the original tripod, fuel stowage was modified and the centre torpedo tube removed from each mounting. During

The twelve 'light scouts' of the 'Navigatori' class were the successors to the *Leone* class. Smaller and with one less gun mounting, they were capable of extremely high speeds when first completed, and had two triple tubes for the more powerful, longer-ranged 533mm torpedo. This is *Usodimare* in 1938. Since completion she has been fitted with a heavy fire control director above the bridge and a funnel cap. In part compensation the height of the funnels and bridge have been reduced and a short pole mast has replaced the original tripod (see drawing). Note the low freeboard amidships and aft, and the straight bow with its lack of flare and sheer; the bows of the surviving ships were modified during the Second World War to improve sea-keeping. (Erminio Bagnasco collection)

the Second World War even more drastic measures were adopted: the hull was widened by one metre, and a raised clipper bow was fitted.

Even while these ships were building it became apparent that they would be outclassed by the second series of French *contre-torpilleurs*. The 138.6mm Model 1923 guns of the *Guépard/Valmy* classes fired a shell almost twice the weight of the Italian 120mm, and the new 550mm Model 1923D torpedo, which was now replacing the Model 1919D in the Marine Nationale, was a formidable weapon with more than double the effective range (13,000–14,000m at 35 knots vs. 6,000m), and completely outclassed Italian torpedoes of the period. If the French ships proved to be lively gunnery platforms, that was even more true of their smaller Italian counterparts. In 1938, like their predecessors of the *Mirabello* and *Leone* classes, the 'Navigatori' would be downgraded and reclassified as *cacciatorpedinieri* ('destroyers') by the Italian Navy.

The Further Development of the Contre-Torpilleur

Despite the technical problems which were already beginning to emerge and the consequent delays in the construction of the early classes of *contre-torpilleur*, the French were convinced that this was the right path to pursue, and were to show considerable commitment and determination in attempting to bring the concept to fruition.

The 1924 *Statut Naval* which succeeded the post-Washington 1922 programme was an ambitious six-year programme intended to rebuild the Marine Nationale as a modern force. The 1924 tranche comprised the first two treaty cruisers of the *Duquesne* class, plus six 1,500-tonne *torpilleurs d'escadre* of the *L'Adroit* class (see Chapter 10); the 1925 tranche comprised the treaty cruiser *Suffren*, the three *contre-torpilleurs* of the *Guépard* class, and four more 1,500-tonne destroyers; and the 1926 tranche would be virtually identical, comprising the cruiser *Colbert*, the three *contre-torpilleurs* of the *Valmy* class, and the final four 1,500-tonne destroyers. However, with the *torpilleur d'escadre* programme now complete there would be a renewed focus on the *contre-torpilleur*; it was planned to build a class of six, together with a single 10,000-ton cruiser, over each of the three remaining years, 1927–29.

The six ships of the 1927 programme, the *Aigle* class (also known in the Marine Nationale as '*les rapaces*', 'the birds of prey'), were essentially repeats of the *Guépard/Valmy* type. The major difference was the main gun, the 138.6mm Model 1927, based on the earlier Model 1923 but with the sliding breech of the German 15cm KL/45-calibre gun, which gave the new weapon a much faster firing cycle. In theory the Model 1927 was capable of 14–15rpm, although in practice the rate of fire continued to be hampered by manual loading of the shells and their separate charges, the slow resupply rate of the (unmodified) hoists, and by the liveliness of the platform in any sort of seaway. These limitations, however, were yet to become apparent when the ships were designed, as the earliest *contre-torpilleurs* of the *Jaguar* class were only just beginning sea trials.

Orders for four of the six ships were placed with private shipyards, and these units were eventually laid down between late 1928 and early 1929. However, the backlog of construction in the naval dockyards was becoming even more serious than in the private yards, and the scheduled workload at the Arsenal de Lorient, to which the remaining two ships had been allocated, meant that they could not be laid down until late 1929 at the earliest. It was therefore resolved that *Milan* and *Epervier* would be laid down in 1930 and would follow the plans of the next series, the *Vauquelin* class. It was subsequently decided to take advantage of this delay in construction by installing prototype high-pressure superheated steam turbines in these ships with a view to adopting machinery of this type for the final series of six.

The six ships of the *Vauquelin* class were originally to have been authorised as part of the 1928 tranche. Had previous practice been adhered to, the two lead ships would have been built in the naval dockyards of Brest or Lorient, which were also responsible for supplying the drawings, with the remaining four being contracted out to private shipyards.[4] However, the result had been that the naval dockyards had become totally overloaded, and there was now a massive backlog of work at Lorient in particular. In order to clear these production bottlenecks the Marine Nationale was compelled to revoke its earlier decisions, and thereby to accept some loss of control with regard to 'quality assurance'. The six units of the *Vauquelin* class, together with the six units of the 1929

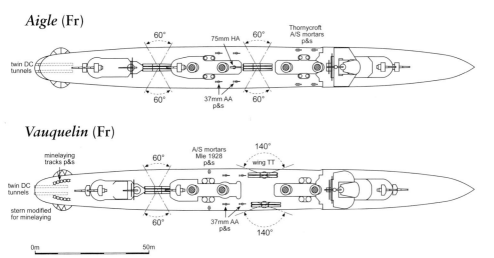

The four-funnelled *contre-torpilleurs* of the *Aigle* and *Vauquelin* classes showed a number of incremental improvements over the *Guépard/Valmy* type. All were armed with the 138.6mm Model 1927, which had a horizontal sliding breech and a much faster firing cycle. In the *Vauquelin* class the arcs of the forward torpedo tubes were improved by replacing the triple centre-line mounting by two pairs of tubes mounted on the deck edge. The later ships were also fitted for minelaying, the short fixed tracks being supplemented by dismountable tracks carried in an after magazine for a total of forty mines.

Tartu, one of six ships of the *Vauquelin* class. Despite their apparent similarity to the earlier *contre-torpilleurs* of the *Guépard/Valmy* and *Aigle* classes, the *Vauquelin*s incorporated a number of technical improvements and were more stable gunnery platforms. Note the twin torpedo tubes mounted port and starboard between the paired funnels, and the concentration dial on the face of the bridge structure. (Courtesy of Robert Dumas)

tranche, would all be ordered from private shipbuilders. Moreover, in order to clear the backlog the 1928 tranche would now become the 1929 tranche, and a further year would be added to the original six-year programme, with the final series of six *contre-torpilleurs* being postponed until 1930.

Although in appearance the *Vauquelin*s were very like the four-funnelled *contre-torpilleurs* of the *Guépard/Valmy* and *Aigle* classes, in terms of performance and technology they represented a major advance. The hull was still largely of traditional riveted construction, but there was extensive use of welding for joints and internal compartmentation, and light duralumin alloys were used for the superstructures – in the Lorient-built *Milan* and *Epervier* it was estimated that these new construction techniques produced savings of sixty-five tons in hull weight. Since much of the weight saving was relatively high in the ship, and freeboard was slightly reduced as compared with the earlier types, they were steadier in adverse sea conditions. Sea-keeping performance was also improved by fitting 49m bilge keels, and the rounded, more streamlined bridge structure reduced the tendency of the earlier ships to heel in strong winds.[5] The improved stability of the ships permitted the reintroduction of the anti-submarine mortar – two of a new Model 1928 of French design being fitted abeam the fourth funnel.

The *cul de poule*[6] stern was adopted with a view to preserving trim at speed and to facilitate minelaying. All ships easily surpassed their designed speed of 37 knots on trials. *Cassard* (and *Milan/Epervier*, which benefited from high-pressure steam machinery) all attained 43 knots, while the other ships all exceeded 39.75 knots. Even in service a 'raid' speed of 37–38 knots by a three-ship division in formation was considered practical.

By the early 1930s, when these ships were under construction, combat operations with three-ship divisions of *contre-torpilleurs* had been practised regularly in annual exercises and had become highly evolved. The practical range of engagement was now set at 10,000–14,000m (beyond 14,000m it was difficult to spot fall of shot). Because the relatively slow rate of replenishment was no longer able to keep pace with the rapid firing cycle of the guns (the electrical hoists were largely unmodified), it had become custom to open fire using ready-use ammunition stowed close to the gun. Concentrated bursts of fire of perhaps ten to fifteen minutes would be punctuated by periods when the ships would move out of combat range to replenish the ready-use parks. The latter had been established at twenty-four rounds per gun, with forty-eight rounds being provided for the centre mounting, which had to be supplied by overhead cable from the after distribution post. During 1933 *Cassard* trialled circular brass guttering (*glissières*) for shells, which was fixed around each of the gun mountings. This enabled the guns to be reloaded rapidly on any bearing by the guncrews, and circular guttering was subsequently adopted for all new *contre-torpilleur* construction and retrofitted to earlier types.

Firing in formation was a key procedure, and was practised throughout the 1930s. Concentration dials were trialled in the *Jaguar*s from 1929, and production models installed in all *contre-torpilleurs* from 1930–31; the forward dial or 'clock' was fixed to the forward face of the bridge structure, and there was either a single (trainable) dial on the after side of the mainmast, or twin dials fixed to the after corners of the bridge wings, which were angled at 45°. The dials enabled other ships in the formation whose rangefinders might be disabled or hampered by smoke to take their firing data from another ship (similar dials had been fitted in British capital ships during the First World War, and the technique had subsequently been widely adopted). They remained in service with the flotilla craft of the Marine Nationale until the late 1930s, when they were replaced by short-range tactical radio. From 1936 the Marine Nationale introduced shells with colorants which enabled each ship in a three-ship division to identify its own shell splashes. Initially the colours were red for the lead ship in the formation, green for the second ship, and white for the third; yellow (which was more distinctive) was substituted for white from 1937.[7]

There were two important modifications to the armament of the *Vauquelin*s as compared with the earlier French *contre-torpilleurs*. The Marine Nationale, in contrast to the Italian Navy, had always envisaged that its ships might need to fight in low visibility or at night, and the earlier *contre-torpilleurs* were well equipped with powerful 75cm remote-controlled searchlight projectors, illuminating shell (generally seventy-five per ship) and flashless charges.[8] With the *Vauquelin* class close-combat capabilities were improved by a revised layout of the torpedo tubes. In previous types these had been mounted on the centre-line with a view to broadside firing in daylight conditions, and had arcs of only 30° either side of the beam. Low-visibility conditions might involve enemy vessels coming into view just ahead or astern, a situation requiring a rapid response, so the forward bank of tubes was replaced in the *Vauquelins* by two twin trainable mountings capable of launching their torpedoes at 20° to the ship's axis, the starboard pair normally being trained ahead and the port-side mounting trained astern.

The other important modification was the provision for the first time of a minelaying capability. When it had still been envisaged that the North Sea would be the primary theatre for the laying of minefields, as in the First World War, it was feasible to imagine that this task could be performed by relatively slow purpose-built ships with a large mine capacity. However, by the late 1920s, with a different enemy in prospect, the Marine Nationale was inclining towards the idea of high-speed minelaying 'raids' close to the northern Italian ports. It was at this time that the fast minelaying cruiser *Emile Bertin* was designed, her conventional cruiser characteristics being complemented by the capacity to carry eighty-four mines, and a similar capability was built into the *Vauquelins* and their successors of the *Le Fantasque* class. Short fixed rails, each with a capacity of five 80kg Bréguet B4 mines, were fitted directly above the stern, and removable sections of track for a further thirty mines were stowed between decks.

The 'Condottieri'

The Reggia Marina was quick to recognise that the small *esploratori* of the 'Navigatori' class were outclassed by the latest French *contre-torpilleurs*, with their five powerful 138.6mm guns and their long-range torpedoes. Even the initial speed advantage of the Italian ships was being eroded: the latest French ships were designed for 36 knots, and were registering speeds well in excess of even this figure on trials.

In 1926 the Regia Marina began studies for a small, fast cruiser-type ship, which in 1927 were translated into orders for four *grandi esploratori* ('large scouts'), which were to bear the names of famous leaders of the mercenary bands in Renaissance Italy (the 'Condottieri'). These ships would be armed with 152mm guns which would outrange and outpunch the French 138.6mm gun, and would be designed for exceptionally high speed – 36.5/37 knots – at the expense of protection, which would be sufficient to resist only destroyer shell.

The four ships of the *di Giussano* class had a standard displacement more than twice that of the French *contre-torpilleurs* (which for all their technical sophistication were still essentially 'large destroyers'). Their 152mm/53-calibre guns were in four twin power-operated turrets with full protection for the gun crews, and these were complemented by three twin 100mm/47-calibre dual-purpose mountings which could be used against destroyers or aircraft, and by smaller 40mm and 12.7mm anti-aircraft weapons. They also had a bridge structure similar to the Italian treaty cruisers, with platforms built around a heavy quadruped mast topped by the main battery director, which was complemented by a second director atop an armoured conning tower; both were fitted with the latest 5m stereoscopic rangefinder. There was a secondary fire control position for the main battery aft, and on the upper platform of the bridge there were twin directors with integral 3m rangefinders to provide fire control for the secondary battery and for the twin torpedo tubes, which were located on the upper deck amidships. There were two spotter/reconnaissance aircraft, stowed in twin hangars at the base of the bridge structure and launched from the forecastle from a Magaldi fixed catapult powered by gunpowder. And removable rails could accommodate up to 169 mines to enable the ships to be employed as fast minelayers, albeit at the expense of their after gun and torpedo mountings, which were unable to train with a full complement of mines embarked.

The horsepower necessary for the designed 37 knots was provided by two-shaft Belluzzo impulse turbines rated at 95,000shp, with steam provided by six Yarrow-type boilers built by Ansaldo. The relatively narrow beam of the ship, essential for the high speeds envisaged, meant that the six boilers and the two groups of turbines had to be disposed singly rather than in pairs, with two boiler rooms each housing two boilers forward, and the third between the two engine rooms. The machinery spaces (together with the short midships magazine for the 100mm/47-calibre munitions) occupied almost half of the ship's length. This served not only to compress the main magazines and to push them towards the ends of the ship, but also made for extremely cramped accommodation for the crews.[9]

Protection, such as it was, was provided by hull plating of vanadium steel with a thickness of 24mm over the machinery spaces and 20mm over the magazines,[10] topped by a 20mm armoured deck. Behind the side plating there was a chrome-nickel splinter bulkhead 18mm thick, and the armoured citadel

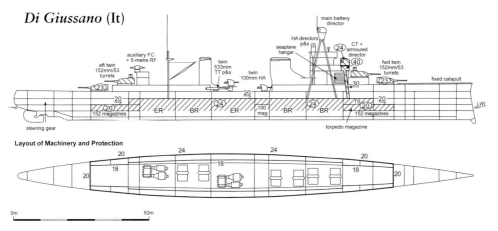

Di Giussano (It)

The early 'Condottieri' sacrificed too much for speed: they were cramped, virtually unprotected and, according to one commanding officer, handled 'like a submarine'. Note the aircraft hangar at the base of the bridge structure and the long, narrow hull form. Beam was insufficient to allow two boilers to be accommodated side by side, hence the extreme length of the machinery spaces. Although these ships were protected by armour-quality steel on the cruiser principle, the thickness of the plating was such that it could be easily penetrated even by destroyer shell.

The Italian *di Giussano*, the first of a series of fast light cruisers armed with eight 6in guns and known collectively as the 'Condottieri'. They were designed to counter the French *contre-torpilleurs*; although well-armed for their size, endurance was sufficient only for operations in the Mediterranean, and the early units had serious stability problems and minimal protection. (Leo van Ginderen collection)

was closed by 20mm transverse bulkheads. The conning tower and its main battery director were protected by 40mm and 25mm walls respectively, and the communications tube by 30mm plating; there was also 23mm protection for the main turrets.

The protection system was designed primarily to resist high-explosive destroyer shell, the theory being that these shells would break up on the hard outer hull plating, and any splinters which entered the ship would be stopped by the internal 18mm bulkhead from entering the ship's vitals. The 138.6mm guns of the French *contre-torpilleurs* fired semi-armour-piercing (SAP) shell, and it is doubtful that the scanty protection of the early 'Condottieri' would have kept these out. However, the 152mm/53-calibre gun adopted for these ships was chosen not only for its superior hitting power but because it outranged the French 138.6mm gun. The latter had a theoretical maximum range of 16,700–18,200m and an effective range of 10,000–14,000m, whereas the maximum range of the Italian 152mm/53-calibre with its original 50kg shell was 28,400m at 45° elevation, and the superior director fire control arrangements of the bigger ship should in theory have resulted in an effective range well outside that of the *contre-torpilleurs*.

All four ships achieved in excess of 38 knots on trials, and *da Barbiano* managed an astonishing 42 knots with 123,500shp, albeit for a period of only thirty minutes. However, this remarkable performance was obtained in ideal sea conditions when the ships were new, and with considerable forcing of the machinery. In July 1940, only nine years after their completion, 31–32 knots was the best speed achieved by *Bartolomeo Colleoni* and *Bande Nere* at the Battle of Cape Spada. The British destroyers present, led by *Jane's Fighting Ships* to believe that the Italian ships were capable of 40 knots, found themselves comfortably outrunning them, and when the 32.5-knot Australian cruiser *Sydney* joined the pursuit at a later stage in the battle she seems to have had no difficulty maintaining the range.

Unfortunately so much had been sacrificed for speed in these ships that they never proved to be effective fighting units, and were not highly rated by either the Italian Navy or the crews who had the misfortune to serve in

The *da Barbiano* in 1935. Note the reconnaissance aircraft on the fixed catapult, which extended from just forward of turret no.1 to the bow, and the door for the hangar in the side of the bridge structure. (Leo van Ginderen collection)

them.[11] Many aspects of the design revealed the customary Italian flair for innovatory solutions, but far too much was attempted on the displacement. There were too many weights high in the ship and they rolled badly in any sort of seaway, a problem which was aggravated by their tumblehome sides. Soon after the first ships were completed the tripod mainmast was replaced by a pole mast and the secondary fire control position aft was suppressed, but they remained unstable gunnery platforms, and their light construction was responsible for severe vibration which adversely affected both the turrets and the fire control systems.

The internal layout of the 152mm turrets was unsatisfactory and the reloading mechanisms were poorly designed, so that the designed firing cycle of 6rpm was never achieved – 4rpm was the maximum rate of fire sustained in service. The guns were also mounted too close together for salvo firing without mutual interference, and the mountings were too lightly built to sustain the recoil which accompanied the high initial muzzle velocity. This was later reduced by employing lighter shells and smaller charges, with a corresponding reduction in maximum range to around 22,600m, but it did not entirely resolve the problem. A high percentage of rounds – up to 10 per cent! – did not fire due to mechanical faults, and when these faults occurred the gun had to cease firing until the problem was resolved. The dispersion problems of the guns have been well documented. During the Battle of Cape Spada the two Italian cruisers managed only one hit over the best part of two hours, even though the later stages of the gunnery duel took place at moderate ranges of 12,000 to 15,000m.

In terms of protection, observers aboard the British ships were surprised

Armando Diaz, the second of the light cruisers of the *Cadorna* class. Note the lower bridge structure, achieved by eliminating the aircraft hangar; this resulted in some improvement in stability. (Leo van Ginderen collection)

that despite numerous hits from 6in and 4.7in shell the *Colleoni* appeared almost undamaged when they closed her towards the end of the engagement. In effect all the shells, including the HE shell of the destroyers, had penetrated the thin outer skin of the hull and burst inside the ship.

Even before the first group of four 'Condottieri' was completed, a further two units were authorised under the 1929–30 programme. The *Cadorna* class was essentially a repeat of the *di Giussano* type but incorporated a number of modifications with a view to improving stability (clearly a concern with the earlier ships even before they were completed). The key modification was the lowering of the height of the bridge structure and the main director, which was achieved by suppressing the aircraft hangar below. The spotter/reconnaissance aircraft were now launched from a fixed catapult atop the after deckhouse and stowed in the open, the tripod mainmast being reinstated and stepped forward of the second funnel.

The tumblehome sides of the earlier ships were eliminated, and the 152mm/53-calibre turrets were of a new more spacious model with improved reloading mechanisms (theoretical rate of fire was now 5–8rpm as compared with only 4rpm in the earlier ships). The *Cadornas* were fitted out as minelayers, but with a slightly reduced capacity of 84–138 mines depending on type (only three of the earlier ships had been so equipped).

The *Cadorna* class cruisers were a marked improvement on their predecessors, but had the same fundamental defects of flimsy construction, poor sea-keeping and instability. The next class of 'Condottieri', authorised after the London Treaty and following trials with the *di Giussano*s, would be of a radically different design.

Table 8.2: The Later Contre-torpilleurs and the 'Condottieri'

	Aigle (Fr)	Di Giussano (It)	Vauquelin (Fr)	Cadorna (It)	Le Fantasque (Fr)
Built	6 ships 1928–34	4 ships 1928–32	6 ships 1930–34	2 ships 1930–33	6 ships 1931–36
Displacement:	2,440tW	4,900tW	2,440tW	5,010tW	2,570tW
Dimensions:	129m × 11.8m	169m × 15.5m	129m × 11.9m	169m × 15.5m	132m × 12m
Machinery:	2-shaft geared turbines; 64,000shp = 36 knots	2-shaft geared turbines; 95,000shp = 36.5 knots	2-shaft geared turbines; 64,000shp = 36 knots	2-shaft geared turbines; 95,000shp = 36.5 knots	2-shaft geared turbines; 74,000shp = 37 knots
Armament:	5–138.6mm/40 (5 × I)	8–152mm/53 (4 × II)	5–138.6mm/40 (5 × I)	8–152mm/53 (4 × II)	5–138.6mm/50 (5 × I)
	4–37mm (4 × I) AA	6–100mm (3 × II) HA	4–37mm (4 × I) AA	6–100mm (3 × II) HA	4–37mm (4 × I) AA
		2–40mm (2 × I) AA		2–40mm (2 × I) AA	
	6–550mm TT (2 × III)	4–533mm TT (2 × II)	7–550mm TT (1 × III, 2 × II)	4–533mm TT (2 × II)	9–550mm TT (3 × III)
	16 DC		16 DC		16 DC
		(78–169 mines)	(40 mines)	(84–138 mines)	(40 mines)
Protection:	(none)	mach and mags: 24mm sides, 20mm deck turrets: 23mm CT: 40mm	(none)	mach and mags: 24mm sides, 20mm deck turrets: 23mm CT: 40mm	(none)

Note: Two ships of the *Aigle* class, *Milan* and *Epervier*, trialled advanced superheated machinery, and completion was delayed; their characteristics were as the *Vauquelin* class.

The Apogee of the Contre-Torpilleur

The last series of *contre-torpilleurs* of the six-year 1924 *Statut Naval* was finally authorised in 1930, although the backlog of construction in the shipyards was such that the first ship was laid down only in August 1931. Originally these ships were to have been repeat *Vauquelins*, but full advantage was taken of the delay in construction to incorporate a number of important modifications. The *Le Fantasque* class featured a new main gun with remote power control (RPC), superheated steam propulsion machinery and a radically different silhouette.

The 138.6mm Model 1929 was a 50-calibre weapon, with similar high-performance loading mechanisms to the Model 1927, but with greater accuracy at longer ranges. The longer barrel, with its higher muzzle velocity, gave the gun a theoretical range of 20,000m at its maximum elevation of 30°, although accurate observation of the fall of shot was still difficult at this range, despite improvements in range-finding (the inadequate 3m base coincidence rangefinder fitted in the early *contre-torpilleurs* had by now been superseded by a stereoscopic model with a 5m base). It also served to increase the recoil forces from 43.5 tonnes to 57 tonnes, which placed additional stresses on the gun mounting, and the blast effect was markedly greater.

It had been envisaged that advanced superheated steam machinery, incorporating boilers operating at a pressure of 27kg/cm², would be trialled in the two Lorient-built *contre-torpilleurs* postponed from the 1927 tranche; these two ships were to be fitted out with competing propulsion units which would then be evaluated during sea trials. In the event *Milan* and *Epervier* were not laid down until late 1930, so decisions regarding the propulsion machinery for the *Le Fantasque* class had to be taken on a purely theoretical

Le Fantasque class (Fr)

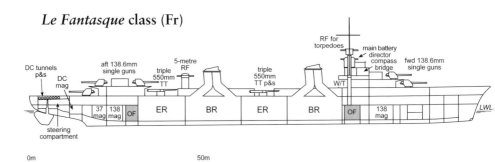

The apogee of the *contre-torpilleur* type was attained with the six ships of the *Le Fantasque* class, which had a new gun with greater range, an embryonic RPC system, and three banks of triple torpedo tubes. For this class a more modern architecture was adopted, with the boiler uptakes being paired in two broad funnels, and a streamlined bridge structure with superimposed directors for the guns and the torpedoes seated around a short pole mast. The *Le Fantasques* were very fast indeed: *Le Terrible* exceeded 45 knots on trials, thereby breaking the world speed record.

Designed as an improved *Vauquelin*, the *Le Fantasque* class was given a radically different silhouette, the paired funnels of their predecessors being combined and reduced in height, and the tall tripod foremast being replaced by a shorter vertical pole mast around the base of which were seated the gunnery and torpedo fire control directors. On completion these were the fastest ships in the world, with *Le Terrible* achieving 45 knots on trials. This is the name-ship of the class in early 1939. (Author's collection)

basis. Despite this, speed performance on trials was remarkable, and sent shock waves through other European navies. *Le Terrible* attained just over 45 knots, thereby breaking the world speed record. All six ships of the class exceeded 43 knots on trials, and comfortably exceeded 40 knots in service. Maximum speed in formation was 40 knots for the ships with Rateau turbines, and 38/39 knots for the Parsons ships.

However, there was a downside to these figures. Because of the economic recession a conscious effort was made to distribute work on the propulsion systems to the largest possible number of subcontractors. It was hoped that this would ensure prompt delivery of components and serve to broaden the military-industrial base, but it also resulted in a marked lack of uniformity and quality of manufacture which was to have a number of adverse consequences. From the outset the *Le Fantasque*s (and, for that matter, the two 'trials' vessels) were plagued by machinery problems, and these were so frequent and so serious that an official enquiry was set up in the mid-1930s headed by the *inspecteur général des machines*.[12]

During trials with the *Guépard/Valmy* class it had become apparent that at speed exhaust gases from the fore-funnel were drawn into the bridge spaces. In late 1930 it was therefore proposed that the fore-funnel of the new ships be moved farther away from the bridge structure. This would have placed it so close to the second funnel that it made sense to combine both uptakes into a single, broader funnel, and to extend this modification to the after pair of funnels. At the same time it was decided that the third 138.6mm mounting, which in all previous *contre-torpilleurs* had been mounted immediately abaft the after funnel, and could therefore be fired only on the broadside, be relocated at the forward end of the after deckhouse. This had the advantage of enabling the gun to fire on forward bearings, and it could also now be served directly from the after shell hoists. Finally, in an effort to reduce the considerable top-hamper of the four-funnelled types, it was decided in July 1933 that the tripod foremast should be replaced by a short pole mast with the gun and torpedo fire control directors seated around its base, and the mainmast by outriggers for radio aerials on the second funnel. It was these final changes which gave the ships a distinctive, 'racy' appearance which matched their high speed.

As for construction, concerns had been expressed regarding the extensive use of duralumin for the superstructures of the *Aigle* and *Vauquelin* classes. The lightweight superstructures of these ships reduced longitudinal strength, and made them vulnerable to damage from heavy seas and from their own gunfire. The external panels of the bridge structure and deckhouses of the *Le Fantasque* class were therefore of steel, and were reinforced where exposed to blast from the main guns; duralumin was used only for partitioning within the superstructures. These improvements were possible because of the considerable weight saved by reducing the height of the superstructures, masts and funnels.

The main problem experienced with the earlier *contre-torpilleurs* during gunnery trials had been that effective, accurate long-range fire had been

The port-side twin 37mm mounting and 550mm torpedo tubes of a ship of the *Le Fantasque* class. The *Vauquelin*s were the first *contre-torpilleurs* to have wing tubes, adopted to enable the ships to launch torpedoes close to the ship's axis in conditions of low visibility; in the *Le Fantasque* class these became triples rather than twins. (Author's collection)

difficult to sustain from a fast-moving, lightweight platform buffeted by the seas, and the interim solutions adopted had served only to reduce the rate of fire. For the *Le Fantasque* class the Naval Staff wanted full remote power control (RPC) for the guns, a system in which electronic motors would automatically compensate for the movement of the platform and keep the gun trained on the target.

RPC systems capable of real-time adjustments in the bearing and elevation of the guns were trialled on the elderly gun training cruiser *Gueydon* in 1928, and subsequently on her successor *Pluton* from 1933. These were all large ships with the weight reserves and electrical generating capacity to accommodate such a system. It would be quite a different matter to install full RPC in a small, lightly built ship where space, weight and generating capacity were at a premium.

RPC for elevation to compensate for the roll of the ship proved to be relatively valueless, because the major problem under these conditions was the manual reloading of the guns by gun crews who were exposed to the elements and hampered by the ship's motions. Moreover, sudden movements of the ship often actuated the circuit-breakers, putting the system out of action when theoretically it should have been of most use.

Four of the six ships entered service with a provisional RPC installation; *Le Terrible* and *L'Indomptable* entered service without. Only the bearing element was thought to show genuine promise. Further installations were made in dribs and drabs over the pre-war years. However, an operational RPC system was never successfully evolved, and for a time the motors were disembarked altogether in *Le Fantasque*.

Table 8.3: The French *Contre-torpilleur* and the Italian *Esploratori* Programmes 1922–30

Estimates	France	Italy
1922	6 *Jaguar* (1922–27)	
1923		
1924		
1925	3 *Guépard* (1927–31)	
1926	3 *Valmy* (1927–31)	12 'Navigatori' (1927–31)
1927	6 *Aigle* (1928–32)	4 *Di Giussano* (1928–32)
1928	6 *Vauquelin* (1930–34)	
1929		2 *Cadorna* (1930–33)
1930	6 *Le Fantasque* (1931–36)	
Total	30 *contre-torpilleurs*	12 'Navigatori'
		+ 6 'Condottieri'

Conclusions

The *Le Fantasque* class marked the high point of the *contre-torpilleur*, and was the last six-ship series to be ordered for the Marine Nationale. Following the London Treaty focus would shift to the construction of light cruisers armed with 152mm guns to perform the fleet scouting role, together with the first of a new generation of capital ships and fleet torpedo boats of modern design with sufficient speed to accompany them. Only two further units of the *contre-torpilleur* type (the *Mogador* class) would be completed before the Second World War, and these would be of a hybrid design, their eight 138.6mm guns being mounted in twin 'pseudo-turrets' to match the early Italian 'Condottieri'.

It would be some years before the performance of the later *contre-torpilleurs* could be properly evaluated, as the first unit of the *Le Fantasque* class was completed only in December 1935, with the other five ships entering service during 1936. They were highly regarded in the Marine Nationale: very fast and capable of sustained high speed in formation, with excellent sea-keeping qualities, and armed with high-performance guns and torpedoes which matched anything in production abroad. On the other hand they were lightly built and sustained damage to plating and superstructures when operated in adverse sea conditions, particularly in the Atlantic; their propulsion machinery and auxiliaries were subject to regular breakdown, and their elaborate RPC systems never worked properly.

In conceptual terms the Marine Nationale was arguably attempting to provide the qualities and performance of a light cruiser in a destroyer hull. Accommodation was cramped, and the *contre-torpilleurs* lacked the necessary endurance for many of the wartime missions they were tasked with. They were well-suited to high-speed raids on enemy shipping and the enemy coastline, but were not ideal gunnery platforms and therefore proved less effective than envisaged in combat situations.

The early light cruisers of the 'Condottieri' type built by the Regia Marina to counter the French *contre-torpilleurs* were poorly conceived and poorly designed. Although in principle a light cruiser with turret-mounted guns should have been a more effective fighting unit than an oversized destroyer equipped with guns in open mountings, the Italians allowed the design of these ships to become totally unbalanced in an attempt to match the exceptionally high speed of the French ships. Their modest protection could easily have been penetrated by the French 138.6mm weapon, and their poor sea-keeping qualities meant that they proved to be far less stable gunnery platforms than the later French ships. There can be little doubt as to the likely outcome of an engagement where a three-ship division of the later French *contre-torpilleurs* was opposed by only a single *di Giussano* or *Cadorna*, and it is questionable whether even two of the Italian ships could have swung the balance. In order to match the French ships with an effective cruiser the Italians would have to accept a major increase in size and cost.

CHAPTER 9

Submarines

Although not as new as the aircraft carrier, the submarine was also a relatively recent category of warship. Experimental prototypes had been built by the French during the nineteenth century, but operational production boats for the major navies had not entered service until the early 1900s, and these were initially capable only of coastal and harbour defence. The first sea-going submarines powered by diesel engines were completed in 1910–11 for the Royal Navy ('D'-class) and in 1913–14 for the Imperial German Navy (*U-19* class). And despite the havoc caused to merchant shipping by the unrestricted U-boat campaign of 1917–18, which was still all too fresh in Anglo-Saxon minds when the Washington Conference was convened, it should be remembered that the Imperial German Navy, having invested huge sums in battleships and cruisers during the early 1900s, had entered the First World War with a mere twenty operational U-boats.

The steam-powered 'K' class marked the culmination of the Royal Navy's wartime efforts to build a submarine with sufficient speed on the surface to operate with surface units of the fleet. The twin funnels were retracted and sealed by watertight hatches on diving. The fast fleet submarine would become something of a Holy Grail for the major navies during the 1920s, but despite considerable expenditure it proved difficult to build a successful production model. (Leo van Ginderen collection)

Although there were numerous successes by submarines in other areas, it had been unrestricted warfare against merchant shipping which made the greatest impact during the First World War. However, the torpedoing of merchant ships without warning was (and would continue to be) contrary to international law. Germany's behaviour was regarded as aberrant by all five signatories of the Washington Treaty, and during the interwar period none of the Washington powers had any compunction about signing further international agreements which outlawed this form of warfare.

This created an anomaly: whilst all of the Washington Treaty powers looked to harness the latest German technology for their postwar submarine development[1] and used the German coastal, sea-going and ocean-going boats that had been completed in 1916–18 as their models, these latter designs had been optimised for commerce warfare and patrols off enemy ports, which required moderate speed and good endurance, not for fleet operations in open waters, for which high surfaced speed and highly developed communications systems were essential. This dichotomy was responsible for a dynamic tension in submarine design which ensured that in the post-Washington era extreme technical solutions, notably in propulsion, would be pursued, and that many of the submarines laid down during the 1920s would be failures – well-intentioned and often spectacular in the scope of their ambition, but failures nonetheless.

German influence on post-Washington developments in submarine warfare was ensured not only by the perceived pre-eminence of the Imperial German Navy in this field following the U-boat campaign of 1917–18, but also by the distribution of German submarines to the victorious Allies as war prizes (see table). Most were scrapped or used as targets following careful examination, but the Japanese incorporated seven of them into their fleet for a short period.[2] Shortly after the former U-boats arrived in Japan in mid-1919, a naval mission headed by a Captain Godo was despatched to Berlin with a view to conducting a study of German submarine construction, obtaining patents and designs for submarines and diesel engines, and engaging the services of submarine designers, engineers and former naval officers to train Japanese personnel and to assist with new IJN submarine building programmes. Many of the higher-ranking personnel were given five-year contracts and were employed directly by the Kawasaki Shipyard in Kobe.[3] The latest large MAN diesels, designed to power the *U-Kreuzer* of the *U-142* class, were to be built under licence.

The impact on IJN submarine construction was immediate. The construction of the prototype 'fleet' submarines of the KD1 and KD2 types (see Chapter 2) was followed by the ocean-going KRS-type minelayers, derived from the German UE II type, and the design of the first series of *Junsen* cruiser submarines was based closely on the uncompleted *U-142* class, with construction being supervised by Dr-Ing H Techel, formerly of the Krupp Germania Shipyard.

Table 9.1: German U-Boat Designs which Influenced Postwar Developments

	UB III (U-48)	UC III (U-80)	Ms Type (U-93)	UE II Type (U-127)	Proj. 46 Type (U-139)
Type:	coastal patrol	coastal minelayer	sea-going patrol	ocean-going minelayer	U-cruiser
Built:	1916–18	1917–18	1916–18	1917–18	1916–18
Displacement:	520t surf.	490t surf.	840t surf.	1,165t surf.	1,930t surf.
Dimensions:	56m × 5.8m	57m × 5.5m	72m × 6.3m	82m × 7.4m	92m × 9.1m
Machinery:	2-shaft diesel/electric; 1,100bhp/790hp = 13.5/7.5 knots	2-shaft diesel/electric; 600bhp/770hp = 11.5/6.5 knots	2-shaft diesel/electric; 2,400bhp/1,200hp = 16.5/8.5 knots	2-shaft diesel/electric; 2,400bhp/1,200hp = 14.5/7 knots	2-shaft diesel/electric; 3,300bhp/1,690hp = 15/7.5 knots
Range:	7,200nm at 6 knots 55nm at 4 knots (dived)	8,300nm at 8 knots 50nm at 5 knots (dived)	8,300nm at 8 knots 50nm at 5 knots (dived)	9,400nm at 8 knots 35nm at 4.5 knots (dived)	17,750nm at 8 knots 53nm at 4.5 knots (dived)
Armament:	5–50cm TT (4B+1S: 10 torpedoes) 1–8.8 or 10.5cm (1 × I)	3–50cm TT (2B+1S: 7 torpedoes) 1–8.8 or 10.5cm (1 × I) 6 mine tubes (14 mines)	6–50cm TT (4B+2S: 12 torpedoes) 1–10.5cm/45 (1 × I)	4–50cm TT (4B: 12 torpedoes) 1–15cm/45 (1 × I) 2 mine tubes (42 mines)	6–50cm TT (4B+2S: 19 torpedoes) 2–15cm/45 (2 × I)
Notes:	three in service France two in service Japan three broken up Italy many broken up GB	three to France & Italy two in service Japan many broken up GB	four in service France two older Ms (Mob) in service Japan	U-117 to USA U-119/121 to France U-120 to Italy U-122–124/126 to GB U-125 to Japan	U-139 to France U-140 to USA U-141 to GB

Key to tables:
B = bow
S = stern
T = trainable

The other major beneficiaries of German submarine expertise were the French. Large numbers of former U-boats were allocated to France, and no fewer than ten were in service with the Marine Nationale until the mid-1930s, despite enormous difficulties in maintenance. All were in poor condition when first handed over, due not only to neglect but to the sabotage of much of their equipment by their former German crews. It was to take between two and four years, and considerable German (and, ironically, British!) technical assistance before they were ready for service again. Nevertheless, early inspection of the hulls, machinery and control systems provided invaluable assistance in the preparation of new submarine designs for the Marine Nationale. Moreover, the qualities of the warbuilt German submarines were found to be precisely those lacking in the French pre-war designs: robust construction, reliable diesel engines, high endurance, rapid diving (as little as thirty-five seconds for some U-boats), and a powerful, well-balanced armament.

In general the five Washington powers took what they required from German U-boat technology and adapted it to their own purposes. The US Navy, for example, appears to have been particularly interested in the highly developed equipment apparent in the later designs, including the hinged masts for long-range radio communications, the net-cutting apparatus and the protective frames around the after control surfaces and propellers, the use of chemicals for air purification, and the apparatus provided for submarine rescue.[4]

The German U-cruisers were also hugely influential. Long-range submersibles armed with two to four medium-calibre guns modelled on the German *U-139* and *U-142* classes were built for all five of the major navies during the interwar period. For the US Navy, which had previously seen the submarine as primarily useful for local area defence, the large German ocean-going boats were a revelation, opening up the possibility of intelligence-gathering and offensive operations in the Western Pacific from bases in Hawaii or on the West Coast. The Italians wanted similar large boats to operate in the Indian Ocean from colonial bases in the Red Sea and East Africa. The French also initiated a series of designs for long-range submarines armed with large-calibre guns, which were eventually to result in the *sous-marins corsaires* of the *Surcouf* class. These large submarine cruisers, some of which were built specifically for commerce raiding, were effectively 'legitimised' by their origins: the Imperial Germany Navy had built them following the abandonment of the first unrestricted U-boat campaign in March 1916, and they were designed to conform to internationally agreed Prize Laws.[5]

The larger German U-boats had double-hull construction, which was adopted to secure the increased fuel bunkerage necessary for oceanic operations, and this was subsequently adopted for many of the larger submarines designed and built during the 1920s, with mixed success. Locating fuel bunkers externally in a relatively light riveted outer hull often resulted in oil leaks, which reduced endurance and gave away the position of the submarine. The Italian and French submarines built on this principle also suffered serious transverse stability problems, and the Italian boats had to be rebuilt with additional lateral saddle tanks which resolved the stability problem at the expense of reduced surface speed. Access for maintenance was also a problem in double-hull boats, and corrosion of pipework and equipment was to shorten the service lives of many of these submarines.

However, the major obstacle to the realisation of large, fast submarines was the limited power of existing diesel engines. Diesels had been employed as the main propulsion unit for submarines only since the immediate pre-war era, earlier submarines having been powered by engines fuelled by petrol or kerosene. Early leaders in the competition to provide an effective diesel engine had been Vickers (GB), MAN (Germany), and Fiat (Italy), all of which favoured six- or eight-cylinder models using a four-stroke cycle. However, the maximum power available for most units was in the 800–900bhp range, and therefore inadequate for large submarines or fast submarines. In order to provide the 3,600bhp required for their early 'fleet' submarines of the 'J' class the British had to go to twelve cylinders and three engines driving three shafts. When their successors of the 'K' class were designed, an initial proposal with diesel power would have required no fewer than eight engines of the same twelve-cylinder model to give the required speed of 24 knots (equivalent to 10,000bhp) – hence the eventual decision in favour of steam turbines.

The German solution to the problem was to build a larger engine with a high power-to-weight ratio. However, this in turn required a much larger submarine with a large-diameter pressure hull to accommodate it. The first *U-Kreuzer* of the *U-139* class had large six-cylinder MAN diesels with a nominal rating of 1,650bhp, but maximum speed on the surface (15 knots plus) was only on a par with the smaller German sea-going boats. The even larger (but untried) ten-cylinder MAN diesel planned for the *U-142* class, which was particularly influential in the postwar Imperial Japanese and US navies, was rated at 3,000bhp, but even so maximum speed for these submarines remained a modest 17.5 knots. This was sufficient for transit to patrol areas for commerce raiding against slow merchant ships, but was inadequate for the fleet operations to which the major navies aspired during the interwar period.

Increasing the length of the engine by adding extra cylinders, as the British had attempted to do with the 'J' class, had the advantage of providing additional brake horsepower without increasing the height and width of the engine, but the downside was the additional torsional stresses, which resulted in engine wear and reduced reliability; the Vickers model does not appear to have been a great success and all but one of the 'J' class had been paid off and broken up by 1924. The alternative was the promise of a significant increase in the power-to-weight ratio of the engine by adopting two-stroke technology. Some of the warbuilt German U-boats had two-stroke diesels built by Germania, but the acknowledged leader in the field by the late-war period was the Swiss company Sulzer. In the immediate postwar period they began to build six-cylinder diesels for merchant ships with a unit power in excess of 3,000bhp. Japan, always quick to seize on promising trends in European technology, signed an agreement to build Sulzer two-stroke engines in its own shipyards as early as 1917. The first fruit of this agreement was the Type 2 single-action, two-cycle diesel rated at 1,300bhp which was used in a multiple (four-shaft) configuration to power the experimental *I-51* (see Chapter 2). More impressive was the Type 3 built from 1921 onwards, which was rated at 3,400bhp and which was to be the main power unit for Japan's first production fleet boats of the KD3 type. The advantage to Sulzer of this arrangement was that it enabled research, development and design to take place at the company's European factory, while manufacture of the diesels was undertaken in or close to the shipyards responsible for installation in Japan. Sulzer two-stroke diesels of 3,000bhp (later 4,000bhp) were also the main propulsion units of the French fleet boats of the *1500-tonnes* type.

It took until the mid-1920s for these higher-powered diesels to come into service, which meant that many of the large submarines built during the early 1920s had multiple engines, implying either multiple shafts or 'composite' drive in which the main diesels and the electric motors – the latter powered by separate 'auxiliary' diesels – were coupled to the same shaft; these complex propulsion plants generally proved to be a maintenance nightmare. Nor did the two-stroke diesels prove particularly reliable, and they required a higher level of maintenance than the traditional four-stroke engines.

The Submarine Cruiser X1

Of the five Washington signatories, the Royal Navy was arguably the least influenced by German submarine technology and the tactical framework for its employment during the period after the First World War. The submarines built for the Royal Navy prior to that conflict were designed firstly to provide for the defence of Britain's harbours and coasts, and secondly to patrol close to enemy coasts and naval bases with a view to providing intelligence in the event of a sortie by the enemy's fleet, as well as taking any opportunity to attack enemy battleships and cruisers as they left their bases. A third mission of mining the approaches to enemy harbours was added to the first two during 1916. Long range was not a priority, as the enemy bases in question were just across the North Sea, so the standard patrol submarines of the 'E' and 'L' classes had ranges of 3,000nm and 3,800nm at 10 knots respectively; for distant deployments (for example, to the Eastern Mediterranean) they were frequently towed part of the way in order to reduce fuel consumption and wear on their diesel engines.

The new types of submarine developed for the Royal Navy during the First World War were a response to a perceived German threat; hence the fleet submarines of the 'J' and 'K' classes were built to counter exceptionally fast (22-knot) German U-boats rumoured to be under construction, and the smaller anti-submarine 'hunter-killer' boats of the 'R' class were designed to intercept and sink anti-commerce U-boats operating in British coastal waters.

The cruiser submarine *X1*, seen here in 1925. Armed with two twin 5.2in guns in shielded open
mountings, she was inspired by the German cruiser submarines of the late-war period. Early post-
Washington plans for the Royal Navy featured up to twelve of these submarines, but although
the Pacific was probably the intended theatre, it was never entirely clear what their mission
would have been, and serious mechanical problems with the first boat meant that the programme
was abandoned. (Author's collection)

By the end of the First World War the British not only had a highly developed
submarine force of its own, but had a far greater variety of submarine types
than any other navy, including 'monitor' submarines armed with a single
12in gun (which inspired a similar proposal for the French Marine Nationale
during the early postwar period).

On 2 November 1921, only days before the opening of the Washington
Conference, the British laid down an experimental large cruiser submarine,
X1. Inspired by the German *U-Kreuzer*, *X1* had been designed in 1920,
when the Royal Navy had already had the opportunity to examine *U-141*,
which had been allocated to Britain as a war prize. *X1* was by no means
a slavish copy of the ex-German boat; she was significantly larger, with a
surfaced displacement approaching 3,000 tons, and a hull-form reminiscent
of the later 'K' class and optimised for high speed on the surface. Like the
German U-cruisers she had a double hull with most of the fuel bunkerage in
the outer hull. She had an even more powerful gun armament, comprising
twin 5.2in QF guns behind shields fore and aft of the conning tower; there
was a rangefinder with a nine-foot base atop the latter, and 100 rounds per
gun were provided in the magazine. The overall impact of the guns on the
design is evidenced by the strength of the gunnery team as a proportion of the
boat's complement: no fewer than fifty-eight out of a crew of 109!

X1 was designed for a diving depth of 400ft, but it took some time before
this figure was realised because she was fitted with torpedo tubes originally
ordered for the later 'L' class, the doors of which could withstand pressures
only up to 200ft depth before they were strengthened. She also had an unusual
'composite' propulsion system with a pair of powerful eight-cylinder diesels
of Admiralty design, each rated at 3,000bhp, supplemented by a pair of
auxiliary six-cylinder MAN diesels removed from the war prize *U-126*, each

with a nominal rating of 1,200bhp. The latter were normally used to charge the batteries via a pair of motor/generators when running on the surface, but could also drive the motors directly when the latter were clutched to the shaft. This complex arrangement gave a theoretical maximum of more than 8,000bhp for a designed speed in excess of 20 knots. On trials, however, the highest recorded power was 7,135bhp for 19.5 knots; neither of the diesels installed achieved its designed rating (the maximum achieved by the MAN units was 940bhp). Worse was to follow: the engine drive wheels had to be replaced in 1926, and both shafts were broken during 1928 and had to be replaced. Both the main and the auxiliary engines gave constant trouble, and *X1* spent most of her operational life in dockyard hands.

Other problems included leaky external fuel tanks and a diving time of fully 3 to 4 minutes. *X1* handled well both on the surface and underwater, and the 5.2in Mk I gun appears to have been a particularly successful weapon, achieving a firing cycle of 6rpm once initial teething troubles were sorted out. With a nominal range of 16,000 yards it should have comfortably met the requirement for the submarine to be capable of sinking a destroyer at 6,000 yards. However, the rationale for this requirement is shrouded in mystery. Although the alleged justification for building this large and costly experimental submarine was 'to study the submerged handling of large vessels and also the practicability of mounting and using a heavy gun armament',[6] it is difficult to see how *X1* fitted in with any existing or projected Royal Navy strategy, and what would be her role in a conflict. This was probably as important a factor in the decision to pay her off in 1930 – less than five years after her completion – as the admittedly serious problems with her machinery; she was scrapped in 1936.

Overseas Patrol Submarines for the Royal Navy

Until the Washington Conference the British continued to hold out for an internationally agreed ban on the submarine as a category of warship. Britain's failure to secure such an agreement, together with the end of the Anglo-Japanese Alliance, had immense consequences for the fleet as a whole and for future submarine policy in particular. As a fleet (as opposed to anti-commerce) submarine force the British submarine fleet of 1918 was second to none. However, the 'E' and 'L' classes, which constituted the 'overseas' component and were hugely influential on other navies (notably that of Japan), were designed to transit the North Sea. The effective radius of 1,700nm of the 'L' was insufficient for oceanic operation, and it could barely reach Japanese waters from Hong Kong. It therefore became apparent in the immediate post-Washington period that a new, larger submarine would need to be developed specifically for operations in the Far East. The result was a new breed of 'Overseas Patrol Submarine' with twice the displacement of the 'L' and an endurance of 8,000–10,000nm.[7]

The prototype, funded under the 1923 Estimates, was the *O1* (later renamed *Oberon*). With a standard displacement of 1,310 tons, *O1* was 40ft longer and

4ft broader than the 'L', and had an exceptionally thick pressure hull which gave her a diving depth of 500ft. Speed on the surface was only 15 knots designed, but she had double the torpedo armament (six bow and two stern tubes – all internal – each with one reload for a total of sixteen), and a 4in deck gun. Power loading was introduced for the bow tubes, enabling a second torpedo salvo to be fired only seven minutes after the first. There was also a new ASDIC set, originally intended to be used in active mode against other submarines, and a long-range low-frequency radio receiver which enabled the submarine to receive instructions together with the latest intelligence updates from command bases ashore. *Oberon*'s much greater endurance (6,500nm at 10 knots) was achieved by carrying a lot of her fuel externally, in the upper half of the saddle tanks. In a move which reflected the rationale behind the design, two further slightly modified boats of the same type were purchased by Australia as *AO1* and *AO2* (later renamed *Otway* and *Oxley*) from Vickers; these were later to revert to Royal Navy control.

Oberon, which was powered by two Admiralty diesels rated at 1,350bhp, failed to make her designed surfaced speed by 1.25 knots and her designed underwater speed by 2 knots, largely due to insufficient care being taken in the design and the alignment of the multitude of external fittings. The production boats which followed had more powerful eight-cylinder diesels, and considerable efforts were made to reduce drag. They also incorporated

The prototype overseas patrol submarine, *Oberon* (centre), flanked by the two 'O'-class boats built for the Royal Australian Navy, *Otway* and *Oxley*. Initially it was envisaged that the Pacific dominion would fund and operate a number of these large patrol submarines, but in the event only these two were built, and they reverted to Royal Navy control in 1931. Note the modified bow of the two Australian boats, designed for higher speed on the surface. (Leo van Ginderen collection)

Oberon (GB)

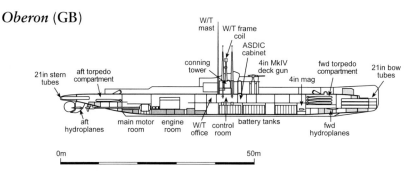

Oberon was the prototype for a series of large overseas patrol submarines designed to be able to operate in the Pacific Ocean against the Japanese. There were reloads for the six bow and two stern tubes, a 4in deck gun in a raised mounting, and long-range radio communications to ensure reliable contact with a shore-based control centre. Endurance was 8,500nm at 10 knots.

a succession of improvements aimed specifically at improving surface performance, including a modified bow better suited to good sea-keeping and raised forward hydroplanes. Six units of the *Odin* class (1926 Estimates) were followed by six units of the *Parthian* class (1927 Estimates) and finally by four – originally six – units of the *Rainbow* class (1928–29 Estimates). All had a maximum surface speed of 17.5 knots and a range in excess of 8,500nm at 10 knots. Armament was unchanged but a much-improved ASDIC set was fitted, which subsequently proved very effective when used in the passive 'detection' mode.

By 1932 the Royal Navy had no fewer than nineteen of these large overseas patrol submarines in commission. They were generally successful in service, although the external fuel bunkers located in the riveted outer hull leaked (a common problem with the large submarines built in the 1920s), and this problem had to be cured by welding. Like many other specialised warships built during the interwar period, they were to suffer grievously during the Second World War from being employed on missions for which they had not been designed. Many of these large, oceanic boats were deployed to the confined and shallow waters of the Mediterranean during 1940 and 1941, and no fewer than nine of them had been lost, from a variety of causes, before Japan even entered the war.

Submarine Minelayers

Minelaying had become an important submarine mission during the First World War. Prior to adopting unrestricted U-boat warfare the Imperial German Navy had taken advantage of its early occupation of Belgium and the Netherlands to build small rail-transportable minelaying submarines of the UC type for offensive operations off the coasts and in the harbour approaches of British ports in the North Sea. Later in the war the navy had embarked on the construction of large sea-going minelayers of the UE type, examples of which came into the possession of all but one of the major Allied

The last of the series of overseas patrol submarines, the 'R' class was to have comprised six boats, but the number was reduced to four as a result of defence economies. In theory, they would have had a key role in delaying the Japanese maritime advance on Singapore, thereby buying time for the British Fleet to arrive from Gibraltar and the Mediterranean. On 1 August 1939 no fewer than fourteen of the nineteen overseas patrol submarines were assigned to the China Station, where they were tended by the purpose-built depot ship *Medway* (1926 Estimates, completed 1929). This is *Rover* shortly after completion in August 1931. (Leo van Ginderen collection)

navies postwar. The small coastal minelayers of the UC type carried their mines externally in vertical tubes located in the saddle tanks, which meant that the mines themselves were exposed to sea corrosion; moreover depth settings had to be made prior to loading the mines and could not be adjusted during transit. The ocean-going minelayers of the UE type, on the other hand, carried forty-two mines internally, within the pressure hull, which were then laid from two horizontal 100cm stern tubes. Settings could be regulated up to the moment of laying – a particular advantage in distant operations, in which the tactical situation prevailing at the time of arrival in the minelaying zone often needed to be taken into account.

The British had traditionally been more interested in minelaying operations for 'area denial' than for sinking enemy shipping. The British 'E'- and 'L'-class submarines modified for minelaying during the First World War carried their 16–20 mines externally in saddle tank tubes modelled on those of the German UC type, but considerable interest was shown in the German UE type in the immediate postwar period. In July 1920 the Naval Staff asked for requirements for a submarine minelayer with mines stowed internally, and these were finally agreed in June 1923, when a submarine with a maximum (submerged) displacement of 2,500 tons and an internal capacity of 36–40 mines was agreed. No further action was taken either on the submarine or the mines it was designed to carry, presumably on grounds of cost. However, there was an on-going requirement for a seagoing minelayer, and in 1924 Rear-Admiral Submarines suggested a boat modelled on surface minelayers, with 100 mines on tracks within a free-flooding superstructure. Maintenance problems would remain, the mines would be exposed to full diving pressure,

Porpoise was the first of six large purpose-built minelayers built for the Royal Navy. The mines were carried atop the pressure hull in an enclosed outer casing, and were laid over the stern using a continuous chain mechanism. In the other five units the mine casing was continued to the bow. Note the periscopes offset to starboard to clear the mines. (Leo van Ginderen collection)

and settings could not be adjusted once the mines were embarked, but such a submarine would have a useful capacity while using existing mine stocks (and thereby minimising cost).

The concept was subsequently tested on a modified 'M'-class monitor submarine. The original 12in gun mounting was removed and mine rails fitted atop the pressure hull from just forward of the conning tower to the stern; the mine stowage area, which had a capacity of 100 'S'-type contact mines, was then enclosed in a free-flooding casing 6ft (1.8m) high. The boat was taken in hand in 1927 for a conversion which lasted fifteen months. Trials were generally successful, although there were some stability problems with a full load of mines, and the submarine took five minutes to dive because of the time it took to flood the additional casing. It was decided to proceed with a purpose-built minelayer based on the 'P' class using the same system, and the first, *Porpoise*, was duly authorised under the 1930 Estimates. The mine conveyor system in the production boats, which had a capacity of fifty mines, was located on the centre-line, so the periscopes were offset to starboard. Careful design of the venting arrangements meant that diving time was reduced to an acceptable ninety seconds. Five more boats of a slightly modified design with improved stability and a greater reserve of buoyancy would be ordered during the early 1930s.

New Sea-going and 'Fleet' Submarines

The Royal Navy had ended the First World War with a large force of medium patrol submarines, both of the overseas type ('E' and 'L' classes) and of the local area/coastal type ('H' class). After Washington the need to address a much-changed strategic situation led to a focus on large submarines of the overseas patrol type. However, as the end of the decade approached the Royal Navy was faced with the prospect of block obsolescence for its warbuilt boats, so studies began in 1928 for a sea-going patrol submarine which would replace the 'H' class in the training and local area role. In comparison to the 'H' class, the submarine was to have higher surfaced speed and greater operating radius, a greater submerged radius to counter improvements in anti-submarine measures, and a heavier armament (at least four, preferably six, bow tubes) to match the submarine's greater endurance. All this was to be achieved without sacrificing the rapid diving and general handiness of the 'H'. The latter proved to be a tall order, particularly when the operational radius requirement was further increased (a transit of 600nm at 9 knots with eight days on station was demanded) during the design stage. The result was the 'S' class, of which the first two units were authorised under the 1929 Estimates with a further pair in 1930.[8] The surfaced speed of these boats was only 13.5 knots, but they had good endurance and an impressive torpedo capacity for their size. However, they did not prove successful in service, due to complex and unreliable fittings, an unsatisfactory internal layout and poor transverse stability: a permanent list of 3° in the normal surface condition was found to increase to 20° when surfacing, which required remedial measures. Later boats of the type would be extensively modified.

The Royal Navy had never abandoned its dream of building fast fleet submarines, and the project was again revived during the late 1920s, when advances in diesel technology finally appeared to offer the prospect of a surface speed comparable to that of a capital ship. It was proposed to adopt a new Admiralty ten-cylinder four-stroke diesel developing a total power of 4,000bhp at 400rev/min on each of the two shafts. Using two auxiliary generators, driven by two Ricardo 400hp sleeve-valve engines, the main diesels could be supercharged to give a total of 10,000bhp for a top speed of 21.75 knots. The submarine would have an unusual 'keyhole' cross-section pressure hull and a surfaced displacement of 1,800 tons standard. The after torpedo tubes had to be omitted to make space for the auxiliary diesel generators, so total torpedo capacity (based on two per tube) was twelve torpedoes, two fewer than in the overseas patrol type. The primary mission of these large, fast submarines, as with their predecessors, was operations against Japan, so endurance was an impressive 10,000nm at 8 knots. This meant that most of the fuel was carried in external bunkers, but these were now welded for the first time, so leakage was not a problem.

The first boat, *Thames*, was authorised under the 1929 Estimates, two further boats followed in 1931–32, and seventeen further units were projected.[9] Designed speed was easily attained on trials (*Thames* attained 22.6 knots on the surface and an impressive 10.6 knots submerged), making these submarines the fastest fleet boats in the world outside the Imperial Japanese Navy.

Table 9.2: Royal Navy Submarine Designs 1920–29

	X1	Odin	Thames	Swordfish	Porpoise
Type:	cruiser	overseas patrol	fleet submarine	sea-going patrol	sea-going minelayer
Built:	1921–25	six 1927–30	three 1931–35	four 1930–33	six 1931–39
Displacement:	2,425tW	1,475tW	1,760tW (des.)	640tW (des.)	1,500tW
Dimensions:	364ft × 30ft	283ft × 30ft	345ft × 28ft	203ft × 24ft	293ft × 26ft
	(111m × 9.1m)	(86m × 9.1m)	(105m × 8.6m)	(62m × 7.3m)	(89m × 7.8m)
Machinery:	2-shaft composite;	2-shaft diesel/electric;	2-shaft diesel/electric;	2-shaft diesel/electric;	2-shaft diesel/electric;
	8,000bhp/2,400hp	4,520bhp/1,390hp	10,000bhp/2,500hp	1,550bhp/1,440hp	3,300bhp/1,630hp
	19.5/8 knots	17.5/8 knots	22/10 knots	13.5/10 knots	15.5/8.5 knots
Range:	14,500nm at 10 knots	8,500nm at 10 knots	10,000nm at 8 knots	3,800nm at 10 knots	7,400nm at 10 knots
	50nm at 4 knots (dived)		90nm at 3 knots (dived)		
Armament:	6–21in TT	8–21in TT	6–21in TT	6–21in TT	6–21in T T
	(6B: 12 torpedoes)	(6B+2S: 14 torpedoes)	(6B: 12 torpedoes)	(6B: 12 torpedoes)	(6B: 12 torpedoes)
	4–5.2in/42 (2 × II)	1–4in/40 (1 × I)	1–4in/40 (1 × I)	1–3in/45 (1 × I)	1–4in/40 (1 × I)
					50 mines

Note: To follow the prototype 'overseas patrol' submarine *Oberon*, the Royal Navy laid down six production boats of the *Odin* class, followed by six slightly improved boats of the *Parthian* class, and finally four repeat *Rainbow* class, all virtually identical in size and performance. Two similar boats were built for the Royal Australian Navy.

The US Navy's 'V'-Boats

All the early submarine types built for the US Navy had been for harbour and coastal defence. However, just before the First World War proposals for large sea-going submarines with sufficient range, endurance and speed to operate with the surface fleet were considered, and these led to *AA1–3* (later *T1–3*), laid down from 1916 to 1917 and completed postwar. With a displacement of 1,100 tons surfaced they were more than twice as large as any existing US Navy submarines, and their four large NLSE diesels, each with a nominal rating of 1,000bhp, drove two shafts for a designed speed of 20 knots. However, this unusual compound propulsion system was a failure: the 'T' class experienced severe torsional vibration problems when running on all four engines, and although they made 20 knots briefly on trials, they could not keep pace with the battle fleet in subsequent exercises. Continuing problems with their propulsion machinery led to their being decommissioned in 1922, when they had been in service for only two years, and they were broken up in 1930.

These problems were still in the future, though, when in 1916, with US entry into the war becoming increasingly likely, Congress authorised a programme which included nine more fleet boats, which would become *V1–9*. The first three of these were duly funded in FY1919 and laid down at the Portsmouth Navy Yard shortly before the Washington Conference. However, funding for these large, expensive submarines then slowed to a virtual halt and only four more were funded before the London Conference of 1930. By the end of 1930 only six 'V'-boats had been completed and these, together with six 'S'-class medium patrol boats (the design of which dated from the late-war period), were the only submarines completed for the US Navy between 1922 and 1930. Moreover, because the building rate was so slow, the design was subject to new requirements, the influence of strategic and technical trends at home and abroad and, from the late 1920s, possible future treaty restrictions. The original 'V'-boat concept became fragmented to such an extent that the nine submarines completed fall into three broad groupings and five distinct classes, with surfaced displacement varying by more than a factor of two between the middle and later groups.

The first three boats, *V1–3*, were essentially a development of the unsuccessful 'T' class but significantly larger, with a surfaced displacement of 2,120 tons and a length of 335ft (102m). They were also designed for 21 knots on the surface, the necessary power being provided by two large Busch-Sulzer six-cylinder diesels of 2,250bhp coupled directly to the twin shafts, with two independent 1,000bhp auxiliary diesels. The latter, located in a separate compartment farther forward, were primarily for charging the batteries via the electric motor generators when running on the surface, but could also drive the main motors directly, enabling both the motors and the main diesels to be clutched to the shafts, as in the British *X1*, to provide a total of 6,200bhp. There were six torpedo tubes (four in the bow, two in the stern) each with a single reload for a total load-out of twelve torpedoes, plus a single 5in/51-calibre deck gun. This was a relatively modest armament for such a large submarine; neither was the designed endurance of 6,000nm at 10 knots particularly impressive when compared with the Japanese prototype fleet boats or the British *Odins*, which were significantly smaller.

It took between three and five years to complete *V1–3*, and their performance both on trials and in service proved disappointing. Maximum speed on the surface was only 18.5 knots, and they also failed to attain their designed underwater speed of 9 knots. Lack of buoyancy in the bow section plus an accumulation of weights forward made them poor seaboats, and the 5in/51-calibre deck gun had to be replaced with the smaller and lighter 3in/50-calibre model. Although the propulsion machinery was an undoubted improvement on that of the earlier 'T's, both the main diesels and the electric motors were notoriously unreliable, so that full-power availability was rare. Renamed *Barracuda*, *Bass* and *Bonita* in 1931, they would be decommissioned in 1937.

Although the General Board continued to favour fast fleet submarines which could operate with the battle fleet, the shift in the strategic focus of the US Navy from the Atlantic to the Pacific after the First World War ensured that the next series of three boats were very different in conception and design. Inspired by the German U-cruisers, *V4–6* were the result of a prolonged series of studies for large, ocean-going submarines capable of independent strategic scouting and offensive operations in the Western Pacific which began in 1918 and continued until the mid-1920s.

Although a German-style campaign against the vulnerable Japanese merchant fleet was prohibited by international law, it was argued that submarines operating off Japanese ports could warn of sorties by IJN fleet units. In addition to this strategic scouting mission, which would be enhanced if seaplanes for reconnaissance were carried, submarines operating in forward areas could attack capital ships and might also be equipped to lay mines.

For such a submarine endurance, not high tactical speed, was the primary consideration. It was estimated that it would take thirty-three days to cover the 7,000nm from the West Coast of the USA to the Western Pacific. The US Navy could not rely on Manila as a forward operating base because it was assumed that the Philippines would fall quickly in a war against Japan, and even submarines operating from Hawaii would have to make a transit of 4,000–5000nm in order to reach patrol areas in the Western Pacific.

The General Board continued to favour the fast fleet submarine, to be deployed in advance of the battle fleet, but was compelled to recognise that only a cruiser type could perform advanced scouting from Hawaiian waters, so it called for a mix of fleet submarines and long-range cruiser and minelaying types. The cruiser was to have an endurance of ninety days,[10] a range of 17,000nm at 10 knots with maximum fuel load, and a load-out of thirty torpedoes. Other requirements were for a diving depth of 300ft (previous submarines could dive to a maximum of 200ft), a continuous reliable speed of 15 knots (transit time was an issue because every additional day spent in transit meant one less day on patrol), an observation aircraft and two large-calibre anti-surface guns.

These characteristics were remarkably close to those of the Project 46 U-cruiser, and the submarines which resulted were heavily influenced by the German design, combining double-hull construction with a 'dory' bow which proved to have far better sea-keeping qualities than earlier bulbous types. The US Navy was also interested in dry stowage for the mines carried by the minelaying variant because of the lengthy Pacific transit, so again a system virtually identical to that of the large German UE II type[11] was adopted, with the mines being carried internally and launched from twin stern tubes. In May 1922 the General Board called for an annual programme of three cruiser submarines and three minelayers per year for FY1923–25, but Congress refused to sanction such an aggressive and costly programme in the wake of the Washington Conference. In April of the following year, alarmed by reports that Japan was embarking on a programme of forty-six large submarines, the General Board requested six cruisers and six minelayers for FY1925. Congress agreed only a single large minelayer.

V4 (later called *Argonaut*), was the largest submarine built for the US Navy until the advent of nuclear power, and was its first purpose-built minelayer. With a submerged displacement of fully 4,160 tons and an overall length of 381ft (116m), she carried almost 700 tons of diesel oil to provide the required range of 18,000 at 10 knots. There were four 21in bow tubes for a total loadout of sixteen torpedoes, two single 6in/53-calibre deck guns, and two horizontal 40in mine tubes aft modelled on the 100cm stern tubes of the German UE II. The sixty Mk XI moored mines were stowed inside the pressure hull in place of the after torpedo tubes and reloads (see drawing). A reconnaissance aircraft was originally to have been accommodated in a pressure-proof tank, but there were concerns about the effect of the latter on control of the submarine when running submerged and on diving, and following disappointing trials with a prototype lightweight (2,000lb) floatplane the concept was abandoned.

V4 was powered by four MAN diesels in a composite drive arrangement similar to that of the earlier 'V'-boats. In service, however, the MAN six-cylinder diesels proved just as unreliable as their Busch-Sulzer predecessors, and the mine stowage compartment occupied so much of the internal volume aft that *Argonaut* suffered from being seriously underpowered, so that the designed speed of 14.5 knots on the surface was never realised. The original diesels were replaced by a more powerful General Motors model early in the Second World War, raising total horsepower to 3,600bhp, but the minelaying system was subsequently stripped out to facilitate conversion to a transport submarine, and *Argonaut* was never to conduct a single minelaying mission.

The General Board requested three cruisers and two minelayers for FY1926, but only two scout/cruisers were authorised. V5–6 (renamed

Stern view of *Argonaut* (ex-*V4*) shortly after her completion. Note the flattening of the casing above the 40in horizontal mine tubes, and the 6in/53-calibre deck gun abaft the conning tower. (US Navy)

Narwhal and *Nautilus* in 1931), were similar in size and general design to *V4*, but had two stern tubes each with four torpedoes in place of the minelaying system. The suppression of the latter also released additional hull volume for propulsion machinery, so that installed horsepower was nearly double that of *V4*, for a designed speed of 17 knots. The main propulsion units were MAN ten-cylinder two-cycle diesels each rated at 2,350bhp, and there were small 450bhp auxiliary diesels for charging the batteries or for supplementing power on the surface. Although 17.5 knots was attained on trials, the diesels proved just as troublesome as earlier models and were replaced by four 1,600bhp GM units early in the Pacific War.

For FY1928 the General Board proposed two (repeat *V4*-type) minelayers and a single (repeat *V5*-type) scout/cruiser, with a view to completing the 'V'-boat programme as originally sanctioned by Congress in 1916. These orders would have created a balanced force of three fleet boats, three cruisers and three minelayers. However, the US Navy's submarine arm, which was by no means as enthusiastic about these large, complex and costly submarines as the General Board, was now getting restive. The submariners argued that at the current rate of authorisation it would take forever to build sufficient 'V'-boats, and proposed building smaller types better suited to wartime mass production. There was considerable support for a US Navy version of the German *U-135* type, which many submariners still considered superior in performance to any US submarine built since the war. A submarine of 1,000–1,400 tons with a hull virtually identical to *U-135* was proposed, with a maximum speed of 16 knots on the surface and 8 knots submerged, a range of 10,000nm at 9 knots, and an armament of a single deck gun and six torpedo tubes (four bow/two stern) each with a single reload.

The Bureau of Construction and Repair (C&R) disagreed strongly, pointing out that the German boat had a number of characteristics which

Argonaut (US)

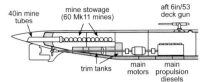

Narwhal (US)

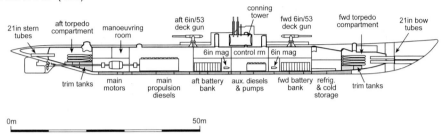

The two cruiser submarines of the *Narwhal* class and their half-sister *Argonaut* were designed to conduct lengthy patrols in the Western Pacific. They were armed with two 6in deck guns and were provided with twenty-four torpedoes for their four bow and two stern tubes; endurance was 18,000nm at 10 knots. In *Argonaut*, designed for minelaying off Japanese harbours, the stern tubes and the corresponding torpedo compartment were replaced by two German-style horizontal tubes with stowage for sixty mines. This impacted on the space available for propulsion machinery, which in turn reduced transit speed and limited the time she could spend on patrol.

made it fundamentally unsuited to long-range Pacific operations, notably insufficient space for stores, a total lack of cold storage or oil coolers, poor habitability, and poor accessibility for maintenance. It was also pointed out that heavier US equipment and engines would be difficult to accommodate in such a cramped design.

Nevertheless, the case for a smaller, 'mobilisation'-type submarine had been made, and over the next two years a number of sketch designs for 1,500-ton cruisers were prepared by C&R. By the end of 1927 it appeared that, with the development of Pearl Harbor as the primary operational base of the US Navy in the Pacific, an endurance of 12,000nm (equivalent to a sixty to ninety-day patrol) was sufficient. It was also now increasingly accepted that submarines would operate independently of the battle fleet, so high 'fleet' speed was unnecessary; a good torpedo battery, machinery reliability and habitability were considered more important requirements for deployment in the Western Pacific. The War Plans division wanted displacement kept to 1,600 tons surfaced, with a sustained sea speed of 12–14 knots (15–17 knots maximum),[12] six torpedo tubes with three torpedoes per tube, and a single 5in deck gun.

The end result of these deliberations was *V7*, a 1,570-ton submarine intermediate in size between the medium patrol submarines of the 'S' class and the large cruiser submarines of the previous group. With a nominal range of 11,000nm at 10 knots and a designed endurance of seventy-five days, the smaller cruiser retained a genuine trans-Pacific capability. It was

The two cruiser submarines of the *Narwhal* class (ex-*V5/6*) and their half-sister *Argonaut* were, with the exception of the French *Surcouf*, the largest submarines of the interwar period. Derived from the late-war German cruiser submarines of the Project 46A type, their primary mission was to conduct lengthy patrols in the Western Pacific with a view to providing intelligence on IJN fleet movements and to sink surface targets of opportunity. Note the flat deck casing and the 'dory' bow, which were also features of the German boats. (US Navy)

The two big 6in/53-calibre deck guns are particularly prominent in this early view of *Narwhal* running at speed on the surface. Note the 'V5' on the bow and the conning tower.

also an insurance policy against possible future treaty restrictions. At the abortive Geneva Conference of 1927 the British had proposed an 1,800-ton limit on individual submarine displacement,[13] and there was every prospect that within a short period of time submarines would be subject to treaty restrictions outlawing submarines above 2,000 tons.

A close-up of *Narwhal* taken during the Second World War, when she received an Oerlikon 20mm AA gun and improved electronic equipment. The big 6in/53-calibre guns are particularly prominent fore and aft of the conning tower; they were located on a raised gunnery platform to keep the crews as dry as possible. (USNHC)

V7 (renamed *Dolphin* in 1931) reverted to the more traditional saddle-tank configuration and had a smaller conning tower modelled on the 'S' class, but retained many of the other features of the large cruisers, having a broad flat deck with a raked bow, and a similar composite drive propulsion system based on four MAN six-cylinder diesels – two main diesels rated at 1,750bhp and two auxiliary diesels each rated at 450bhp – for a maximum speed of 17 knots. Three torpedoes were provided for each of the six torpedo tubes (four bow, two stern), as originally proposed, but the calibre of the single deck gun was reduced to 4in.

It was initially envisaged that *V7* would be a one-off prototype, and that the construction of larger cruisers would then be resumed, but the Wall Street Crash and the London Treaty intervened to ensure that future US submarines would be even smaller. *Dolphin* was the last US Navy submarine to be ordered prior to the London Conference of 1930, and the design of the last two 'V'-boats, *V8–9* (later *Cachalot* and *Cuttlefish*), would be influenced by the limitations agreed at that conference on unit size and on overall submarine tonnage (see Chapter 11).

The performance of *Dolphin* in service was to prove disappointing. Her machinery was unreliable and, despite being completed only in 1932, she would quickly be relegated to training duties during the Second World War. Nevertheless, in terms of her size and general capabilities, she blazed a trail

Table 9.3: The US Navy's 'V'-Boats 1920–29

	V1–3	V4	V5–6	V7–9
	(>Barracuda class)	(>Argonaut)	(>Narwhal class)	(>Dolphin)
Built:	three 1921–26	1925–28	two 1927–30	1930–32
Displacement:	1,910tW	2,660tW	2,730tW	1,550tW (des.)
Dimensions:	341ft × 28ft (104m × 8.4m)	381ft × 34ft (116m × 10.3m)	371ft × 33ft (113m × 10.1m)	319ft × 28ft (97m × 8.5m)
Machinery:	2-shaft composite; 6,500bhp/2,400hp = 21/9 knots (des)	2-shaft composite; 3,250bhp/2,200hp = 15/8 knots (des)	2-shaft composite; 5,600bhp/1,600hp = 17/8 knots	2-shaft composite; 4,200bhp/1,750hp = 17/8 knots
Range:	10,000nm at 10 knots 50nm at 5 knots (dived)	18,000nm at 10 knots 50nm at 5 knots (dived)	18,000nm at 10 knots 50nm at 5 knots (dived)	11,000nm at 10 knots 50nm at 5 knots (dived)
Armament:	6–21in TT (4B+2S: 12 torpedoes) 1–5in/51 (1 × I)	4–21in TT (4B: 16 torpedoes) 2–6in/53 (2 × I) 2 mine tubes (60 mines)	6–21in TT (4B+2S: 24 torpedoes) 2–6in/53 (2 × I)	6–21in TT (4B+2S: 18 torpedoes) 1–4in/50 (1 × I)

for the 1,500-ton 'fleet boats' of the *Gato, Balao* and *Tench* classes which were to make such an impact on the latter stages of the Pacific War.

Large Submarines for Japan

Japan's geostrategic situation was in effect a mirror image of that of the United States. The Japanese fleet could comfortably dominate home waters, but was faced with the prospect of having to face a superior US battle fleet despatched from the West Coast of America or from Pearl Harbor. The medium patrol submarines developed from European models during the late-war period were more than adequate for the defence of the Japanese homeland. However, they had insufficient range to operate outside Japanese waters, and inadequate surfaced speed to operate in conjunction with the Japanese battle fleet.

Like the French, the Japanese saw the submarine as a potential 'force multiplier' capable of compensating for the navy's statutory inferiority in capital ships imposed by the Washington Treaty. The weak point of the US Navy's expeditionary strategy as embodied in Plan Orange was the 5,000–7,000-mile transit across the Central Pacific en route to the 'decisive battle' in the seas south of Japan.[14] During that transit its strength would need to be whittled down in order to give the Combined Fleet a reasonable chance of success. There was a notable precedent to such an action in the Japanese victory over a nominally superior Russian fleet at Tsushima in 1905, and it was envisaged that a determined and well-coordinated campaign of harassment during the lengthy voyage to the Western Pacific would leave the US Fleet as tired and demoralised as its predecessor. The large, long-range submarine was seen as the primary weapon to achieve this: it could operate off Hawaii or the West Coast of America, it could provide strategic intelligence about US Navy movements and strength, and it could harass the US battle fleet, and hopefully cripple two or three of its capital ships as it steamed across the open expanses of the Pacific en route to the decisive battle.

We have already seen in Chapter 2 how the IJN had embarked on the design and construction of large, fast experimental submarines of the *Kaigun-dai* ('fleet') type even before the Washington Conference. Once the treaty was concluded it would put in place a programme for a powerful force of ocean-going submarines of three distinct types backed up by a considerable investment in infrastructure. The Submarine School, which had been founded only in 1920, was moved to new accommodation at Kure in 1924, and provided rigorous training for all submariners.[15] The appointment of Rear-Admiral Suetsugu Nobumasa to command the 1st Submarine Division, comprising the first of the newly developed large submarines, resulted in dramatic progress: older, more conservative officers were replaced by younger, more aggressive and ambitious men; rigorous training methods were instituted and new tactics devised. From 1925 IJN submarines began the surveillance of US ports, and from 1926 they were given the mission of locating the enemy fleet as it sortied from its main base, and of tracking and harassing it en route.

Only one fast fleet submarine of the KD2 type, the first of which had been laid down prior to the Washington Conference, was completed; the other five projected were cancelled in 1922 to allow the IJN time to review its entire post-treaty construction programme. Following this review the navy embarked on the construction of three distinct types: one was a development of the KD2, but the other two were more specialised types which owed much to postwar German influence.

The first production submarines of the KD type were laid down from August 1924. With a length of 100m and a standard displacement of 1,635 tons, the KD3 was powered, like the KD2 prototype, by two large Sulzer Type 3 diesels, each rated at 3,400bhp. These gave a maximum speed of 20 knots on the surface, while endurance was an impressive 10,000nm at 10 knots. Six bow and two stern 53cm torpedo tubes, each provided with two torpedoes, were complemented by a single 12cm deck gun. No fewer than nine submarines of the KD3 type entered service between 1927 and 1930, and these were followed by six slightly modified units of the KD4 and KD5 types, which were laid down from 1926 and 1929 respectively and completed between 1930 and 1932. The major difference was that the latter two classes were powered by 3,000bhp MAN Type 2 diesels, and had only four bow tubes (the torpedo load-out was correspondingly reduced to fourteen). The KD5 also had a smaller 10cm deck gun with a dual-purpose capability. Once significant numbers had been completed the KD submarines were given an organisation similar to IJN destroyers: a typical submarine squadron comprised three divisions each with three submarines, with a light cruiser flagship to provide command, control and communications. This organisation clearly derived from their fleet function.

In March 1923, almost eighteen months before work on the first of the production fleet boats began, the first cruiser submarine of the *Junsen* type was laid down at the Kawasaki Shipyard, Kobe. Derived from the Project 46A *U-Kreuzer* of the *U-142* class,[16] the J1 type was a large, double-hulled submarine with a standard displacement of almost 2,000 tons. Designed for independent operations off Hawaii and the US West Coast, these submarines were powered by two 3,000bhp MAN Type 2 diesels purchased directly from Germany. Maximum speed on the surface was 18 knots, which was lower than that of the fleet boats but meant that a transit speed of around 15 knots could be sustained. Even more impressive were the figures for endurance: 24,000nm at 10 knots.[17] There were six torpedo tubes (four bow, two stern) and twenty torpedoes, while the 15cm guns guns fore and aft of the conning tower in the original German design were replaced by the standard IJN light cruiser weapon, the 14cm gun.

Four large cruisers of the J1 type were completed 1923–29, and these were followed by a slightly modified boat of the J1M type, which was equipped to operate a floatplane for long-range scouting. Experiments using a German Caspar-Heinkel U-1 biplane fitted with floats[18] began in 1923, and a prototype Japanese aircraft based on the U-1, the Yokosuka Type 1, was test-flown from the minelaying submarine *I-21* (later *I-121*). The wings could be folded back for stowage in a cylindrical hangar, and the aircraft had an endurance of two hours. Following the trials with *I-21* it was decided to proceed with the development of a larger and more advanced aircraft, which became the Watanabe E9W1.

In the specially modified J1 design twin cylindrical hangars to house the fuselage/floats and wings respectively were fitted abaft the conning tower, the hangars being retracted into the outer hull when not in use. Assembly of the aircraft was a protracted and difficult operation, and it then had to be lowered onto the water for launch, which could be performed only in relatively calm sea conditions. The aircraft-handling arrangements of the J1M were not considered a success, and the equipment was subsequently removed in 1940. Later cruiser submarines of the *Junsen* type would have catapults and more highly developed aircraft-handling arrangements, but this would be at the expense of one of the two large-calibre guns.

The third new ocean-going submarine type developed for the Imperial Japanese Navy post-Washington was the *Kirai sen* or KRS type. A virtual copy of the German UE II-type ocean minelayer, of which Japan had received one example, *U-125*, as a war prize (she became *O1* in IJN service), the KRS was intended to lay mines off American harbours in the Western and Central Pacific. Characteristics were almost identical to the German boats, the only major difference being the substitution of a 14cm deck gun for the original 15cm. There were four bow tubes for a loadout of twelve

I-53, completed in March 1927, was the first of the Imperial Japanese Navy's fleet submarines of the KD3A type. Like the KD2 prototype (see Chapter 2), the KD3s were powered by two large Sulzer Type 3 diesels, each rated at 3,400bhp, giving them a maximum speed of 20 knots on the surface. (Fukui Shizuo collection)

The four submarines of the J1 type were, like the US *Narwhal*, derived from the German
U-cruisers of the Project 46A type and were powered by MAN 3,000bhp diesels. Although not as
fast as the 'fleet' (KD) types, they had sufficient endurance to enable them to operate off Hawaii
or even the West Coast of the United States. This is *I-3*, completed in 1926; note the 14cm guns
fore and aft of the conning tower.

torpedoes, and two 100cm mine tubes aft for forty-two mines, which were
stowed internally in the after compartments. This restricted the internal
volume available to house the propulsion machinery, as was the case with
both the German UE boats and the US Navy's *Argonaut*, so maximum speed
on the surface was only 14.5 knots. Range was 10,500nm at 8 knots, and
endurance only twenty days; this was less of a disadvantage in a minelayer,
which had a fixed short-term mission, than in a patrol submarine, but it did
mean that the American West Coast was effectively beyond reach without
forward basing.

J1 (Jap)

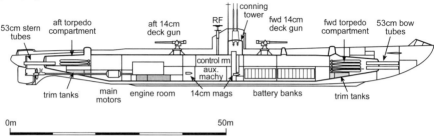

The J1 was the Japanese counterpart to the US Navy's *Narwhal* and *Nautilus*. Derived from
the German Project 46A type, these submarines were likewise intended for long-distance
reconnaissance off enemy bases. They were smaller than the American boats, but were heavily
armed and had an impressive endurance. The 14cm (5.5in) gun was considered handier than the
6in weapon given the smaller stature of the average Japanese seaman. Four boats were built to
the standard configuration before the IJN started experimenting with reconnaissance aircraft.

Table 9.4: IJN Large Submarines 1920–29

	J1	KD3A/B	KRS	KD4/KD5	J1M
Type:	cruiser	fleet submarine	sea-going minelayer	fleet submarine	cruiser
Built:	four 1923–29	nine 1924–30	four 1924–28	six 1926–32	one 1929–32
Displacement:	1,955tW	1,635tW	1,140tW	1,638tW	1,955tW
Dimensions:	97.5m × 9.2m	100m × 8m	85m × 7.5m	98m × 7.8m	(as J1)
Machinery:	2-shaft diesel/electric; 6,000bhp/2,600hp = 18/8 knots	2-shaft diesel/electric; 6,800bhp/1,800hp = 20/8 knots	2-shaft diesel/electric; 2,400bhp/1,100hp = 14.5/7 knots	2-shaft diesel/electric; 6,000bhp/1,800hp = 20/8 knots	(as J1)
Range:	24,000nm at 10 knots 60nm at 3 knots (dived)	10,000nm at 10 knots 90nm at 3 knots (dived)	8,000nm at 12 knots 40nm at 4.5 knots (dived)	10,000nm at 10 knots 60nm at 3 knots (dived)	(as J1)
Armament:	6–53cm TT (4B+2S: 20 torpedoes) 2–14cm/40 (2 × I)	8–53cm TT (6B+2S: 16 torpedoes) 1–12cm/45 (1 × I)	4–53cm TT (4B: 12 torpedoes) 1–14cm/40 (1 × I) 2 mine tubes (42 mines)	6–53cm TT (4B+2S: 14 torpedoes) 1–12cm/10cm (1 × I)	6–53cm TT (4B+2S: 20 torpedoes) 2–14cm/40 (2 × I) 1 floatplane

Four submarines of the KRS type were built, the first being laid down in October 1924; they were completed in 1927–28. They would be the last purpose-built minelaying submarines built for the IJN, leaving the large *Junsen* cruisers and the fast *Kaigun dai* fleet boats as the two main strands of Japanese submarine construction during the early 1930s.

The Marine Nationale

French interest in the submarine as a means of countering Britain's numerically superior battle fleet was longstanding, and the perceived inequity of the Washington Treaty, which restricted the Marine Nationale to a third of Britain's capital ship tonnage, served only to reinforce France's determination to create a force of modern submarines which would be second to none. In the absence of an agreement on tonnage limits at Washington, the French felt fully justified in adhering to the overall figure of 90,000 tons which they considered essential to national maritime security, and which they had placed on the table at the conference only for it to be rejected by the British delegation.

Unfortunately, as was the case with the remainder of France's ambitious postwar naval modernisation programme, such a force would have to be created virtually from scratch. The early French boats built during the pre-war period were short-range submarines designed for underwater operation in the approaches to harbours; they were plagued by poor-quality equipment and unreliable diesels. The Entente Cordiale with Britain had effectively undermined the harbour defence mission, while the larger French submarines deployed to the Adriatic to assist the Italians in blockading the Austro-Hungarian Fleet had proved relatively ineffectual, and had sustained more losses than they had inflicted. German development of the 'submersible', a submarine designed to operate on the surface of the seas and oceans, submerging only to attack, was every bit as great a revelation to the French as it was to the Americans and the Japanese, and the submarines designed and built for the Marine Nationale following the First World War would bear little resemblance to their predecessors.

A review of the future naval programme in the aftermath of Washington established an overall requirement for eighty-four submarines, of which forty-six would be large submarines of the patrol or fleet type, thirty would be for coastal defence, and eight would be ocean-going cruisers armed with two 8in guns for commerce protection and deployment in defence of the colonies. In a move which reflected French indignation at the unfairness of the Washington Treaty the French parliament insisted on an *increase* in the number of coastal defence boats to forty-eight!

The design of the 1,100-tonne large patrol submarines of the *Requin* class was based on that of the German Ms type. It was a double-hull design with moderate speed on the surface and a range of 6,650nm at 10 knots. The major difference lay in the armament, which was altogether more powerful. There were four bow and two stern tubes, all with a single reload, and four external tubes in twin trainable mountings (which were to become a feature of all French interwar submarines), together with a single 100mm deck gun. The torpedo tubes were all of the new 550mm diameter, and fired a torpedo with a 310kg warhead to a range of 3,000m at 45 knots or 7,000m at 35 knots – impressive figures for the day.

Nine of these submarines were built under the 1922 *Statut Naval*, with six being authorised in 1922 and three in 1923. As might be expected with a completely new type, they were not a great success. Lightweight machinery and construction resulted in regular equipment failures, the conning tower was cramped, and handling characteristics were not good. Worse still, they were too heavy, and could not dive in water with a density greater than 1,021kg/m³ (1,025kg/m³ was standard in the Atlantic); remedial measures included disembarking the reserve torpedoes and reducing external fuel bunkerage (thereby reducing range and endurance). They were rebuilt with a remodelled conning tower and new machinery during the late 1930s.

French submarines had traditionally been built in the naval dockyards. Had this practice been adhered to for the post-Washington submarine programme the naval dockyards would have had insufficient capacity to deliver the numbers required. For the coastal patrol submarines the Marine Nationale therefore turned to three private shipyards, each of which was contracted to design and build four submarines to general specifications provided by the STCN. The three shipyards selected employed former constructors as consultants, and came up with quite different designs.

The resulting submarines were well-armed for their size: there was a single internal bow tube with two fixed external tubes (designated *tubes-canons*) angled outwards forward of the conning tower, two stern tubes, and a trainable twin mounting immediately abaft the conning tower, for a total of seven ready-use torpedoes plus a reserve torpedo for the single bow tube. There was also a 75mm deck gun (several units received a 100mm).

The *600 tonnes* were manoeuvrable and well adapted to operations in shallow waters. However, the double hull (also a feature of the German UB III

The submarines of the *600-tonnes* type were designed for local area defence and were funded under the coast defence budget. They packed a considerable punch for their size but were cramped and unsuited to prolonged patrols. This is *Eurydice*: note the '*tubes canons*' – fixed external torpedo tubes angled outboard – close to the bow.

Table 9.5: French Submarines of the 1922 *Statut Naval*

	Requin	*600 tonnes*
Type:	sea-going patrol	coastal patrol
Built:	nine 1923–28	twelve 1924–28
Displacement:	975tW	550–575tW
Dimensions:	78m × 6.8m	66m × 5.2/6.2m
Machinery:	2-shaft diesel/electric;	2-shaft diesel/electric;
	2,900bhp/1,800hp	1,250bhp/1,000hp
	= 15/9 knots	= 14/7.5 knots
Range:	7,700nm at 9 knots	3,000nm at 9 knots
	70nm at 5 knots (dived)	75nm at 5 knots (dived)
Armament:	10–550mm TT	7–550mm TT
	(4B+2S+4T: 16 torpedoes)	(3B+2S+2T: 8 torpedoes)
	1–100mm/40 (1 × I)	1–100mm/40 (1 × I)

on which these boats were closely modelled) meant that crew accommodation was particularly cramped. They were not good divers, experienced stability problems, and had a maximum underwater speed of only 7.5 knots. They also shared many of the defects of the *Requin* class with regard to the layout and reliability of their machinery. The Normand-Fenaux sub-group proved to be the most successful of the three, but the Marine Nationale clearly considered the experiment of putting out contracts to three competing shipyards worth repeating, as it was to adopt the same procedure with the next class of coastal boats.

The 1924 Programme

The ambitious six-year 1924 *Statut Naval* which followed on from the 1922 programme aimed to bring French overall submarine tonnage to more than 94,000 tonnes. It included two large cruiser submarines, six minelaying submarines, and no fewer than twenty-eight 1,500-tonne patrol submarines for the fleet, alongside an on-going programme of patrol submarines for coastal defence.

The *Requin* class, modelled as it was on a German design intended for commerce warfare, was considered too slow for operations with and against surface warships. A series of studies for a new submarine with sufficient speed to scout for the fleet (designated 'M') was therefore put in motion in December 1922. The Naval General Staff wanted 17 knots sustained on three-quarters power – a forty-eight-hour trial was required! – with an endurance of 4,000nm (or thirty days) at 10 knots surfaced, and 100nm at 5 knots submerged. The armament was to comprise four bow torpedo tubes with reloads plus two trainable twin mountings (one of which replaced the stern tubes to free up internal volume for the powerful machinery required), complemented by a single 100mm gun, an anti-aircraft gun and two machine guns. The submarine was to be capable of diving in less than sixty seconds, would have a maximum diving depth of 80m (260ft), and a 25 per cent reserve of buoyancy. Displacement was to be the minimum compatible with these requirements.

July 1924 saw the adoption of project M5 as the basis for the new submarines, which were significantly larger than the *Requin* class and were to become known as the '*1500 tonnes*'. Power was provided by a new Sulzer diesel with a nominal rating of 3,000bhp (twice that of the model in the *Requin* class) and the first two boats, *Redoutable* and *Vengeur*, had a separate generator to charge the batteries. In the M6 design which superseded it the generator was abandoned, and later boats of the series had even more powerful diesels rated at 3,375bhp, rising to 4,000bhp, which raised maximum surface speed from 17 to 20 knots.

The torpedo armament was modified during the design process, and was even more powerful than that originally specified. The trainable mounting abaft the conning tower had three 550mm tubes, while the stern mounting had two 550mm tubes outside two smaller 400mm tubes for lightweight, short-range torpedoes intended for use against 'targets of opportunity'. The total loadout was nine 550mm torpedoes in the tubes plus two reloads, and two 400mm torpedoes in the stern tubes.

The *1500 tonnes* was numerically the largest class of submarines built by any navy during the interwar period. No fewer than thirty-one, in four

The *1500-tonnes* submarine *Le Centaure* completing at Brest Naval Dockyard during the early 1930s. Note the trainable torpedo tubes above the stern, so located in order to free up the after end of the pressure hull for the large diesel engines; there were two 550mm tubes outboard of a pair of 400mm tubes.

Pascal (Fr)

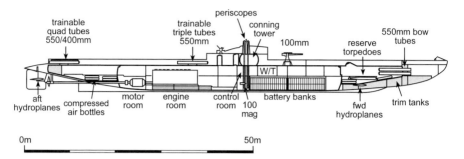

The *1500-tonnes* type (the drawing is of *Pascal*) was numerically the largest class of submarine built by any of the five contracting powers between the wars, and was designed to have sufficient surface speed to accompany the battle fleet. In order to free up space in the after part of the pressure hull for the powerful propulsion machinery the after torpedo tubes were in trainable external mountings. The early boats of the class had a maximum speed on the surface of 17 knots, but with the adoption of more powerful diesels this was increased in the later boats to 20 knots.

sub-groups, were authorised between 1924 and 1930, although serious congestion in the shipyards and delays in the delivery of key equipment – especially diesels – meant that two of the submarines in the last series, allocated to the Cherbourg Naval Dockyard, took almost eight years to build. Despite double-hull construction they could dive in 40–45 seconds. Handling when dived was excellent, and they could stay submerged for eighteen hours consecutively, surfacing only at night to replenish batteries. Sea-keeping on the surface was adjudged superior to that of the torpedo boats of the *Bourrasque* class (also designated *1500 tonnes*), although there were problems with the forward diving planes, which were mounted low and close to the bow, when running on the surface in heavy seas.

Nevertheless, there was still inadequate attention to habitability, and the *1500 tonnes* never attained their designed thirty-day patrol. There was insufficient ventilation in the early boats, supplies of bottled oxygen were inadequate, and fresh stores were provided for the equivalent of 2½ days! (This last defect was corrected by the installation of additional refrigeration power at later refits.) Wartime experience was to reveal that insufficient attention had been given to protecting the submarines against the shocks experienced during depth-charging. Problems were experienced with water-tight hatches and battery integrity; electrically operated systems such as lighting circuits and the external torpedo mountings frequently failed because switchboards and control systems were not seated on flexible mountings. The *1500 tonnes* were inferior in this respect to the earlier *Requin* because a greater proportion of their equipment was located between the pressure hull and the outer casing. The 400mm torpedo also proved unsuccessful; many failures were to be experienced in action, and in 1943–44 surviving boats of the series had their original stern trainable mounting replaced by a second triple 550mm mounting.

The coastal patrol submarines ordered as part of the 1924 programme were similar in size and conception to the *600 tonnes* of the 1922 programme. Like their predecessors, the sixteen boats of the *630-tonnes* type were built in private shipyards to a specification provided by the STCN. Half were powered by Normand-Vickers four-stroke diesels, the remainder by either Schneider-Carel or Sulzer two-stroke diesels, and the fixed stern tubes were replaced, as in the *1500 tonnes*, by an external trainable mounting – in this instance comprising a single 550mm tube flanked by two 400mm tubes.

The *630 tonnes* were better divers than their predecessors. The stability problems experienced with the *600 tonnes* were corrected, the hydraulically operated control surfaces proved more reliable than the electric controls of the latter, and underwater speed was increased from 7.5 knots to 9 knots. However, the *630 tonnes* suffered from the traditional French vice of over-elaboration in the pursuit of high performance, and the sheer quantity of new equipment meant that they were even more cluttered and less habitable than the *600 tonnes*.

With the completion of the *630-tonnes* series the Marine Nationale clearly felt that private competition had delivered as much as could reasonably be expected in terms of innovation and improvements in performance, and that it was time to incorporate the lessons learned in a simpler, standard design. The next class, authorised in 1930 (a further two boats would follow in 1936), was designed by the STCN and was to be known as the *Amirauté* ('Admiralty') type. The armament of these submarines was greatly simplified: four 550mm bow tubes, two 550mm internal stern tubes, and a triple 400mm trainable mounting abaft the conning tower; reserve torpedoes were suppressed altogether in order to maximise internal volume. Other performance parameters were similar to the *630 tonnes*, the four-stroke Normand-Vickers diesel being adopted in preference to the Sulzer/Schneider units.

Authorised at the rate of one per year between 1925 and 1930, the six minelayers of the *Saphir* class were contemporaries of the *630 tonnes*. Designed to lay mines in the shallow waters of the Mediterranean and the North Sea, they were relatively small submarines with a surfaced displacement of 760 tonnes. The thirty-two mines were carried externally in sixteen vertical tubes located in the saddle tanks, as in the Royal Navy's wartime 'E'- and 'L'-class conversions. The minelaying system, developed by Normand-Fenaux, proved safe and reliable, and the relatively small size of these boats made them particularly well-suited to operations in shallow waters. *Rubis*, which served with the Free French Naval Forces from June 1940, was arguably the outstanding minelaying submarine of the Second World War.

Table 9.6: French Submarines of the 1924 *Statut Naval*

	1500 tonnes	*630 tonnes*	*Saphir*	*Surcouf*
Type:	fleet submarine	coastal patrol	coastal minelayer	cruiser
Built:	thirty-one 1924–39	sixteen 1927–35	six 1926–37	1927–34
Displacement:	1,380tW	560–570tW	670tW	2,880tW
Dimensions:	92m × 8.2m	64m × 6.2m	66m × 7.2m	110m × 9m
Machinery:	2-shaft diesel/electric; 6,000–8,000bhp/2,000hp = 17–20/8 knots	2-shaft diesel/electric; 1,300bhp/1,000hp = 14/9 knots	2-shaft diesel/electric; 1,300bhp/1,000hp = 12/9 knots	2-shaft diesel/electric; 7,600bhp/3,400hp = 18.5/8.5 knots
Range:	10,000nm at 10 knots 100nm at 5 knots (dived)	3,000nm at 10 knots 85nm at 5 knots (dived)	7,000nm at 7.5 knots 80nm at 4 knots (dived)	10,000nm at 10 knots 60nm at 5 knots (dived)
Armament:	9–550mm, 2–400mm TT (4B+7T: 13 torpedoes) 1–100mm/40 (1 × I)	6–550mm, 2–400mm TT (3B+5T: 9 torpedoes) 1–75mm/35 (1 × I)	3–550mm, 2–400mm TT (2B+3T: 9 torpedoes) 1–75mm/35 (1 × I) 16 mine chutes (32 mines)	6–550mm, 4–400mm TT (4B+6T: 22 torpedoes) 2–203mm/50 (1 × II) 1 floatplane

The Submarine Cruiser Surcouf

Of the four submarine types projected under the French 1924 programme, the one which undoubtedly made the greatest political impact was the large commerce raiding cruiser (the official designation was *croiseur corsaire submersible*), the first of which was authorised in 1926. Laid down the following year, *Surcouf* was to take some seven years to build and on completion was the world's largest submarine – a position she was to hold until 1942.

In conception she derived from the German U-cruisers, although the design was also closely influenced by the British *X1*, completed in September 1925. With a surfaced displacement of 3,300 tonnes *Surcouf* was armed with two 203mm (8in)/50-calibre guns in a fully-enclosed, watertight rotating twin turret. In contrast to the *1500 tonnes* the torpedo armament was weighted in favour of the smaller 400mm torpedo, which was considered adequate for use against small mercantile targets. There were four 550mm bow tubes, and two triple trainable mountings each of one 550mm tube and two 400mm tubes set into the after-deck casing. Eight reserve torpedoes were provided for the internal bow tubes, and a reload magazine containing four 400mm torpedoes was located within the pressure hull beneath the trainable mountings, the tubes being reloaded by the crew via a hoist and deck crane while the boat was surfaced.

Two large Sulzer diesels, each rated at 3,800bhp, provided a maximum speed of 18.5 knots on the surface, and the designed endurance was 10,000nm at 10 knots; stores were sufficient for a ninety-day patrol. A floatplane intended to locate potential targets on the high seas was carried (broken

The submarine cruiser *Surcouf* showing her massive 203mm twin turret to good effect. The turret was completely water- and pressure-tight, to enable the gun crew to be closed up and ready to open fire as soon as the boat surfaced. (Leo van Ginderen collection)

Surcouf (Fr)

Surcouf was the ultimate cruiser submarine of her generation. Her design owed little to the German late-war cruisers. The large cylindrical turret for the twin 203mm (8in) guns was water- and pressure-tight, as was the smaller cylinder aft which housed the broken-down reconnaissance floatplane. The 400mm torpedo tubes in the two trainable mountings fired torpedoes capable of sinking a small merchantman at close range, and were provided with reloads stowed in a magazine within the pressure hull. In order to conform to international law, *Surcouf* was equipped with a ten-metre motor launch to rescue the ship's crew, and had accommodation for forty prisoners.

down) in a watertight hangar abaft the conning tower and, to conform with Prize Laws, there was accommodation for forty prisoners.

The construction of *Surcouf*, with the prospect of a new generation of commerce-raiding cruisers – two sisters were projected by the Marine Nationale – could not fail to cause concern on the other side of the Channel, and the British made a second attempt to secure the prohibition of submarine warfare against merchant shipping at the London Conference of 1930. On this occasion, however, the French delegation came better prepared, and a compromise was reached whereby France would be permitted to complete the *Surcouf* in return for an agreement to limit future submarines to 2,000 tons standard displacement and 5.1in (130mm) guns.

The most serious weaknesses of the *Surcouf* design were arguably conceptual rather than technical. By the time the submarine was completed France was again in a close political alliance with Britain, and the potential enemies were Germany and Italy. Italy's mercantile trade was focused on the Mediterranean, while the trans-Atlantic operations of the small German merchant fleet would be quickly and effectively snuffed out by a Royal Navy blockade as soon as hostilities commenced, leaving few worthwhile targets for a large commerce-raiding submarine. When war broke out in 1939 *Surcouf* was a submarine in search of a mission, and was to spend a substantial part of her remaining service life as a trans-Atlantic convoy escort.

It is a measure of the French achievement that during the period 1922–30 the total tonnage of submarines authorised for the Marine Nationale was 84,180 tonnes (surfaced displacement), which breaks down as follows: forty large patrol or fleet submarines of 56,400 tonnes, thirty coastal patrol submarines of 19,920 tonnes, six minelayers of 4,560 tonnes and one cruiser of 3,300 tonnes.[19] Major improvements were made in infrastructure, especially in the production of diesels, batteries and mines, as well as in repairs. Regular training cruises of 5–10 days were implemented, with longer 20–30 day 'endurance' cruises every eighteen months, an attack teacher was installed at Cherbourg, and a course for submarine commanders proposed (but not implemented). A Naval Staff note of February 1925 even proposed funding for trials with closed-cycle propulsion.

Ocean-Going Submarines for the Regia Marina

As with the French Marine Nationale, Italian submarine development prior to the First World War had focused on small submarines for coastal and harbour defence, and these had been employed to good effect for blockade of the Austro-Hungarian Fleet in the confined waters of the northern Adriatic. Despite chronic shortages of steel, Italy had been able to continue to build small diesel-propelled boats of around 250 tons surfaced displacement in significant numbers during 1914–18. The most recent types, the twenty-one-strong 'F' class designed by Laurenti and the six boats of the 'N' class designed by Bernardis, were armed with two bow tubes for four 450mm torpedoes plus a 76mm deck gun, and had surfaced and submerged speeds of 12 knots and 8 knots respectively.

During the First World War attention turned to medium and large submarines, which were, however, built in relatively small numbers. The four submarines of the *Provana* class were laid down in late 1915 and completed postwar. With a surfaced displacement of 760 tons and an armament of six 450mm torpedo tubes (four bow, two stern) plus two 76mm deck guns, they were fast and manoeuvrable, but diving depth was only 50m, which made them vulnerable to anti-submarine measures. The six large submarines of the *Micca* class, three of which were originally laid down in Venice in 1914 but which were not completed until 1919–20, had a surfaced displacement of 842 tons, and were originally to have had two additional external torpedo tubes in a trainable mounting similar to those adopted by the Marine Nationale postwar. Their endurance was impressive, but they were failures in most other respects; poor manoeuvrability and unreliable diesel engines led to partial rebuilding in 1923.

The Regia Marina also purchased a number of small British- and Canadian-built submarines of the 'S', 'W' and 'H' classes to supplement domestic construction during the First World War, so that by 1920 the navy was well-stocked with submarines for coastal and harbour defence. With the defeat and dismantling of the Austro-Hungarian Empire and Italy's acquisition of the key northern Adriatic ports of Fiume, Pola and Trieste, however, the geostrategic situation of the Regia Marina had changed dramatically. In the postwar era Italy's primary focus would be on consolidating and expanding its colonial foothold in East Africa and the Red Sea, and on counterbalancing French naval power in the Mediterranean. The new strategy would require submarines of much greater size and range than hitherto, and like the other major Allied navies Italy would look to German technology to provide suitable models.

The ex-German and ex-Austro-Hungarian war prizes allocated to the Italians were predominantly coastal submarines, the surviving ocean-going boats having been divided between the other allies. Three of the late-war UB III-type and three UC III minelayers, together with the larger UE II-type minelayer *U-120* were handed over to the Regia Marina, and these were thoroughly examined prior to being broken up. The Italians also had the opportunity to examine the hulls of the German Ms-type ocean-going submarines building for the Austro-Hungarian Navy at the end of the war following the occupation of Fiume and Pola. Like other Allied navies, the Regia Marina was impressed with the U-cruiser concept, which it saw as the basis for a large submarine with the necessary endurance for long-range operations in the Indian Ocean.

The Washington Treaty gave Italy naval parity with France not only in terms of capital ship and aircraft carrier tonnage, but also in terms of status. The Regia Marina now looked to 'cover' every French move in order to secure a strategic and tactical balance between the two navies. So when the Marine Nationale embarked on a major submarine building programme post-Washington, it was inevitable that the Regia Marina would invest heavily in sea-going and ocean-going submarines of modern design.

There were two main strands to Italian submarine construction in the immediate aftermath of the Washington Treaty: a series of large submarine cruisers intended to operate in the Red Sea and the Indian Ocean from Italy's East African colonies; and a series of large sea-going submarines similar to the German Ms type for operations in the Mediterranean and, in the event of conflict with France, the North Atlantic. They were the largest submarines built for the Italian Navy to date, and all were armed with new-model 533mm torpedoes with greater range, speed and power than their 450mm predecessors.

The four cruiser submarines of the *Balilla* class were laid down in 1925–26. They had an overall length of 87m and displaced 1,425 tons surfaced. Derived from the ex-German *U-120*, they were double-hulled boats with very strong hull construction designed for a diving depth of 100m. The two Fiat main propulsion diesels were complemented, as in the French M5 fleet type, by an auxiliary diesel of 425bhp, which in addition to charging the batteries when running on the surface could be used to provide a cruise radius of 13,000nm at 7 knots. There were four bow tubes, each with two reloads, and two stern torpedo tubes, each with a single reload, but only a single 120mm deck gun in a shielded mounting. Originally there were to have been four mines, stowed internally and launched by gravity from a single stern tube, but only *Sciesa* was fitted with this system. The *Balillas* were designed for the relatively high surfaced speed of 17.5 knots, but never attained

The Italian cruiser submarine *Antonio Sciesa* of the *Balilla* class during the early 1930s. The Italian cruisers were smaller than their foreign counterparts, and carried only a single 120mm main gun – seen here in a 'redoubt' forward of the conning tower – but endurance was impressive and there were ten reloads for the six internal torpedo tubes. Note the raised W/T masts, essential for long-range communication with the shore when on patrol. (Maurizio Brescia collection)

more than 16 knots in service. It took the Italians a long time to master the transverse instability problems inherent in double-hull construction, and these boats were particularly unsuccessful in this respect.

A fifth cruiser submarine, *Fieramosca*, was built to a design by the engineer Bernardis. Like other Bernardis boats (see below) she was of partial double-hull construction with external saddle tanks. The initial project featured a 203mm gun at the forward end of the conning tower, and a hangar for a floatplane, intended for long-range scouting, was incorporated into its after end. A second project had two internal stern tubes for twenty-four 1,000kg mines, and two external stern torpedo tubes in addition to the four internal tubes in the bow. In the final project the minelaying system was suppressed and the mines and external torpedo tubes replaced by four internal stern tubes; the deck gun was the 120mm/45-calibre fitted in the *Balillas*. *Fieramosca* was completed with the aircraft hangar, but no suitable aircraft was developed and it was removed in 1931.

Despite more powerful Tosi two-stroke diesels rated at 2,750bhp, *Fieramosca* failed to attain her designed speed of 20 knots by a significant margin. She was also slow to dive, difficult to manoeuvre when submerged, and her machinery was unreliable (she was taken out of active service early in the Second World War following a battery explosion which caused a number of fatalities).

The early collapse of France in 1940 removed the primary mission of these large submarine cruisers, which were intended to operate against French sea lines of communication in the Indian Ocean. Like the large 'overseas patrol' submarines built by the British for operations against the Japanese, they were too large to operate effectively in the Mediterranean, and were either laid up or employed as supply submarines during the Second World War.

The other major Italian submarine of the period was a sea-going type of similar size and capabilities to the German Ms series, of which no fewer than eighteen were laid down between 1925 and 1929. There were two completing prototype designs – one from Cavallini and Tosi, the other from Bernardis – which became the *Mameli* and *Pisani* classes respectively, each comprising four boats. Both were built to the same general specifications: a maximum speed of 17 knots surfaced, a diving depth of 100m, and an armament comprising four bow torpedo tubes (each with a single reload) and two stern tubes, with a 102mm/35-calibre deck gun. However, their respective designers opted for quite different hull forms. The *Mameli* was a robust saddle tank design with a pressure hull that was of cylindrical cross-section throughout, resulting in a diving depth twice that of earlier Italian submarines (100m designed, 115m in trials). Bernardis, however, chose a partial double-hull form in which a second resistant hull containing the diving tanks, emergency diving tanks and fuel bunkers extended outside the inner pressure hull over two-thirds of the length of the submarine.

The *Mameli* class proved very successful: fast, manoeuvrable, stable in depth-keeping, spacious and comfortable. The *Pisani* class, on the other hand, had serious transverse stability problems as completed. They were immediately taken in hand for the fitting of additional saddle tanks on the upper part of the hull, which resolved the stability problems at the expense of a significant reduction in speed and endurance.

The eight submarines of the *Bandiera* and *Squalo* classes which succeeded them (both from Bernardis) had an additional two stern tubes but were otherwise little modified, so suffered from the same stability problems and were subjected to the same remedial action. They also proved to be poor seaboats, and had their bows reconstructed to provide greater freeboard and buoyancy.

The last two submarines of the series, the Cavallini–Tosi boats of the *Settembrini* class, were contemporaries of the *Squalo* class. They were larger than the *Mameli*s, and had the four stern tubes of the later Bernardis boats but were much more successful – they were the only boats of the eighteen built to achieve their designed surface speed of 17.5 knots.

Contemporary with the *Bandiera* class, and sharing the same basic hull design, were the two minelaying submarines of the *Bragadin* class. The 16–24 mines were stowed internally in the after part of the pressure hull, and were laid by gravity via two vertical tubes in the underside of the stern. There were also four 533mm torpedo tubes in the bow, together with the standard

The two *Settembrini*s were the most successful of the early Italian sea-going boats. They were well armed, but endurance was unimpressive by foreign standards. (USMM)

102mm/45-calibre deck gun; endurance rather than speed was a priority. The *Bragadin*s experienced the same sea-keeping problems as the *Bandiera*s on completion, and the bow had to be similarly modified. The position of the mine tubes aft also proved unsatisfactory, and the stern was completely rebuilt during the mid-1930s to ensure that the mines were laid clear of the after control surfaces.

By the end of the decade the Regia Marina, despite its considerable investment in submarine construction, still lagged behind the French. Twenty large patrol submarines (including the two *Bragadin*s) and five cruisers had been completed or laid down, and only the latter were comparable in size and capabilities to the French *1500-tonnes* type, which were being laid down at the rate of six per year during the period 1925–30. Moreover, there was no Italian counterpart to the French coastal submarines, of which no fewer than twenty-eight were being completed with a further six projected. The Regia Marina's own smaller coastal submarines completed at the end of the First World War were now ageing, and would soon need to be replaced.

In 1929 the Italians therefore embarked on the first of a series of coastal submarines of comparable size to the French *600-tonnes* and *630-tonnes* classes, designed specifically for shallow-water operations in the Mediterranean. The seven-boat *Argonauta* class was designed by Bernardis, and despite the marked reduction in dimensions and displacement these submarines were little inferior to the larger sea-going boats in offensive power, although maximum diving depth was reduced to around 80m and

The coastal patrol submarine *Fisalia* of the *Argonauta* class during the early 1930s. The 102mm
deck gun serves to emphasise the small size of these submarines. They nevertheless proved to
be most effective in the confined waters of the Mediterranean, and spawned many successors.
(Maurizio Brescia collection)

no reloads were provided for the four bow and two stern torpedo tubes. The
much less powerful propulsion machinery was still capable of 14 knots on
the surface (after modification the larger patrol submarines could only make
15 knots), and endurance was on a par with the *Pisani* series and the two
later Cavallini–Tosi boats.

Argonauta (It)

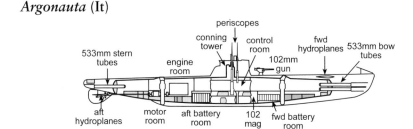

The *Argonauta* design proved so successful and so well suited to the narrow and shallow waters
of the Mediterranean that it became the basis of successive classes of small submarine built for
the Regia Marina during the 1930s, many of which served with distinction during the Second
World War. Well armed and quick-diving, they lacked the endurance (including the torpedo
reloads) of the larger Italian boats, but the proximity of their bases, particularly when operating
in the central Mediterranean, made this relatively insignificant.

Table 9.7: Italian Submarines 1922–29

	Balilla	Mameli	Bandiera	Bragadin	Argonauta
Type:	cruiser	sea-going patrol	sea-going patrol	sea-going minelayer	coastal patrol
Built:	four 1925–29	four 1925–29	four 1928–30	two 1927–31	seven 1929–33
Displacement:	1,370tW	770tW	815tW	800tW	600tW
Dimensions:	87m × 7.8m	65m × 6.5m	70m × 7.2m	68m × 7.2m	62m × 5.7m
Machinery:	2-shaft diesel/electric;	2-shaft diesel/electric;	2-shaft diesel/electric;	2-shaft diesel/electric;	2-shaft diesel/electric;
	4,900bhp/2,200hp	3,000bhp/1,000hp	3,000bhp/1,300hp	1,500bhp/1,000hp	1,500bhp/800hp
	= 16/7 knots	= 15/7.5 knots	= 15/8 knots	= 11.5/7 knots	= 14/8 knots
Range:	13,000nm at 7 knots	4,360nm at 8 knots	4,740nm at 8.5 knots	4,180nm at 6.5 knots	5,000nm at 8 knots
		65nm at 4 knots (dived)	60nm at 4 knots (dived)	72nm at 4 knots (dived)	74nm at 4 knots (dived)
Armament:	6–533mm TT	6–533mm TT	8–533mm TT	4–533mm TT	6–533mm TT
	(4B+2S: 16 torpedoes)	(4B+2S: 10 torpedoes)	(4B+4S: 12 torpedoes)	(4B: 6 torpedoes)	(4B+2S: 6 torpedoes)
	1–120mm/27 (1 × I)	1–102mm/35 (1 × I)	1–102mm/35 (1 × I)	1–102mm/35 (1 × I)	1–102mm/35 (1 × I)
				2 tubes (16–24 mines)	

Notes:

- The four *Balillas* were followed by *Fieramosca*, of similar size and capabilities but designed to operate a floatplane.
- Eighteen seagoing patrol submarines were built for the Regia Marina during the 1920s to two basic competing designs. The four *Mamelis*, designed by Cavallini and Tosi, were followed by two boats of the *Settembrini* class; the four *Bandieras*, designed by Bernardis, were preceded by four boats of the *Pisani* class, and superseded by a further four boats of the *Squalo* class.

Table 9.8: Submarine Authorisations 1922–30

Estimates	British Empire	USA	Japan	France	Italy
1922				6 *Requin* (1922–28) 6 *600-tonnes* (1923–29)	
1923	*Oberon* (1924–27) 2 *Oxley* (Aus: 1925–27)		4 *J1* (1923–29) 4 *KD3A* (1924–28) 5 *KD3B* (1926–30) 3 *KD4* (1926–30)	3 *Requin* (1923–28) 6 *600-tonnes* (1923–30)	4 *Ballila* (1925–29) 3 *Mameli* (1925–29) 3 *Pisani* (1925–29)
1924				2 *1500-tonnes* (1924–31)	1 *Mameli* (1925–29) 1 *Pisani* (1925–29)
1925		*V4* (1925–28)		7 *1500-tonnes* (1925–32) 2 *Saphir* (1925–30)	1 *Fieramosca* (1926–31) 2 *Bragadin* (1927–31)
1926	6 *Odin* (1927–30)	*V5–6* (1927–30)		1 *Surcouf* (1927–34) 5 *1500-tonnes* (1927–34) 4 *630-tonnes* (1927–33) 1 *Saphir* (1927–31)	
1927	6 *Parthian* (1928–31)		1 *J1M* (1930–32) 3 *KD5* (1929–32)	5 *1500-tonnes* (1928–34) 4 *630-tonnes* (1928–34) 1 *Saphir* (1928–33)	4 *Bandiera* (1928–30) 2 *Settembrini* (1928–32)
1928	4(+2) *Rainbow* (1929–32)			4 *630-tonnes* (1928–33)	4 *Squalo* (1928–31)
1929	1 *Thames* (1931–32) 2 *Swordfish* (1930–32)			6 *1500-tonnes* (1929–37) 4 *630-tonnes* (1930–35) 1 *Saphir* (1929–34)	7 *Argonauta* (1929–33)
1930	1 *Porpoise* (1931–33) 2 *Swordfish* (1931–33)	*V7* (1930–32)		6 *1500-tonnes* (1930–39) 4 *Minerve* (1931–37) 1 *Saphir* (1931–37)	1 *Micca* (1931–35) 3 *Calvi* (1932–36) 4 *Archimede* (1931–35) 12 *Sirena* (1931–34)
Total	20 Large 4 Medium 1 M/L	4 Large	20 Large	32 Large 9 Medium 32 Small 6 M/L	9 Large 22 Medium 19 Small 2 M/L

The *Argonauta* class would be the forerunners of a long series of coastal submarines which would dominate Italian submarine construction during the next decade. They would be the mainstay of the Regia Marina's submarine force during the Second World War, and would be responsible for many of its successes.

Conclusion

For the five Washington navies, the 1920s were characterised by the construction of large ocean-going submersibles, often derived from the German U-boat designs of the late-war period. This reflected a change in the likely arena of future naval conflicts from the relatively confined waters of the North Sea and the Mediterranean to the broad expanses of the Pacific and Indian oceans.

The major concerns for the Royal Navy and for the US Navy (and to a certain extent the IJN and the Italian Regia Marina) were endurance and transit speed on the surface; their cruiser and overseas patrol submarines were intended for independent long-range operations in enemy-dominated waters. However, the Japanese and the French also wanted high tactical speed for their large fleet boats to enable the latter to operate effectively in conjunction with their surface squadrons, and were prepared to invest considerable resources in pursuing the necessary high-power diesel technology. For both these nations a large force of fleet submarines was perceived as a potential 'equaliser' or 'force multiplier' which could compensate for their statutory inferiority in capital ships over their most likely opponents in any future conflict.

All of the Washington navies except the French Marine Nationale found themselves well provided with medium and coastal submarines of modern design at the end of the First World War: the British had the 'H' and 'L' classes, the Americans the 'S' class, the Japanese the competitive foreign-derived 'F', 'K' and 'L' series, and the Italians the 'F' and 'N' classes together with some Canadian-built 'H'-class boats. Only the French invested heavily in smaller submarines in the immediate post-Washington era, with thirty-two coastal defence submarines of the *600-tonnes*, *630-tonnes*, and *Amirauté* types being authorised between 1922 and 1930. By the end of the decade both the British and the Italians had laid down medium/coastal boats of new design to operate in the confined and shallow waters of the North Sea and the Mediterranean respectively. However, the Americans and the Japanese would continue to focus their attention on large ocean-going submarines to operate in the broad expanses of the Pacific, and would experiment with smaller designs only as possible 'mobilisation' types for the local defence of island territories and forward bases.

CHAPTER 10

Destroyers

The British and the Americans ended the First World War with large numbers of destroyers of modern design either recently completed or still on the stocks. The immediate needs of both fleets were more than met by these, as the orders placed during the last two years of the war had included large numbers of ships for anti-submarine and convoy escort duties in the North Atlantic, missions which would be less relevant to peacetime operations.

The US Navy's inventory by the time of the Washington Conference included no fewer than three hundred of the 1,000-ton 'flush-deckers', built in private shipyards using mass production techniques during the late-war period. They carried an impressive complement of torpedoes but were too small and fragile for ocean operations, and their low freeboard and heavy topweight combined to make them poor seaboats. Even before they were completed they were outclassed by the latest British designs. However, the massive investment made in these ships, together with their numerical strength, provided a powerful argument in Congress against new destroyer construction throughout the 1920s, and during that period not a single destroyer of modern design was authorised for the US Navy.

The British were in a far better position with regard to destroyers. The latest ships of the 'V' and 'W' classes were universally recognised as the best of their type, and the 1,300-ton 'Modified W's, with their powerful armament of four 4.7in guns and two triple banks of 533mm torpedo tubes, not only provided the model for the British destroyers built during the late 1920s and early 1930s but set the standard for postwar destroyer construction outside Britain. Their flotilla leader counterparts of the *Scott* and *Shakespeare* classes were even larger at 1,550 tons (normal), and had an additional 4.7in gun as well as a faster speed of 36 knots. Although not as numerous as the US Navy's flush-deckers, the British destroyers were high-quality ships, available in sufficient numbers to accompany the battle squadrons throughout the 1920s and well into the 1930s before block obsolescence would become an issue. This meant that the British could adopt a rational approach to destroyer development during the immediate post-Washington period, investing purely in development prototypes which would become the precursors of the new-build destroyers that would be needed by the 1930s.

Progress in the Imperial Japanese Navy during the First World War was less spectacular in terms of the number of destroyers built, but in the three-year period 1918–21 no fewer than twenty-four large 'first class' destroyers of the *Minekaze* and *Asakaze* classes had been laid down. Fast and well armed, these ships were comparable with the British 'Modified W' class, despite the German influence apparent in their overall layout. They would be followed in the post-Washington era by the similar *Mutsuki* class, before the much larger and more powerful 'special type' of the *Fubuki* class revolutionised Japanese destroyer construction, while at the same time laying down a gauntlet to the rest of the world.

The French, in stark contrast to their competitors, found themselves without a single modern destroyer type of indigenous design and construction. The situation in the French shipyards during the First World War had been so dire that in 1917, faced with a disastrous shortage of destroyers, France had ordered twelve small second-class destroyers of the *Kaba* class from Japan. Yet there can be no doubting the Marine Nationale's commitment to building a new generation of powerful flotilla craft during the postwar period. The French made a point of keeping in touch with the latest British developments (the acquisition of incomplete 'Modified W' hulls was contemplated in 1919 as a short-term measure), and the new fleet torpedo boats of the post-Washington 1922 programme would be among the largest and most powerful in the world on completion. They would, moreover, be ordered in numbers: twelve in the 1922 programme, with a further fourteen units of a slightly modified design during the first three years of the 1924 programme.

The Italian Regia Marina had a rather better base on which to build, with eight large two-funnelled destroyers based on the Yarrow-built *Audace* building during the postwar period. Both the *Palestro* and *Curtatone* classes had originally been ordered in 1915, but their construction had been delayed by a shortage of steel. The former displaced 1,035 tonnes (normal), the latter 1,170 tonnes, and they were armed with four 102mm guns and four/six 450mm torpedo tubes, the main guns being in paired mountings in the later ships. These ships would provide the baseline for Italian destroyers of post-Washington design. However, the Italians would also need to take account of the latest British and French destroyers, so gun calibre would increase to 120mm, and 533mm torpedoes would replace the older 450mm models. Italian destroyer construction during the 1920s would be steady if unspectacular, with a class of four ordered in most years.

High-pressure Steam for the Royal Navy

Following the First World War the Royal Navy cancelled four flotilla leaders and forty destroyers. The remaining ships still on the stocks, which included sixteen large destroyers of the 'Modified W' type and twelve 1,550-ton flotilla leaders, were completed over the next five years. In the extensive 'cull' which took place in 1921, all older destroyers up to the 'R' class were paid off. This left large numbers of the smaller 'R' and 'S' types – which displaced 1,000 tons (normal), were capable of 36 knots, and were armed with three single 4in guns plus two twin trainable 21in torpedo mountings – and forty-eight of the larger 'V' and 'W' classes, armed with four single 4in guns and two twin or triple torpedo mountings. These were all modern ships ordered from 1915 onwards, and many would go on to serve in the Second World War, for which they formed the bedrock of the anti-submarine escort forces.

In the immediate aftermath of Washington, it was estimated that no new replacements would be needed before the end of the decade. However, the construction of powerful new-build destroyers was continuing in other navies (notably the French Marine Nationale and the IJN), and the Royal Navy was anxious to keep abreast of new technological developments, so it adopted the wise course of using this breathing space to build experimental prototypes which could provide the basis for a new improved destroyer design that would come into service during the 1930s.

For the new prototypes the Admiralty turned to the two foremost private builders of destroyers, Yarrow and Thornycroft. The new ships were to be based on the successful 'Modified W' design, and were to trial superheated steam machinery and new fire control systems. *Amazon* (Thornycroft) and *Ambuscade* (Yarrow) were duly authorised under the 1924–25 Estimates, and were laid down in 1924–25. Both ships took less than two years to complete.

Amazon was one of two competing designs commissioned by the Royal Navy during the mid-1920s as prototypes for new destroyers powered by superheated steam machinery. Built by Vosper Thornycroft, she created a huge impression abroad, resulting in orders for similar ships for the Chilean Navy. Note the old-style shields on the main guns. (Royal Naval Museum)

The Admiralty's speed requirement was for 35 knots, but Yarrow's design specified 37 knots, so Thornycroft felt compelled to follow. *Amazon* had three Yarrow four-drum boilers of equal size, rated at 260lb/in² using superheated steam, but *Ambuscade* had two large and one small boiler rated at an even more impressive 290lb/in². She achieved her designed speed with only 33,000shp, whereas *Amazon* required 39,500shp to equal this performance (she was also the heavier of the two ships). Both ships had separate cruise turbines to improve fuel economy at lower speeds. Despite her more flexible boiler arrangements *Ambuscade* proved less economical than *Amazon* below 25 knots, but she was more fuel efficient at higher speeds.

The armament of four single 4.7in/45-calibre guns and two triple torpedo mountings was essentially unchanged from the 'Modified W' class; indeed the ships retained the Mk I gun mounting, which had the traditional screw breech. Fire control arrangements, however, were far superior to those of the warbuilt destroyers. A rangefinder was allied to the new 'destroyer director sight', and both were in a raised position at the after end of the bridge with good views forward. The rangefinder and director sight were linked to a fire control table in a transmitting station at the after end of the forecastle. A more substantial secondary control position and searchlight platform was fitted between the torpedo tubes. There was no anti-submarine provision as completed.

These were handsome ships which made a considerable impact abroad. The Yarrow design was subsequently adopted by the Royal Netherlands Navy, which built eight similar units, and by the Portuguese Navy, which purchased two slightly modified units directly from Yarrow and built a further five under licence in Lisbon Naval Dockyard. Thornycroft built six smaller versions of *Amazon* for Chile.

When the resumption of destroyer construction for the Royal Navy was considered during the mid-1920s it was decided that a flotilla of eight standard ships, together with a larger leader, which would have enlarged command spaces and an additional gun, would be ordered each year, starting from 1927.[1] The first class of eight destroyers of the 'A' class, together with their flotilla leader *Codrington*, were duly authorised under the 1927–28 Estimates, and they were followed by the eight 'B's, with their leader *Keith*, ordered under the 1928–29 Estimates.

The design of the new ships was able to take into account lessons learned from trials with *Amazon* and *Ambuscade*, and the Admiralty requested a number of modifications. The gun mountings of the two prototypes had an elevation of only 30°, so it was now envisaged that 'B' mounting would be given an elevation of 60° in order to improve anti-aircraft capabilities. The bridge was to be relocated farther aft in order to lighten the forward part of the ship and improve sea-keeping. And the Admiralty wanted a heavier armament, which included quadruple torpedo mountings, a full anti-submarine outfit comprising the newly developed ASDIC equipment, two depth-charge throwers and four depth charge (DC) racks. It also wanted to fit

Codrington (GB)

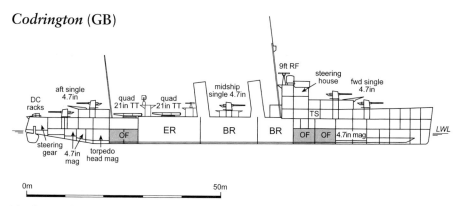

The first 'production' destroyers built for the Royal Navy in the post-Washington era were a development of the late-war 'Modified W' type, but with more advanced superheated steam turbine machinery. A new QF variant of the 4.7in gun with a sliding breech was fitted, and quadruple torpedo mountings replaced the triples of earlier British destroyers. The 'A'-class leader, *Codrington*, depicted here, was 20ft (6m) longer than the standard destroyer and mounted an additional 4.7in gun between the funnels. *Keith*, the leader of the 'B' class, on the other hand, was similar to her sisters but with additional command facilities.

the new two-speed destroyer sweep (TSDS) system, designed for high-speed minesweeping ahead of the battle fleet. In the event it proved impossible to fit both, for reasons of topweight and deck space (essential for handling the sweep), so the 'A' class was given the TSDS sweep and a small depth-charge rack, while the 'B' class had the full ASW oufit, with the four small DC racks originally envisaged being replaced by a single larger rack, and twenty-five depth charges being provided. This pattern would be repeated in future classes, with TSDS alternating with ASW weaponry.

Boreas, one of the eight 'B'-class destroyers authorised for the Royal Navy under the 1928 Estimates. Unlike the 'A's they had the full anti-submarine outfit, comprising Type 119 ASDIC, two depth-charge throwers and a single large depth-charge rack. (Leo van Ginderen collection)

The 4.7in Mk IX gun was a new quick-firing (QF) model incorporating a sliding breech, and was fitted with a more substantial shield which provided better protection against wind and spray for the gun crews. A new mounting with 60° elevation was trialled in *Bulldog*, but was unsuccessful and thus abandoned.

The propulsion machinery was a development of the system in *Ambuscade*, although the separate cruise turbines of the two prototypes were abandoned; instead a cruise stage was incorporated in the HP turbine. Most ships had Admiralty three-drum boilers rated at 300lb/in² (21kg/cm²), but two of the 'A's had Yarrow boilers with a slightly lower steam pressure, and *Acheron* was given a prototype high-pressure boiler rated at 500lb/in² (35kg/cm²). The increase in topweight accepted in order to accommodate quad torpedo mountings and the TSDS/ASW outfit had to be compensated for by a slightly broader hull – maximum speed was correspondingly reduced by two knots to thirty-five knots.

In keeping with First World War practice the flotilla leader of the 'A' class, *Codrington*, was a larger ship with specialised command spaces and an additional 4.7in gun amidships. For the 'B' class, however, the leader *Keith* was to be a standard hull, the original intention being to omit 'Y' gun to provide the additional accommodation needed for flotilla staff. This latter measure was not implemented, which meant that the staff had to be distributed among other vessels, with *Blanche* being fitted as a divisional leader. The practice of adapting a standard hull to provide command facilities, which was evidently the cheaper option, was repeated for the 'C's and 'D's, but it was not successful and later classes would revert to enlarged flotilla leaders of separate design, built in pairs or threes for economy.

The 'A' and 'B' classes proved to be robust, seaworthy ships, and set the pattern for the next seven flotillas, comprising fifty-two standard destroyers plus seven leaders. Two similar ships, specially fitted for Arctic operations, were built for Canada.

The next series, the 'C' and 'D' classes, were ordered under the 1929–30 and 1930–31 Estimates respectively. They had a lightly larger hull to secure a greater radius of action (5,500nm vs. 4,800nm at 15 knots), which entailed a slight increase in horsepower to compensate, but were otherwise little modified. In accordance with the now-established pattern the 'C' class were fitted with TSDS, while the 'D's had the full anti-submarine outfit; they would be the first British destroyers to receive the new retractable ASDIC keel dome. Orders for the 'C' class had to be reduced to four ships plus a leader due to the financial crisis, and once sufficient full flotillas were available they were sold to Canada (1937–38). However, the 'D' class which followed under the 1930–31 Estimates would again comprise eight ships plus a flotilla leader, with *Daring* and *Decoy* fitted as divisional leaders.

Leaders for the US Navy

The massive investment made in the three hundred flush-decker destroyers built during 1917–20 meant that Congress resolutely refused to countenance any US Navy request for further destroyer construction for the next decade. Even when the destroyer design issue was reopened in 1927 by C&R, which wanted ships to trial high-pressure steam and to consolidate the experience acquired since the war with the flush-deckers, the proposal failed to get beyond paper studies. The US Navy thereby passed up an opportunity to build prototypes which could serve as test-beds for the new generation of destroyers to be built during the 1930s – an opportunity which had been readily grasped by the British Royal Navy. The British destroyers of the 'A'–'I' classes would prove to be robust ships with reliable machinery and weapon systems; in contrast the first postwar US destroyers of the *Farragut* class, authorised only in FY1932, would be much criticised for their lightweight construction and the fragility of their equipment, despite their advanced machinery and modern dual-purpose guns.

The one area of need which the navy attempted to use as a lever with Congress was that of flotilla leaders. The US Navy had previously built no specialised ships in the destroyer class comparable to the British flotilla leaders, and had no small, fast cruisers suitable to perform this role comparable to those of the Imperial Japanese Navy. On the other hand, joint fleet operations with the British during the late-war period had convinced the US Navy of the value of command ships which could keep pace with, and direct the operations of, the destroyer flotillas operating with the battle fleet.

Leader design 1919 (US)

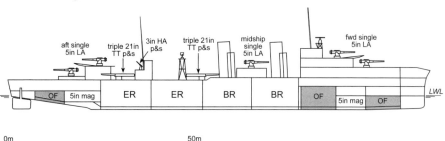

On a displacement more than twice that of the standard 'flush-decker', the US Navy leader design of 1919 would have been armed with five 5in/51-calibre guns in single mountings, and like the destroyers would have had twelve 21in torpedoes in four triple broadside mountings, the principle being that a salvo of six torpedoes would be launched to port or to starboard, and the ship would then turn through 180° to launch a second salvo. The leaders would have had a raised forecastle to improve sea-keeping, and the uptakes for the four boilers would have been paired, resulting in two funnels of broadly equal cross-section. Like their British counterparts they would have been faster than standard destroyers, with a maximum speed of 37 knots.

The *Omaha* class cruisers were fast enough to operate with the destroyers, but had been designed specifically as scouts, and in the absence of any other ships which might perform this latter mission would have to be employed as such, at least until the advent of the more powerful treaty cruisers during the 1930s. In 1919 the US Navy therefore proposed the construction of large destroyer-type flotilla leaders displacing 2,200 tons, armed with five single 5in/51-calibre guns and twelve torpedo tubes, disposed in four triple wing mountings. The new leaders (as they were classified in the US Navy) would have a raised forecastle for improved sea-keeping, and the General Board also wanted a small scout floatplane for observation. Five leaders were duly incorporated into the proposed FY1921 programme, but Congress refused to fund them, arguing that existing destroyers were adequate for work with the battle fleet, and that with the advent of fast carriers only large cruisers would be suitable as escorts for their high-speed runs.

Not to be discouraged, the US Navy persisted with its attempts to design and build an effective leader, and during the mid/late-1920s studies were conducted for ships of 1,600, 1,700, 2,000 and even 2,900 tons (normal) – the latter apparently influenced by the latest French *contre-torpilleur* designs. The larger ships now had a mix of 6in/53-calibre anti-surface guns and 5in/25-calibre dual-purpose guns, twelve torpedo tubes disposed as previously, and a speed of 36.5 knots. However, the US Navy – influenced by British proposals at Geneva to limit flotilla leaders to 1,850 tons standard – would come to favour designs in the middle range of 1,700–2,000 tons, and existing designs were reviewed following the London Conference of 1930, when it was felt that Congress might look more favourably on new proposals.

The IJN Raises the Stakes

The standard 'first-class' destroyer building for the Imperial Japanese Navy during the immediate postwar period was a large, fast ship displacing around 1,370 tonnes (normal), armed with four single 12cm guns and six 53cm torpedoes in three twin mountings. The twenty-four units of the *Minekaze* and *Asakaze* classes were unusual in adopting a layout reminiscent of German destroyers of the period, with the forward bank of torpedo tubes in a well between the forward gun mounting and the bridge. However, they were otherwise comparable in size and power to the large British destroyers building in 1918.

The first Japanese destroyers to be authorised and built post-Washington, the twelve-ship *Mutsuki* class, were designed around the same hull and machinery as the earlier types, to which they bore a close resemblance externally. However, there was one significant modification: in place of the three paired 53cm torpedo mountings there were two triple mountings for the new Type 8 61cm torpedo, which combined a powerful 346kg warhead with alternative range settings of 20,000m at 27 knots, 15,000m at 32 knots, and 10,000m at 38 knots. Beam was increased slightly to compensate for the additional topweight, which resulted in a reduction in speed to about

36 knots, with 33.5 knots the maximum achieved in deep load condition. Most ships had Parsons reaction turbines, but one unit was fitted with Rateau and another with Zoelly impulse turbines for comparison. These French-built turbines do not appear to have been a conspicuous success (unsurprisingly, as the Marine Nationale itself experienced serious reliability problems with the Zoelly models, while the Rateau types proved heavy on fuel consumption), and later Japanese destroyers reverted to Parsons turbines.

In the same year that the *Mutsuki*s were authorised, authorisation was given for the construction of a large, advanced destroyer of a completely new type. The *Fubuki* class, of which nine would be built under the naval replenishment programme of 1923, with a further fifteen under the 1927 programme, would become known as the 'special type'. They were to be armed with six 12.7cm/50-calibre guns disposed in three twin mountings (one forward, two aft) with fully enclosed, gas-tight gunhouses to protect their crews – the first such mounting in the world for a ship of this size. The tactical importance accorded to torpedo attacks against a superior battle line by the IJN was reflected in a torpedo armament well in advance of anything contemplated outside Japan. There were three triple 61cm torpedo tubes on the centre-line between and abaft the funnels, with a further five torpedoes housed in lockers served by rails and reloading gear: three abeam the second funnel and two in the port side of the after deckhouse (see drawing).[2] Geared turbines rated at 50,000shp gave the 'special type' a designed speed of 38 knots.

'Special Type' (Jap)

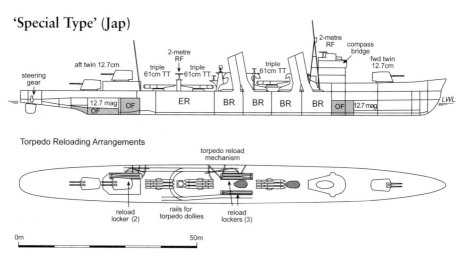

The *Fubuki* and *Akatzuki* classes, known collectively by the designation 'special type', were built to a completely new design, and were by some margin the largest and most powerful destroyers of their generation. They were armed with three twin 12.7cm guns in enclosed mountings and three triple 61m torpedo mountings. In the lower drawing, note the five ready-use reloads in lockers and the system of rails employed to line them up with the tubes. The London Treaty of 1930 called a halt in the construction of destroyers of this size. However, the special type set the standard for later classes of Japanese destroyers.

The first destroyers designed for the IJN after the Washington Conference were the twelve *Mutsuki*s (the lead ship is seen here). Although they bore a superficial resemblance to their predecessors of the *Minekaze* and *Kamikaze* classes, they had the powerful new 61cm torpedo Type 8, which had a range of 10,000m at 37 knots.

The hull form marked a complete break from previous destroyers, having a raised forecastle with marked flare and sheer for improved sea-keeping with moderate freeboard amidships. The bridge was significantly larger than in previous destroyers to provide improved command spaces, and there was a light tripod foremast and a short pole mainmast.

Of the twenty-strong *Fubuki* class the first five units were authorised in 1923, followed by four in 1926, and eleven in 1927 as part of the 1927 naval replenishment programme. The last ten were built to a slightly modified design, with gunhouses which permitted a maximum elevation of 75° and enabled the ships to engage aircraft at long range (the single-purpose guns of the first ten ships elevated to only 40°). This development reflected similar modifications to the guns of the *Atago*-class cruisers (see Chapter 6), which were also built under this programme, and furthered the adoption of British-style 'layered' air defence to protect the battle fleet against aerial attack. However, the slow training speed of the mounting, the lack of power ramming for the guns, and the failure to develop a high-angle fire control system meant that these weapons would be relatively ineffectual against the high-speed monoplane aircraft developed during the 1930s.

The last four destroyers of the 'special type', the *Akatsuki* class, also authorised under the 1927 programme but not laid down until 1930, had further modifications. They had three larger, more powerful boilers in place of the four of earlier ships, and this was reflected in a small fore-funnel of circular cross-section and a large flat-sided second funnel which gave them their distinctive appearance. *Hibiki*, the last to be laid down, was the IJN's first all-welded ship.

The exceptionally powerful armament of the 'special type' came at a cost. These would be the largest conventional destroyers in the world for many years; they were 20m longer than the contemporary British destroyers of the 'A' and 'B' classes, and had a standard displacement as completed of 1,750 tons.

The Japanese destroyers of the 'special type' were so called because they represented an attempt on the part of the IJN to break with previous destroyer designs and to build ships which outclassed all foreign types. With their six 12.7cm guns and nine 61cm torpedo tubes (plus five reloads), they made an instant impact on the world stage. Displacement was comparable to that of the British leaders, and they would have to be classified as such following the London Treaty of 1930. This is *Shirayuki* shortly after completion in 1930. (Leo van Ginderen collection)

The marked difference in size between the standard postwar IJN destroyer and the 'special type' is particularly evident in this view. The destroyer moored outboard belongs to the *Ayanami* sub-group, in which the main guns could elevate to 75°, giving them a theoretical anti-aircraft capability. In practice training and elevation of the guns was too slow, and no specialised HA fire control system was provided. (Stephen Dent Collection)

Table 10.1: British, US and Japanese Destroyers 1922–30

	'A'/'B' class (GB)	1919 Leader (US)	Mutsuki (Jap)	Fubuki (Jap)
Built:	16 + 2L 1928–30	(not built)	12 ships 1924–27	10 ships 1926–29
Displacement:	1,330tW	1,940tW	1,315tW	1,700tW
Dimensions:	320ft × 32ft (98m × 9.8m)	366ft × 36ft (112m × 11.1m)	103m × 9.2m	118m × 10.4m
Machinery:	2-shaft geared turbines; 34,000shp = 35 knots	2-shaft geared turbines; 55,000shp = 37 knots	2-shaft geared turbines; 38,500shp = 37 knots	2-shaft geared turbines; 50,000shp = 38 knots
Armament:	4–4.7in/45 (4 × I)	5–5in/51 (5 × I)	4–12cm/45 (4 × I)	6–12.7cm/50 (3 × II)
	2–2pdr (2 × I)	2–3in HA (2 × I)	2–7.7mm MG (2 × I)	2–7.7mm MG (2 × I)
	8–21in TT (2 × IV)	12–21in TT (4 × III)	6–61cm TT (2 × III)	9–61cm TT (3 × III)
	1 DC rack		18 DC	18 DC

Notes:
• The British 'B' class was followed by the 'C' and 'D' classes, built to a slightly modified design.
• The ten ships of the Japanese *Fubuki* class were followed by ten slightly modified ships of the *Ayanami* sub-group (1928–31) and four of the *Akatsuki* class (1930–32).

Even so they proved to be too lightly constructed for their size, and the excessive topweight of the enclosed gun mountings (32.5 tonnes as compared with 8.9 tonnes for the single 12cm mountings of their predecessors), the torpedo tubes and reload lockers, and the enlarged bridge were to result in serious stability problems. Following the capsizing of the modern torpedo boat *Tomozuru* in a gale off Sasebo in 1934, and the damage sustained by the Fourth Fleet in the great storm of 1935, the class was taken in hand for serious remedial work. The longitudinal members of the hull were strengthened and permanent ballast added, which had the effect of raising standard displacement by 340 tons; maximum speed was correspondingly reduced from 38 knots to 34 knots.

The 'special type' would be the last IJN destroyers of their size to be built under the Washington Treaty. At the London Conference of 1930 it was agreed that the upper limit on individual destroyer displacement (including the flotilla leader category) was to be 1,850 tons, and that only 16 per cent of total destroyer tonnage should exceed 1,500 tons individual displacement (ships already on the stocks could be retained). Since the overall allocation of destroyer tonnage for the IJN established by the conference was 105,500 tons, and the tonnage of the twenty-four 'special type' destroyers completed or building was 41,720 tons (or 39.5 per cent), it was clear that these large destroyers would have to be abandoned in favour of a smaller design: the *Hatsuharu* design which followed would have a standard displacement of 1,490 tons.

Fleet Torpedo Boats for the Marine Nationale

In 1913 the Marine Nationale had assessed its future needs as 115 fleet torpedo boats (*torpilleurs d'escadre*) of 1,000–1,220 tonnes minimum, to be completed by 1920. The outbreak of the First World War promptly put an end to these discussions, and when the Armistice came into force on 10 November 1918 France had the least adequate force of destroyers of any of the five major navies: eight 800-tonne ships of the *Bouclier* class completed 1912–14, a further seven similar ships of the *Bisson* and *Enseigne Roux* classes completed during the first two years of the war, four slightly larger ships of the *Aventurier* class building for Argentina and requisitioned for the Marine Nationale, and the twelve small destroyers of the *Arabe* class purchased from Japan. The *800 tonnes*, which constituted the bedrock of the French postwar destroyer forces, were poorly constructed, with a shallow draught (intended to protect them against mines when operating close to shore) and low freeboard. The *Bouclier*s had been built in a multitude of private shipyards to general specifications provided by the STCN, so there was a wide variation in the manufacture of the propulsion machinery and a correspondingly wide variation in performance. Moreover, by 1918 the armament of two 100mm guns and two twin 450mm torpedo tubes was totally inadequate and outmoded.

Although many of the above ships would remain in service until the 1930s, together with a handful of German and Austro-Hungarian prizes,

Forbin, seen here in the Mediterranean shortly after her completion, was one of the second series of fourteen 'fleet torpedo boats' laid down for the Marine Nationale during the mid-1920s. They and their twelve half-sisters of the *Bourrasque* class carried the largest-calibre gun of all the destroyers built during the 1920s, and also had an impressive complement of torpedoes and anti-submarine weaponry. (Courtesy of Robert Dumas)

the need for new destroyers of modern design in the postwar period was desperate. In the study paper entitled *Note sur les destroyers* approved on 12 March 1919 (see also Chapter 2) the baseline destroyer proposed was to have a normal displacement of 1,500 tonnes, was to be seaworthy, robust and habitable, with command spaces which favoured all-weather operation, and was to be capable of a rapid response. Preliminary studies were subsequently conducted for this type and for a larger 1,700-tonne *contre-torpilleur*, and the first of these were presented to the Naval Staff in April 1920, by which time the latter type had grown to 2,360 tonnes, and was intended to operate independently, not as a flotilla leader (see Chapter 8). In contrast the *torpilleur d'escadre* was now a smaller ship of 1,350 tonnes with a relatively modest performance: four single 100mm guns, two single 75mm HA guns, two or three twin torpedo mountings, 33 knots maximum speed and an endurance of 3,000nm at 15 knots.

Whilst these characteristics were on a par with the British 'V' and 'W' classes, the US Navy's flush-deckers and the Regia Marina's latest destroyers of the *Curtatone* class, they lagged seriously behind the British 'Modified W's and the Japanese *Kamikaze* and *Minekaze* types, which were armed with 4.7in/12cm guns, and it was already becoming apparent that it would be the latter which would set the standard for the new generation of destroyers to be built during the 1920s. The French Naval Staff therefore pressed for an intermediate gun calibre between the 100mm of the initial designs and the 140mm guns under consideration for the larger *contre-torpilleurs* – a new 120mm gun or a lightweight version of the existing 130mm/40-calibre gun being the favoured options. In the event the 130mm Model 1919 was approved in June 1921, and to compensate for the increased weight of the mounting displacement was increased to 1,425 tonnes. However, little account was taken of the potential adverse effects on stability of these guns, which would be the largest-calibre guns mounted in destroyers until the German destroyers of the 1936A type were completed during the Second World War. The 130mm Model 1919 gun mounting weighed 12.7 tonnes, almost 50 per cent more than the standard British 4.7in Mk IX (8.6 tons/8.8 tonnes). Moreover, the bridge had to be raised to clear the superimposed no.2 mounting, and the older-type 450mm torpedo tubes were superseded by the new, heavier 550mm mountings. These weights were all concentrated high in the ship.[3]

The project was approved in its final form in December 1921, when the Washington Conference was already underway, and twelve ships were included in the 1922 programme, the intention being to order a further six of a slightly modified design in 1924, and four in each of the next two years, for a total of twenty-six. This was an impressive and ambitious programme considering the poor state of France's postwar infrastructure and the quantity of new equipment incorporated into the design.

Because of the sheer scale of the programme, and because the naval dockyards were fully occupied with building the new cruisers and *contre-torpilleurs*, the twelve ships of the *Bourrasque* class were ordered from private shipbuilders. They were to be built to identical hull plans drawn up by the STCN. However, the same degree of uniformity was not possible for the propulsion machinery. Six ships had Parsons reaction turbines, two had Rateau impulse turbines, and four had Zoelly impulse turbines.[4] The boilers, designed by A C de St Nazaire-Penhoët, were built by seven different companies in ten different shipyards, so there were many detail differences in the build of ships, and tactical groupings after completion were often based, as with their *800-tonnes* predecessors, on the particular machinery installation.

The designed speed of 33 knots was comfortably attained for a short period on trials, but most ships struggled to maintain 32.5 knots over the nine-hour trial, and sustained speed in service was naturally lower. The designed endurance of 3,000nm at 15 knots also proved optimistic, and in service the figure was probably closer to 1,500nm, which was to pose serious problems when the ships were deployed as convoy escorts in 1939–40.

The new improved hull form was a shortened version of that of the contemporary *contre-torpilleurs* of the *Jaguar* class (see Chapter 8); it featured a raised forecastle with prominent sheer and flare, and greater hull depth and higher freeboard amidships than earlier French destroyers. There was a tripod foremast and a pole mainmast, and three slim, tall funnels raked at a similar angle, each of which served one of the three boilers. The *Bourrasque* class had the same virtues and defects as the *Jaguar*s: they were good seaboats but lively, with a rapid roll period (*Mistral* recorded 43° over five seconds on trials) which made them poor gunnery platforms in heavy seas. The original lightweight gunshields were replaced by a more substantial model soon after completion, further adding to topweight. The height of the funnels was lowered by 1.5–2m following trials, in part as a topweight reduction measure, but also because of concerns about the high, distinctive silhouette of the ships.

The weapons mounted were also identical to those of the *Jaguars*, although there was one fewer 130mm gun mounting and only a single 75mm HA gun. The *Bourrasques*, which were intended to accompany the battle fleet, were to have been fitted with a comprehensive anti-submarine outfit comparable to that of the *contre-torpilleurs*. There was provision for ultrasonic detection apparatus, and the 200kg depth charges (in 'tunnels' as in the *Jaguars*) were to have been complemented by four Thornycroft A/S mortars and Italian Ginocchio torpedoes. However, the mortars were suppressed in 1924 because of topweight concerns, the ultrasonic apparatus failed to materialise (installation was abandoned in 1929), and trials using the Ginocchio torpedo were equally unsuccessful and led to the equipment being disembarked in 1933. When the anti-submarine issue was again addressed in 1939, ASDIC equipment had to be ordered from Britain, and no.4 gun mounting had to be suppressed in order to embark A/S mortars and external depth-charge racks.

The fourteen-ship *L'Adroit* class which followed under the 1924 naval programme was built to essentially the same design, but there were a number of small modifications. The 130mm main guns were of an improved Model 1924 which had more automatic features than the Model 1919. The trunnion was lowered by 16cm to make reloading easier, which in theory should have increased the firing cycle to 8–9rpm – in practice it remained at 5rpm. Reloading the guns on a lively platform was still an issue, newly installed inhibitors permitted firing only in the middle of the ship's roll, and

Bourrasque (Fr)

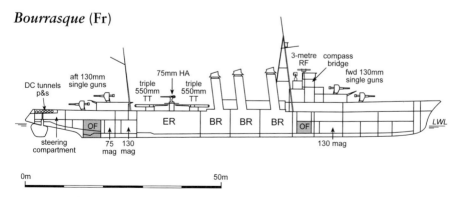

Forming two distinct classes totalling twenty-six ships, the *1500-tonnes* type were intermediate in size between the British 'A' class and the IJN 'special type'. However, whereas in the British and Japanese destroyers the torpedo was pre-eminent, the focus in the French design was on gun power. The 130mm Model 1919 and its successor, the Model 1924, were the largest-calibre guns to be mounted on destroyers during the 1920s, and fired a shell 50 per cent heavier than any of their competitors. The drawing shows the funnels as completed; their height was subsequently lowered by 1.5–2m in order to reduce the silhouette.

the additional safety mechanisms had the effect of slowing or halting firing when they malfunctioned.

The *L'Adroit* class had slightly greater beam and were fitted with longer bilge keels than the *Bourrasques*, which resulted in some improvements in stability, but they still rolled badly in heavy seas and heeled alarmingly under maximum rudder. The Rateau turbines of the *Bourrasques* were superseded by an improved Rateau-Bretagne model, but the Zoelly turbines had a tendency to strip their blades and were abandoned for later construction. The auxiliary machinery, especially the turbo-pumps and the compressors, was also subject to frequent breakdown.

The single 75mm HA gun of the *Bourrasques* was criticised as over-complex and unreliable, and was incapable of sustained anti-aircraft fire. It was therefore replaced in the *L'Adroit* class by two single 37mm Model 1925 AA guns. Two of the four Thornycroft mortars originally projected were fitted on completion, but the installation of effective submarine detection equipment had to wait until 1940.

Steady Progress in the Regia Marina

The standard Italian destroyer type building at the time of the Washington Conference was the *Curtatone*, a two-funnelled design with a displacement of 1,170 tonnes normal, a top speed of 32 knots, and an armament comprising two twin 102mm gun mountings and two triple 450mm torpedo mountings. Like other Italian destroyers these ships were designed to operate primarily in the confined waters of the Adriatic, so there was provision for up to forty mines, and endurance was limited to 1,400nm at 10 knots.

The original design of the *Curtatone* class dated from 1915, and although the armament had been revised before the ships were finally laid down in 1920–21, few modifications were made to the hull and propulsion system. After Washington the Regia Marina was no longer an Adriatic navy, and its greatest potential rival was the French Marine Nationale, which was already projecting a series of large, heavily armed destroyers. New Italian ships in this category would therefore need to be armed with heavier guns and larger torpedoes than their predecessors, and would need to combine high speed with good endurance. These were the considerations which dominated the design of the first post-Washington generation of Italian destroyers which, although they resembled the *Curtatone*s in their internal layout and external appearance, were altogether more powerful in terms of their military characteristics.

The first four ships of the *Sella* class were laid down in 1922–23. They were closely followed by the four ships of the *Sauro* class laid down in 1924 and the eight units of the *Turbine* class laid down in 1925. They were all two-funnelled ships like their immediate predecessors, but were designed for 35–36 knots, with installed horsepower rising progressively from 35,000shp (more than 50 per cent greater than in the *Curtatone*s) to 40,000shp. There was a slight increase in hull size from one group to the next, so that by the *Turbine* class displacement had grown from 970 to 1,110 tonnes standard. There were also continual improvements in endurance, from 1,800nm at 14 knots in the *Sella*s to an impressive 3,200nm at 14 knots in the *Turbine*s.

All were armed with the new 120mm/45-calibre Model 1924/1926 gun and had torpedo tubes for the more powerful 533mm torpedo. The layout of the armament was identical to that of the *Curtatone*s, with the guns in two twin mountings fore and aft[5] and the triple torpedo mountings on a raised centre-line platform between the second funnel and the after guns. Two single 40mm/39-calibre Vickers AA guns were also mounted in all ships as first completed.

There was no anti-submarine weaponry, but as with earlier Italian destroyers one of the designed missions of the new ships was minelaying. Two sets of mine rails capable of accommodating 32–40 mines in the *Sella*s, and up to fifty-two in the later ships, were fitted aft in all three types, the after 120mm gun mounting being raised on a small deckhouse to clear the mine rails.

These were the first Italian destroyers to have superheated steam, and all largely exceeded their contractual speeds on trials, with the fastest, *Aquilone*, sustaining 39.5 knots over four hours. The experimental Belluzzo lightweight impulse turbine on *Crispi* was a failure, and the machinery installation of the early units was fragile, but the installation in later ships was more successful and two of the *Turbine* class were to serve throughout the Second World War (the remaining six ships were lost during the first three months). However,

The name-ship of the *Sauro* class, *Nazario Sauro*, at Taranto. Fast and well armed, these two-funnelled destroyers more than matched their foreign counterparts on paper, but too much was attempted on the displacement, and with the fitting of new fire control directors during the early 1930s topweight/stability became a serious problem and speed declined. (Leo van Ginderen collection)

as with Italian cruisers of the period, the speed of these destroyers in service never matched their performance during trials, and it further declined with later weight additions and with age, so that by the mid-1930s sustained service speed was little better than 30 knots. The destroyers also suffered from their lightweight construction, and they regularly sustained hull and superstructure damage in adverse sea conditions. Hull subdivision was also less well developed than in their larger French counterparts, making them particularly vulnerable to torpedo and mine damage.

Arguably the greatest weakness of these ships, however, lay in their poor stability, which was particularly marked in the early units and necessitated remedial action when they were first completed. The difficulties of upgunning an existing successful design were almost certainly underestimated. The twin 102mm mounting of the *Curtatone*s weighed ten tonnes; the 120mm/45-calibre twin mounting which replaced it 16.7 tonnes – an increase of 67 per cent. Moreover, the 533mm torpedoes, at around 1,700kg, were double the weight of the 450mm models they superseded. All these weights were high in the ship, and when new fire control systems with heavy directors were fitted atop the bridge structures in the early 1930s the topweight problems became even more pronounced.

By the late 1920s it was becoming apparent that a larger type of high-speed destroyer with greater endurance would be required to accompany the new treaty cruisers. The eight units of the *Freccia* and *Folgore* classes, ordered in 1928 and 1929 respectively, were therefore built to a new design showing a marked increase in dimensions and displacement. Whilst they retained the general layout of the *Turbine* class in terms of their main armament and propulsion machinery, they were completed with a modern fire control system, and internal arrangements were markedly improved.

The three boilers, larger and more powerful than those of their predecessors, had their uptakes led into a broad single funnel, giving these ships clean, handsome lines which would be adopted for all subsequent Italian destroyer designs. The four *Freccia*s had the customary Parsons turbines, but the *Folgore*s had turbines of a new lightweight Belluzzo model.

The twin 120mm mountings fore and aft were of the new 50-calibre model introduced in the *esploratori* of the 'Navigatori' class (see Chapter 8). They had an impressive range (18,200m as compared with 15,500m for the 45-calibre gun), but suffered from the same dispersion problems as the earlier guns. They were matched for the first time by a sophisticated modern fire control system which combined a heavyweight director atop the bridge structure with a mechanical computer in a protected compartment beneath the compass bridge (see drawing), and there was also a secondary fire control position fitted with an enclosed rangefinder between the torpedo tubes.

The bridge was considerably enlarged in order to accommodate the new director and improved command spaces, and it was relatively close to the bow. The new ships were therefore not only poor seaboats, but experienced serious stability problems, which were even more marked in the second series due to a reduction in beam. Remedial measures shortly after completion included the embarkation of ninety tonnes of permanent ballast (thirty tonnes beneath the after turbines and sixty beneath the boiler rooms), and lengthening the bilge keels. Stability was still inadequate once 50 per cent of the fuel had been consumed, so there was also provision for replacing fuel with seawater.

The *Freccia*s slightly exceeded their designed speed on trials, but once the measures undertaken to improve their stability had been undertaken there was a marked reduction in performance both in terms of speed and endurance. It was proposed to lengthen these ships to compensate during the 1930s, but because the Regia Marina was in an almost constant state of mobilisation between 1935 and 1939 and the shipyards were fully occupied with new construction, this proposal proved impossible to implement. Wartime equipment additions in the form of minesweeping gear and AA guns served only to exacerbate their stability problem.

Sauro (It)

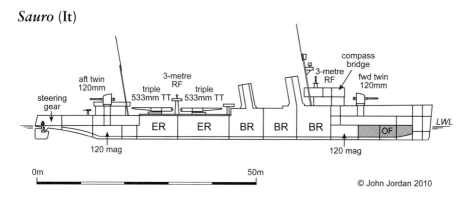

© John Jordan 2010

Freccia (It)

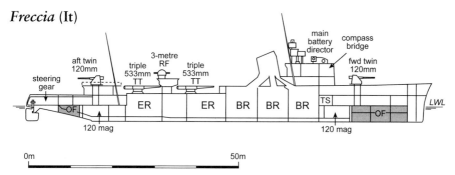

The first generation of destroyers built for the Regia Marina post-Washington were upgunned versions of the postwar *Curtatone* class, with twin 120mm gun mountings and triple banks of 533mm torpedoes. They were smaller than their foreign contemporaries, and early ships of the series were poor seaboats and suffered from serious stability problems. The later ships (the *Sauro* class is depicted here) were an improvement, but their small size meant that they had insufficient endurance to accompany the new treaty cruisers. The Regia Marina therefore went to a larger hull for the *Freccia* and *Folgore* classes which succeeded them in the late 1920s. Unfortunately the decision to take advantage of the larger hull to provide enlarged command spaces and a modern cruiser-style fire control system meant that these ships also suffered from excessive topweight and poor stability. The after twin gun mounting was located on a raised deckhouse to permit the carrying of mines.

The destroyers of the *Freccia* and *Folgore* classes were significantly larger than previous types, and their broad single funnel would become a feature of all subsequent destroyers and escorts built for the Regia Marina. Despite the increase in size, the adoption of the heavyweight 120mm/50-calibre twin mounting – the same as in the 'Navigatoris' – and the incorporation into the design of large command spaces and a modern fire control director meant that these ships suffered from the same topweight/stability problems as their predecessors. This is *Dardo* in 1934. (Leo van Ginderen collection)

Table 10.2: French and Italian Destroyers 1922–30

	Bourrasque (Fr)	*Sauro* (It)	*Freccia* (It)
Built:	12 ships 1923–28	4 ships 1924–27	4 ships 1929–32
Displacement:	1,320tW	1,060tW	1,205tW
Dimensions:	106m × 9.9m	90m × 9.2m	96m × 9.8m
Machinery:	2-shaft geared turbines;	2-shaft geared turbines;	2-shaft geared turbines;
	31,000shp = 33 knots	36,000shp = 35 knots	44,000shp = 38 knots
Armament:	4–130mm/40 (4 × I)	4–120mm/45 (2 × II)	4–120mm/50 (2 × II)
	1–75mm/50 HA (1 × I)	2–40mm AA (2 × I)	2–40mm AA (2 × I)
	6–550mm TT (2 × III)	6–533mm TT (2 × III)	6–533mm TT (2 × III)

Notes:
- The twelve *Bourrasque*s were followed by fourteen slightly modified ships of the *L'Adroit* class.
- The four *Sauro*s were preceded by the four ships of the *Sella* class and followed by eight slightly modified ships of the *Turbine* class.
- The four *Freccia*s were followed by four slightly modified ships of the *Folgore* class.

Conclusions

By the end of the decade the destroyers being designed and built by the major navies were generally larger, more heavily armed and more technologically sophisticated than their wartime predecessors. Propulsion machinery employing higher steam pressure and lightweight turbines were beginning to make their appearance, as were more advanced fire control systems. However, there were already tensions: between complexity and reliability; between heavyweight high-performance weapons systems and stability – exacerbated in the destroyer type because it featured a narrow, lightweight hull designed for high speed; and between high unit cost and numbers.

Paired gun mountings were adopted by the Japanese and the Italians as a means of increasing firepower while economising on deck space. However, paired mountings in destroyers proved to be less effective than two single mountings, in part because the guns were mounted so close together that there were inevitable dispersion problems. Neither could they be said to have saved weight: the Italian 120mm/45-calibre twin mounting weighed 17 tonnes, almost twice the weight of the British 4.7in/45-calibre single mounting (see table); and the IJN's 12.7cm Type 3 mounting weighed 32.5 tonnes, more than twice as much as the French 130mm Mod.1919 single mounting. Paired mountings theoretically permitted more guns to be mounted, with fewer superimposed mountings and a lower bridge structure, resulting in a reduction in topweight. However, the Italians chose to raise their after mountings in order to accommodate a full load of mines, and the IJN destroyers of the 'special type' were given high bridges simply because of the current Japanese obsession with large command spaces.

Only the Italians developed high-performance cruiser-type fire control systems for their destroyers during this period, and there is little indication that they greatly improved the hitting power of these ships. The British had long accepted that destroyers did not make good long-range gunnery platforms, and their experience during the First World War would be largely borne out during the Second. Destroyers were lively ships in any sort of a sea due to their small size and light construction, and the increase in topweight which accompanied director towers with integral rangefinders mounted high in the ship tended to contribute to the liveliness of the platform.

The destroyer of the 1920s was still essentially a 'fleet torpedo boat' in conception. The French, the Italians and, to a certain extent, the Japanese were interested in improving the gunnery capabilities of the type, but the British and the Americans still viewed destroyers as ships which could be 'thrown in' against the enemy battle line without regard to consequences – in a word they were 'expendable'. For the British, cost versus numbers would be a major issue throughout the 1930s and indeed the Second World War; there was a legitimate fear that the more costly and sophisticated the destroyer, the fewer hulls could be afforded, and that these ships would then become too valuable to be endangered in the face of almost certain loss to the enemy's guns at the close range necessary for effective torpedo launch. The focus on the development of long-range torpedoes by the IJN was an implicit recognition of this fact; torpedo attacks at long range were seen as a key factor not only in conducting surprise attacks on the enemy at night, but in securing better coordination of attacks by the flotillas and a higher rate of survival among the destroyers (essential for an effective 'second strike' following reloading of the

Table 10.3: Destroyer Guns of the 1920s

	4in/50	4.7in/45	12cm/45	12.7cm/50	130mm/40	120mm/45	120mm/50
	Mk 9 (US)	Mk IX (GB)	Type 3 (Jap)	Type 3 (Jap)	M1919 (Fr)	M1924 (It)	M1926 (It)
Weight of projectile:	15kg	22.7kg	20.4kg	23kg	32.1kg	23.2kg	23.2kg
Range:	14,560m at 20°	15,500m at 40°	16,000m at 33°	17,600m at 40°	18,900m at 36°	15,500m at 33°	18,200m at 35°
Weight of mounting:	4.6 tonnes (S)	8.8 tonnes (S)	8.9 tonnes (S)	32.5 tonnes (T)	12.5 tonnes (S)	16.9 tonnes (T)	20.2 tonnes (T)

Key:
S = single mounting
T = twin mounting

Table 10.4: Destroyer Authorisations 1922–30

Estimates	British Empire	USA	Japan	France	Italy
1922			12 *Mutsuki* (1924–27)	12 *Bourrasque* (1923–28)	4 *Sella* (1922–27)
1923					4 *Sauro* (1924–27)
1924	2 'A' proto. (1924–26)			6 *L'Adroit* (1925–29)	2 *Turbine* (1925–28)
1925			9 *Fubuki* (1926–29)	4 *L'Adroit* (1926–31)	6 *Turbine* (1925–28)
1926				4 *L'Adroit* (1927–31)	
1927	8 'A' + 1 FL (1928–30)		11 *Fubuki* (1928–32)		
1928	8 'B' + 1 FL (1929–31) 2 *Saguenay* (Can: 1929–31)		4 *Akatsuki* (1930–32)		4 *Freccia* (1929–32)
1929	4 'C' + 1 FL (1930–32)				4 *Folgore* (1929–32)
1930	8 'D' + 1 FL (1931–33)				4 *Maestrale* (1931–34)

torpedo tubes from the special lockers which were a feature of all the postwar IJN destroyers). The French also wanted the capability to conduct torpedo attacks at longer range, hence their adoption of the 550mm torpedo, which approached the early Japanese 61cm models in performance.

There was as yet no serious thought of using destroyers for fleet air defence, even though the IJN paid lip-service to the principle by developing a dual-purpose 12.7cm gun mounting for the later series of the 'special type', and the British considered giving one of the four 4.7in guns on the 'A' and 'B' classes a similar capability. Effective long-range anti-aircraft fire from destroyers would require heavy and sophisticated high-angle control systems, which the British in particular thought inappropriate for ships designed primarily for torpedo attack and defence; these systems would entail precisely the increase in hull size, cost, and technical sophistication to which the Royal Navy was resolutely opposed.

Given that the primary mission of the submarines built during the post-Washington period was to sink large surface warships, and that there was a particular emphasis on penetrating the screen of the enemy battle fleet to target capital ships, one might have expected a greater focus on anti-submarine weaponry in the destroyers built during the 1920s. However, in the quest for greater firepower and a more powerful torpedo armament on hulls of restricted size and cost, deck space and stability margins were often insufficient for an effective outfit of anti-submarine weapons.

Both the British and the Americans were experimenting with submarine detection equipment using sound waves generated by quartz crystals throughout the 1920s, and operational devices under the acronyms ASDIC (Allied Submarine Detection Investigation Committee)[6] for the Royal Navy, and SONAR (Sound Navigation and Ranging) for the US Navy had entered service aboard destroyers, sloops and submarines during the late 1920s. The British had also developed a thin steel dome to protect the equipment, which permitted search operations to be carried out at up to 12 knots, and by 1929 twenty-five ships had been fitted with ASDIC. However, only alternate classes of fleet destroyer were so fitted in the early days, and it would be the 1930s before ASDIC would be fitted as standard. The development of SONAR in the US Navy would take even longer to mature, and it would be the late 1930s before the equipment was widely fitted in American destroyers. The other major navies conspicuously failed to develop anti-submarine sensors which could reliably detect a submarine from a moving ship.

The lack of attention given to anti-submarine warfare is surprising as all five Washington navies were convinced, following the devastating U-boat campaign of 1917–18, that the submarine had now 'come of age' and was a threat to be taken seriously. The anti-submarine technology developed in haste during the late-war period can best be described as embryonic, and investment in research and development during the 1920s would have paid dividends later; as it was, the major navies would begin the Second World War with first-generation underwater sensors and the anti-submarine weaponry of the First.

CHAPTER 11

Geneva and London

According to Article XXI of the Washington Treaty, a further conference would take place after eight years to review the provisions of the treaty. However, by the mid-1920s it was already apparent that the agreement to call a halt to battleship construction until 1931, and the failure to agree on an overall tonnage limit for smaller vessels, had had the effect of releasing funding for cruisers, submarines and destroyers to an extent which had not been anticipated. The United States, which had been the architect of 'collective security' and which at the Washington Conference had secured theoretical parity with the British Royal Navy, had remained aloof from this frenzy of construction, and the US Navy had elected to spend the limited funding allocated to it by Congress on the modernisation of the battle fleet and the conversion of the two big carriers *Lexington* and *Saratoga*. Despite unrelenting pressure from the 'Big Navy' lobby, strongly supported by the steel and armaments industries, Congress preferred to use the breathing space provided by the arms limitation treaties and the new collective security arrangements to reduce expenditure on the US armed forces to a minimum.

It was the US president, Calvin Coolidge, who in February 1927 issued a call for the other four Washington contracting powers to meet in Geneva to confront the issue of naval rivalries, and to agree new limits on the overall tonnage of warships below the battleship and aircraft carrier categories. The contrast between the US naval programmes of 1922–26 and those of the other four powers is clearly shown in Table 1. In the cruiser category, which was the one of most concern to the United States, the British had authorised no fewer than fourteen treaty cruisers over the past three years, and the Japanese eight, with a further four 10,000-ton ships projected for the 1927 programme. During the same period the US Navy had authorised only five ships, with a further three projected for FY1927. Given that the only other modern cruisers built for the US Navy were the ten *Omaha*s built under the 1916 programme, whereas both Britain and Japan had large numbers of cruisers armed with 6in/14cm guns in service dating from the late-war and early postwar periods, this placed the US Navy in a position of marked inferiority.

Table 11.1: Authorisations of Ships outside the Capital Ship/Aircraft Carrier Categories 1922–26

Category	Great Britain	United States	Japan	France	Italy
8in-gun cruisers	14	5	8	4	2
6.1in-gun cruisers	–	–	–	3	–
Large destroyers	–	–	9	12	12
Standard destroyers	2	–	12	26	16
Large submarines	9	3	16	24	5
Medium/small submarines	–	–	–	19	10

The British were equally keen to participate in a new conference, although for quite different reasons. A paper of 1923 by the Plans Division, subsequently adopted as policy by the Admiralty, had stated that British fleet and imperial commitments necessitated a minimum of seventy cruisers,[1] which it was estimated would require the construction of forty-five new ships by the late 1930s. This posed two problems. It had become apparent by the mid-1920s that, even with the funding released by the 'battleship holiday', there would be insufficient funding forthcoming for forty-five new treaty cruisers, and that the only possible solution was to build smaller and less costly ships (a 7,500-ton cruiser armed with 6in guns was proposed) which could be built in the requisite numbers. However, there would be little point in pitting such ships against 10,000-ton Japanese (or French?) cruisers armed with 8in guns. Such a proposal was therefore workable only if the upper limits on unit displacement and armament agreed at Washington were reduced.

The Japanese also agreed to send a delegation to the proposed conference, largely in the hope that the two major powers might be persuaded to accept the 10:7 ratio for cruisers that Japan had failed to secure for capital ships and carriers at Washington and which she considered essential for her security. France and Italy, however, declined to attend, citing their current involvement in disarmament efforts being conducted under the aegis of the League of Nations. This was a calculated snub to the United States, which, having been instrumental in setting up the League of Nations, had promptly withdrawn into its own isolationist cocoon. As if to further emphasise the point, the French foreign minister, Aristide Briand, after prior consultation with the US Secretary of State Frank B Kellogg, submitted a draft treaty to outlaw war altogether to the League of Nations at Geneva on 20 June, the same day that the US-sponsored naval conference began.

The primary motivation for France's refusal to take part in the Geneva Conference was arguably rooted in French dissatisfaction with the terms of the Washington Treaty, and a fear that Anglo-Saxon pressure might now be applied to secure a reduction in the very forces in which the Marine Nationale was currently investing in an attempt to compensate for the inferiority in capital ships imposed at the 1922 conference. The large programme of flotilla craft and submarines had only just got under way, and the French were anxious to ensure that large numbers of these ships were in service before the statutory review of Washington scheduled for 1930–31, thereby enabling their delegation to negotiate from a position of strength which had been denied them in the immediate postwar period. For their part the Italians, somewhat alarmed by the scale of French naval rearmament, were not prepared to attend a conference at which restrictions might be imposed on them but not on their major Mediterranean rival.

The Geneva Conference 1927

The conference, which took place from 20 June to 4 August, was doomed from the outset. It was weakened by the non-attendance of France and Italy, and the three major powers dispatched only second-rank diplomats to represent them.[2] However, the key factor in its failure was the impossibility of reconciling the very different agendas of the participants. The Americans, whose interest was primarily in limiting naval construction, wished to have overall limits imposed on cruiser construction in line with the 5:5:3 ratio established for capital ships and carriers at Washington. The British, citing extensive and onerous commitments to the defence of the Empire and the trade routes, considered parity in cruisers with the United States (which had no such commitments) iniquitous, but needed limits on the size and armament of individual cruisers if it was to afford them in the required numbers. They therefore proposed a 5:5:3 tonnage ratio for 8in-gun cruisers with an upper limit of fifteen hulls for Great Britain and the United States, and twelve for Japan. Once these levels were reached – and Britain and Japan were already close to the limit – new cruiser construction would be limited to ships of 7,500-ton maximum displacement armed with 6in guns, with an overall limit of seventy cruisers being suggested for Britain and the United States.

The United States was unwilling, for reasons of status, to accept a limit on overall cruiser tonnage which was inferior to that accorded to the Royal Navy; on the other hand, the US Navy simply did not have a requirement for cruisers in the numbers the Royal Navy considered essential for its own purposes, and viewed any cruiser of less than 10,000 tons as being of limited value for trans-Pacific operations. The Japanese did not need the long-range operational capability of the US Navy, and, although they favoured the large 8in-gun cruiser for strategic scouting, were quite happy with smaller types for fleet work; by supporting the British position the Japanese felt there was an opportunity to secure the desired 10:7 ratio which would help to compensate for their statutory inferiority in capital ships.[3]

The long-term programme for the US Navy was for twenty-five treaty cruisers of 10,000 tons, for an overall tonnage of 250,000 tons. If the ten 6in-gun cruisers of the *Omaha* class, each of which had a standard displacement of around 7,100 tons, were added to this total, this gave a figure of 321,000 tons. This was far below the Royal Navy's minimum requirements. Given that it was already committed to a programme of fifteen 8in-gun cruisers, including two of a smaller 8,250-ton design, the acceptance of parity with the United States at the levels projected by the US Navy would mean that only 174,500 tons remained for further new construction; even if all the new ships were of 7,500-ton individual displacement then only twenty-three could be built. This would give the Royal Navy a total of thirty-eight cruisers, little more than half the number recommended by the Jellicoe Report of 1919 and totally insufficient for its needs. Moreover, the issue of qualitative inferiority would remain, since the Royal Navy would have only fifteen treaty cruisers with 8in guns to the US Navy's twenty-five.

In an attempt to find a compromise solution, the American delegation proposed a maximum figure of 400,000 tons of cruiser construction, of which 250,000 tons was available for 8in-gun, 10,000-ton types. This met US Navy aspirations for twenty-five cruisers for trans-Pacific scouting operations, but if this latter figure was to be matched by the Royal Navy only 150,000 tons would remain for the construction of smaller types. If these ships were of 7,500 tons displacement twenty could be built, for a total of forty-five cruisers – still far short of British requirements. The American and British positions therefore proved fundamentally irreconcilable.

The naval disarmament talks dragged on for six weeks, but the conference broke up without agreement on any of the key issues, the impasse on cruisers effectively precluding any serious discussion of other categories of warship. Recriminations inevitably followed: the United States blamed Britain and Japan for prevaricating and for countering every proposal with pleas for 'special circumstances'; Britain blamed the United States for failing to understand her imperial defence needs; and Japan blamed the inflexibility of the Americans and, in particular, their rigid insistence on the 5:5:3 ratio, which was designed to keep Japan in a position of statutory military inferiority.

Arguably the most important political consequence of the failure of the conference was that the United States realised that it could no longer afford to hold back from building cruisers, and that further arms limitation could be accomplished only by resuming the naval construction race. If Congress were prepared to fund a new building programme and use US economic clout to outspend the other major maritime powers, then the latter would be compelled to seek an accommodation which would again, it was calculated, be on US terms. The result was the 1929 naval programme, which envisaged the construction of five treaty cruisers in each of the fiscal years FY1929, FY1930 and FY1931, and which when added to the eight ships already under construction would mean twenty-three 8in-gun cruisers in service by 1935. The impact of this programme would be all the greater because 1928–30 was the period when Britain finally exhausted her coffers, and began to acknowledge the extent of the mismatch between her naval aspirations and her ability to deliver. When the London Treaty was signed on 22 April 1930 the British would agree to an overall tonnage ceiling of 339,000 tons for cruisers, a figure well below the one offered by the United States at Geneva.

The Road to London

According to the terms agreed at the Washington Conference, the treaty on the limitation of naval armaments was due for review at a conference to be held by the beginning of 1931. If no modifications were made to the original proposals the construction of capital ships would be resumed according to the agreed replacement programme. In the absence of any agreement on new limits on cruiser, destroyer and submarine construction, current developments would inevitably result in an unmanageable 'free-for-all' in which construction was limited only by a combination of finance and ambition – a situation at odds with the concept of collective security through restraint and respect for the interests of other nations. The world would again be riven by political and economic rivalries which would spawn a new arms race.

The British were not prepared to wait that long for a review of Washington. Once naval programmes were underway they tended to develop a momentum all their own, and were difficult to stop. Under the terms of the Washington Treaty the four older battleships of the *Iron Duke* class were due to be replaced by two new ships by 1934. These would have to be laid down by 1931, so general requirements would have to be agreed by early 1929. Moreover Admiralty thinking was now moving towards the idea that the navy's requirements could be met by a smaller capital ship. A new limit of 28,000 tons and 13.5in guns had been proposed by the British delegation at Geneva, but the proposal had been received unenthusiastically by the United States, and the acrimonious discussions on cruisers completely overshadowed the capital ship issue. By March 1929 the Sea Lords were proposing an even smaller ship of 25,000 tons with 12in guns, and this would become the British 'official position' in the lead-up to the Washington Treaty review. In the interim the Royal Corps of Naval Constructors was instructed to prepare designs for ships of 35,000 tons and 16in guns, 28,000 tons and 14in guns (which it was thought would be attractive to the Japanese as well as to the smaller European navies), and 25,000 tons and 12in guns.

The dire economic straits in which Britain found herself in the years 1928–30 gave added impetus to her efforts to secure further limitations in naval armaments. The heady years of the mid-1920s, when the Royal Navy could lay down five treaty cruisers per year, now seemed a long way away. Only a single 8in-gun cruiser had been authorised in 1927, and the two heavily armoured ships of the *Surrey* class which had initially been put forward in the 1928 Estimates were first postponed until the 1929 Estimates and then cancelled altogether. The only cruiser ordered under the 1929 Estimates was the 7,500-ton *Leander*, armed with eight 6in guns, which was authorised specifically to provide a template for a new treaty-limited cruiser for which

Britain hoped to secure agreement at the Washington Treaty review. Even so, the authorisation of this ship had to be balanced against a reduction of the annual destroyer flotilla[4] to only four ships (the 'C' class – see Chapter 10). Some British naval historians have blamed the treaty era for preventing the Royal Navy from building the ships it wanted in the numbers it required, but this viewpoint is unsupported by the evidence. By the end of the 1920s Britain was desperate for even more restrictive treaty measures to constrain the development of her naval rivals. The prospect of having to deliver a total of seventy cruisers *and* a new generation of capital ships when there was barely enough money to sustain the existing fleet in its peacetime operations was not an enticing one.

In June 1929 a new Labour government came into power under Ramsay MacDonald. The latter was strongly committed to achieving continuous peace by international negotiation, and from the outset declared his intention to reduce the size of the Royal Navy. It was now the British who were driving the naval arms limitation process, and the British government at once communicated to the United States its desire for a new naval conference to take place in London at the beginning of 1930 which would then constitute the statutory eight-year review of the Washington Treaty. The US Government, which had been concerned at the souring of Anglo-American relations which resulted from the failure at Geneva, readily agreed, and invitations were then extended to the other contracting powers.

HMS *Leander*, authorised just before the London Conference, was the first of a series of smaller cruisers armed with 6in guns which the British hoped would serve as a template for new construction in the other major navies. However, the US Navy opposed any reduction in the qualitative cruiser limits, arguing that a ship of less than 10,000 tons would have inadequate range for trans-Pacific operations. (Leo van Ginderen collection)

Table 11.2: HMS *Leander* Characteristics

Laid down:	Sept. 1930
Displacement:	7,000tW (designed)
Dimensions:	555ft × 56ft (169m × 16.8m)
Machinery:	4-shaft geared turbines;
	72,000shp = 32.5 knots
Armament:	8–6in/50 (4 × II)
	4–4in/45 (4 × I) HA
	8–21in TT (2 × IV)
Protection:	mach: 3in belt, 1¼in deck
	mags: 3½in sides, 2in crowns
	turrets: 1in

'Philosophical' Issues

James Ramsay McDonald spent most of the autumn of 1929 preparing the ground for the conference, talking to all the major players and trying to resolve any issues which might otherwise result in failure before the conference opened. These overtures were received favourably by the American Hoover administration, and the Japanese, while insisting on a 10:7 ratio for cruisers, were prepared to listen and negotiate as they had been at Geneva in 1927. However, it became clear that the French position had hardened considerably. There had been much soul-searching in France following the disappointing outcomes of the Washington Conference, and the French Navy was determined not to be caught unprepared a second time.

Britain favoured an extension of the ratios established for capital ships and carriers at Washington to all the other recognised categories of warship: cruisers, destroyers and submarines – a position which was referred to as 'limitation by categories'. The French had been opposed to this from the outset, and their tardy ratification of the Washington Treaty had been accompanied by a formal warning that any future attempt to impose the ratios established for capital ships on 'auxiliary' warships and submarines would be resolutely opposed. Informally, the French were of the opinion that limitation by categories constituted an attempt on the part of the Royal Navy to ensure a statutory and permanent inferiority of the Marine Nationale in *all categories.*

At Washington the French had been boxed into a corner: if they had refused to accept the capital ship ratio with which they had been presented as a fait accompli, they would have been pilloried by the Western press for having brought about the collapse of the conference. They were determined not to be put in this invidious position again, and under the dynamic navy minister, Georges Leygues, the Marine Nationale had drawn up counter-proposals backed up by carefully considered arguments.

The French proposed an alternative formula which would become officially known as 'global limitation'. Under this formula, each of the five contracting powers would be allocated an overall tonnage allocation which they could dispose of as they wished. Qualitative limitations could still be established for each of the categories the conference chose to define, but there would not be separate quantitative limits for each of those categories, thereby enabling a country to opt to build more submarines, or more cruisers and fewer destroyers, depending on its particular defence requirements. Moreover, the global limitation figure – which the French would have preferred to see determined by the League of Nations under its own arms limitation machinery rather than in a separate five-power conference[5] – would have to reflect each country's naval defence obligations.

The French noted potential European security problems which were of particular concern to them: increasing German opposition to the Treaty of Versailles; a possible *Anschluss* between German and Austria; a possible entente between Germany and Italy; the interference of the latter in Poland and Yugoslavia; Soviet imperialism; and Italian efforts towards a rapprochement with Spain. From a strictly naval point of view the French pointed out that it needed to operate both in the Atlantic (possibly against a resurgent Germany) and in the Mediterranean (against an increasingly hostile Italy), that the French empire had 18,109nm of coastline[6] and 33,850nm of sea lines of communication, and that 66 per cent of France's trade was transported by sea.

Finally, the French made it clear that because of their greater naval commitments, parity with Italy was not acceptable. At the same time the Italians were making it equally clear that although they were flexible on the 'global limitation' and 'limitation by categories' formulae – they inclined towards the former – parity with France was a *sine qua non*.

Following lengthy discussions with President Hoover, Ramsay MacDonald managed to secure US backing for limitation by categories, but it was becoming increasingly evident that there were major obstacles in the path towards a new five-power treaty.

'Technical' Issues

As if these 'political' problems were not enough, there were a number of 'technical' difficulties to confront.

Whilst the ground-breaking agreements on limiting the construction of capital ships and aircraft carriers at Washington were generally seen as successful, and had held throughout the decade – to the extent that neither the French nor the Italians had felt the need to use their specially granted new tonnage allocation – the absence of parallel agreements for smaller surface ships and for submarines had effectively distorted the development of the three 'lesser' navies, which had attempted to compensate for their statutory inferiority in capital ships by accelerated building in other categories of warship. This had already resulted in serious anomalies which would be difficult to regulate by attempting to extend the 5:3:1.75 ratio agreed in 1922 for capital ships to cruisers, destroyers and submarines.

Between 1922 and 1929 the French had authorised thirty-five large and twenty-nine coastal submarines, while the Japanese had ordered twenty even larger ocean-going boats; during the same period the US Navy authorised only three submarines. Between 1922 and 1929 the French had authorised twenty-four *contre-torpilleurs* and twenty-six standard destroyers and the Japanese thirty-six destroyers, of which twenty-four were of a new large-displacement type; during the same period the US Navy authorised no flotilla craft whatsoever. Clearly the French and the Japanese were not about to be 'put in their place' in categories in which they had invested so heavily.

Moreover, the absence of any qualitative limits below 10,000 tons and 8in guns had resulted in innovative developments which had effectively blurred what were previously quite distinct categories, making the establishment of acceptable limits on size and armament fraught with difficulty. Whereas 800 tons was a relatively large displacement for a submarine of First World War vintage, the standard fleet submarine now being built for Japan displaced twice that amount, while the IJN's cruiser submarines displaced more than 2,000 tons; even that figure was dwarfed by the US Navy's *V4–6* (2,900 tons surfaced) and the French *Surcouf* (3,250 tons surfaced).

The latest French *contre-torpilleurs* had a standard displacement of 2,600 tons and were armed with 138.6mm guns. Since the Marine Nationale was the only navy of the five building such ships, there was no justification for creating a new category of warship, so they had to be classed either as destroyers (in which case they largely exceeded any displacement or gun-calibre figure the conference was likely to agree to) or as cruisers (in which case their tonnage would have to be counted as part of France's cruiser allocation, thereby limiting the number of protected ships armed with 8in or 6in guns with which the Marine Nationale might oppose the Italian Navy).

Even within the proposed 'destroyer' category there were potential problems. The Japanese destroyers of the 'special type' were so much larger and more powerful than the standard destroyers built by Britain, France and Italy during the 1920s that they would have to be classified as 'leaders', even though they were nothing of the sort. The leader sub-category, however, would have to be subjected to strict limits which would inevitably take the twenty-four Japanese ships above the permitted percentage of destroyer tonnage.

These were difficult issues which would make for fraught negotiations between the five contracting powers, at least three of which (Japan, France and Italy) came to the conference more resolute and better prepared than had been the case at Washington.

The London Treaty

The London Conference began on 21 January 1930. Aware of the potential stumbling blocks to agreement, and anxious that the conference should get off to a positive start, Ramsay MacDonald ensured that the early meetings were 'front-loaded' with items which appeared to enjoy a strong consensus, and that the more difficult issues concerning quantitative limits for auxiliary vessels and submarines were held back until the latter part of the conference, in the hope that the momentum created by early agreement would better dispose the different parties to compromise in the interests of international harmony.

Part I

Part 1 of the treaty was relatively straightforward, despite the importance of its conclusions. The United States was predictably unhappy with the British proposal to reduce the qualitative limit for capital ships to 25,000 tons and 12in guns; on the other hand there was little general enthusiasm for an imminent resumption in capital ship construction. It was therefore agreed that the ten-year 'battleship holiday' agreed at Washington be extended for a further five years, until 31 December 1936 (Article 1). Ships lost or destroyed could still be replaced, and French and Italian concerns regarding their elderly dreadnoughts were addressed by reaffirming their allocation of 70,000 tons of new ships which remained unused from 1927 and 1929.

USS *Utah* would be one of the elderly American battleships to be disarmed following the London Treaty of 1930; she became a target ship. The photo was taken in 1935. (US Navy)

Table 11.3: Capital Ships to be Retained under the London Treaty

British Empire
i) To be retained (15 ships):

	Built	Displ.	Main guns	Speed
2 *Nelson*	1922–27	33,500tW	9–16in (3 × III)	23 knots
Hood	1916–20	41,200t	8–15in (4 × II)	31 knots
2 *Renown*	1915–16	26,500t	6–15in (3 × II)	30 knots
5 *Revenge*	1913–17	25,750t	8–15in (4 × II)	22 knots
5 *Queen Elizabeth*	1912–16	27,500t	8–15in (4 × II)	24 knots

ii) Gunnery Training ship: **iii) To be discarded:**
Iron Duke   *Tiger*
                                       3 *Iron Duke*

Note: Displacement figures do not include 3,000 tons available for modifications. The figure for *Nelson* is Washington standard; the officially declared figure for sister *Rodney* was 33,900 tons.

United States
i) To be retained (15 ships):

	Built	Displ.	Main guns	Speed
3 *Colorado*	1917–23	32,600t	8–16in (4 × II)	21 knots
2 *Tennessee*	1916–21	32,300t	12–14in (4 × III)	21 knots
3 *New Mexico*	1915–19	32,000t	12–14in (4 × III)	21 knots
2 *Pennsylvania*	1913–16	31,400t	12–14in (4 × III)	21 knots
2 *Nevada*	1912–16	27,500t	10–14in (2 × III, 2 × II)	21 knots
2 *New York*	1911–14	27,000t	10–14in (5 × II)	21 knots
Arkansas	1910–12	26,000t	12–12in (6 × II)	21 knots

ii) Gunnery Training ship: **iii) To be discarded:**
Wyoming   2 *Florida*

Note: Of the 2 *Florida*s, *Utah* became a target ship.

Japan

i) To be retained (9 ships):

	Built	Displ.	Main guns	Speed
2 *Nagato*	1917–21	33,800t	8–16in (4 × II)	26 knots
2 *Ise*	1915–18	31,260t	12–14in (6 × II)	23 knots
2 *Fuso*	1912–17	30,600t	12–14in (6 × II)	22 knots
3 *Kongo*	1911–15	27,500t	8–14in (4 × II)	26 knots

ii) Gunnery Training ship:

Hiei

France

i) To be retained (5 ships):

	Built	Displ.	Main guns	Speed
3 *Bretagne*	1912–16	23,500t	10–13.4in (5 × II)	20 knots
2 *Courbet*	1910–12	23,500t	12–12in (6 × II)	20 knots

ii) Gunnery Training ship:

Paris

Italy

i) To be retained (4 ships):

	Built	Displ.	Main guns	Speed
2 *Andrea Doria*	1912–16	22,700t	13–12in (3 × III, 2 × II)	22 knots
2 *Conte di Cavour*	1910–15	22,500t	13–12in (3 × III, 2 × II)	22 knots

However, as the older capital ships in service with all five navies were now of little military value, it was agreed that all powers should reduce the number of capital ships in service to the long-term levels prescribed at Washington: fifteen each for Britain and the United States, nine for Japan and five each for France and Italy (Article 2 – see table for details). There was also an informal understanding that, in view of the age of the ships which remained in service, no objection would be raised to their modernisation provided the 3,000-ton Washington allowance for this purpose was respected. The Japanese and the Italians would take advantage of this to undertake a radical reconstruction of their elderly dreadnoughts which would include modern propulsion machinery and improved fighting qualities.[7]

The two elderly Italian dreadnoughts of the *Cavour class* were completely rebuilt during the mid-1930s; this is *Conte di Cavour* at Taranto in 1938, shortly after her recommissioning. The reconstruction involved not only additional horizontal protection and an underwater protection system featuring the Pugliese shock-absorbing cylinder, but completely new machinery and a new bow to raise speed from the original 21.5 knots to 27–28 knots. The centre turret was removed, the remaining main guns were bored out to 320mm, and new secondary and HA guns fitted. The superstructures were completely rebuilt, and incorporated modern fire control systems. Similar modifications were made to all nine of the surviving Japanese battleships from the early 1930s. The former battlecruiser *Hiei*, relegated to a gunnery training ship under the London Treaty, would follow on the expiry of the Washington Treaty. (Erminio Bagnasco)

The rules governing aircraft carriers were tightened up in Articles 3–5 of the treaty. Britain and the United States would already have been aware that the Imperial Japanese Navy had recently laid down a carrier of less than 10,000 tons standard displacement (*Ryujo*) which did not therefore count as part of Japan's overall tonnage allocation under the Washington Treaty, so this loophole was effectively closed by replacing the wording 'in excess of 10,000 tons' which formed part of the Washington definition of an aircraft carrier with the words: 'whatever its displacement' (Article 3). Capital ships, cruisers and destroyers with either a landing-on or a flying-off platform were exempt from the aircraft carrier classification, although no capital ship in existence on 1 April 1930 could be fitted with a landing-on platform or deck. This was to lead to some exotic carrier/cruiser projects for the US Navy and for the IJN during the early 1930s, none of which however came to fruition.

Under Article 4 the maximum gun calibre for an aircraft carrier of 10,000 tons or less was 6.1in (155mm), while larger ships remained subject to the limit of eight/ten 8in guns prescribed by Articles IX and X of the Washington Treaty (Article 5).

Part II

In Part II of the treaty an attempt was made to establish qualitative boundaries and definitions for surface ships under 10,000 tons and for submarines.

Under Article 6 the definition of 'standard' displacement adopted at Washington for capital ships and carriers was extended to all surface vessels, but there was a new definition for standard displacement specifically for submarines; this displacement excluded not only fuel (reserve feed water for boilers was not an issue!) but also lubricating oil, fresh water and ballast water. It was further stated that the figure for standard displacement should be used for the official registration/notification of all naval combatants for treaty purposes.

Article 7 stated that the maximum displacement for a submarine (including any boat built for export) should be 2,000 tons, and that the maximum gun calibre should be 5.1in (130mm). This was certainly a higher displacement figure than Britain wanted, and France and Italy would have also been happy with a figure closer to 1,500 tons, but for both the Pacific navies size was equated with range, and 1,650–2,000 tons was now the norm for Japanese submarine construction. Even with a proposed limit of 2,000 tons there were a number of submarines either building or in service which largely exceeded both the displacement and the maximum gun calibre figures.[8] Two exceptions to the above rules were therefore made: each nation would be permitted to retain, complete or acquire up to three submarines of 2,000–2,800 tons displacement armed with guns up to 6.1in (155mm); and submarines of less than 2,000 tons displacement but with guns of a calibre greater than 5.1in could be retained. These exceptions, the first of which was intended to placate the US Navy and the second the Japanese, embraced all submarines in service or building except the French *Surcouf*, which France was permitted to complete on the understanding that two projected sisters were to be cancelled.

At Geneva the United States and Japan had proposed a 'treaty-exempt' category of ships, to embrace sloops and gunboats and other types intended for the local defence of remote colonial stations. The United States felt that such a category would meet the demands of the imperial navies (particularly Britain and France) for 'special treatment', and remove the pressure from these powers for special consideration with regard to cruisers. Such ships could be used for 'presence' missions and for the protection of trade, particularly in time of peace. They were purely defensive in capability, and therefore presented no threat to another power. The concept was revived again at the London Conference, and this time received a more favourable hearing. The qualitative definition of these ships was by no means easy, given that in terms of their displacement and armament they had many of the features of destroyers or small cruisers. However, after much discussion, a form of wording was finally agreed which defined them (Article 8) as surface units in the 600–2,000 tons standard range which:

- did not have guns of 6.1in (155mm) calibre and above;
- did not mount four or more guns greater than 3in (76mm);
- could not launch torpedoes;
- could not exceed 20 knots.

Any other surface warship of 600–2,000 tons standard was (by implication) either a destroyer or a cruiser. Ships below 600 tons, which by definition lacked the range and sea-keeping qualities for offensive, open-ocean operations, were not subject to treaty limits.[9]

The characteristics adopted were undoubtedly influenced by the contemporary French 'colonial sloops' (*avisos coloniaux*) of the *Bougainville* class, of which eight had been ordered 1927–30. Displacing just under 2,000 tons standard, these ships were powered by diesels which gave them a maximum speed of 15 knots, and were armed with three single 138mm guns; they were designed to operate 'on station'.

Article 9 extended the Washington rules for the replacement of capital ships and aircraft carriers to cruisers, destroyers and submarines; these were detailed in Annex I. Surface ships exceeding 3,000 tons but not exceeding 10,000 tons displacement laid down before 1 January 1920 could be replaced after sixteen years, and those laid down from that date after twenty years. The corresponding figures for surface ships up to 3,000 tons were twelve and sixteen years, while submarines could be replaced after thirteen years. Replacements could be laid down three years in advance for the larger 'cruiser' category, and two years for smaller surface ships and submarines.

The decision to draw the dividing line at 3,000 tons rather than 2,000 tons appears to have been made at the insistence of the French; although the *contre-torpilleurs* fell outside the 'destroyer' category agreed at London because of their elevated displacement and large-calibre guns, they remained large destroyers in terms of their hull construction and machinery, and could not therefore be expected to have the service-lifespan of a more sturdily built cruiser. The latest ships of the *Le Fantasque* class displaced 2,610 tons standard; their post-London successors of the *Mogador* class would displace 2,885 tons.

The remaining articles in Part II of the treaty outlined formal notification procedures (Article 10), established rules for the disposal of superannuated warships (Article 11 and Annex II), and dealt with 'special vessels' which became anomalous under Article 8 (Article 12 and Annex III). The length and complexity of this section and its associated annexes is evidence of the protracted and difficult nature of the negotiations. Every elderly training cruiser, monitor, minelayer, seaplane carrier, destroyer tender, sloop, yacht and despatch vessel in service with any of the five contracting powers which did not comply with the provisions of Article 8 had to be formally registered and named in order to prevent its being classified as a 'cruiser' or 'destroyer' and therefore subject to agreed overall tonnage limits.

Part III

Part III of the London Treaty was concerned with quantitative limitations on ships in the cruiser, destroyer and submarine categories, and was agreed only by Britain, the United States and Japan. The issues involved proved particularly intractable, and the respective positions taken by the three major powers – which were essentially those responsible for the failure of the Geneva Conference – proved almost impossible to reconcile. Following prolonged and often acrimonious negotiations a compromise was hammered out which, if not particularly well liked by any of the participants, was at least broadly acceptable to each of them.

Article 14 established the principle of overall tonnage limitations for naval combatant vessels other than capital ships and aircraft carriers, while Article 15 attempted to define the 'cruiser' and 'destroyer' categories in terms of individual displacement and gun calibre as a necessary precondition to establishing agreed overall tonnage limits for each category. For these purposes a cruiser was defined as a surface vessel of war other than a capital ship or aircraft carrier with a displacement exceeding 1,850 tons or a gun calibre exceeding 5.1in/130mm, the latter figures becoming the maximum displacement/gun calibre for a ship classified as a destroyer.

The cruiser issue, which on the evidence of Geneva again promised to be the most contentious, had been the subject of 'pre-negotiations' between Britain and the United States in the autumn of 1929, before the conference opened. The British now offered to reduce their own total number of cruisers to fifty in return for an agreement to freeze 8in-gun cruiser construction. Britain would retain her existing fifteen 8in-gun ships to the Japanese twelve, and the US Navy would be permitted to build up to the same level. The British delegation also tried again to secure acceptance for a smaller type of cruiser, armed with 6in guns and with a maximum displacement of 7,500 tons (i.e. equivalent to the recently authorised *Leander*).

The initial American response was little more favourable than at Geneva. The US delegation pushed hard for the completion of the twenty-three 8in-gun ships authorised in 1924 and 1929. Moreover, the US Navy made it abundantly clear that it had no use whatsoever for the smaller cruiser proposed, and insisted that 10,000 tons was a minimum displacement for effective trans-Pacific strategic scouting and fleet operations. However, whereas the General Board favoured the 8in gun, there were others in the US Navy, including Admiral William V Pratt, who headed their delegation in London, who felt that a cruiser armed with rapid-firing 6in guns in triple turrets would be able to match an 8in gun ship at normal battle ranges. There was also a view that a 10,000-ton ship armed with 6in guns could be better protected.

The third party to this discussion, the Imperial Japanese Navy, had become an enthusiastic convert to the 8in-gun treaty cruiser; it had eight 10,000-ton ships built or building in addition to the four smaller ships of the *Furutaka* and *Aoba* classes, and expected to lay down a further class of four in its next construction programme. These were the ships which, together with the large fleet and cruiser submarines, the Japanese envisaged would compensate for her inferiority in capital ships in any conflict with the United States. The Japanese wanted to use their existing superiority in treaty cruisers as a lever to secure the 10:7 ratio which had been a fundamental tenet of IJN policy prior to Washington, and they insisted that the proposed figure of twenty-three US treaty cruisers would have to be matched by sixteen 8in-gun Japanese ships – a figure which was totally unacceptable to Britain.[10]

The negotiations were again fraught with difficulty. Britain wanted Japan restricted to its twelve existing ships, and was prepared to allow the US Navy to go to a maximum of eighteen to compensate. The United States responded by offering to reduce its demand to twenty-one, and in order to accommodate Britain's demand for numbers to police the trade routes was prepared to accept fifteen smaller cruisers against thirty-five for Britain. Britain countered by offering eighteen 8in-gun ships plus an additional 30,000 tons for 6in cruisers. This offer was in turn rejected.

The solution eventually agreed was to split the cruiser category into two sub-categories, the first of which had guns with a calibre exceeding 6.1in/155mm, the second of which had guns with a maximum calibre of 6.1in (Article 15). These were referred to in the treaty as 'sub-category (a)' and 'sub-category (b)' respectively. There was no new formal displacement limit on the latter type, which was subject only to the Washington maximum of 10,000 tons. This left open the possibility of building smaller ships, as desired by the British, or large 10,000-ton types (in effect treaty cruisers armed with 6in guns) as desired by the United States.

Article 16 established the overall tonnage limitations which each of the three major powers should work to by 31 December 1936. These were:

	Great Britain	United States	Japan
Cruisers (a)	146,800tW	180,000tW	108,400tW (=60%)
Cruisers (b)	192,200tW	143,500tW	100,450tW (=70%)
Destroyers	150,000tW	150,000tW	105,500tW (=70%)
Submarines	52,700tW	52,700tW	52,700tW (=100%)

Note: tW = tons (Washington) standard.

There could be a transfer of tonnage allocation not exceeding 10 per cent between the cruiser (b) and the destroyer categories (Article 17). Otherwise vessels which took these totals above the permitted levels were to be disposed of before the due date.

With regard to cruisers, the construction of the 8in sub-category (a) type was effectively frozen except for the United States, which could retain seven

Savannah, seen here in 1939, was one of nine 10,000-ton cruisers armed with 6in guns the US Navy opted to build following the London Conference; only ships of this size were considered useful for the Pacific theatre. The fifteen 6in guns in triple turrets were intended to match those of their Japanese counterparts of the *Mogami* class. The construction of these ships by the two Pacific navies compelled the British to respond with the twelve-gun *Southampton*s, thereby disrupting the Royal Navy's plans to maximise numbers by building only 6in-gun cruisers of 5,000–7,000 tons. (Leo van Ginderen collection)

ships from its current programme (for a total of fifteen), and which would then be permitted to lay down additional ships in 1933, 1934 and 1935 respectively (Article 18). The maximum number of 8in-gun ships in service with each of the three navies in the longer term was therefore: United States eighteen; Britain fifteen; Japan twelve. Should the United States elect to do so, 15,166 tons (standard) of sub-category (b) tonnage could be substituted for the 10,000 tons of each of the additional three sub-category (a) ships – a clause aimed at preserving US 'face' on the key issue of parity with Great Britain.

Within these overall limits 25 per cent of cruisers could be fitted with a landing-on platform or a flight deck (Article 16.5). This was at the insistence of the US delegation, which had Rear-Admiral Moffett of the Bureau of Aeronautics, a keen proponent of putting flight decks on both cruisers and capital ships, as its naval aviation adviser. It would lead during the early 1930s to a series of US 'flying deck cruiser' designs, with a view to boosting the number of available flight decks while using up the navy's 'superfluous' 6in cruiser allowance.[11]

With regard to destroyers, point no.4 of Article 16 effectively created two sub-categories: a large destroyer (or leader) with a maximum displacement of 1,850 tons, and a 'standard' destroyer with a maximum displacement of 1,500 tons. A maximum of 16 per cent of overall destroyer tonnage could be allocated to ships above 1,500 tons. This effectively endorsed Royal Navy doctrine of having an enlarged destroyer 'leader' with enhanced command spaces and superior communications as flagship for a destroyer flotilla. The figure of 16 per cent allowed the construction of one leader of 1,850 tons for a flotilla of eight standard destroyers of 1,250–1,500 tons, which reflected exactly Royal Navy practice.

Flying Deck Cruiser 1930 (US)

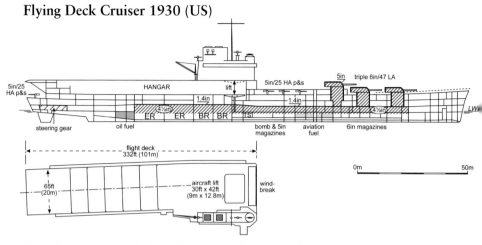

General arrangement of the flying deck cruiser of 1931, one of the more unusual designs to come out of the Washington Treaty. There was considerable enthusiasm for the project in Congress, and in December 1930 the Bureau of Construction and Repair (C&R) produced several studies, one of which had a double hangar. However, at this point the various US Navy bureaux began to present contradictory demands. The aviators of BuAer wanted a ship optimised for air operations with the longest possible unobstructed flight deck and hinged funnels; BuOrd and C&R insisted that cruiser characteristics (i.e. gunnery, fire control and protection) should be prioritised, while BuEng and C&R wanted a fixed funnel.

The design finally selected was inevitably a compromise, with the guns and their respective magazines all forward, the flight deck, hangar and machinery occupying the after end of the ship, and the aviation fuel tanks and bomb magazines amidships. The flight deck was 332ft long with a single elevator at its forward end, and there was a fixed funnel and an island carrying the fire control installations to starboard. The take-off/landing area was angled at 2° to maximise the width of the flight deck abeam the island. The three triple 6in turrets were close to the bow, with the third turret superimposed, the main HA battery (comprising eight single 5in/25-calibre guns) was amidships, and there was to be an air group of twenty-four dive-bombers or fighters. All the aircraft could be spotted on deck, and could then be flown off in the 130ft remaining with 30 knots of wind over the deck (although the dive-bombers would have to be under-fuelled).

War games at the Naval War College established that in a contest between the flight deck cruiser (or CLV) and a conventional gun-armed cruiser the aircraft-carrying ship would generally fare better because of its ability to strike first and at longer range. Also, unlike a fully fledged carrier the CLV would still be a useful fleet asset even after the destruction of its flight deck. It was judged to be particularly valuable for scouting and convoy escort missions. The General Board had strong reservations about this hybrid type of vessel, which did not have the balanced air group necessary to allow it to scout independently, and which it considered vulnerable even to destroyer fire. However, there was sufficient interest and enthusiasm to justify building a prototype, and this went as far as contract plans before the Depression intervened. In 1934 a new project for a cruiser with a less substantial flight deck, the CF, was undertaken, but by this time the General Board had lost interest in the type and it was abandoned.

The Americans were doubly happy with the proposal: on the one hand it provided political support for the US Navy's own proposed leaders, while on the other it effectively called a halt to the IJN's construction of the large and powerful 'special type' destroyers. Since the displacement of the twenty ships of the *Fubuki* class was being declared as 1,750 tons (standard) and that of the four *Akatsuki*s as 1,680 tons, the Japanese already had 41,720 tons of destroyers in the 1,501–1,850 ton bracket – equivalent to almost 40 per cent of their total destroyer tonnage allocation.

The IJN had no intention of using these large destroyers as flotilla leaders, as the latter function would be performed for the foreseeable future by the light cruisers completed postwar (thereby eating into their cruiser sub-category (b) allocation). Although the British and the Americans were prepared to concede that the IJN should retain the ships already on the stocks, the Japanese would from now on be compelled to build destroyers comparable in size and power to their Anglo-Saxon counterparts. Nor would the IJN be permitted to build replacements for the 'special type' destroyers until the total tonnage of the latter declined to the statutory 16 per cent. This would become yet another grievance to add to the ever-growing Japanese list, as the ruling effectively undermined the IJN's policy of countering the US Navy's numerical superiority by the qualitative superiority of its individual units.[12]

With regard to submarines it was made clear that the three 'over-sized' boats permitted in Article 7 would need to be counted in the overall tonnage

The Imperial Japanese Navy responded to the quantitative limits placed on cruisers and destroyers by attempting to pack the superior military qualities of their existing ships into smaller or lighter hulls, relying on new shipbuilding techniques such as the introduction of welding to achieve the necessary reduction in weight. This policy was a failure, and produced a succession of classes in the early 1930s which suffered stability and structural problems; the ships subsequently had to be rebuilt at great expense, losing much of their original qualitative superiority in the process. This is the destroyer *Hatsuharu* at Sasebo in October 1933, shortly after her completion; the superimposed turret would have to be relocated aft and the massive bridge structure reduced, among other remedial measures. (Fukui Shizuo collection)

allocation. Thus there was a powerful incentive to replace these submarines with smaller boats when they approached the end of their statutory thirteen-year lifespan.

Article 19 insisted that the overall tonnage limits agreed in Article 16 should be respected when replacing vessels which would be over-age by 31 December 1936, and outlined the rules for the replacement of ships due to become over-age in 1937–39, while Article 20 incorporated some detailed exceptions to Article 19. The British were anxious to be able to discard the large cruisers of the *Hawkins* class, two of which had been completed as late as 1924–25, to provide the necessary tonnage for new light cruisers armed with 6in guns. The Japanese had similar concerns regarding the medium patrol submarines completed postwar, which the IJN now wished to replace with large cruiser and fleet boats; it also wished to be able to substitute new tonnage for the oldest and smallest of its light cruisers. It was therefore agreed that the British could dispose of the cruisers *Frobisher* and *Effingham* during 1936, while the Japanese would be permitted to decommission the cruiser *Tama* in the same year. In a more significant concession the IJN would be permitted to lay down 19,200 tons of replacement submarine tonnage before 31 December 1936, and to complete 12,000 tons prior to that date.

The final article of Part III, Article 21, was drawn up at the insistence of the British, who were concerned that the failure to secure the agreement of France and Italy to any quantitative restrictions within the new categories might result in escalatory building programmes which the Royal Navy would then have to match. Article 21 permitted any of the three signatories to respond proportionately to any security threat posed by any non-signatory provided formal notification was given to the other two contracting powers. Whilst it was still hoped at this stage that subsequent talks between France and Italy, with Britain acting as mediator, would result in a binding agreement on new naval construction between these two powers, Britain was effectively reserving the right to act in its own security interests should the talks come to nothing. It was no doubt also felt that the potential damage to the treaty system implicit in this undermining of the quantitative limits so painfully negotiated at the London Conference would give Britain leverage, particularly against France, in the negotiations to follow.

Part IV

The British again attempted to outlaw the submarine at the London Conference, and again failed; this time opposition to abolition was universal, with the Japanese and the Italians, who had invested heavily in this category since the Washington Treaty had been signed, standing firm with the French. Indeed the Japanese managed to secure parity with Britain and the USA (see Part III) in the submarine category – although even this tonnage allocation was dwarfed by the current strength of the French submarine arm. The French, however, were now prepared to sign up to a new version of the Root Resolution outlawing unrestricted submarine warfare.

Thus Part IV of the London Treaty comprised just a single article. Article 22 reaffirmed established international law concerning submarine warfare against mercantile shipping. It re-emphasised that a submarine could not sink or disable a merchant vessel 'without having first placed passengers, crew and ship's papers in a place of safety', and that 'the ship's boats are not regarded as a place of safety unless the safety of the passengers and crew is assured, in the existing sea and weather conditions, by the proximity of land, or the presence of another vessel which is in a position to take them on board.' This effectively precluded unrestricted oceanic commerce warfare; even a cruiser submarine the size of the French *Surcouf*, which had accommodation for forty prisoners, would soon find its capacity exceeded and would have to curtail its operations and return to base.

The British government also offered to communicate the provisions of the Article to all 'Powers which are not signatories of the said [i.e. London] Treaty, inviting them to accede thereto definitely and without limit of time'. It would subsequently be signed by many countries outside the five-power treaty system, including Hitler's Germany.

Part V

Part V of the treaty outlined the statutory duration of the various clauses agreed, and the arrangements for ratification (plus the dissemination of Article 22 – see above). The London Treaty was to remain in force until 31 December 1936, and was then to be replaced by a new treaty for which a conference would take place in 1935. At the insistence of the Japanese delegation it was agreed that 'none of the provisions of the present treaty shall prejudice the attitude of any of the High Contracting Parties at the conference agreed to'. This effectively served notice on Britain and the USA that the days of the Washington Treaty were numbered, and that at the next conference Japan would be looking for an agreement which reflected her new status as a major world naval power.

There were two exceptions to the six-year time limit of the London Treaty. Part IV/Article 22 was agreed indefinitely: it had a lifespan outside the framework of the Washington Treaty (indeed it could be argued that the League of Nations, rather than the London Conference, was a more appropriate forum for its discussion, agreement and implementation). And the articles which related to aircraft carriers (i.e. Articles 3–5 and Article 11) were deemed to supplement or supersede the carrier clauses of the Washington Treaty and were therefore to remain in force for the same period of time as the latter.

In view of the failure to secure the accession of France and Italy to the provisions of Part III, it was agreed that the London Treaty should come into force as soon as it had been ratified by the governments of Britain, the United States and Japan. However, it was still anticipated that the governments of France and Italy would ratify those parts of the treaty which their delegations had agreed and signed (i.e. Parts I, II, IV and V), and that these parts would come into force for those powers either on the same date, or on whatever date ratification was deposited with the British government. The US Congress duly ratified the treaty on 21 July 1930, and the Japanese Diet followed suit in October. The treaty came into force on 27 October 1930.

Postscript

The British government was reasonably happy with the outcome of the London Conference, although Ramsay MacDonald very much regretted the failure to lock the French and Italian navies into the quantitative limitations for cruisers, destroyers and submarines.[13] The Royal Navy, on the other hand, was unhappy that the cruiser tonnage allocation agreed between the three major powers would not permit Britain to build the number of ships it required to patrol the trade routes; the figure of 192,200 tons for sub-category (b) cruisers would furnish a maximum twenty-five cruisers of 7,500 tons, which when added to the existing fifteen 8in-gun ships would make for a total of forty – little more than half the seventy demanded by the Admiralty to meet operational requirements.

From an American perspective the London Treaty achieved three fundamental goals. It reduced the need for massive expenditure on naval armaments at a time when the United States was about to see the economic prosperity of the 1920s tumble into the Great Depression of the early 1930s.[14] It reaffirmed the principle of parity of force and esteem with Britain by extending the 5:5 ratio in capital ships and carriers to all other surface and underwater combatants, including cruisers, while securing long-term superiority in the 8in cruisers considered essential for trans-Pacific operations by the US Navy. It also put a cap on Japanese attempts to compensate for the 5:3 ratio for capital ships and carriers agreed at Washington by building large numbers of 'auxiliary' vessels.

American satisfaction with its success in restraining Japanese naval ambitions was more than matched by Japanese dissatisfaction with the outcomes of the conference. Securing parity in submarine tonnage was achieved only at the cost of an overall reduction in the size of the submarine fleet to a level well below the IJN's operational requirements. The failure to secure the desired 10:7 ratio in 8in-gun cruisers was regarded as a national humiliation, and the restrictions on the building of large destroyers threatened the IJN's quest for qualitative superiority in this category of warship. In more general terms, the overall tonnage limitations agreed at London meant that all Japan's efforts to compensate for the inferiority in capital ships and carriers imposed by the Washington Treaty had come to nothing. Early investment in large treaty cruisers, long-range fleet and cruiser submarines, and powerful destroyers meant that the IJN was already close to its permitted ceilings of construction, while the United States, which had under-invested in these ships during the 1920s, could now close the gap at its own leisurely pace,[15] in the secure knowledge that numerical superiority was guaranteed and could not be threatened by the qualitative superiority of individual Japanese ships.[16] Ratification of the London Treaty by the Japanese Diet was therefore preceded by prolonged and acrimonious debate, and it was only at the end of October 1930 that Japan was able to notify the British government of its willingness to accept the agreed terms. The perceived injustices of the treaty would provide ammunition for increasingly vociferous nationalist and militarist factions which served to undermine, and ultimately overthrow democratic government in Japan.

Although the French and the Italian delegations signed the London Treaty at the closing session on 22 April 1930, their respective governments subsequently declined to ratify it. However, despite the evident dissatisfaction of these two powers with the outcomes of the conference, there is every indication that both strictly adhered to the terms of the treaty with regard to Parts I, II, and IV during the period 22 April 1930 to 31 December 1936, and that neither wished to destabilise the naval armaments limitation system by embarking on immoderate and escalatory building programmes.

The capital ships which the French and the Italians laid down in 1932 and 1934 were strictly in accordance with the provisions of the Washington/London treaties – indeed, the French *Dunkerque* and *Strasbourg*, which displaced 26,500 tons standard and were armed with 330mm (13in) guns, reflected the British proposals for smaller battleships. No cruisers armed with 8in/203mm guns were authorised by either power after 1930, so that the eventual total of these ships in service in both the Marine Nationale and the Regia Marina was seven.[17] To follow *Algérie* (Fr) and *Pola* (It) both countries embarked on the construction of category (b) cruisers of less than 8,000 tons displacement armed with 152mm (6in) guns. Despite the refusal of the French and Italian delegations to have anything to do with Part III of the London Treaty,[18] the 5:3:1.75 ratio with respect to the other major Washington powers was not significantly breached as far as 'auxiliary' surface ships were concerned. With both countries affected by the world recession, building programmes were scaled down during the period 1930–36 and limited largely to replacements for warbuilt cruisers and destroyers.

The major issues for France continued to be the failure of the London Treaty to acknowledge her global tonnage requirements as an imperial power, the attempt to impose limits on her submarine force, which she regarded as crucial to her defensive security, and the anomalous position of the *contre-torpilleur*, which straddled the destroyer and '(b)' cruiser categories of the London Treaty. France had conceded parity in capital ship and aircraft carrier tonnage with Italy at Washington on the strict understanding that the same 'inequitable' ratio could not be accepted for 'auxiliary' surface vessels or submarines. Italy, on the other hand, was now nurturing her own imperial ambitions, and would not be prepared to accept less than parity with France in the newly defined categories. Prolonged negotiations in Paris, Rome and London over the next two years would fail to resolve this impasse.

APPENDIX 1

Treaty between the British Empire, France, Italy, Japan and the United States of America for the Limitation of Naval Armament – Washington, February 6, 1922

Declared Purpose: 'to contribute to the maintenance of the general peace, and to reduce the burdens of competition in armament.'

Chapter I – General Provisions relating to the Limitation of Naval Armament

Articles

I   The Contracting Powers agree to limit their respective naval armament as provided in the present Treaty.

II   The Contracting Powers may retain respectively the capital ships which are specified in Chapter II, Part I. On the coming into force of the present Treaty, but subject to the following provisions of this Article, all other capital ships, built or building, of the United States, the British Empire and Japan shall be disposed of as prescribed in Chapter II, Part II.

In addition to the capital ships specified in Chapter II, Part I, the United States may complete and retain two ships of the *West Virginia* class now under construction. On the completion of these two ships the *North Dakota* and *Delaware* shall be disposed of as prescribed in Chapter II, Part II.

The British Empire may, in accordance with the replacement table in Chapter II, Part III, construct two new capital ships not exceeding 35,000 tons (35,560 metric tons) standard displacement each. On the completion of the said two ships the *Thunderer*, *King George V*, *Ajax* and *Centurion* shall be disposed of as prescribed in Chapter II, Part II.

III   Subject to the provisions of Article II, the Contracting Powers shall abandon their respective capital ship building programmes, and no new capital ships shall be constructed or acquired by any of the Contracting Powers, except replacement tonnage, which may be constructed or acquired as specified in Chapter II, Part III.

Ships which are replaced in accordance with Chapter II, Part III, shall be disposed of as prescribed in Part II of that Chapter.

IV   The total capital ship replacement tonnage of each of the Contracting Powers shall not exceed in standard displacement: for the United States, 525,000 tons (533,400 metric tons); for the British Empire, 525,000 tons (533,400 metric tons); for France, 175,000 tons (177,800 metric tons); for Italy, 175,000 tons (177,800 metric tons); for Japan, 315,000 tons (320,040 metric tons).

V   No capital ship exceeding 35,000 tons (35,560 metric tons) standard displacement shall be acquired by, or constructed by, for, or within the jurisdiction of, any of the Contracting Powers.

VI   No capital ship of any of the Contracting Powers shall carry a gun with a calibre in excess of 16 inches (406 millimetres).

VII   The total tonnage for aircraft carriers of each of the Contracting Powers shall not exceed in standard displacement: for the United States, 135,000 tons (137,160 metric tons); for the British Empire, 135,000 tons (137,160 metric tons); for France, 60,000 tons (60,960 metric tons); for Italy, 60,000 tons (60,960 metric tons); for Japan, 81,000 tons (82,296 metric tons).

VIII   The replacement of aircraft carriers shall be effected only as prescribed in Chapter II, Part III, provided, however, that all aircraft carrier tonnage in existence or building on the 12th November, 1921, shall be considered experimental, and may be replaced, within the total tonnage limit prescribed in Article VII, without regard to its age.

IX   No aircraft carrier exceeding 27,000 tons (27,432 metric tons) standard displacement shall be acquired by, or constructed by, for, or within the jurisdiction of, any of the Contracting Powers.

However, any of the Contracting Powers may, provided that its total tonnage allowance of aircraft carriers is not thereby exceeded, build not more than two aircraft carriers, each of a tonnage of not more than 33,000 tons (33,528 metric tons) standard displacement, and in order to effect economy any of the Contracting Powers may use for this purpose any two of their ships, whether constructed or in course of construction, which would otherwise be scrapped under the provisions of Article II. The armament of any aircraft carriers exceeding 27,000 tons (27,432 metric tons1 standard displacement shall be in accordance with the requirements of Article X, except that the total number of guns to be carried in case any of such guns be of a calibre exceeding 6 inches (152 millimetres), except anti-aircraft guns and guns not exceeding 5 inches (127 millimetres), shall not exceed eight.

X   No aircraft carrier of any of the Contracting Powers shall carry a gun with a calibre in excess of 8 inches (203 millimetres). Without prejudice to the provisions of Article IX, if the armament carried includes guns exceeding 6 inches (152 millimetres) in calibre, the total number of guns carried, except anti-aircraft guns and guns not exceeding 5 inches (127 millimetres), shall not exceed ten. If, alternatively, the armament contains no guns exceeding 6 inches (152 millimetres) in calibre, the number of guns is not limited. In either case the number of anti-aircraft guns and of guns not exceeding 5 inches (127 millimetres) is not limited.

XI   No vessel of war exceeding 10,000 tons (10,160 metric tons) standard displacement, other than a capital ship or aircraft carrier, shall be acquired by, or constructed by, for, or within the jurisdiction of, any of the Contracting Powers. Vessels not specifically built as fighting ships nor taken in time of peace under Government control for fighting purposes, which are employed on fleet duties or as troop transports or in some other way for the purpose of assisting in the prosecution of hostilities otherwise than as fighting ships, shall not be within the limitations of this Article.

XII   No vessel of war of any of the Contracting Powers, hereafter laid down, other than a capital ship, shall carry a gun with a calibre in excess of 8 inches (203 millimetres).

XIII   Except as provided in Article IX, no ship designated in the present Treaty to be scrapped may be reconverted into a vessel of war.

XIV   No preparations shall be made in merchant ships in time of peace for the installation of warlike armaments for the purpose of converting such ships into vessels of war, other than the necessary stiffening of decks for the mounting of guns not exceeding 6-inch (152 millimetres) calibre.

XV   No vessel of war constructed within the jurisdiction of any of the Contracting Powers for a non-Contracting Power shall exceed the limitations as to displacement and armament prescribed by the present Treaty for vessels of a similar type which may be constructed by or for any of the Contracting Powers; provided, however, that the displacement for aircraft carriers constructed for a non-Contracting Power shall in no case exceed 27,000 tons (27,432 metric tons) standard displacement.

XVI   If the construction of any vessel of war for a non-Contracting Power is undertaken within the jurisdiction of any of the Contracting Powers, such Power shall promptly inform the other Contracting Powers of the date of the signing of the contract and the date on which the keel of the ship is laid; and shall also communicate to them the particulars relating to the ship prescribed in Chapter II, Part III, Section I (b), (4) and (5).

XVII   In the event of a Contracting Power being engaged in war, such Power shall not use as a vessel of war any vessel of war which may be under construction within its jurisdiction for any other Power, or which may have been constructed within its jurisdiction for another Power and not delivered.

XVIII   Each of the Contracting Powers undertakes not to dispose by gift, sale or any mode of transfer of any vessel of war in such a manner that such vessel may become a vessel of war in the Navy of any foreign Power.

XIX   The United States, the British Empire and Japan agree that the *status quo* at the time of the signing of the present Treaty, with regard to fortifications and naval bases, shall be maintained in their respective territories and Possessions specified hereunder:-

1. The insular Possessions which the United States now holds or may hereafter acquire in the Pacific Ocean, except (a) those adjacent to the coasts of the United States, Alaska and the Panama Canal Zone, not including the Aleutian Islands, and (b) the Hawaiian Islands.

2. Hong Kong and the insular Possessions which the British Empire now holds or may hereafter acquire in the Pacific Ocean, east of the meridian of 110° east longitude, except (a) those adjacent to the coast of Canada, (b) the Commonwealth of Australia and its territories, and (c) New Zealand.

3. The following insular territories and Possessions of Japan in the Pacific Ocean, to wit: the Kurile Islands, the Bonin Islands, Amami-Oshima, the Loochoo Islands, Formosa and the Pescadores, and any insular territories or Possessions in the Pacific Ocean which Japan may hereafter acquire.

The maintenance of the *status quo* under the foregoing provisions implies that no new fortifications or naval bases shall be established in the territories and Possessions specified; that no measures shall be taken to increase the existing naval facilities for the repair and maintenance of naval forces; and that no increase shall be made in the coast defences of the territories and Possessions above specified. This restriction, however, does not preclude such repair and replacement of worn-out weapons and equipment as is customary in naval and military establishments in time of peace.

XX   The rules for determining tonnage displacement prescribed in Chapter II, Part IV, shall apply to the ships of each of the Contracting Powers.

Chapter II – Rules relating to the Execution of the Treaty – Definition of Terms

PART I – Capital Ships which may be Retained by the Contracting Powers
[These tables are reproduced, in edited form, in Chapter 3 of this book.]

PART II – Rules for Scrapping Vessels of War
The following rules shall be observed for the scrapping of vessels of war which are to be disposed of in accordance with Articles II and III:-

I   A vessel to be scrapped must be placed in such condition that it cannot be put to combatant use.

II   This result must be finally effected in any one of the following ways:-
    (a) Permanent sinking of the vessel.
    (b) Breaking the vessel up. This shall always involve the destruction or removal of all machinery, boilers and armour, and all deck, side and bottom plating.
    (c) Converting the vessel to target use exclusively. In such case, all the provisions of paragraph III of this Part, except sub-paragraph (6), in so far as may be necessary to enable the ship to be used as a mobile target, and except sub-paragraph (7), must be previously complied with. Not more than one capital ship may be retained for this purpose at one time by any of the Contracting Powers.
    (d) Of the capital ships which would otherwise be scrapped under the present Treaty in or after the year 1931, France and Italy may each retain two sea-going vessels for training purposes exclusively, that is, as gunnery or torpedo schools. The two vessels retained by France shall be of the *Jean Bart* class. and of those retained by Italy one shall be the *Dante Alighieri*, the other of the *Giulio Cesare* class. On retaining these ships for the purpose above stated, France and Italy respectively undertake to remove and destroy their conning-towers and not to use the said ships as vessels of war.

III   (a) Subject to the special exceptions contained in Article IX, when a vessel is due for scrapping, the first stage of scrapping, which consists in rendering a ship incapable of further warlike service, shall be immediately undertaken.
    (b) A vessel shall be considered incapable of further warlike service when there shall have been removed and landed, or else destroyed in the ship:-
        1. All guns and essential portions of guns, fire control tops and revolving parts of all barbettes and turrets;
        2. All machinery for working hydraulic or electric mountings;
        3. All fire control instruments and rangefinders;
        4. All ammunition, explosives and mines;
        5. All torpedoes, war-heads and torpedo tubes;
        6. All wireless telegraphy installations;
        7. The conning-tower and all side armour, or alternatively all main propelling machinery; and
        8. All landing and flying-off platforms and all other aviation accessories.

IV   The periods in which scrapping of vessels is to be effected are as follows:-
    (a) In the case of vessels to be scrapped under the first paragraph of Article II, the work of rendering the vessels incapable of further warlike service, in accordance with paragraph III of this Part, shall be completed within six months from the coming into force of the present Treaty, and the scrapping shall be finally effected within eighteen months from such coming into force.
    (b) In the case of vessels to be scrapped under the second and third paragraphs of Article II, or under Article III, the work of rendering the vessel incapable of further warlike service, in accordance with paragraph III of this Part, shall be

commenced not later than the date of completion of its successor, and shall be finished within six months from the date of such completion. The vessel shall be finally scrapped, in accordance with paragraph II of this Part, within eighteen months from the date of completion of its successor. If, however, the completion of the new vessel be delayed, then the work of rendering the old vessel incapable of further warlike service, in accordance with paragraph III of this Part, shall be commenced within four years from the laying of the keel of the new vessel, and shall be finished within six months from the date on which such work was commenced, and the old vessel shall be finally scrapped, in accordance with paragraph II of this Part, within eighteen months from the date when the work of rendering it incapable of further warlike service was commenced.

PART III – Replacement

The replacement of capital ships and aircraft carriers shall take place according to the rules in Section I and the tables in Section II of this Part.

Section I – Rules for Replacement

(a) Capital ships and aircraft carriers twenty years after the date of their completion may, except as otherwise provided in Article VIII and in the tables in Section II of this Part, be replaced by new construction, but within the limits prescribed in Article IV and Article VII. The keels of such new construction may, except as otherwise provided in Article VIII and in the tables in Section II of this Part, be laid down not earlier than seventeen years from the date of completion of the tonnage to be replaced: provided, however, that no capital ship tonnage, with the exception of the ships referred to in the third paragraph of Article II, and the replacement tonnage specifically mentioned in Section II of this Part, shall be laid down until ten years from the 12th November, 1921.

(b) Each of the Contracting Powers shall communicate promptly to each of the other Contracting Powers the following information:-

1. The names of the capital ships and aircraft carriers to be replaced by new construction.

2. The date of governmental authorisation of replacement tonnage.

3. The date of laying the keels of replacement tonnage.

4. The standard displacement in tons and metric tons of each new ship to be laid down, and the principal dimensions, namely, length at waterline, extreme beam at or below water-line, mean draft at standard displacement.

5. The date of completion of each new ship and its standard displacement in tons and metric tons, and the principal dimensions, namely, length at waterline, extreme beam at or below waterline, mean draft at standard displacement, at time of completion.

(c) In case of loss or accidental destruction of capital ships or aircraft carriers, they may immediately be replaced by new construction, subject to the tonnage limits prescribed in Articles IV and VII, and in conformity with the other provisions of the present Treaty, the regular replacement programme being deemed to be advanced to that extent.

(d) No retained capital ships or aircraft carriers shall be reconstructed except for the purpose of providing means of defence against air and submarine attack, and subject to the following rules: The Contracting Powers may, for that purpose, equip existing tonnage with bulge or blister or anti-air attack deck protection, providing the increase of displacement thus effected does not exceed 3,000 tons (3,048 metric tons) displacement for each ship. No alterations in side armour, in calibre, number or general type of mounting of main armament shall be permitted except:-

1. In the case of France and Italy, which countries within the limits allowed for bulge may increase their armour protection and the calibre of the guns now carried on their existing capital ships so as not to exceed 16 inches (406 millimetres); and

2. The British Empire shall be permitted to complete, in the case of the *Renown*, the alterations to armour that have already been commenced but temporarily suspended.

Section II – Replacement and Scrapping of Capital Ships
[These tables are reproduced, in edited form, in Chapter 3 of this book.]

PART IV – Definitions
For the purposes of the present Treaty, the following expressions are to be understood in the sense defined in this Part:-

Capital Ship
A capital ship, in the case of ships hereafter built, is defined as a vessel of war, not an aircraft carrier, whose displacement exceeds 10,000 tons (10,160 metric tons) standard displacement, or which carries a gun with a calibre exceeding 8 inches (203 millimetres).

Aircraft Carrier
An aircraft carrier is defined as a vessel of war with a displacement in excess of 10,000 tons (10,160 metric tons) standard displacement – designed for the specific and exclusive purpose of carrying aircraft. It must be so constructed that aircraft can be launched therefrom and landed thereon, and not designed and constructed for carrying a more powerful armament than that allowed to it under Article IX or Article X, as the case may be.

Standard Displacement
The standard displacement of a ship is the displacement of the ship complete, fully manned, engined and equipped ready for sea, including all armament and ammunition, equipment, outfit, provisions and fresh water for crew, miscellaneous stores and implements of every description that are intended to be carried in war, but without fuel or reserve feed water on board.

The word 'ton' in the present Treaty, except in the expression 'metric tons', shall be understood to mean the ton of 2,240 pounds (1,016 kilog.).

Vessels now completed shall retain their present ratings of displacement tonnage in accordance with their national system of measurement. However, a Power expressing displacement in metric tons shall be considered for the application of the present Treaty as owning only the equivalent displacement in tons of 2,240 pounds.

A vessel completed hereafter shall be rated at its displacement tonnage when in the standard condition defined herein.

Chapter III – Miscellaneous Provisions

Articles
XXI   If during the term of the present Treaty the requirements of the national security of any Contracting Power in respect of naval defence are, in the opinion of that Power, materially affected by any change of circumstances, the Contracting Powers will, at the request of such Power, meet in conference with a view to the

reconsideration of the provisions of the Treaty and its amendment by mutual agreement.

In view of possible technical and scientific developments, the United States, after consultation with the other Contracting Powers, shall arrange for a conference of all the Contracting Powers, which shall convene as soon as possible after the expiration of eight years from the coming into force of the present Treaty, to consider what changes, if any, in the Treaty may be necessary to meet such developments.

XXII   Whenever any Contracting Power shall become engaged in a war which in its opinion affects the naval defence of its national security, such Power may, after notice to the other Contracting Powers, suspend for the period of hostilities its obligations under the present Treaty other than those under Articles XIII and XVII, provided that such Power shall notify the other Contracting Powers that the emergency is of such a character as to require such suspension.

The remaining Contracting Powers shall in such case consult together with a view to agreement as to what temporary modifications, if any, should be made in the Treaty as between themselves. Should such consultation not produce agreement, duly made in accordance with the constitutional methods of the respective Powers, any one of said Contracting Powers may, by giving notice to the other Contracting Powers, suspend for the period of hostilities its obligations under the present Treaty, other than those under Articles XIII and XVII.

On the cessation of hostilities the Contracting Powers will meet in conference to consider what modifications, if any, should be made in the provisions of the present Treaty.

XXIII   The present Treaty shall remain in force until the 31st December, 1936, and in case none of the Contracting Powers shall have given notice two years before that date of its intention to terminate the Treaty, it shall continue in force until the expiration of two years from the date on which notice of termination shall be given by one of the Contracting Powers, whereupon the Treaty shall terminate as regards all the Contracting Powers. Such notice shall be communicated in writing to the Government of the United States, which shall immediately transmit a certified copy of the notification to the other Powers and inform them of the date on which it was received. The notice shall be deemed to have been given and shall take effect on that date. In the event of notice of termination being given by the Government of the United States, such notice shall be given to the diplomatic representatives at Washington of the other Contracting Powers, and the notice shall be deemed to have been given and shall take effect on the date of the communication made to the said diplomatic representatives.

Within one year of the date on which a notice of termination by any Power has taken effect, all the Contracting Powers shall meet in conference.

XXIV   The present Treaty shall be ratified by the Contracting Powers in accordance with their respective constitutional methods, and shall take effect on the date of the deposit of all the ratifications, which shall take place at Washington as soon as possible. The Government of the United States will transmit to the other Contracting Powers a certified copy of the *procès-verbal* of the deposit of ratifications.

The present Treaty, of which the French and English texts are both authentic, shall remain deposited in the archives of the Government of the United States, and duly certified copies thereof shall be transmitted by that Government to the other Contracting Powers.

APPENDIX 2

International Treaty for the Limitation and Reduction of Naval Armament – London, April 22, 1930

Part I

Articles

1. The high contracting parties agree not to exercise their rights to lay down the keels of capital ship replacement tonnage during the years 1931–36 inclusive, as provided in chapter II, part 3, of the treaty for the limitation of naval armament, signed between them at Washington on the 6th February, 1922, and referred to in the present treaty as 'the Washington Treaty'.

   This provision is without prejudice to the disposition relating to the replacement of ships accidentally lost or destroyed, contained in chapter II, part 3, section I, paragraph (c), of the said treaty.

   France and Italy may, however, build the replacement tonnage which they were entitled to lay down in 1927 and 1929 in accordance with the provisions of the said treaty.

2. (1) The United States, the United Kingdom of Great Britain and Northern Ireland and Japan shall dispose of the following capital ships as provided in this article:
   - United States: *Florida, Utah, Arkansas* or *Wyoming.*
   - United Kingdom: *Benbow, Iron Duke, Marlborough, Emperor of India, Tiger.*
   - Japan: *Hiyei.*

   (a) Subject to the provisions of sub-paragraph (6), the above ships, unless converted to target use exclusively, in accordance with chapter II, part 2, paragraph II (c), of the Washington Treaty, shall be scrapped in the following manner:

   One of the ships to be scrapped by the United States and two of those to be scrapped by the United Kingdom shall be rendered unfit for warlike service, in accordance with chapter II, part 2, paragraph III (b), of the Washington Treaty, within 12 months from the coming into force of the present treaty. These ships shall be finally scrapped, in accordance with paragraph II (a) or (b) of the said part 2, within 24 months from the said coming into force. In the case of the second of the ships to be scrapped by the United States, and of the third and fourth of the ships to be scrapped by the United Kingdom, the said periods shall be 18 and 30 months respectively from the coming into force of the present treaty.

   (b) Of the ships to be disposed of under this article, the following may be retained for training purposes:
   - By the United States: *Arkansas* or *Wyoming.*
   - By the United Kingdom: *Iron Duke.*
   - By Japan: *Hiyei.*

These ships shall be reduced to the condition prescribed in section V of annex II to part II of the present treaty. The work of reducing these vessels to the required condition shall begin, in the case of the United States and the United Kingdom, within 12 months, and in the case of Japan, within 18 months from the coming into force of the present treaty; the work shall be completed within 6 months of the expiration of the above-mentioned periods.

Any of these ships which are not retained for training purposes shall be rendered unfit for warlike service within 18 months, and finally scrapped within 30 months, of the coming into force of the present treaty.

(2)   Subject to any disposal of capital ships which might be necessitated, in accordance with the Washington Treaty, by the building by France or Italy of the replacement tonnage referred to in article 1 of the present treaty, all existing capital ships mentioned in chapter II, part 3, section II, of the Washington Treaty and not designated above to be disposed of may be retained during the term of the present treaty.

(3)   The right of replacement is not lost by delay in laying down replacement tonnage, and the old vessel may be retained until replaced, even though due for scrapping under chapter II, part 3, section II, of the Washington Treaty.

3.   (1)   For the purposes of the Washington Treaty, the definition of an aircraft carrier given in chapter II, part 4, of the said treaty is hereby replaced by the following definition:

The expression 'aircraft carrier' includes any surface vessel of war, whatever its displacement, designed for the specific and exclusive purpose of carrying aircraft, and so constructed that aircraft can be launched therefrom and landed thereon.

(2)   The fitting of a landing-on or flying-off platform or deck on a capital ship, cruiser or destroyer, provided such vessel was not designed or adapted exclusively as an aircraft carrier, shall not cause any vessel so fitted to be charged against or classified in the category of aircraft carriers.

(3)   No capital ship in existence on the 1st April, 1930, shall be fitted with a landing-on platform or deck.

4.   (1)   No aircraft carrier of 10,000 tons (10,160 metric tons) or less standard displacement, mounting a gun above 6.l-inch (155mm) calibre, shall be acquired by or constructed by or for any of the high contracting parties.

(2)   As from the coming into force of the present treaty in respect of all the high contracting parties, no aircraft carrier of 10,000 tons (10,160 metric tons) or less standard displacement, mounting a gun above 6.1-inch (155mm) calibre, shall be constructed within the jurisdiction of any of the high contracting parties.

5.   An aircraft carrier must not be designed and constructed for carrying a more powerful armament than that authorised by article 9 or article 10 of the Washington Treaty, or by article 4 of the present treaty, as the case may be.

Wherever in the said articles 9 and 10 the calibre of 6 inches (152 mm) is mentioned, the calibre of 6.1 inches (155mm) is substituted therefor.

Part II

6.   (1)   The rules for determining standard displacement prescribed in chapter II, part 4, of the Washington Treaty shall apply to all surface vessels of war of each of the high contracting parties.

(2)   The standard displacement of a submarine is the surface displacement of the vessel complete (exclusive of the water in non-watertight structure), fully

manned, engined, and equipped ready for sea, including all armament and ammunition, equipment, outfit, provisions for crew, miscellaneous stores, and implements of every description that are intended to be carried in war, but without fuel, lubricating oil, fresh water or ballast water of any kind on board.

(3) Each naval combatant vessel shall be rated at its displacement tonnage when in the standard condition. The word 'ton', except in the expression 'metric tons', shall be understood to be the ton of 2,240 pounds (1,016 kilos).

7. (1) No submarine, the standard displacement of which exceeds 2,000 tons (2,032 metric tons) or with a gun above 5.1-inch (130mm) calibre, shall be acquired by or constructed by or for any of the high contracting parties.

(2) Each of the high contracting parties may, however, retain, build or acquire a maximum number of 3 submarines of a standard displacement not exceeding 2,800 tons (2,845 metric tons); these submarines may carry guns not above 6.1-inch (155mm) calibre. Within this number, France may retain one unit, already launched, of 2,880 tons (2,926 metric tons), with guns the calibre of which is 8 inches (203mm).

(3) The high contracting parties may retain the submarines which they possessed on the 1st April, 1930, having a standard displacement not in excess of 2,000 tons (2,032 metric tons) and armed with guns above 5.1-inch (130mm) calibre.

(4) As from the coming into force of the present treaty in respect of all the high contracting parties, no submarine the standard displacement of which exceeds 2,000 tons (2,032 metric tons), or with a gun above 5.1-inch (130mm) calibre, shall be constructed within the jurisdiction of any of the high contracting parties, except as provided in paragraph (2) of this article.

8. Subject to any special agreements which may submit them to limitation, the following vessels are exempt from limitation:

(a) Naval surface combatant vessels of 600 tons (610 metric tons) standard displacement and under.

(b) Naval surface combatant vessels exceeding 600 tons (610 metric tons), but not exceeding 2,000 tons (2,032 metric tons) standard displacement, provided they have none of the following characteristics:

(1) Mount a gun above 6.1-inch (155mm) calibre.

(2) Mount more than four guns above 3-inch (76mm) calibre.

(3) Are designed or fitted to launch torpedoes.

(4) Are designed for a speed greater than 20 knots.

(c) Naval surface vessels not specifically built as fighting ships which are employed on fleet duties or as troop transports or in some other way than as fighting ships, provided they have none of the following characteristics:

(1) Mount a gun above 6.1-inch (155mm) calibre.

(2) Mount more than four guns above 3-inch (76mm) calibre.

(3) Are designed or fitted to launch torpedoes.

(4) Are designed for a speed greater than 20 knots.

(5) Are protected by armour plate.

(6) Are designed or fitted to launch mines.

(7) Are fitted to receive aircraft on board from the air.

(8) Mount more than one aircraft-launching apparatus on the centre line; or two, one on each broadside.

(9) If fitted with any means of launching aircraft into the air, are designed or adapted to operate at sea more than 3 aircraft.

9. The rules as to replacement contained in annex I to this part II are applicable to vessels of war not exceeding 10,000 tons (10,160 metric tons) standard displacement with the exception of aircraft carriers, whose replacement is governed by the provisions of the Washington Treaty.

10. Within 1 month after the date of laying down and the date of completion respectively of each vessel of war, other than capital ships, aircraft carriers and the vessels exempt from limitation under article 8, laid down or completed by or for them after the coming into force of the present treaty, the high contracting parties shall communicate to each of the other high contracting parties the information detailed below:

    (a) The date of laying the keel and the following particulars:
    - Classification of the vessel.
    - Standard displacement in tons and metric tons.
    - Principal dimensions, namely: length at water-line, extreme beam at or below water-line.
    - Mean draft at standard displacement.
    - Calibre of the largest gun.

    (b) The date of completion together with the foregoing particulars relating to the vessel at that date.

    The Information to be given in the case of capital ships and aircraft carriers is governed by the Washington Treaty.

11. Subject to the provisions of article 2 of the present treaty, the rules for disposal contained in annex II to this part II shall be applied to all vessels of war to be disposed of under the said treaty, and to aircraft carriers as defined in article 3.

12. (1) Subject to any supplementary agreements which may modify, as between the high contracting parties concerned, the lists in annex III to this part II, the special vessels shown therein may be retained and their tonnage shall not be included in the tonnage subject to limitation.

    (2) Any other vessel constructed, adapted or acquired to serve the purposes for which these special vessels are retained shall be charged against the tonnage of the appropriate combatant category, according to the characteristics of the vessel, unless such vessel conforms to the characteristics of vessels exempt from limitation under article 8.

    (3) Japan may, however, replace the minelayers *Aso* and *Tokiwa* by two new minelayers before the 31st December, 1936. The standard displacement of each of the new vessels shall not exceed 5,000 tons (5,080 metric tons); their speed shall not exceed 20 knots, and their other characteristics shall conform to the provisions of paragraph (b) of article 8. The new vessels shall be regarded as special vessels, and their tonnage shall not be chargeable to the tonnage of any combatant category. The *Aso* and *Tokiwa* shall be disposed of in accordance with section I or II of annex II to this part II, on completion of the replacement vessels.

    (5) The *Asama, Yakumo, Izumo, Iwate* and *Kasuga* shall be disposed of in accordance with section I or II of annex II to this part II when the first three vessels of the *Kuma* class have been replaced by new vessels. These three vessels of the *Kuma* class shall be reduced to the condition prescribed in section V, sub-paragraph (b) 2, of annex II to this part II, and are to be used for training ships, and their tonnage shall not thereafter be included in the tonnage subject to limitation.

13. Existing ships of various types, which, prior to the 1st April, 1930, have been used as stationary training establishments or hulks, may be retained in a non-seagoing condition.

[**Part II** of the treaty had the following annexes:
I – Rules for Replacement
II – Rules for Disposal of Vessels of War
III – Special Vessels (listed)]

Part III

The President of the United States of America, His Majesty the King of Great Britain, Ireland and the British dominions beyond the Seas, Emperor of India, and His Majesty the Emperor of Japan, have agreed as between themselves to the provisions of this part III.

14. The naval combatant vessels of the United States, the British Commonwealth of Nations and Japan, other than capital ships, aircraft carriers and all vessels exempt from limitation under article 8, shall be limited during the term of the present treaty, as provided in this part III, and, in the case of special vessels, as provided in article 12.

15. For the purpose of this part III the definition of the cruiser and destroyer categories shall be as follows:

    Cruisers
    Surface vessels of war, other than capital ships or aircraft carriers, the standard displacement of which exceeds 1,850 tons (1,880 metric tons), or with a gun above 5.1-inch (130mm) calibre.

    The cruiser category is divided into two sub-categories, as follows:
    (a) Cruisers carrying a gun above 6.1-inch (155mm) calibre.
    (b) Cruisers carrying a gun not above 6.1-inch (155mm) calibre.

    Destroyers
    Surface vessels of war the standard displacement of which does not exceed 1,850 tons (1,880 metric tons), and with a gun not above 5.1-inch (130mm) calibre.

16. (1) The completed tonnage in the cruiser, destroyer and submarine categories which is not to be exceeded on the 31st December, 1936, is given in the following table:

Categories	United States	British Common- wealth of Nations	Japan
Cruisers: (a) with guns of more than 6.1-inch (155mm) calibre	180,000 tons (182,880mt)	146,800 tons (149,149mt)	108,400 tons (110,134mt)
(b) with guns of 6.1-inch (155mm) calibre or less	143,500 tons (145,796mt)	192,200 tons (195,275mt)	100,450 tons (102,057mt)
Destroyers	150,000 tons (152,400mt)	150,000 tons (152,400mt)	105,500 tons (107,188mt)
Submarines	52,700 tons (53,543mt)	52,700 tons (53,543mt)	52,700 tons (53,543mt)

(2) Vessels which cause the total tonnage in any category to exceed the figures given in the foregoing table shall be disposed of gradually during the period ending on the 31st December, 1936.

(3) The maximum number of cruisers of sub-category (a) shall be as follows: for the United States, 18; for the British Commonwealth of Nations, 15; for Japan, 12.

(4) In the destroyer category not more than 16 per cent of the allowed total tonnage shall be employed in vessels of over 1,500 tons (1,524 metric tons) standard displacement. Destroyers completed or under construction on the 1st April, 1930, in excess of this percentage may be retained, but no other destroyers exceeding 1,500 tons (1,524 metric tons) standard displacement shall be constructed or acquired until a reduction to such 16 per cent, has been effected.

(5) Not more than 25 per cent of the allowed total tonnage in the cruiser category may be fitted with a landing-on platform or deck for aircraft.

(6) It is understood that the submarines referred to in paragraphs (2) and (3) of article 7 will be counted as part of the total submarine tonnage of the high contracting party concerned.

(7) The tonnage of any vessels retained under article 13 or disposed of in accordance with annex II to part II of the present treaty shall not be included in the tonnage subject to limitation.

17. A transfer not exceeding 10 per cent of the allowed total tonnage of the category or sub-category into which the transfer is to be made shall be permitted between cruisers of sub-category (b) and destroyers.

18. The United States contemplates the completion by 1935 of 15 cruisers of sub-category (a) of an aggregate tonnage of 150,000 tons (152,400 metric tons). For each of the three remaining cruisers of sub-category (a) which it is entitled to construct, the United States may elect to substitute 15,166 tons (15,409 metric tons) of cruisers of sub-category (b). In case the United States shall construct one or more of such three remaining cruisers of sub-category (a), the sixteenth unit will not be laid down before 1933 and will not be completed before 1936; the seventeenth will not be laid down before 1934 and will not be completed before 1937; the eighteenth will not be laid down before 1935 and will not be completed before 1938.

19. Except as provided in article 20, the tonnage laid down in any category subject to limitation in accordance with article 16 shall not exceed the amount necessary to reach the maximum allowed tonnage of the category, or to replace vessels that become 'over-age' before the 31st December, 1936. Nevertheless, replacement tonnage may be laid down for cruisers and submarines that become 'over-age' in 1937, 1938 and 1939, and for destroyers that become 'over-age' in 1937 and 1938.

20. Notwithstanding the rules for replacement contained in annex I to part II:

(a) The *Frobisher* and *Effingham* (United Kingdom) may be disposed of during the year 1936. Apart from the cruisers under construction on the 1st April, 1930, the total replacement tonnage of cruisers to be completed, in the case of the British Commonwealth of Nations, prior to the 3lst December, 1936, shall not exceed 91,000 tons (92,456 metric tons).

(b) Japan may replace the *Tama* by new construction to be completed during the year 1936.

(c) In addition to replacing destroyers becoming 'over-age' before the 31st December, 1936, Japan may lay down, in each of the years 1935 and 1936, not more than 5,200 tons (5,283 metric tons) to replace part of the vessels that become 'over-age' in 1938 and 1939.

(d) Japan may anticipate replacement during the term of the present treaty by laying down not more than 19,200 tons (19,507 metric tons) of submarine tonnage, of which not more than 12,000 tons (12,192 metric tons) shall be completed by the 31st December, 1936.

21. If, during the term of the present treaty, the requirements of the national security of any high contracting party in respect of vessels of war limited by part III of the present treaty are, in the opinion of that party, materially affected by new construction of any Power other than those who have joined in part III of this treaty, that high contracting party will notify the other parties to part III as to the increase required to be made in its own tonnages within one or more of the categories of such vessels of war, specifying particularly the proposed increases and the reasons therefore, and shall be entitled to make such increase. Thereupon the other parties to part III of this treaty shall be entitled to make a proportionate increase in the category or categories specified; and the said other parties shall promptly advise with each other through diplomatic channels as to the situation thus presented.

Part IV

22. The following are accepted as established rules of international law:
    (1) In their action with regard to merchant ships, submarines must conform to the rules of international law to which surface vessels are subject.
    (2) In particular, except in the case of persistent refusal to stop on being duly summoned, or of active resistance to visit or search, a warship, whether surface vessel or submarine, may not sink or render incapable of navigation a merchant vessel without having first placed passengers, crew and ship's papers in a place of safety. For this purpose the ship's boats are not regarded as a place of safety unless the safety of the passengers and crew is assured, in the existing sea and weather conditions, by the proximity of land, or the presence of another vessel which is in a position to take them on board.

    The high contracting parties invite all other Powers to express their assent to the above rules.

Part V

23. The present treaty shall remain in force until the 31st December, 1936, subject to the following exceptions:
    (1) Part IV shall remain in force without limit of time.
    (2) The provisions of articles 3, 4 and 5, and of article 11 and annex II to part II, so far as they relate to aircraft carriers, shall remain in force for the same period as the Washington Treaty.

    Unless the high contracting parties should agree otherwise by reason of a more general agreement limiting naval armaments, to which they all become parties, they shall meet in conference in 1935 to frame a new treaty to replace and to carry out the purposes of the present treaty, it being understood that none of the provisions of the present treaty shall prejudice the attitude of any of the high contracting parties at the conference agreed to.

24. (1) The present treaty shall be ratified by the high contracting parties in accordance with their respective constitutional methods, and the ratifications shall be deposited at London as soon as possible. Certified copies of all the *procès-verbaux* of the deposit of ratifications will be transmitted to the Governments of all the high contracting parties.

(2) As soon as the ratifications of the United States of America, of His Majesty the King of Great Britain, Ireland and the British dominions beyond the Seas, Emperor of India, in respect of each and all of the members of the British Commonwealth of Nations as enumerated in the preamble of the present treaty, and of His Majesty the Emperor of Japan have been deposited, the treaty shall come into force in respect of the said high contracting parties.

(3) On the date of the coming into force referred to in the preceding paragraph, parts I, II, IV and V of the present treaty will come into force in respect of the French Republic and the Kingdom of Italy if their ratifications have been deposited at that date; otherwise these parts will come into force in respect of each of those Powers on the deposit of its ratification.

(4) The rights and obligations resulting from part III of the present treaty are limited to the high contracting parties mentioned in paragraph (2) of this article. The high contracting parties will agree as to the date on which, and the conditions under which, the obligations assumed under the said part III by the high contracting parties mentioned in paragraph (2) of this article will bind them in relation to France and Italy; such agreement will determine at the same time the corresponding obligations of France and Italy in relation to the other high contracting parties.

25. After the deposit of the ratifications of all the high contracting parties, His Majesty's Government in the United Kingdom of Great Britain and Northern Ireland will communicate the provisions inserted in part IV of the present treaty to all Powers which are not signatories of the said treaty, inviting them to accede thereto definitely and without limit of time.

Such accession shall be effected by a declaration addressed to His Majesty's Government in the United Kingdom of Great Britain and Northern Ireland.

26. The present treaty, of which the French and English texts are both authentic, shall remain deposited in the archives of His Majesty's Government in the United Kingdom of Great Britain and Northern Ireland. Duly certified copies thereof shall be transmitted to the Governments of all the high contracting parties.

[Signatures]
In faith whereof the above-named plenipotentiaries have signed the present treaty and have affixed thereto their seals.

Done at London, the 22nd day of April, 1930.
[Signed on behalf of the United Kingdom and parts of the British Empire not separate members of the League of Nations, Australia, Canada, Irish Free State, New Zealand, South Africa, India, France, Italy, Japan and United States.]

Bibliography

Historical

BOOKS

Asada, Sadao, *From Mahan to Pearl Harbor*, US Naval Institute Press (Annapolis, Maryland 2006)

Espagnac du Ravay, *Vingt Ans de Politique Navale (1919–1939)*, B Arthaud (Grenoble, 1941)

Evans, David C and Peattie, Mark, *Kaigun: Strategy, Tactics and Technology in the Imperial Japanese Navy 1887–1941*, US Naval Institute Press (Annapolis, Maryland 1997)

Greene, Jack and Massagnani, Alessandro, *The Naval War in the Mediterranean 1940–43*, Chatham Publishing (London 1998)

Hone, Thomas C, Friedman, Norman and Mandeles, Mark D, *American and British Aircraft Carrier Development*, US Naval Institute Press (Annapolis, Maryland 1999)

McIntyre, W David, *The Rise and Fall of the Singapore Naval Base*, Macmillan Press (London 1979)

Miller, Edward S, *War Plan Orange*, US Naval Institute Press (Annapolis, Maryland 1991)

Minardi, Salvatore, *Il Disarmo Navale (1919–1936)*, Ufficio Storico della Marina Militare (Rome 1999)

Peattie, Mark, *Sunburst: the Rise of Japanese Naval Air Power, 1909–1941*, US Naval Institute Press (Annapolis, Maryland 2001)

Roskill, Stephen, *Naval Policy Between the Wars*, Collins (London 1968)

PERIODICALS AND OTHER RESOURCES

Papers and Record of Meetings of the Committee of Experts, London Conference

Papers and Record of Meetings of the First Committee, London Conference

Record of Meetings of the British Empire Delegation, Washington and London (1930) Conferences

Record of Plenary Sessions, London Conference

Contemporary articles published in the following:

Annals of the American Academy of Political and Social Science (AAAPS)

Proceedings of the Academy of Political Science in the City of New York

Pacific Affairs

Pacific Historical Review

Political Science Quarterly

Foreign Affairs

Far Eastern Survey

The American Journal of International Law

Technical

GENERAL

Campbell, John, *Naval Weapons of World War Two*, Conway Maritime Press (London 1985)

Chesneau, Roger (ed.), *Conway's All the World's Fighting Ships 1922–1946*, Conway Maritime Press (London 1980)

Friedman, Norman, *Battleship: Design and Development 1905–1945*, Conway Maritime Press (London 1978)

— *Submarine: Design and Development*, Conway Maritime Press (London 1984)

Gray, Randal (ed.), *Conway's All the World's Fighting Ships 1906–1921*, Conway Maritime Press (London 1985)

GREAT BRITAIN

Akermann, Paul, *Encyclopaedia of British Submarines 1901–1955*, Maritime Books (Liskeard 1989)

Brown, David K, *Nelson to Vanguard: Warship Design and Development 1923–1945*, Chatham Publishing (London 2006)

Campbell, N J M, 'Washington's Cherrytrees: The Evolution of the British 1921–22 Capital Ships', *Warship Nos.1-3*, Conway Maritime Press (London 1977)

Friedman, Norman, *British Carrier Aviation*, Conway Maritime Press (London 1988)

— *British Destroyers: From Earliest Days to the Second World War*, Seaforth Publishing (Barnsley 2009)

Raven, Alan and Roberts, John, *British Battleships of World War Two*, Arms & Armour Press (London 1976)

— *British Cruisers of World War Two*, Arms & Armour Press (London 1980)

UNITED STATES

Friedman, Norman, *US Aircraft Carriers: An Illustrated Design History*, US Naval Institute Press (Annapolis, Maryland 1983)

— *US Battleships: An Illustrated Design History*, US Naval Institute Press (Annapolis, Maryland 1985)

— *US Cruisers: An Illustrated Design History*, US Naval Institute Press (Annapolis, Maryland 1985)

— *US Submarines Through 1945: An Illustrated Design History*, US Naval Institute Press (Annapolis, Maryland 1995)

— *US Destroyers: An Illustrated Design History*, US Naval Institute Press (Annapolis, Maryland 1982)

Hone, Thomas C and Hone, Trent, *Battle Line: The United States Navy 1919–1929*, US Naval Institute Press (Annapolis, Maryland 2006)

Stern, Robert C, *The Lexington Class Carriers*, Arms & Armour Press (London 1993)

JAPAN

Boyd, Carl and Yoshida, Akihiko, *The Japanese Submarine Force and World War II*, US Naval Institute Press (Annapolis, Maryland 1995)

Jentschura, Hansgeorg, Jung, Dieter and Mickel, Peter, *Warships of the Imperial Japanese Navy, 1869–1945*, Arms & Armour Press (London 1977)

Lacroix, Eric and Wells, Linton, *Japanese Cruisers of the Pacific War*, US Naval Institute Press (Annapolis, Maryland 1997)

Lengerer, Hans, '*Akagi* and *Kaga*', Parts 1–3, *Warship Nos.22–24*, Conway Maritime Press (London 1982)

— 'The Japanese Destroyers of the *Hatsuharu* Class', *Warship 2007*, Conway Publishing (London 2007)

Polmar, Norman and Carpenter, Dorr B, *Submarines of the Imperial Japanese Navy 1904–1945*, US Naval Institute Press (Annapolis, Maryland 1986)

FRANCE

Dumas, Robert and Guiglini, Jean, *Les Cuirassés de 23 500 tonnes*, Lela Presse (Outreau 2005)

Garier, Gérard and du Cheyron, Patrick, *Les croiseurs lourds français de 10 000TW Duquesne & Tourville*, Lela Presse (Outreau 2003)

Huan, Claude, *Les Sous-Marins Français, 1918–1945*, Marines Edition (Bourg en Bresse 1995)

Jordan, John, 'French Submarine Development Between the Wars', *Warship 1991*, Conway Publishing (London 1991)

— 'French Treaty Cruisers: The Middle Period', *Warship 2006*, Conway Publishing (London 2006)

— 'The French Flotilla Programme of 1922', *Warship 1992*, Conway Publishing (London 1992)

— and Dumas, Robert, *French Battleships 1922–1956*, Seaforth Publishing (Barnsley 2009)

Lassaque, Jean, *Les CT de 2 400 tonnes du type Jaguar*, Marines Edition (Bourg en Bresse 1994)

— *Les CT de 2 700 tonnes du type Vauquelin*, Marines Edition (Nantes 2000)

— *Les CT de 2 800 tonnes du type Le Fantasque*, Marines Edition (Nantes 1998)

Le Masson, Henri, *Histoire du Torpilleur en France 1872–1940*, Académie de la Marine (Paris 1963).

Moulin, Jean and Maurand, Patrick, *Le croiseur Algérie*, Marines Edition (Nantes 1999)

Moulin, Jean, Morareau, Lucien and Picard, Claude, *Le Béarn et le Commandant Teste*, Marines Edition (Bourg en Bresse 1997)

Saibène, Marc, *Les Torpilleurs de 1500 tonnes du type Bourrasque*, Marines Edition (Nantes 2001)

ITALY

Bargoni, Franco, *Esploratori Italiani*, Ufficio Storico della Marina Militare (Rome 1996)

Giorgerini, Giorgio and Nani, Augusto, *Gli Incrociatotori Italiani*, Ufficio Storico della Marina Militare (Rome 1964)

— *Le Navi di Linea Italiane*, Ufficio Storico della Marina Militare (Rome 1966)

Pollina, Paolo M, *I Sommergibili Italiani*, Ufficio Storico della Marina Militare (Rome 1963)

Tignelli, Rear-Admiral V E (ed.), *I Cacciatorpedinierei Italiani*, Ufficio Storico della Marina Militare (Rome 1966)

Notes

Preface

1. The French *Statut Naval* (lit. Naval Law) was similar in principle. However, although mention is made in the text of the six-year *Statut Naval* of 1924, the Marine Nationale failed to secure parliamentary approval for the programme, and the navy was compelled to break it down into six 'slices' (tranches) – voted annually – in order to secure the necessary funding.
2. Some ships, notably the British submarines of the 1929 Estimates, were authorised but orders were delayed pending the outcomes of the conference.

Chapter 1

1. All the displacements in the this chapter are 'normal' (for submarines, 'surfaced'). Most have been rounded up or down to give an approximation for comparative purposes.
2. The *Nagato* was officially stated at the time to have a maximum speed of 23 knots, but was apparently designed for at least 25 knots and achieved 26.7 knots on trials. The two ships of the *Kaga* class which would have followed the two *Nagato*s were designed for a similar speed, while the other twelve ships of the projected postwar programme were to have been even faster.
3. The speed matched that of the FY17 'battle scouts' and scout cruisers.
4. Night action by the battle fleet was regarded as inadvisable, because of the uncertainties of combat in conditions of poor visibility (a view shared by the Royal Navy at that time).
5. Twelve identical ships were built for the French Marine Nationale as the *Algérien* class.
6. By contrast, HMS *Dreadnought* herself was completed in the record time of fourteen months. For subsequent battleships built for the Royal Navy the time between laying down and completion was about two years. US Navy dreadnoughts took around two and a half years to build, German dreadnoughts three years.
7. In 1914 total tonnage was 690,000 tonnes, including twenty-one battleships and seventeen cruisers; in 1921 tonnage was 485,000 tonnes, with ten battleships and eighteen cruisers – a 47 per cent reduction.
8. The heavy bow armour of these ships, allied to the closeness of their superimposed turrets to the bow, made them exceptionally wet forward, and was removed postwar.
9. Even at 10,000m large-calibre shells would have a relatively flat trajectory.
10. A solution to this problem, which persisted into the interwar period, was the grouping in divisions of ships according to their machinery (see Chapter 10).
11. Two ships were cancelled in 1921.
12. The Italian ships were named: *Leone, Leopardo, Lince, Pantera, Tigre*. Their French counterparts were *Léopard, Lynx, Panthère*, and *Tigre*, the class of six being completed by *Jaguar* and *Chacal*. One of the following class was given the name *Lion*.
13. Cuniberti subsequently wrote an impassioned advocacy entitled 'An ideal battleship for the British Fleet' for the 1903 edition of *Jane's Fighting Ships*.
14. Others were built in Britain and Canada.

Chapter 2

1. There was no 'technical' input into the committee's deliberations.
2. Presumably the lowest level would have been acceptable only for the battlecruisers which, because of their higher speed, could choose whether or not to engage; for the battleships it would imply vulnerability to the shellfire of the American and Japanese battleships currently under construction.
3. Other important bureaux with input into the design process of US Navy warships were: the Bureau of Ordnance (BuOrd), the Bureau of Engineering (BuEng) and the Bureau of Aeronautics (BuAer).
4. She was not, however, the first to be completed; that honour went to the IJN's *Hosho*, completed in December 1922.
5. The 14cm shell had proved to be the largest that could be comfortably handled by the Japanese seaman, who was smaller than his Western counterpart, hence the IJN's unwillingness to move to the 6in/15cm QF gun standard in British and US Navy cruisers.

6. Data from Lacroix and Wells, *Japanese Cruisers of the Pacific War*, on which this account is largely based.
7. Memorandum no.21 May 1918, planning section (quoted in Friedman, *US Cruisers*, p.106).
8. It was still US Navy practice to locate the magazines in the bowels of the ship, well beneath the waterline, where they were relatively immune to shell fire but vulnerable to underwater explosions from torpedoes or mines.
9. As we shall see in a later chapter, the Imperial Japanese Navy came to quite different conclusions. The view taken by the French reflects operational requirements in the European theatre, where ships would normally return to their home port after each engagement; the Pacific powers were faced with longer campaigns over vast expanses of ocean, and therefore had a different perspective.

Chapter 3

1. For the precise wording of the treaty, see Appendix I.
2. In the wording of the treaty these ships are referred to as the *West Virginia* class. This is odd in that *West Virginia* (BB-48) was technically the last ship of the class (she was also the last to enter service). The only ship completed prior to the conference was *Maryland* (BB-46). According to US Navy custom and practice *Colorado* (BB-45) should have been the name-ship of the class.
3. This is strictly incorrect: in mathematical terms the true ratio is 5:3:1.66. The reason for the anomaly lies in Secretary Hughes's original proposals, which were for 500,000 tons, 300,000 tons and 175,000 tons. When quantitative limits were agreed, it became clear that the first two figures were not divisible by 35,000 tons, so they were increased accordingly. However, the British strongly objected to the French total being raised to 210,000 tons, so it remained at 175,000 tons.
4. The British delegation pushed for a limit of 43,000 tons with a view to preserving the first two G3s, but this was really a non-starter as ships of this size would have outclassed the latest battleships being completed for the US Navy and the IJN, and it represented precisely the escalation that the United States was anxious to nip in the bud.
5. The displacements used in this chapter are those which appear in Chapter II of the Washington Treaty document.
6. The battlecruisers *Amagi* and *Akagi* being built for the the Imperial Japanese Navy had been laid down in December 1920 and were 40 per cent complete when the Washington Conference opened. The US Navy, for its own part, had already initiated studies for the conversion of the *Lexington*s to carriers prior to the conference.
7. The ulterior motivation for the British objection was that its delegation was still pushing for a 45,000-ton limit on capital ships to enable the Royal Navy to complete at least two of the projected G3 battlecruisers.
8. The British 'light battlecruiser' conversions (*Furious*, *Courageous* and *Glorious*) and the French conversion of the hull of the *Normandie*-class battleship *Béarn*, would all have a standard displacement of 22,000–22,500 tons.
9. ASW carriers had already been proposed by Admiral Charles Madden at a Royal Navy conference in 1920 – see Friedman, *British Carrier Aviation*, p.90.
10. The carrier tonnage ratio is often stated to have been the same as that for battleships. This was patently not the case: the agreed ratio was 5:3:2.2.
11. Curiously this latter figure was reduced to eight for carriers above 27,000 tons (Article IX). Thus the Japanese *Akagi* and *Kaga*, which as first completed were just within the 27,000-ton margin, could be armed with ten 20cm guns while their 'overweight' US counterparts, *Lexington* and *Saratoga*, had only eight 8in guns.
12. The British remained concerned that the looseness of the treaty wording might be seen as permitting carriers armed with both 8in and 6in guns, and that this might lead to aircraft carriers being used for commerce raiding (presumably using their aircraft to scout for potential mercantile targets).
13. The original Hughes proposal had been for 450,000 tons for the two major powers, 270,000 tons for Japan and, presumably, 157,500 tons for France and Italy. (The Americans were almost totally focused on the navies of the three major powers, regarding the French and Italian figures as a side issue to be settled later).
14. A paper by the Conseil Supérieur de la Marine of September 1920 proposed the construction of eleven battleships of 40,000 tons and fifteen cruisers of 12,000 tons by 1940. The latter would probably have been armed with guns of at least 194mm.
15. The British wanted separate categories established for 'fleet' and 'trade' cruisers, with only the former constrained by quantitative limits. This was clearly a non-starter, with the United States arguing that there was nothing preventing ships whose declared mission was trade protection being used to bolster an attacking fleet.
16. British paranoia in this regard appears to have been focused on the French. In June 1922 (i.e. only four months after the signing of the Washington Treaty) a report of the Salisbury Committee for National and Imperial Defence to the Committee for Imperial Defence stated that the French armed forces presented a real danger for world peace and a threat to Britain and the Empire.

17. A further concern may have been a purely commercial one: in the absence of capital ship orders from their own government, shipyards might need to rely on orders for new-build ships for foreign powers. These were to be subject to the same qualitative limits as vessels built for the contracting powers under the treaty (Article XV).
18. Note that in the wording of this article (see Appendix I) there was no specific mention of the former German island groups mandated to Japan by the League of Nations: the Marshalls, the Carolines and the (northern) Marianas. The terms of the mandate expressly forbade the construction of fortifications or the raising of an army within the territory, so a specific reference in the Washington Treaty was unnecessary.
19. One submarine on patrol for every three counted in force strengths was the official French estimate of the time.
20. The practical difficulties of achieving this in vessels of obsolescent design, together with the cost, were such as to make this course of action a non-starter, but the conference clearly thought it necessary to provide this theoretical sop to the French and Italian delegations.
21. Quoted in full in Raven and Roberts, *British Battleships of World War II*, p.128.
22. The definition was to be amended in the London Treaty of 1930 to include ships of less than 10,000 tons (see Chapter 11).

Chapter 4

1. The American Strategist Alfred Thayer Mahan, quoted in Asada, *From Mahan to Pearl Harbor*, p. 89.
2. The Italian delegation had been instructed to settle if offered 80 per cent of the French total.

Chapter 5

1. This was still 2 knots faster than the US Navy's *Colorado*s, and was thought to be on a par with the IJN's *Nagato*s. Neither the British nor the Americans were aware that the Japanese ships, which had been inspired by the 'fast battleships' of the *Queen Elizabeth* class, had a designed speed of 26.5 knots (the US Navy only learned of this when the ships emerged from a major reconstruction during the late 1930s, and redesigned its own battleships of the *South Dakota* class accordingly).
2. The warheads of torpedoes then in service with flotilla craft were significantly smaller. Those on contemporary British destroyers were 515lb (234kg).
3. The metacentric height (GM) of the previous class of British battleship, the *Royal Sovereign*s, was 5.1ft; in the *Queen Elizabeth* class, which was not bulged, it was 7.8ft.
4. The barrel life of the 16in weapon was estimated at only 200 rounds even after the adoption of a reduced charge, as compared with 350 rounds for its 15in predecessor.
5. The US Navy insisted prior to the London Conference of 1930 that one or both would need to be matched by new US construction if its theoretical equal status with the Royal Navy was to be preserved.
6. The bulges of the first ships to receive them had not been particularly successful, and had produced excessive roll. The later conversions were fitted with bulges of different design, without the steel 'crushing tubes'.
7. The same individual also claimed that firing had been carried out at a range of 30,000 yards – only *Hood* had this capability.
8. Memorandum by Capt Frank H Schofield to the secretary of the navy.
9. Letter to the Chairman of the House of Representatives Committee on Naval Affairs, 6 January 1925.
10. In the *Nagato* class this proved ineffectual so the fore-funnel was trunked back into a distinctive 'S' shape.
11. The Japanese adopted metric measurements from the early 1920s, so all subsequent figures for Japanese ships will conform to this system.
12. This development seems to have gone unnoticed in Europe, where the British and the French still worried about the Japanese battlecruisers being employed to hunt down their own treaty cruisers.
13. In a footnote to Part 3, Section 1(d), France and Italy were permitted to modify both the main battery and the armour belts of their elderly dreadnought battleships provided the 16in-gun restriction and the 3,000-ton ceiling on reconstruction were adhered to.
14. The fourth ship, *France*, became a total loss following a grounding off the coast of Brittany in 1922.
15. In *Paris* the funnels were simply moved together without trunking.
16. Draft plans for 'Battlecruisers of 37,000 tonnes' dating from 1927–28 have recently been discovered, but there was never the political will to build ships of this size for the reasons outlined above.
17. The French appear to have been more heavily influenced by contemporary British practice than any of the other major powers.

18. Although 16in/406mm guns were also considered, the weight of the guns and their associated turrets was felt to be excessive on the displacement. Moreover, 15in/381mm guns had already been designed and built for the uncompleted *Caracciolo* class of the late war period.

Chapter 6

1. Not all of these would have been treaty cruisers, however. There was also interest in building smaller cruisers armed with 6in guns. The 'Special Programme of Naval Construction' drawn up in December 1923 called for eight 10,000-ton cruisers and ten smaller ones to be completed by 1929. In the event construction had to be focused on the treaty cruiser type in response to the wholehearted enthusiasm shown for these ships abroad.
2. The original staff requirement for the British Vickers Mk I mounting was for a firing cycle of 12rpm! This proved impossible to attain, and attempts by Vickers to provide even the minimum 5rpm in sustained firing that was considered acceptable by the navy added considerably to the weight and complexity of the mounting.
3. Single mountings were briefly considered by the Royal Navy, but were quickly rejected because of the problem of accommodating enough of them on the centre-line.
4. The length overall of the *Myoko* was 204m, 12–13m longer than the British and French first-generation treaty cruisers, and 25m longer than the US Navy's *Pensacola*.
5. An impression only heightened when they served in the Far East, and carried the traditional China Station livery of white hull and buff funnels.
6. The weight of an 8in/203mm shell was around 120–130kg – that of a standard 6in shell only 50–55kg.
7. The American, British and Italian first-generation treaty cruisers all had their boilers grouped in fours. The exceptionally large boiler rooms of the *Pensacolas* were much-criticised, and in their successors they were subdivided by additional bulkheads.
8. In the later 'Counties' the shell rooms were given the same level of protection as the magazines.
9. However, one would have thought that the massive 14 per cent overweight figure recorded on *Yubari*'s completion in 1923 should have served as a warning.
10. This was, in principle, no different to the British failure to declare the 2,870-ton weight of the liquid (water) anti-torpedo filling in the *Nelson* class.
11. Significantly, the figure of 350 tons is not far short of the difference in the weight allocated to protection in the French and Italian cruisers.
12. This was not a conspicuous success, as the elevating and recoil mechanism proved to be fragile, and 55° was acknowledged to be the maximum elevation at which the gun could deliver sustained high-angle fire.
13. The torpedo body was strengthened and the angle of entry changed.
14. Even when the fixed tubes were subsequently replaced by trainable mountings located at upper-deck level these were still housed within superstructure decks in order to maximise reloading capabilities, and exploding torpedo warheads would be responsible for the loss of several IJN 'A'-type cruisers during the Second World War. All five navies were aware of the serious risks posed by exploding torpedo warheads. The French solution was to stow the warheads in lockers of HT steel on the deck edge so that any explosion would be vented upwards and outwards, thereby minimising damage to the ship's vitals.
15. In order to model for a ship's performance in service, it was common practice for designers to set a figure for a 'normal', 'trial' or 'legend' displacement which would correspond to the 10,000-ton 'standard' displacement to enable them to perform the necessary calculations for powering, stability, etc. For the *Myokos* that figure had originally been set at 11,850 tons (although the metric system had been adopted by the Japanese Diet in 1920–21, imperial measurements had been retained for the design calculations of the *Myoko*).
16. *Japanese Cruisers of the Pacific War*, pp.88–90.
17. In the interim the IJN experimented with a two-part take-off platform 26.6m long in the *Furutaka* class, one part being fixed to no.4 20cm 'semi-turret' and rotating with it, the other part being mounted on semicircular rails ahead of the turret. However, this proved to be particularly hazardous; it never became operational and was removed in 1930.
18. Raven and Roberts, *British Cruisers of World War Two*, p.130.
19. When the Japanese admiral Takagi, with the treaty cruisers *Nachi* and *Haguro* in command, took advantage of a lull in the Battle of the Java Sea in February 1942 to recover the five seaplanes he had employed for spotting earlier in the battle, his two cruisers were surprised at only 12,000m in the dying light by the Allied cruiser force which was heading north in search of the convoy he was protecting, and he was fortunate to emerge from this difficult situation unscathed. Subsequently the IJN came to regard the aircraft as expendable.
20. Raven and Roberts, *British Cruisers*, p.211.
21. The classification of the early treaty cruisers by the different navies is confused (and confusing to the reader). Most of the navies concerned classified them initially either as 'light cruisers' (to distinguish them from the numerous 'armoured cruisers' still extant) or simply as 'cruisers'. The

IJN, however, referred to all its 20cm-gun post-Washington cruisers as 'first class' or 'A class' cruisers, including the *Furutaka* and *Aoba* classes, the second of which was strikingly similar in armament and general configuration to the British 'B-type'. The issue was further complicated by the London Treaty of 1930, which differentiated between cruisers armed with 8in guns, referred to as 'category (a)', and those with a maximum calibre of 6.1in (155mm), referred to as 'category (b)'. At this point classification again diverged, with the IJN adding a 'B class' category to its existing 'A class', and other navies opting either for the 'heavy' (8in) and 'light' (6.1in and below) categories commonly used by modern reference sources, or for a 'first/second class' classification.

22. These 'immunity' figures (14,000m against 140mm shell for *Foch*, 18,000m against 155mm for *Dupleix*) clearly reflect French views regarding the combat ranges envisaged for these ships. They also reflect the likely opposition; by the time *Dupleix* was being designed the Italians were about to lay down the first of a series of modern light cruisers armed with 152mm guns, the 'Condottieri' (see Chapter 8). Earlier French treaty cruisers had had to contend only with large destroyer types armed with 120mm guns.

23. The view often expressed by Anglo-Saxon commentators that only the 'foreigners' cheated is disingenuous. When the British *London* class was designed it was proposed to save weight by reducing the number of 8in rounds from 130rpg (rounds per gun) in the *Kents* to 100rpg, but to provide space for 150rpg, to be carried only in time of war. This measure was specifically prohibited by the treaty, which stated that standard displacement should include 'all armament and ammunition … that are intended to be carried in war'. The Americans seem to have been confused about which liquids were excluded from standard displacement, and excluded drinking water, which should have been included. In the event the British and the Americans got away with it because their early treaty cruisers all turned out underweight due to the adoption of advanced shipyard practices and the careful control of weights during construction. By the time the second generation of treaty cruisers was designed, however, all the navies concerned were submitting pared-down figures for munitions, provisions and fresh water which related to peacetime operations and manning levels, and other, even more serious, breaches such as the overweight of the Italian and Japanese ships were being deliberately concealed.

24. According to Giorgerini (*Gli Incrociatori Italiani* – see Bibliography), the constructors were instructed to prioritise protection over the 10,000-ton treaty limit, and the Regia Marina was prepared to accept that an effective ship would displace around 12,000 metric tons. Like the IJN Naval Staff, the Italian Navy regarded 'qualitative superiority' over foreign cruisers as having a higher priority than conformity to 'political' treaty obligations.

25. Ironically, when the *Zara*s were put to the test in combat during the Second World War they faced not French treaty cruisers at combat ranges of 18,000–25,000m, but British battleships armed with 15in guns firing at point-blank range, which blew three of them apart in the space of a few minutes. However, given that the US Navy suffered grievous losses among its own later (and heavily protected) treaty cruisers to Japanese cruisers in similar circumstances at Savo Island, the Italian losses at Matapan have to be viewed in the context of the hazards of night action rather than any conceptual error in the design of the ships themselves.

26. The Guyot du Temple boilers fitted in earlier French treaty cruisers were rated at 20kg/cm²; those in *Algérie* operated at a steam pressure of 27kg/cm².

27. For a thoroughgoing and provocative analysis, see the late David K Brown's excellent article 'WWII Cruisers: Was Armour Really Necessary?', *Warship 1992*, Conway (London 1992).

Chapter 7

1. *Vindictive*, an 'Elizabethan' class cruiser, had undergone similar modifications to *Furious* but was no longer in service following a grounding incident in the Baltic in 1919.

2. *Hosho* had an unusual 'split-level' hangar, which could accommodate nine fighter aircraft at its forward end, and six large bomber aircraft, together with six broken-down reserve aircraft, in the broader after section.

3. Wind-over-deck speed would also become an increasingly important consideration as heavier, faster aircraft were developed.

4. Since ten 8in guns was regarded as the maximum feasible armament for the new cruisers, this also became the limit for carriers.

5. See, for example, the proposals of Admiral Charles Madden in Norman Friedman, *British Carrier Aviation*, pp.59–60, p.90.

6. In the US Navy it was estimated that it took nine minutes to launch a bomber stowed in the hangar; the equivalent figure for a fighter was six minutes. It was these concerns that led the US Navy to adopt large deck parks for *Lexington* and *Saratoga*.

7. This became a problem during the Second World War when it was decided to embark high-performance land-based fighters adapted for carrier operations, such as the Seafire. The latter had to be kept on deck because the early models did not have folding wings.

8. Freeboard – and topweight – was an issue for all carriers designed with multiple hangars.

9. By 1933 this had evolved into: two flights each of six spotters, two flights each of six torpedo attack aircraft, a single flight of reconnaissance aircraft, and a single flight of fighters (thirty-six aircraft).
10. Standard displacements of the ships to be replaced were: *Argus* 14,000 tons; *Eagle* 21,000 tons; *Hermes* 10,500 tons. Scrapping all three would have added 45,500 tons to the 20,500 tons already available, thereby permitting the construction of four new carriers of 16,500 tons.
11. Both ships were completed with a slightly reduced HA battery of sixteen guns, and these were supplemented by two eight-barrel pom-poms (on the lower flight deck) in 1934.
12. Ironically *Glorious* was the only major carrier in any navy to be sunk by surface action during the Second World War. Whether a handful of 8in guns would have made much difference against the 11in (28cm) weapons of the German fast battleships *Scharnhorst* and *Gneisenau* is debatable.
13. She was moved from Rosyth Naval Dockyard to Devonport for completion. The six years that it took to rebuild her compares with the Royal Navy's estimate of three years to build a new carrier, and is an indication of the heavy workload on the naval dockyards imposed by the battleship modernisation programme.
14. These procedures were developed aboard uss *Langley* during 1925–26 under the driving influence of Captain (later Rear-Admiral) Joseph M Reeves. Reeves first doubled the air complement of *Langley* from eight to fourteen aircraft and then, following the adoption of a crash-barrier and fore-and-aft arrester wires, doubled it again to twenty-eight. *Lexington* and *Saratoga* were subsequently modified while building to enable aircraft to be fuelled and rearmed on deck.
15. 'Fleet Problem' was the term used by the US Navy to describe each of twenty-one large-scale naval exercises conducted between 1923 and 1940.
16. *Kaga*'s sister *Tosa* was used to test capital ship protection systems before being sunk in the Bungo Strait in 1925.
17. 'Reserve' aircraft and spares could not be suspended between the hull girders beneath the flight deck as on the US Navy carriers because the adoption of a double hangar meant much-reduced deck height.
18. A similar system had been devised by the French for the carrier *Béarn* (q.v.).
19. As a battleship *Béarn* would have been the only ship of the class to have all-turbine propulsion machinery. However, as completed she was fitted out with the machinery intended for her sister *Normandie*, whose construction was more advanced.
20. Interestingly, it doesn't seem to have occurred to the US Navy that the additional 3,000 tons claimed for the *Lexington*s under the anti-submarine/anti-aircraft provisions for existing capital ships should still have been counted against its total carrier tonnage allowance.
21. The bomb, delivered in a high-angle dive, was the weapon of choice against enemy carriers; the torpedo was needed only against capital ships, and for a short period during the mid-1930s the torpedo bomber fell out of favour with the US Navy.

Chapter 8

1. Raoul Castex, *Théories Stratégiques, tome III*, Société d'éditions géographiques, maritimes et coloniales, 1931. Translation by the author.
2. The new ships were referred to as *torpilleurs-éclaireurs* ('scout torpedo boats') when first projected in 1920, and were subsequently designated *contre-torpilleurs* ('torpedo-boat destroyers')
3. The Marine Nationale acquired the large German destroyer *S113*, which served under the name *Amiral Sénès* until 1936, and was quick to appreciate the benefits of the sliding breech of the Krupp 15cm KL/45-calibre lightweight gun installed in the latter. This lesson was applied to later models of the 138.6mm gun, but it came too late for the Model 1923.
4. This policy was duly adopted by the Marine Nationale for major types of warship following the Great War to secure a greater degree of uniformity in standards and equipment.
5. *Milan* and *Epervier* were credited with a heel of only 4–10° at 32 knots on maximum rudder.
6. Literally: 'hen's arse'. Earlier *contre-torpilleurs* had a traditional 'cruiser' stern, which tended to bury itself at high speed.
7. This technology was duly transferred to the British Royal Navy in 1939 as part of an exchange agreement which gave the Marine Nationale access to British anti-submarine detection equipment.
8. Of the 745 charges provided in the *Jaguar* class, eighty-five were specifically for night firing. In the later *contre-torpilleurs*, which had provision for one hundred rounds per gun in peacetime and double that figure in wartime, a quarter of the charges were for night firing.
9. This was further exacerbated by the adoption of a hull form with marked 'tumblehome', which meant that compartments in the upper part of the hull were narrower than at the waterline.
10. In order to save weight, the armour plating, as in contemporary Japanese cruisers, was an integral part of the longitudinal strength of the ships.
11. In the Regia Marina they apparently acquired the nickname '*cartoni animati*' ('cartoon ships').
12. Despite the high formation speed of these ships, the regulation *combat* speed decreed following their entry into service was fixed at only 28 knots. This was to avoid the vibrations experienced at different speeds by individual vessels due to the variations in their machinery installations.

Chapter 9

1. Of the five major powers the British, with their own well-developed submarine arm, were arguably the least enthusiastic, and had grave concerns about the dissemination of German U-boat technology to the other navies.
2. All seven were stricken in 1922, following brief active service.
3. Boyd and Yoshida, *The Japanese Submarine Force and World War II*, p.14.
4. *Ibid.*, p.13.
5. Ironically, the Imperial German Navy seems to have been less enthusiastic about the *U-Kreuzer*, which attracted criticism because of their size, cost and protracted building times, the time it took for them to reach their operational areas, and the lengthy periods of maintenance between patrols necessitated by their complex machinery.
6. D K Brown, 'X1 – Cruiser Submarine', *Warship* 23 (July 1982).
7. The 'Special Programme of Naval Construction' of December 1923 called for seven overseas patrol submarines plus a single fleet- or cruiser-type submarine to be laid down each year beginning in 1926.
8. None would be laid down until after the London Conference, at which the British government still hoped to secure the abolition of the submarine.
9. In the event only three would be built.
10. The endurance of *V1–3* was estimated at only forty days, with a sixty-day rest and maintenance period between sorties.
11. The US Navy was allocated *U-117* as a war prize.
12. In contrast to turbines, which had rotors not pistons, diesels did not like being run at maximum power for sustained periods, and were more liable to breakdown.
13. As was customary with such British proposals, the limitation was framed with a view to permitting the Royal Navy to build the fleet submarines it wanted, while banning the large cruiser submarines building for the USA, Japan, France and Italy, which it suspected would be used for commerce warfare in the event of conflict. The future Royal Navy fleet submarine design which would become the *Thames* class would have a standard displacement of 1,800 tons as completed. The fleet submarines of the KD type currently building for the IJN, and which had a standard displacement of 1,635 tons, would fall comfortably within this figure, as would the French fleet submarines of the *1500-tonnes* type. There was therefore a good chance that the US Navy would find itself isolated if it insisted on continuing the construction of large cruiser submarines.
14. Planning for a war against Japan (Orange) began in 1906; all the war plans developed under this name embodied an expeditionary strategy which aimed to project US naval power into the Western Pacific.
15. There had been considerable input to the submarine training establishment by German U-boat personnel.
16. Plans of *U-142* were purchased from Krupp's Germaniawerft, Kiel.
17. 25,000nm was comfortably achieved on the trial cruise.
18. The same model was used in experiments by the US Navy.
19. During this same period the British Royal Navy laid down or completed a single cruiser of 2,800 tons and seventeen large overseas patrol submarines of 30,000 tons surfaced displacement, and the US Navy laid down or completed only seven large fleet/cruiser submarines of 17,000 tons. Note that 84,180 tonnes = 82,850 tons.

Chapter 10

1. The 1923 'Special Programme of Naval Construction' had proposed two flotillas per year (plus leaders), but by the mid-1920s it was recognised that this was not realistic in the prevailing political and financial climate.
2. It was estimated that in moderate sea conditions the later IJN destroyers, which could transfer their torpedoes directly into the tubes, could effect a complete reloading in as little as fifteen minutes, making possible two closely spaced multiple-torpedo attacks on the enemy battle line. The arrangements aboard the destroyers of the 'special type' had more primitive handling arrangements which made far greater demands on the crews, and could not have matched this; destroyers would have been obliged to retire from combat to replenish their tubes.
3. During the early 1930s the British installed an experimental 5.1in the (130mm)/50-calibre mounting on the flotilla leader *Kempenfelt*, which although slightly shorter than the French *1500-tonnes* type had a similar beam and displacement, and judged that the gun was too heavy for a ship of this size.
4. France had no experience with geared turbines until they were trialled aboard the modified 800-tonne *Enseigne Gabolde* during 1923, so there was a long learning curve.
5. The *Sella*s were completed with a single mounting forward, but this was replaced by a twin lightweight mounting in 1929.
6. The precise origins of this acronym have been disputed.

Chapter 11

1. The figure of seventy was based on a requirement for thirty-one fleet cruisers to match twenty-five Japanese ships (a 25 per cent margin was allowed for refits), and thirty-nine ships for trade protection. Of the fifty-one cruisers then in service with the Royal Navy twenty-six were small, short-ranged vessels designed for North Sea operations and therefore suited neither to fleet operations in the Pacific nor to patrolling the trade routes. The seventy-ship cruiser standard remained Royal Navy policy until 1937, when the navy estimated that a hundred cruisers would be required if Britain was to fight a war in Europe and take on Japan in the Far East.

2. There were nevertheless strong naval delegations, on whom much of the detailed negotiation devolved. When the conference failed to achieve the desired positive outcomes, with recriminations on both sides, both the British and the US governments concluded that admirals were the last people to be trusted to secure naval arms limitation, and should in future be excluded from face-to-face negotiations, accompanying their political masters purely in the role of advisers.

3. Even taking into account the lower displacement of the Japanese 8in-gun cruisers of the *Furutaka* and *Aoba* classes (officially 7,100 tons standard), twelve cruisers gave Japan a total of 108,400 tons compared to 150,000 tons for Britain and the United States (equivalent to approximately 72 per cent).

4. In the immediate post-Washington period Royal Navy requirements had originally been projected as two eight-ship destroyer flotillas per year!

5. This was an implicit criticism of the United States, which had chosen to remain aloof from the League of Nations. The French felt strongly that naval arms limitation should be subsumed into the ongoing League of Nations arms limitation process, and that it was illogical to separate naval weaponry from air and land forces in assessing a nation's defensive needs. They would also have liked more 'security guarantees' from the United States, which they saw as becoming increasingly remote and isolationist.

6. Many of the French overseas territories were small islands in the Caribbean, the Indian Ocean and the south Pacific, so this was a carefully selected figure; the coastline of metropolitan France, although substantial, was only 2,430nm.

7. Under Part III Section I(d) of the Washington Treaty, Italy was permitted to upgrade the armament and protection of its elderly dreadnoughts, but there was no provision for reconfiguring and upgrading propulsion machinery.

8. The British *X1* (2,425tW/5.2in), the US Navy's *V4–6* (2,710–2,730tW/6in), the IJN's cruiser submarines of the *Junsen* type (14cm guns), and the French *Surcouf* (2,880tW/203mm) – see Chapter 9.

9. Britain would take advantage of this provision to build sub-chasers. Japan, France and Italy, on the other hand would attempt to build torpedo boats for coastal defence; all the latter types turned out either overweight, unstable or both.

10. Although the United States was viewed by Britain as a political rival, Japan was now potentially a hostile power.

11. The US delegation also tried to secure permission for flight decks on capital ships, but this was strongly opposed by Britain. As a compromise it was agreed that landing-on or flying-off platforms might be fitted on future capital ships (Article 3.2) but that conversion of existing ships was prohibited (Article 3.3).

12. An unforeseen consequence would be that the IJN would now attempt to build destroyers with the armament of the 'special type' on a displacement of only 1,400 tons; the result was the disastrous *Hatsuharu* class.

13. The French submarine programme had in fact largely 'shot its bolt', although the British would not have been aware of this at the time. The congestion in the French naval dockyards was such that the *1500-tonnes* submarines authorised in 1930 would take between six and eight years to enter service. It would be Italy that increased its submarine production during the 1930s.

14. The Wall Street Crash, which began on 24 October 1929, preceded the London Conference by little more than two months.

15. This process would begin with the Vinson-Trammell Act of 1934, which aimed to bring the US Navy up to the quantitative limits permitted by the London Treaty.

16. By the beginning of the London Conference the IJN had twelve 8in-gun cruisers built or building to the US Navy's eight, had laid down or completed thirty-six fleet destroyers without any American response, and had laid down or completed twenty large fleet or cruiser submarines to the US Navy's six. The overall tonnage for destroyers and submarines allocated to Japan under the treaty actually implied a *reduction* in current force levels, from 132,495 tons to 105,500 tons and from a projected 78,000 tons to 52,700 tons respectively.

17. A strict application of the Washington ratios would have permitted six 8in-gun cruisers for each of the two powers, a figure proposed by the British prior to the conference.

18. Their respective delegations withdrew before the discussions on quantitative limits between Britain, the United States and Japan took place.

Index

For ease of reference, ships are listed under **category** (order: Capital Ships, Cruisers, Aircraft Carriers, Scouts, Submarines and Destroyers), and within each category by **nationality** (order: GB, US, Jap, Fr, It and 'other'). Page numbers in **bold** refer to the main entries.